CAMUS

A BIBLIOGRAPHY

CAMUS

A BIBLIOGRAPHY

Compiled
and edited by

ROBERT F. ROEMING

THE UNIVERSITY OF WISCONSIN PRESS

Madison, Milwaukee, and London
1968

Published by
THE UNIVERSITY OF WISCONSIN PRESS
Box 1379
Madison, Wisconsin 53701
The University of Wisconsin Press, Ltd.
27–29 Whitfield Street, London, W. 1

Printed in the United States of America by
Kingsport Press, Inc.
Kingsport, Tennessee

Library of Congress Catalog Card Number 68–9835

CONTENTS

INTRODUCTION

This bibliography has two purposes, one the compilation of references to the works of Albert Camus and to critical and historical material about these works and their author, the other the development of a computerized bibliographical system. The research to achieve these purposes, unfortunately, impeded rapid progress toward publication as it revealed new and varied directions of inquiry.

When I began to compile this bibliography after the awarding of the Nobel Prize for Literature to Albert Camus in December, 1957, I assumed that, although the body of literature involved was extensive, the author's growing status as a writer was sufficient to ensure that his own work and that of his critics would be well documented and the record would be easily accessible. In fact this misconception of the task of compilation naturally gave greater importance to the form in which the bibliography was to be cast.

As I began work one bibliography had already been published, that of Renate Bollinger; another, by Simone Crépin, was about to appear.[1] Both of these were compiled to complete requirements for degrees in library science. The former is limited in scope because it antedates world-wide recognition of Camus. The latter has proved itself unreliable because of its innumerable errors. In addition, both bibliographies are simple compilations of references from other standard bibliographical sources and as such are exercises in librarianship rather than products of analytical inquiry and verification. It was thus imperative to seek original or supporting documentation for each entry. The two bibliographies served only as guides to available material, not as sources of documentation. Because many entries in these bibliographies and some in later compilations differ from those listed here, cross-references have been given in the print-out, after the main entry, to facilitate comparison. A list of abbreviated bibliographical titles follows the Introduction.

The search for documentation stimulated what was originally a side-interest, a scholarly curiosity concerning what had already been written about Albert Camus. Establishing the authenticity of all bibliographical entries involved voluminous correspondence and a number of personal visits to those who might most readily be able to supply reliable information about

---

1. Renate Bollinger, *Albert Camus: Eine Bibliographie der Literatur über ihn und sein Werk* (Köln: Greven Verlag, 1957); abbreviated as BO in the bibliography. Simone Crépin, *Albert Camus: Essai de Bibliographie* (Bruxelles: Commission Belge de Bibliographie, 1960); abbreviated as CR in the bibliography.

original material. Trips to France and to major cities in Europe and South America gave me opportunities to investigate local libraries and publishing houses, and to broaden the network of my relations with those who were in some way occupied with the writings of Camus. Were I to attempt to list the hundreds who during the past decade have offered me citations, copies of articles, bibliographies of their critical writings, copies of original manuscripts, or just names and addresses of persons for further inquiries, I might offend by inadvertent omission, but even more seriously, be accused of name-dropping.

The ravages of World War II have created lacunae in documentation which we may never be able to close. It is, however, justifiable to claim that the major portion of this bibliography rests upon the evidence of the original items. This is especially true of the many translations, or partial translations, of Camus' works; references to these, if reported at all, had been compiled in a manner so confusing that they had to be examined directly in order to establish their true nature and the facts of their publication.

The death of Albert Camus in 1960 caused extensive reconsiderations of his life and writings, and the task of verifying earlier works had to proceed concurrently with the constant addition of new material which could readily be obtained in the original. Not wishing to sacrifice thoroughness in an effort to keep up with the tempo of new publications, I have included in this bibliography only works published in 1966 or before. Though critical writing and the publication of previously unprinted Camus items continue, this is lesser in bulk and generally much more manageable in extent, not appearing as before in many obscure journals and newspapers or from virtually unknown publishing houses.

A further limitation has been imposed on this bibliography by the expedient use of available time. Dr. Emmett Parker, in completing the basic research for his book *Albert Camus: The Artist in the Arena* (1965), made an exhaustive compilation of all the newspaper articles and editorials that could possibly be attributed to Albert Camus. I was at the time aware of his work, and saw no justification for duplicating his very authoritative bibliography of these items.[2] Some of these, to be sure, do appear as individual items republished elsewhere, as items related to the three volumes of *Actuelles*, in collections or in translations which were specifically excluded from Parker's list.

The publication in the same year of the second and final volume of the complete works of Albert Camus, compiled and edited by Roger Quilliot, offered a second listing of newspaper articles and editorials by Camus.[3] The variations between these two major compilations clearly indicate that a definitive listing will require further intensive and arduous research. As Roger Quilliot indicates in his prefatory note to the bibliography, I assisted him, but primarily in establishing the authenticity and dates of the translations.[4] Here again there are many variations because originally references

2. See Appendix B, "Articles and Editorials by Camus," in *Albert Camus: The Artist in the Arena* (Madison: The University of Wisconsin Press, 1965), pp. 185–204.

3. *Essais* (Paris: Gallimard, Bibliothèque de la Pléiade, 1965).

4. *Ibid.*, p. 1933.

to translations came from bibliographical sources in which the dates of original publication are confused with those of successive printings.

Brian T. Fitch in *Calepins de bibliographie, Albert Camus, 1937– 1962*, listed critical articles in French by year.[5] The bibliography contains two indexes, one an index of authors, the other an index of periodicals of all types; both are cross-referenced by year to the body of the bibliography. To find a specific item one must consult the indexes or search through the various years.

The present bibliography is only the first step toward a definitive compilation. I have, therefore, devoted much time and effort to evolving a bibliographical computerized system which would establish for each entry a precise and permanently error-free format. A review of other efforts to establish linguistically—and, by extension, nationally—orientated bibliographies made it evident that the electronic computer could be used to group the bibliographical entries into different categories.[6]

Bibliographies, in general, address themselves to those with specialized knowledge in a given field and with considerable experience in the use of the tools of scholarship—it is, for instance, improbable that anyone quite unfamiliar with Albert Camus would consult this volume. Furthermore, the adaptability of this system to the greatest possible number of existing computer installations was important. Although print-outs in the more conventional and attractive upper- and lower-case style would have been possible, they were hardly essential to understanding, and upper-case letters have accordingly been used throughout. However, in the interests of accuracy diacritical marks have been added, since the bibliography contains references in many languages, some requiring transliteration into the Roman alphabet.

As much information as possible has been given in the references, especially for periodical literature. The original investigation revealed errors by publishers in recording volumes or numbers of journals, in numbering pages, and in recording titles of articles. Very often, too, the initial error has been compounded by library binding practices, further complicating the search for documents if only scant information is available. Acquiring correct articles or book pages, particularly through interlibrary loan, often necessitates a much more detailed citation than is normally offered in bibliographies, as my own experience in trying to obtain information from distant sources has convincingly demonstrated.

Finally, it must be emphasized that punctuation and spacing in this system serves both its traditional function, and supports coding. Thus the format of entries here is essentially different from that of recognized guides.

The bibliography as such is stored on magnetic computer tape and thus in its raw state is easily transported and duplicated. A control is maintained

---

5. Paris: Minard, Lettres Modernes, 1965.

6. E.g., that by Brian Fitch, previously mentioned; see J. H. Matthews, "Configuration critique d'Albert Camus, I: *L'Etranger* à l'étranger: Camus devant la critique anglo-saxonne," *La Revue des Lettres Modernes*, Vol. VIII, Nos. 64–66 (automne 1961); and Richard Thieberger, "Configuration critique d'Albert Camus, II: Camus devant la critique de langue allemande," *La Revue des Lettres Modernes*, Nos. 90–93 (hiver 1963).

on typewritten cards with a numbering system with sufficient breadth and flexibility to allow additional citations to be added in the proper sequences. This numbering system, designed for control purposes only, is not sequential and is a seven-digit number, the first of which is a category classification designating either an original Camus work or a publication by an author other than Camus. Items on the tape can, therefore, be periodically revised by additions, deletions, and corrections to conform to the control card file.

The unique characteristic of the computer program is the renumbering of items while the print-out is being produced. The control numbering system is revised in this process to a sequential numbering system, and all cross-references are brought into conformity with the new numbers. This marks a tremendous step forward in the compilation of bibliographies. In preparing a manuscript of a bibliography it has been almost impossible to make any changes once the typing began; correcting errors in the sequential numbering and renumbering the cross-references have required constant alertness and immense labor. In this bibliography new entries, deletions, and corrections have been made to the very day of its being produced in printed form. For easy reference the first item on an even-numbered page and the last item on an odd-numbered page are registered on the upper outside corners of the pages.

The ordering of the items of a bibliography has always been a vexing problem since only one form was feasible. In this bibliographical system it is possible to order the citations in one manner and then reorder them in the supplementary indexes with a cross-reference to the original number of the entry. Thus collections of essays are listed under the general title with cross-reference listings to the individual essays included in the volume. All critical works about Camus and his writings are catalogued under the name of the author. The latter are in alphabetical order, while multiple items by the same author are listed in chronological order. The original works by Camus present a very difficult ordering problem. Much of his work appeared as small individual items and was reassembled into larger volumes; and these had to be coordinated with innumerable translations. Therefore, Camus' writings have been listed under the individual titles in alphabetical order, followed by other groupings which for easy reference coordinate a large number of items not included in the major works.

Three supplementary indexes, organized first by country of publication and next by language, are included. The first index lists the authors under these two categories, showing the geographical and linguistic distribution not only of Camus' works but also of the critical writings. The second index lists journals, offering a ready evaluation of library resources in any given language. Newspapers and popular magazines have not been included in this index, although they are included in the bibliography itself; such materials are generally not of a kind to support Camus scholarship at the graduate or undergraduate level, and are now mostly kept only on microfilm in very large libraries or central depositories. The third index, a chronological listing by country and language, reveals the distribution of all items on a triple basis. It offers, therefore, the information contained in bibliographies which used either a chronological or a national linguistic organization, or a combination of these, but which were limited to one nation or language.

The last tabulation reveals that consistent serious attention was paid to the writings of Camus in France and in the rest of Western Europe from 1946 on. By 1956 the number of items had approximately doubled and the number of countries represented had also kept pace, primarily through the translation of Camus' most widely read books in the major countries of the world.

As might be anticipated translation and criticism accelerated in 1957 and 1958, after Camus was awarded the Nobel Prize. Much of the 1957 material was of course journalistically oriented—a factor which led me to include only journals in the second index—while the more critical evaluations appeared in 1958. Camus' accidental death in 1960 quite naturally increased the sum of writings, both journalistic and critical, about him in that year to approximately the total of 1957 and 1958 combined. Since 1960 translation has slackened; this combined with intensive and sober scholarship has tended to reduce publication to about 175 items worthy of citation each year.

The search has, however, widened, as writers in an ever more extensive orbit of human knowledge have felt the inclination to show at least an intellectual acquaintance with Camus. In this bibliography citations from such academic disciplines as law, medicine, education, political science, and sociology are evidence of the wide currency of his name. Many authors, of course, drop the name "Camus" once or twice without showing more than shallow familiarity. Yet wide-ranging investigation has been essential, since a number of discerning essays have appeared in books not exclusively devoted to Camus. I cannot indeed be sure that I have exhausted all possible lines of inquiry for the years after 1960, or that the citations herein contained constitute an exhaustive list. However, the present system of accumulating data provides for the possibility of supplementary lists.

Though I have already confessed my complete inability to give specific thanks to all those who have assisted in what has been essentially a common effort, I must acknowledge my indebtedness to those who have sustained me and made this project possible. Among these are the various administrators of the Graduate Schools both of the University of Wisconsin and University of Wisconsin-Milwaukee, Deans John E. Willard, Robert A. Alberti and Karl Krill, as well as Associate Deans Maxwell M. Freeman, Eric R. Rude, and J. Thomas Shaw; the successive Deans of the College of Letters and Science of the University of Wisconsin-Milwaukee, Joseph G. Baier and Roy G. Francis; Fred Harvey Harrington, President of the University of Wisconsin, who as Vice President of the University offered me the initial potential to undertake this work; the directors and personnel of the libraries of both the University of Wisconsin and the University of Wisconsin-Milwaukee; the administrators and consultants of the Computer Centers of the University of Wisconsin where the technological facilities were first made available and of the University of Wisconsin-Milwaukee where the print-out was finally produced; William H. Brady, Jr., and Harold F. Falk, industrialists of Milwaukee, for their personal kindness and material support; and the Harnischfeger Corporation, where much of the initial experience in computer utilization was obtained.

Robert F. Roeming

Milwaukee, Wisconsin
June, 1968

ABBREVIATIONS OF
BIBLIOGRAPHICAL REFERENCES

BDZ—*Bibliographie der Deutschen Zeitschriftenliteratur* (Osnabrück: Verlag Felix Dietrich).

BFZ—*Bibliographie der Fremdsprachigen Zeitschriftenliteratur* (Osnabrück: Verlag Felix Dietrich).

BIBLIO—*Catalogue des ouvrages parus en langue française au monde entier* (Paris: Hachette).

BNI—*Bibliografia Nazionale Italiana* (Firenze: Centro Nazionale per il Catalogo Unico delle Biblioteche Italiane e per le Informazioni Bibliografiche).

BO—Bollinger, Renate, *Albert Camus: Eine Bibliographie der Literatur über ihn und sein Werk* (Köln: Greven Verlag, 1957).

BPI—*Bolletino delle Pubblicazioni Italiane* (Firenze: Biblioteca Nazionale Centrale).

BR—Brisville, Jean-Claude, *Camus* (Paris: Gallimard, 1959).

BRHT—Bibliography of *Revue de l'Histoire du Théâtre.*

BTA—*Bibliographie des traductions allemandes d'imprimés français* (Baden-Baden: Kunst und Wissenschaft).

BUL SIGN—*Bulletin Signalétique* (Paris: Centre Nationale de la Recherche Scientifique).

CBI—Cumulative Book Index (New York: H. W. Wilson).

CR—Crépin, Simone, *Albert Camus: Essai de Bibliographie* (Bruxelles: Commission Belge de Bibliographie, 1960).

DR—Drevet, Marguerite L., *Bibliographie de la littérature française, 1940–1949: Complément à la bibliographie de H. P. Thieme* (Genève: Librairie E. Droz, 1954).

FITCH—Fitch, Brian T., *Calepins de Bibliographie, Albert Camus, 1937–1962* (Paris: Minard, 1965).

FR VII—*French VII Bibliography* (New York: French Institute).

KL—Klapp, Otto, *Bibliographie der Französischen Literaturwissenschaft* (Frankfurt-am-Main: Vittorio Klostermann).

INB—*Indian National Bibliography* (Calcutta: National Library).

I.T.—*Index Translationem* (New York: UNESCO).

LF—Librairie Française, *Les Livres de l'Année* (Paris: Cercle de la Librairie).

MA—Matthews, J. H., "Configuration critique d'Albert Camus, I: *L'Etranger* à l'étranger: Camus devant la critique anglo-saxonne," *La Revue des Lettres Modernes*, Vol. VIII, Nos. 64–66 (automne 1961).

PMLA—Quarterly bibliographies in *Publications of the Modern Language Association* (New York: Modern Language Association of America).

WORKS
BY CAMUS

ACTUELLES

ACTUELLES. CHRONIQUES 1944-1948. PARIS, GALLIMARD (N.R.F.), 0001
    1950. CR 176, FR VII 4065, BIBLIO (1950), P. 121.

ACTUELLES. CHRONIQUES 1944-1948. ÉDITION RELIÉE D'APRÈS LA 0002
    MAQUETTE DE MARIO PRASSINOS. PARIS, GALLIMARD, 1950. CR
    175, BIBLIO (1950), P. 121.

JIYU NO SHONIN. TOKYO, SHINCHO-SHA, 1952. CR 179, I.T. 0003
    (1953) 8380. YANAIHARA, ISAKU.

LE TÉMOIN DE LA LIBERTÉ. LA GAUCHE, DECEMBER 20, 1948. SEE 0004
    NO. 1.

L'ARTISTE EST LE TÉMOIN DE LA LIBERTÉ. EMPÉDOCLE, VOL. 1, NO. 0005
    1, (APRIL 1949), PP. 71-76. CR 352. SEE NO. 4.

DE KUNSTENAAR IS DE GETUIGE DER VRIJHEID. VLAM, VOL. 5, NO. 5 0006
    (JAN. 29, 1949), P. 8. CR 356. SEE NO. 4.

ARTIST AS WITNESS OF FREEDOM. COMMENTARY, VOL. 8, NO. 6 (DEC. 0007
    1949), PP. 534-538. CR 353, IIP (APRIL 1949-MARCH 1952),
    279. SEE NO. 4. FRECHTMAN, BERNARD.

DAS BLUT DER FREIHEIT (DIE BEFREIUNG VON PARIS). IN FRAGEN DER 0008
    ZEIT, PP. 40-41. SEE NO. 630, 1.

THE BLOOD OF FREEDOM (THE LIBERATION OF PARIS). IN RESISTANCE, 0009
    REBELLION AND DEATH, PP. 27-28. SEE NO. 633, 1.

THE BLOOD OF FREEDOM (THE LIBERATION OF PARIS). IN RESISTANCE, 0010
    REBELLION AND DEATH, PP. 35-37. SEE NO. 647, 1.

DIE NACHT DER WAHRHEIT (DIE BEFREIUNG VON PARIS). IN FRAGEN 0011
    DER ZEIT, PP. 42-45. SEE NO. 630, 1.

THE NIGHT OF TRUTH (THE LIBERATION OF PARIS). IN RESISTANCE, 0012
    REBELLION AND DEATH, PP. 29-30 SEE NO. 633, 1.

THE NIGHT OF TRUTH (THE LIBERATION OF PARIS). IN RESISTANCE, 0013
    REBELLION AND DEATH, PP. 38-40. SEE NO. 647, 1.

GIORNALISMO CRITICO (CRONACHE 1944-1958). IN RIBELLIONE E 0014
    MORTE, PP. 45-54. SEE NO. 634, 1.

RENÉ LEYNAUD. IN FRAGEN DER ZEIT, PP. 46-48. SEE NO. 630, 1. 0015

THE FLESH. IN RESISTANCE, REBELLION AND DEATH, PP. 31-32. SEE 0016
    NO. 633, 1.

0017   THE FLESH.   IN RESISTANCE, REBELLION AND DEATH, PP. 41-54.   SEE
          NO. 647, 1.

0018   PESSIMISMUS UND MUT (PESSIMISMUS UND TYRANNEI).   IN FRAGEN DER
          ZEIT, PP. 62-65.   SEE NO. 630, 1.

0019   PESSIMISM AND COURAGE (PESSIMISM AND TYRANNY).   IN RESISTANCE,
          REBELLION AND DEATH, PP. 41-43.   SEE NO. 633, 1.

0020   PESSIMISM AND COURAGE (PESSIMISM AND TYRANNY).   IN RESISTANCE,
          REBELLION AND DEATH, PP. 57-60.   SEE NO. 647, 1.

0021   DEN GEIST HOCHHALTEN (PESSIMISMUS UND TYRANNEI).   IN FRAGEN DER
          ZEIT, PP. 66-70.   SEE NO. 630, 1.

0022   DEFENCE OF INTELLIGENCE (PESSIMISM AND TYRANNY).   IN
          RESISTANCE, REBELLION AND DEATH, PP. 44-46.   SEE NO. 633,
          1.

0023   DEFENSE OF INTELLIGENCE (PESSIMISM AND TYRANNY).   IN
          RESISTANCE, REBELLION AND DEATH, PP. 61-65.   SEE NO. 647,
          1.

0024   NI VICTIMES, NI BOURREAUX.   CALIBAN,   NO. 11 (NOVEMBER 1947),
          PP. X-XX11.   CR 330, DR 116.   SEE NO. 1.

0025   NOCH BEUL, NOCH OFFER, I.   VLAM,   VOL. 3, NO. 19 (MAY 16,
          1947), PP. 5-6.   CR 331.   SEE NO. 24.

0026   NOCH BEUL, NOCH OFFER, II.   VLAM,   VOL. 3, NO. 20 (MAY
          23,1947), P. 9.   CR 332.   SEE NO. 25.

0027   NOCH BEUL, NOCH OFFER, III.   VLAM,   VOL. 3, NO. 21 (MAY 30,
          1947), P. 9.   CR 333.   SEE NO. 25.

0028   NOCH BEUL, NOCH OFFER, IV.   VLAM,   VOL. 3, NO. 22 (JUNE 6,
          1947), P. 9.   CR 334.   SEE NO. 25.

0029   NOCH BEUL, NOCH OFFER, V.   VLAM,   VOL. 3, NO. 23 (JUNE 13,
          1947), P. 10.   CR 335.   SEE NO. 25.

0030   NOCH BEUL, NOCH OFFER, VI.   VLAM,   VOL. 3, NO. 24 (JUNE 20,
          1947), P. 10.   CR 336.   SEE NO. 25.

0031   NOCH BEUL, NOCH OFFER, VII.   VLAM,   VOL. 3, NO. 25 (JUNE 27,
          1947), P. 10.   CR 337.   SEE NO. 25.

0032   NOCH BEUL, NOCH OFFER, VIII.   VLAM,   VOL. 3, NO. 26 (JULY 4,
          1947), P. 10.   CR 338.   SEE NO. 25.

0033   NEITHER VICTIMS NOR EXECUTIONERS.   ADELPHI,   VOL. 24, NO. 3
          (APRIL-JUNE 1948), PP. 135-146.   CR 349, DR 116.   SEE NO.
          24.   MACDONALD, DWIGHT.

0034   NÉ VITTIME NÉ CARNEFICI (CRONACHE 1944-1958).   IN RIBELLIONE E
          MORTE, PP. 55-86.   SEE NO. 634, 24.

0035   KVERKEN OFFER ELLER BØDLER.   IN DEN UOVERVINNELIGE SOMMER, PP.
          89-117. SEE NO. 639, 24.

0036   OÙ EST LA MYSTIFICATION?   RÉPONSE À D'ASTIER DE LA VIGERIE.
          CALIBAN,   NO. 16 (JUNE 1948), PP. 67-75.   CR 350.   SEE NO.
          1.

0037   ATEISTI JA KRISTITYT.   IN ESSEITÄ (VALIKOIMA), PP. 108-114   SEE

NO. 627, 1.

DER UNGLÄUBIGE AN DIE CHRISTEN. ECKART, VOL. 27, NO. 8   0038
  (OCT.-DEC. 1958), PP. 275-278. SEE NO. 1.

DER UNGLÄUBIGE UND DIE CHRISTEN. IN FRAGEN DER ZEIT, PP.   0039
  72-78. SEE NO. 630, 1.

THE UNBELIEVER AND CHRISTIANS. IN RESISTANCE, REBELLION AND   0040
  DEATH, PP. 49-53. SEE NO. 633, 1.

THE UNBELIEVER AND CHRISTIANS. IN RESISTANCE, REBELLION AND   0041
  DEATH, PP. 67-74. SEE NO. 647, 1.

TRE INTERVISTE (CRONACHE 1944-1958). IN RIBELLIONE E MORTE,   0042
  PP. 87-99. SEE NO. 634.

WARUM SPANIEN? IN FRAGEN DER ZEIT, PP. 79-87. SEE NO. 630, 1.   0043

WHY SPAIN? IN RESISTANCE, REBELLION AND DEATH, PP. 57-61. SEE   0044
  NO. 633, 1.

WHY SPAIN? IN RESISTANCE, REBELLION AND DEATH,   PP. 75-83.   0045
  SEE NO. 647, 1.

ACTUELLES II

0046   ACTUELLES II. CHRONIQUES 1948-1953. PARIS, GALLIMARD, 1953.
        CR 214.
0047   ACTUELLES II. CHRONIQUES 1948-1953. ÉDITION ORIGINALE RELIÉE
        D'APRÈS LA MAQUETTE DE MARIO PRASSINOS. PARIS, GALLIMARD,
        1953. CR 213, BIBLIO (1953) 142.
0048   SOZO TO JIYU TOKYO, SHINCHO-SHA, 1955. I.T. (1956) 12646.
        SEE NO. 46. YANAIHARA, ISAKU.
0049   RIVOLTA E CONFORMISMO I (CRONACHE 1944-1958). IN RIBELLIONE E
        MORTE, PP. 101-103. SEE NO. 634, 46.
0050   RIVOLTA E CONFORMISMO II (CRONACHE 1944-1958). IN RIBELLIONE E
        MORTE, PP. 104-108. SEE NO. 634, 46.
0051   CONVERSAZIONE SULLA RIVOLTA (CRONACHE 1944-1958). IN
        RIBELLIONE E MORTE, PP. 109-117. SEE NO. 634, 46.
0052   EPURAZIONE DEI PURI (CRONACHE 1944-1958). IN RIBELLIONE E
        MORTE, PP. 118-120. SEE NO. 634, 46.
0053   RIVOLTA E POLIZIA (CRONACHE 1944-1958). IN RIBELLIONE E MORTE,
        PP. 121-126. SEE NO. 634, 46.
0054   RIVOLTA E ROMANTICISMO (CRONACHE 1944-1958). IN RIBELLIONE E
        MORTE, PP. 127-132. SEE NO. 634, 46.
0055   RIVOLTA E SERVITÚ (CRONACHE 1944-1958). IN RIBELLIONE E MORTE,
        PP. 133-159. SEE NO. 634, 46.
0056   L'ESPAGNE ET LA CULTURE. LECTURE; PARIS, SALLE WAGRAM, 1952
        SEE NO. 46.
0057   SPANIA OG KULTUREN. IN DEN UOVERVINNELIGE SOMMER, PP. 118-125.
        SEE NO. 639, 56.
0058   LE PAIN DE LA LIBERTÉ. LECTURE; PARIS, BOURSE DU TRAVAIL DE
        SAINT-ÉTIENNE, 1953. SEE NO. 46.
0059   BROT UND FREIHEIT (VERTEIDIGUNG DER FREIHEIT). IN FRAGEN DER
        ZEIT, PP. 90-101. SEE NO. 630, 46.
0060   BREAD AND FREEDOM (DEFENCE OF FREEDOM). IN RESISTANCE,
        REBELLION AND DEATH, PP. 65-71. SEE NO. 633, 1.
0061   BREAD AND FREEDOM (DEFENSE OF FREEDOM). IN RESISTANCE,
        REBELLION AND DEATH, PP. 87-97. SEE NO. 647, 46.
0062   THE ARTIST AND HIS TIME. IN THE MYTH OF SISYPHUS AND OTHER
        ESSAYS, PP. 163-169. SEE NO. 645, 46.
0063   THE ARTIST AND HIS TIME. IN THE MYTH OF SISYPHUS AND OTHER
        ESSAYS, PP. 1-109. SEE NO. 646, 46.

ACTUELLES III

ACTUELLES III. CHRONIQUE ALGÉRIENNE 1939-1958. PARIS,   0064
    GALLIMARD (COLL. BLANCHE), 1958. CR 270.
ACTUELLES III. CHRONIQUE ALGÉRIENNE. 1939-1958. ÉDITION   0065
    ORIGINALE RELIÉE D'APRÈS LA MAQUETTE DE MARIO PRASSINOS.
    PARIS, GALLIMARD, 1958. CR 269, BIBLIO (1958) 156, BIBLIO
    (1959) 160.
PROBLEMAS DE NUESTRA ÉPOCA. CRÓNICA ARGELINA. BUENOS AIRES,   0066
    LOSADA, 1960. SEE NO. 64. BIXIO, ALBERTO LUIS.
CRONACHE 1944-1958. IN RIBELLIONE E MORTE. SEE NO. 634, 64.   0067
ESIPUHE KOKOELMAAN ACTUELLES III. (AVANT-PROPOS TO ACTUELLES   0068
    III). IN ESSEITÄ (VALIKOIMA), PP. 73-88. SEE NO. 627, 64.
VORWORT ZUR ALGERISCHEN CHRONIK (ALGERIEN). IN FRAGEN DER   0069
    ZEIT, PP. 184-200. SEE NO. 630, 64.
PREFACE TO ALGERIAN REPORTS (ALGERIA). IN RESISTANCE,   0070
    REBELLION AND DEATH, PP. 81-90. SEE NO. 633, 64.
PREFACE TO ALGERIAN REPORTS (ALGERIA). IN RESISTANCE,   0071
    REBELLION AND DEATH, PP. 111-125. SEE NO. 647, 64.
KIRJE ALGERIALAISELLE TAISTELIJALLE. IN ESSEITÄ (VALIKOIMA),   0072
    PP. 89-93. SEE NO. 627, 64.
BRIEF AN EINEN ALGERISCHEN AKTIVISTEN (ALGERIEN). IN FRAGEN   0073
    DER ZEIT, PP. 200-205. SEE NO. 630, 64.
LETTER TO AN ALGERIAN MILITANT (ALGERIA). IN RESISTANCE,   0074
    REBELLION AND DEATH, PP. 91-94. SEE NO. 633, 64.
LETTER TO AN ALGERIAN MILITANT (ALGERIA). IN RESISTANCE,   0075
    REBELLION AND DEATH, PP. 126-130. SEE NO. 647, 64.
AUFRUF FÜR EINEN BURGFRIEDEN IN ALGERIEN (ALGIERIEN). IN   0076
    FRAGEN DER ZEIT, PP. 205-219. SEE NO. 630, 64.
APPEAL FOR A CIVILIAN TRUCE IN ALGERIA. (ALGERIA). IN   0077
    RESISTANCE, REBELLION AND DEATH, PP. 95-102. SEE NO. 633,
    64.
APPEAL FOR A CIVILIAN TRUCE IN ALGERIA (ALGERIA). IN   0078
    RESISTANCE, REBELLION AND DEATH, PP. 131-142. SEE NO. 647,
    64.
ALGERIEN 1958 (ALGERIEN). IN FRAGEN DER ZEIT, PP. 219-226.   0079
    SEE NO. 630, 64.
DAS NEUE ALGERIEN (ALGERIEN). IN FRAGEN DER ZEIT, PP. 226-230.   0080
    SEE NO. 630, 64.
ALGERIE 1958. IN DEN UOVERVINNELIGE SOMMER, PP. 126-136. SEE   0081
    NO. 639, 64.
ALGERIA 1958. IN RESISTANCE, REBELLION AND DEATH, PP. 103-107.   0082
    SEE NO. 633, 64.
NEW ALGERIA. IN RESISTANCE, REBELLION AND DEATH, PP. 108-110.   0083
    SEE NO. 633, 64.

0084   ALGERIA 1958 (ALGERIA).   IN RESISTANCE, REBELLION AND DEATH,
          PP. 143-153. SEE NO. 64, 647.

0085   INTRODUZIONE ALL ALGERIA (CRONACHE 1944-1958).   IN RIBELLIONE E
          MORTE, PP. 161-176. SEE NO. 64, 634.

0086   MISERIA DELLA CABILIA (CRONACHE 1944-1958).   IN RIBELLIONE E
          MORTE, PP. 177-223. SEE NO. 64, 634.

0087   CRISI IN ALGERIA (CRONACHE 1944-1958).   IN RIBELLIONE E MORTE,
          PP. 225-247. SEE NO. 64, 634.

0088   LETTERA A UN MILITANTE ALGERINO (CRONACHE 1944-1958).   IN
          RIBELLIONE E MORTE, PP. 249-253. SEE NO. 64, 634.

0089   L'ALGERIA STRAZIATA (CRONACHE 1944-1958).   IN RIBELLIONE E
          MORTE, PP. 255-281. SEE NO. 64, 634.

0090   ALGERIA 1958 (CRONACHE 1944-1958). IN RIBELLIONE E MORTE, PP.
          283-293. SEE NO. 64, 634.

0091   L'ART. BRUXELLES-PARIS, PRESSES ANCIENNES DE GEORGES-MARIE
          DUTILLEUL (COLL. MÉTAMORPHOSES), 1955. CR 230, BIBLIO
          (1955) 138.

CALIGULA

CALIGULA. PIÈCE EN QUATRE ACTES. IN LE MALENTENDU. PIÈCE EN   0092
    TROIS ACTES. SUIVIE DE CALIGULA. PIÈCE EN QUATRE ACTES.
    CR 90. SEE NO. 414.
CALIGULA. PIÈCE EN QUATRE ACTES. PARIS, GALLIMARD, 1946. CR   0093
    91.
CALIGULA. PIÈCE EN QUATRE ACTES. NEW YORK, SCHIFFRIN   0094
    (PANTHEON BOOKS), 1946. CR 93.
CALIGULA-PIÈCE EN QUATRE ACTES. NEW YORK, SCHIFFRIN (PANTHEON   0095
    BOOKS), 1947. CR 94.
CALIGULA-PIÈCE EN QUATRE ACTES. NOUVELLE EDITION. PARIS,   0096
    PARIS-THÉÂTRE (NO. 135), 1958. CR 95.
CALIGULA (ÉDITION ILLUSTRÉE PAR P.-Y. TRÉMOIS). IN RÉCITS ET   0097
    THÉÂTRE. SEE NO. 618.
CALIGULA. PIEZA EN CUATRO ACTOS. IN TEATRO, PP. 55-114. CR   0098
    185 SEE NO. 622. BERNARDEZ, AURORA.
CALIGULA. IN CALIGULA AND THREE OTHER PLAYS. CBI (1961-1962),   0099
    415. SEE NO. 624.
CALIGULA. SKUESPIL I FIRE AKTER. COPENHAGEN, GYLDENDAL,   0100
    1947. CR 97. SEE NO. 93. LA COUR, PAUL.
CALIGULA IN DRAMEN PP. 15-73. CR 183 SEE NO. 628.   0101
CALIGULA AND CROSS PURPOSE. LONDON, H. HAMILTON, 1947. CR   0102
    105, I.T. (1948-1950) 6587. SEE NO. 430. GILBERT, STUART.
CALIGOLA. DRAMMA IN QUATTRO ATTI. IN TEATRO, PP. 71-154.   0103
    I.T. (1963) 15502. SEE NO. 636. LODOVICI, CESARE VICO.
KARIGYURA. GOKAI. TOKYO, SHINCHO-SHA, 1951. CR 108, I.T.   0104
    (1952) 9775. SEE NO. 424. KATO, MICHIO.
CALIGULA. AMSTERDAM, BEZIGE BIJ, 1961. SEE NO. 93. VAN   0105
    VRIESLAND, VICTOR E.
CALIGULA. O EQUIVOCO. LISBON, LIVROS DO BRASIL, N.D. (1959).   0106
    I.T. (1961), 17703. SEE NO. 426. CARVALHO, RAUL DE.
CALIGULA. SKADESPEL I FYRA AKTER. MISSFÖRSTÅNDET. SKADESPEL I   0107
    TRE AKTER. STOCKHOLM, BONNIERS, 1949. CR 109. SEE NO.
    427. JOHNSON, EYVIND.
CALIGULA. IN CALIGULA, MISSFÖRSTÅNDET, DE RÄTTFÄRDIGA. SEE   0108
    NO. 641. JOHNSON, EYVIND.
CALIGULA. A PLAY IN FOUR ACTS. IN CALIGULA AND THREE OTHER   0109
    PLAYS, PP. 1-74. SEE NO. 643.
CALIGULA. IN CALIGULA AND THREE OTHER PLAYS, PP. 1-74. SEE   0110
    NO. 644.
CALIGULA. (IV. AKT VON SCENE 9 AB). KARUSSELL, VOL. 1, NO. 12   0111
    (1947), PP. 15-22. CR 329, BTA (VOL C-E), 4430. GLAESER,
    ERNST. HAUSER, HANS H.

CARNETS

0112   PAGES DE CARNETS. SYMPOSIUM,   VOL. 12, NOS. 1-2 (SPRING-FALL,
          1958), PP. 1-6. FR VII 19411.
0113   CARNETS MAI 1935-FEVRIER 1942. PARIS, GALLIMARD (NRF), 1962.
0114   CARNETS, 1935-1942. LONDON, HAMISH HAMILTON, 1963. SEE NO.
          113. THODY, PHILIP.
0115   TACCUINI. MILAN, BOMPIANI, 1963. SEE NO. 113. CAPRIOLO,
          ETTORE.
0116   NOTEBOOKS 1935-1942. NEW YORK,   KNOPF, 1963. SEE NO. 113.
          THODY, PHILIP.
0117   CARNETS JANVIER 1942-MARS 1951. PARIS, GALLIMARD (NRF), 1964.

LA CHUTE

LA CHUTE. RÉCIT. (COLL. BLANCHE) PARIS. GALLIMARD, 1956.   0118
    CR 231, BIBLIO (1956) 146.

LA CHUTE. RÉCIT. ÉDITION ORIGINALE RELIÉE D'APRÈS LA MAQUETTE   0119
    DE MARIO PRASSINOS. PARIS, GALLIMARD, 1956. CR 231,
    BIBLIO (1957) 150.

LA CHUTE. RÉCIT. PARIS, CLUB DU MEILLEUR LIVRE, 1958. CR   0120
    237, BIBLIO (1958) 156.

LA CHUTE (ÉDITION ILLUSTRÉE PAR ANDRÉ MASSON). IN RÉCITS ET   0121
    THÉÂTRE. SEE NO. 618.

LA CHUTE. RÉCIT. PARIS, GALLIMARD (COLL. SOLEIL), 1960.   0122
    BIBLIO (1960) 162.

LA CAÍDA. BUENOS AIRES, LOSADA, 1957. I.T. (1963) 3742. SEE   0123
    NO. 118. BIXIO, ALBERTO LUIS.

THE FALL. TORONTO, MCCLELLAND AND STEWART. CR 243, CBI   0124
    (1957). SEE NO. 118. O'BRIEN, JUSTIN.

THE FALL. TORONTO, RANDOM HOUSE (VINTAGE), 1963. SEE NO.   0125
    145. O'BRIEN, JUSTIN.

PAD. IN CIZINEC-PAD, PP. 95-179. SEE NO. 625, 118.   0126

FALDET. COPENHAGEN, GYLDENDAL, 1958. CR 244, I.T. (1959)   0127
    4946, I.T. (1960) 6170, I.T. (1962) 6243. SEE NO. 118.
    JAEGER, FRANK.

PUTOAMINEN. HELSINKI, OTAVA, 1957. CR 245, I.T. (1959) 7446,   0128
    I.T. (1960) 8574, I.T. (1964) 9400. SEE NO. 118.
    AUTERINEN, MAIJALIISA.

DER FALL. ROMAN. HAMBURG, ROWOHLT, 1957. CR 238, I.T.   0129
    (1959) 898, I.T. (1963) 1298. SEE NO. 118.

DER FALL. AUGSBURG, SUHRKAMP, 1964. SEE NO. 118. MEISTER,   0130
    GUIDO, G.

DER FALL. DARMSTADT, DEUTSCHE BUCH-GEMEINSCHAFT, 1959. I.T.   0131
    (1962) 1286. SEE NO. 118. MEISTER, GUIDO G.

THE FALL. LONDON, H. HAMILTON, 1956. CR 241, I.T. (1959)   0132
    18727. SEE NO. 118. O'BRIEN, JUSTIN.

THE FALL. IN THE COLLECTED FICTION OF ALBERT CAMUS. SEE NO.   0133
    632.

FALLID. AKUREYRI, BÓKAFORLAG ODDS BJÖRNSSONAR, 1961. CR 135,   0134
    I.T. (1963) 14182. SEE NO. 118. GUDMUNDSSON, LOFTUR.

PATAN. DELHI, RAJKAMAL PRAKASAN, 1960. I.T. (1963) 13498.   0135
    SEE NO. 118. RAO, UMA.

HA-NEFILA. GALUT U-MALCHUT. MERHAVYA, SIFRIYAT POALIM, 1959.   0136
    I.T. (1961) 12136. SEE NO. 118, 308. ARAD, ZEVI.

LA CADUTA. L'ESILIO E IL REGNO. MILAN, BOMPIANI, 1958. CR   0137
    246, I.T. (1960) 12966. SEE NO. 118, 309. MORANDO,
    SERGIO.

0138   TENRAKU.   IN IHOJIN, TENRAKU   SEE NO. 118, 278.   SATO, SAKU.

0139   DE VAL. AMSTERDAM, BIZIGE BIJ, 1957.   CR 247, I.T. (1959)
          15154, I.T. (1962) 17154, I.T. (1964) 17628.   SEE NO. 118.
          PONT, ANNE MACLAINE.

0140   FALLET. OSLO, ASCHEHOUG, 1957.   CR 248, I.T. (1959) 14274.
          SEE NO. 118.   MARTENS, JOHANNES SKANCKE.

0141   UPADEK. WARSAW, PANSTWOWY INSTYTUT WYDAWNICZY, 1957.   CR 249,
          I.T. (1959) 16410.   SEE NO. 118.   GUZE, JOANNA.

0142   A QUEDA. LISBON, LIVROS DO BRASIL, N.D. (1957).   CR 250, I.T.
          (1959) 16998.   SEE NO. 118.   TERRA, JOSE.

0143   FALLET. STOCKHOLM, BONNIERS (PANACHE), 1957.   CR 251, I.T.
          (1959) 19389.   SEE NO. 118.   ALEXANDERSSON, EVA.

0144   THE FALL. NEW YORK, KNOPF, 1957.   CR 243, I.T. (1958) 5751.
          SEE NO. 118.   O'BRIEN, JUSTIN.

0145   THE FALL. NEW YORK, VINTAGE BOOKS, 1963.   SEE NO. 125.
          O'BRIEN, JUSTIN.

0146   PAD (PRIPOVIJEST). ZAGREB, MLADOST, 1958.   I.T. (1961) 29036.
          SEE NO. 118.   LALIĆ, IVAN V.

0147   DER FALL. (EXCERPT). MERKUR, VOL. 11, NO. 1 (JAN. 1957), PP.
          60-65.   CR 417.

DISCOURS DE SUÈDE

DISCOURS DE SUÈDE. (CONTIENT AUSSI L'ARTISTE ET SON TEMPS).   0148
    PARIS, GALLIMARD, 1958. CR 271, BIBLIO (1958) 156.
DISCOURS DE SUÈDE. (CONTIENT AUSSI L'ARTISTE ET SON TEMPS).   0149
    PARIS, GALLIMARD, (COLL. BLANCHE), 1958. CR 272.
DISCOURS DE SUÈDE. (CONTIENT AUSSI L'ARTISTE ET SON TEMPS).   0150
    PARIS, GALLIMARD (COLL. RELIURE D'EDITEUR), 1958. CR 273.
DISCOURS DE SUÈDE. (CONTIENT AUSSI L'ARTISTE ET SON TEMPS).   0151
    PARIS, N.R.F., 1958. CR 274.
KUNSTNEREN OG HANS SAMTID. IN SOMMER, ESSAYS, PP. 125-155.   0152
    SEE NO. 626.
JOULUKUUN NELJÄNNENTOISTA PUHE VUODELTA 1957. IN ESSEITÄ   0153
    (VALIKOIMA), PP. 175-200. SEE NO. 627.
REDE ANLÄSSLICH DER ENTGEGENNAHME DES NOBELPREISES AM 10   0154
    DEZEMBER 1957 IN STOCKHOLM. HAMBURG, ROWOHLT, 1957. 1.T.
    (1960) 135. SEE NO. 148. MEISTER, GUIDO G.
NOBELPREISREDE (DER KÜNSTLER UND SEINE ZEIT). IN FRAGEN DER   0155
    ZEIT, PP. 261-267. SEE NO. 630.
NOBELPREISREDE. IN KLEINE PROSA, PP. 5-11. SEE NO. 631.   0156
REDE IN STOCKHOLM ZUR VERLEIHUNG DES NOBELPREISES AM 10   0157
    DEZEMBER 1957. IN NOBELPREISTRÄGER DER LITERATUR. EIN
    KAPITEL WELTLITERATUR DES ZWANZIGSTEN JAHRHUNDERTS, PP.
    31-35. SEE NO. 154. MEISTER, GUIDO G.
DER KÜNSTLER UND SEINE ZEIT (DER KÜNSTLER UND SEINE ZEIT). IN   0158
    FRAGEN DER ZEIT, PP. 268-294. SEE NO. 630.
DISCORSI DI SVEZIA. IN RIBELLIONE E MORTE, PP. SEE NO. 634.   0159
KUNSTNEREN OG HANS TID. IN DEN UOVERVINNELIGE SOMMER, PP. 139-   0160
    163. SEE NO. 639.
DISCURSO DA SUÉCIA. IN O AVESSO E O DIREITO. DISCURSO DA   0161
    SUÉCIA. SEE NO. 640.
THE NOBEL PRIZE SPEECH. LONDON MAGAZINE, VOL. 5, NO. 6 (JUNE   0162
    1958), PP. 11-14. CR 432. SEE NO. 148. STEWART, JEAN.
SPEECH OF ACCEPTANCE UPON THE AWARD OF THE NOBEL PRIZE FOR   0163
    LITERATURE. NEW YORK, KNOPF, 1958. PP. XIV. CR 275, 1.T.
    (1960) 7959. SEE NO. 148.
DER KÜNSTLER UND SEINE ZEIT. IN KLEINE PROSA, PP. 13-31. SEE   0164
    NO. 631.
ARTYSTA I WSPÓŁCZESNOŚĆ. TWÓRCZOŚĆ, VOL. 13, NO. 4 (APRIL   0165
    1957), PP. 96-108. SEE NO. 148. NATANSON, WOJCIECH.
KONSTNÄREN OCH HANS SAMTID. BONNIERS LITTERARA MAGASIN, VOL.   0166
    27, NO. 1 (JAN. 1958), PP. 34-44. SEE NO. 148.
    ALEXANDERSSON, EVA.
CREATE DANGEROUSLY. IN RESISTANCE, REBELLION AND DEATH, PP.   0167
    176-191. SEE NO. 633, 148.

0168   DISCORSO DEL 10 DICEMBRE 1957 (DISCORSI DI SVEZIA).   IN
         RIBELLIONE E MORTE, PP. 299-305.   SEE NO. 634.

0169   CONFERENZA DEL 14 DICEMBRE 1957 (DISCORSI DI SVEZIA).   IN
         RIBELLIONE E MORTE, PP. 305-328.   SEE NO. 634.

L'ENVERS ET L'ENDROIT

L'ENVERS ET L'ENDROIT. ALGER, CHARLOT (COLL. MÉDITER-   0170
RANÉENNE), 1937. CR 1, BIBLIO (1937) 149.

L'ENVERS ET L'ENDROIT. PREFACE DE L'AUTEUR. PARIS, GALLIMARD   0171
(COLL. LES ESSAIS), 1958. CR 2, BIBLIO (1958) 156, BIBLIO
(1959) 161.

L'ENVERS ET L'ENDROIT (ÉDITION ILLUSTRÉE PAR C. CAILLARD). IN   0172
RÉCITS ET THÉÂTRE. SEE NO. 618.

EL REVÉS Y EL DERECHO. BUENOS AIRES, LOSADO, 1958. I.T.   0173
(1961) 2329. SEE NO. 170. BIXIO, ALBERTO L.

LICHT UND SCHATTEN. IN LITERARISCHE ESSAYS, PP. 7-74. SEE NO.   0174
629, 171. MEISTER, GUIDO G.

LICHT UND SCHATTEN. IN KLEINE PROSA, PP. 33-76. SEE NO. 631.   0175

IL ROVESCIO E IL DIRITTO. IN SAGGI LETTERARI, PP. 5-58. SEE   0176
NO. 635.

URA TO OMOTE. TSUIHO. TOKYO, SHINCHO-SHA, 1958. CR 4, I.T.   0177
(1960) 14290. SEE NO. 170. KUBOTA, KEISAKU.

PYORI. SEOUL, LEE WHI YEONG, 1958. CR 3. SEE NO. 170.   0178
BULMUNWHA YEONGUHOE CHULPANBU.

KEER EN TERUGKEER. AMSTERDAM, BEZIGE BIJ, 1960. I.T. (1963)   0179
16797. SEE NO. 170. PONT, ANNE MACLAINE.

O AVESSO E O DIREITO. IN O AVESSO E O DIREITO. DISCURSO DA   0180
SUÉCIA. SEE NO. 640.

FRAMSIDAN OCH FRÅNSIDAN. IN SOMMAR, PP. SEE NO. 642, 170.   0181

ESIPUHE KOKOELMAAN (PREFACE). IN ESSEITÄ (VALIKOIMA), PP.   0182
151-165. SEE NO. 627.

KYLLÄ JA EI (ENTRE OUI ET NON). IN ESSEITÄ (VALIKOIMA), PP.   0183
19-29. SEE NO. 627.

MELLOM JA OG NEI (ENTRE OUI ET NON). IN DEN UOVERVINNELIGE   0184
SOMMER, PP. 29-40. SEE NO. 170, 639.

BETWEEN YES AND NO. PARTISAN REVIEW, VOL. 16, NO. 2 (NOV.   0185
1949), PP. 1090-1097. CR 354. FRECHTMAN, BERNARD.

L'ENVERS ET L'ENDROIT. NOUVELLE REVUE FRANÇAISE, VOL. 6, NO.   0186
61 (JAN. 1958), PP. 1-12. FR VII 19410.

FORSIDEN OG BAGSIDEN (L'ENVERS ET L'ENDROIT). IN SOMMER,   0187
ESSAYS, PP. 23-28. SEE NO. 186, 626.

NURJA JA OIKEA. IN ESSEITÄ (VALIKOIMA), PP. 97-101. SEE NO.   0188
186, 627.

IRONIEN. IN DEN UOVERVINNELIGE SOMMER, PP. 17-28. SEE NO.   0189
170, 639.

L'ÉTAT DE SIÈGE

0190 L'ÉTAT DE SIÈGE. SPECTACLE EN TROIS PARTIES. ÉDITION
      ORIGINALE RELIÉE D'APRÈS LA MAQUETTE DE MARIO PRASSINOS.
      PARIS, GALLIMARD, 1948. CR 167.

0191 L'ÉTAT DE SIÈGE. SPECTACLE EN TROIS PARTIES. PARIS,
      GALLIMARD, 1948. CR 168, BIBLIO (1949) 126.

0192 L'ÉTAT DE SIÈGE. SPECTACLE EN TROIS PARTIES. PARIS,
      GALLIMARD (N.R.F.), 1948. CR 169.

0193 L'ÉTAT DE SIÈGE. SPECTACLE EN TROIS PARTIES. ÉDITION RELIÉE
      D'APRÈS LA MAQUETTE DE MARIO PRASSINOS. PARIS, GALLIMARD,
      1949. CR 170.

0194 L'ÉTAT DE SIÈGE. SPECTACLE EN TROIS PARTIES. ÉDITION RELIÉE
      D'APRÈS LA MAQUETTE DE MARIO PRASSINOS. PARIS, GALLIMARD,
      1950. CR 171.

0195 L'ÉTAT DE SIÈGE (ÉDITION ILLUSTRÉE PAR MARIANO ANDREU). IN
      RÉCITS ET THÉÂTRE. SEE NO. 618.

0196 EL ESTADO DE SITIO. ESPECTÁCULO EN TRES PARTES. IN TEATRO,
      PP. 115-189. SEE NO. 622. BERNARDEZ, AURORA.

0197 L'ÉTAT DE SIÈGE. IN CALIGULA AND THREE OTHER PLAYS. SEE NO.
      624.

0198 BELAGERUNGSZUSTAND. DRAMA IN 3 ABTEILUNGEN. VIENNA, MUNICH,
      BASEL, DESCH, 1955. CR 172, 173, I.T. (1957) 855.
      HAUSER, HANS H.

0199 DER BELAGERUNGSZUSTAND. IN DRAMEN, PP. 117-186. CR 183. SEE
      NO. 628, 190.

0200 DAR MOHÄSERE (L'ÉTAT DE SIÈGE). TEHERAN, 1962. SEPANLU,
      MOHAMMED-ALI.

0201 LO STATO D'ASSEDIO. SPETTACOLO IN TRE ATTI. IN TEATRO, PP.
      233-325. SEE NO. 636. LODOVICI, CESARE VICO.

0202 KAIGENREI. TOKYO, SHINCHO-SHA, 1952. CR 174. SEE NO. 190.
      MIYAZAKI, MINEO.

0203 STATE OF SIEGE. A PLAY IN THREE PARTS. IN CALIGULA AND THREE
      OTHER PLAYS, PP. 135-232. SEE NO. 643.

0204 STATE OF SIEGE. IN CALIGULA AND THREE OTHER PLAYS, PP.
      135-232. CR 96. SEE NO. 644.

L'ÉTÉ

L'ÉTÉ. ESSAIS. ÉDITION ORIGINALE. PARIS, GALLIMARD (COLL.   0205
    LES ESSAIS, 68), 1954. CR 219, BIBLIO (1954) 128.

L'ÉTÉ. ESSAIS. ÉDITION RELIÉE D'APRÈS LA MAQUETTE DE MARIO   0206
    PRASSINOS. PARIS, GALLIMARD (COLL. LES ESSAIS, 68), 1954.
    CR 220, BIBLIO (1954) 128.

L'ÉTÉ. ESSAIS. PARIS. GALLIMARD N.R.F., (COLL. LES ESSAIS,   0207
    68), 1954. CR 221.

L'ÉTÉ. ESSAIS. PARIS. GALLIMARD, N.R.F. (COLL. LES ESSAIS,   0208
    68), 1954. CR 222.

L'ÉTÉ (ÉDITION ILLUSTRÉE PAR P.-E. CLAIRIN). IN RÉCITS ET   0209
    THÉÂTRE. SEE NO. 618.

EL VERANO. BUENOS AIRES, SUR, 1957. CR 225, I.T. (1960)   0210
    2775. SEE NO. 205. BIXIO, ALBERTO L.

SOMMER (ESSAYS). COPENHAGEN, GYLDENDAL, 1961. I.T. (1963)   0211
    6657. SEE NO. 205. HANSEN, THORKILD.

HEIMKEHR NACH TIPASA. IN LITERARISCHE ESSAYS, PP. 123-203.   0212
    SEE NO. 629, 205. REPRINT OF NO. 214. LANG, MONIQUE.

NATSU. TOKYO, SHINCHO-SHA, 1956. CR 226, I.T. (1957) 10939.   0213
    SEE NO. 205. KUBOTA, KEISAKU.

HEIMKEHR NACH TIPASA. ZURICH, VERLAG DER ARCHE, 1957. SEE   0214
    NO. 205. LANG, MONIQUE.

L'ESTATE. IN SAGGI LETTERARI, PP. 99-169. SEE NO. 635.   0215

SOMMAR. IN SOMMAR, PP. 123-211. SEE NO. 642, 205.   0216

LETO. BELGRADE, NOLIT, 1957. CR 227, I.T. (1958) 27209. SEE   0217
    NO. 205. MARKOVIC, IVANKA.

MANDELTRÄEET. (L'ÉTÉ). IN SOMMER, ESSAYS, PP. 92-96. SEE NO.   0218
    626.

MANTELIPUUT. (L'ÉTÉ). IN ESSEITÄ (VALIKOIMA), PP. 115-118.   0219
    SEE NO. 627.

ZAGADKA. (THE RIDDLE OR THE ENIGMA). NOWA KULTURA, NO. 513   0220
    (1961). GUZE, JOANNA.

ARVOITUS (L'ÉNIGME). IN ESSEITÄ (VALIKOIMA), PP. 166-174. SEE   0221
    NO. 627.

L'EXIL D'HÉLÈNE. (ESSAI). IN PERMANENCE DE LA GRÈCE. PARIS,   0222
    ÉDITIONS DES CAHIERS DU SUD, 1948. SEE NO. 205.

L'EXIL D'HÉLÈNE. IN PERMANENCE DE LA GRÈCE, PP. 381-386.   0223
    MARSEILLE, CAHIERS DU SUD, 1948. CR 279. SEE NO. 205.

HELEN'S EXIL. IN THE MYTH OF SISYPHUS, PP. 145-151. SEE NO.   0224
    645, 222.

DEN LANDFLYGTIGE HELENA. IN SOMMER, ESSAYS, PP. 103-111. SEE   0225
    NO. 626, 222.

HELENAN MAANPAKO. IN ESSEITÄ (VALIKOIMA), PP. 124-130. SEE   0226
    NO. 627, 222.

0227   HELENA I LANDFLYKTIGHET.   IN DEN UOVERVINNELIGE SOMMER, PP.
          164-169.   SEE NO. 639, 222.

0228   LA MER AU PLUS PRÈS.   NOUVELLE REVUE FRANÇAISE,   VOL. 2, NO.
          13 (JAN. 1954), PP. 1-10.   CR 376.

0229   NÄRMAST INTILL HAVET.   BONNIERS LITTERÄRA MAGASIN,   VOL. 26,
          NO. 10 (DEC. 1957), PP. 848-852.   SEE NO. 228.   BJURSTRÖM,
          G. G.

0230   ALLTID NAERMERE HAVET.   IN DEN UOVERVINNELIGE SOMMER, PP. 181-
          191.   SEE NO. 639, 228.

0231   LE MINOTAURE OU LA HALTE D'ORAN.   PARIS,   CHARLOT, 1950.   CR
          188, BIBLIO (1950) 122.   SEE NO. 205.

0232   LE MINOTAURE OU LA HALTE D'ORAN.   L'ARCHE,   VOL. 3, NO. 13
          (FEB. 1946), PP. 3-23.   CR 327.

0233   MINOTAUROS ELLER OPHOLD I ORAN.   IN SOMMER, ESSAYS, PP. 58-91.
          SEE NO. 626, 231.

0234   THE MINOTAUR OR THE STOP IN ORAN.   IN THE MYTH OF SISYPHUS AND
          OTHER ESSAYS, PP. 123-144.   SEE NO. 645, 232.

0235   PIENI OPAS MATKALLE KAUPUNKEIHIN, JOILLA EI OLE MENNEISYYTTA.
          IN ESSEITÄ (VALIKOIMA), PP. 53-58.   SEE NO. 627.

0236   PROMÉTHÉE AUX ENFERS.   PARIS,   PALIMURGE, 1947.   CR 166.   SEE
          NO. 205.

0237   PROMETHEUS I HELVEDE.   IN SOMMER, ESSAYS, PP. 97-102.   SEE NO.
          626, 236.

0238   PROMETHEUS MANALASSA.   IN ESSEITÄ (VALIKOIMA), PP. 119-123.
          SEE NO. 627, 236.

0239   TILBAGE TIL TIPASA.   IN SOMMER, ESSAYS, PP. 112-124   SEE NO.
          626.

0240   PALUU TIPASAAN.   IN ESSEITÄ (VALIKOIMA), PP. 56-69.   SEE NO.
          627.

0241   RETURN TO TIPASA.   IN THE MYTH OF SISYPHUS AND OTHER ESSAYS,
          PP. 153-162.   SEE NO. 645, 205.

0242   GJENSYN MED TIPASA.   IN DEN UOVERVINNELIGE SOMMER, PP. 170-180.
          SEE NO. 639.

0243   ÅTER TILL TIPASA.   BONNIERS LITTERÄRA MAGASIN,   VOL. 29, NO. 2
          (FEB. 1960), PP. 97-101.   BJURSTRÖM, C. G.

0244   HEIMKEHR NACH TIPASA.   ZURICH,   VERLAG DER ARCHE, 1957.   CR
          223, I.T. (1959) 20352.   LANG, MONIQUE.

0245   L'ÉTÉ (EXTRAIT).   LES NOUVELLES LITTÉRAIRES,   NO. 1573 (OCT.
          24, 1957), P. 6.   SEE NO. 464.

L'ÉTRANGER

L'ÉTRANGER. ROMAN. ÉDITION ORIGINALE. PARIS, GALLIMARD   0246
    (NRF), 1942. CR 24, BIBLIO (1942) 98.

L'ÉTRANGER. ROMAN. RELIÉ D'APRÈS LA MAQUETTE DE MARIO   0247
    PRASSINOS. PARIS, GALLIMARD, 1944. CR 26, BIBLIO (1945)
    104.

L'ÉTRANGER. ROMAN. NEW YORK, SCHIFFRIN, PANTHEON BOOKS,   0248
    1946. CR 27, DR 116, BIBLIO (1946) 116.

L'ÉTRANGER. ROMAN. AVEC 29 EAUX-FORTES DE MAYO. PARIS,   0249
    GALLIMARD (N.R.F.), 1946. CR 28, BIBLIO (1946) 116.

L'ÉTRANGER. ROMAN. PARIS, CLUB DU MEILLEUR LIVRE, 1954. CR   0250
    31.

L'ÉTRANGER. ROMAN. RELIÉ D'APRÈS LA MAQUETTE DE MARIO   0251
    PRASSINOS. PARIS, GALLIMARD (COLL. RELIURE D'ÉDITEUR),
    1954. CR 32, L.F. (1946-1955) I. 368.

L'ÉTRANGER. ROMAN. EDITED BY GERMAINE BRÉE AND CARLOS LYNES, 0252
    JR. NEW YORK, APPLETON-CENTURY-CROFTS, 1955. CR 33, FR
    VII 15331, BIBLIO (1956) 146.

L'ÉTRANGER. ROMAN. SUIVI D'UN ÉCRIVAIN QUI VIENT. ALBERT   0253
    CAMUS PAR MARCEL ARLAND. PARIS, CLUB DE LIBRAIRES DE
    FRANCE, (COLL. FICTION NO. 67), 1957. CR 34, BIBLIO (1958)
    156.

L'ÉTRANGER. ROMAN. EDITED BY GERMAINE BRÉE AND CARLOS LYNES. 0254
    LONDON, METHUEN, 1958. CR 35, BIBLIO (1958) 156.

L'ÉTRANGER. PARIS, GALLIMARD (COLL. SOLEIL), 1958.   0255

L'ÉTRANGER (ÉDITION ILLUSTRÉE PAR EDY LEGRAND). IN RÉCITS ET 0256
    THÉÂTRE. SEE NO. 618.

L'ÉTRANGER. ROMAN. PARIS, LIBRAIRIE GÉNÉRALE FRANÇAISE   0257
    (LIVRE DE POCHE), 1959. CR 36.

L'ÉTRANGER. ROMAN. NEW YORK, RANDOM HOUSE (PANTHEON BOOKS), 0258
    1963. SEE NO. 721.

L'ÉTRANGER. ROMAN. EDITED BY FRANZ-RUDOLF WELLER. FRANKFURT 0259
    AM MAIN, DIESTERWEG, 1964. STERWEG, 1964.

EL EXTRANJERO. BUENOS AIRES, EMECE, 1949. CR 46, B.B.A.   0260
    (1949) 692. CARRIL, BONIFACIO DEL.

CIZINEC. IN CIZINEC-PAD, PP. 7-93. SEE NO. 625.   0261

DEN FREMMEDE. COPENHAGEN, GYLDENDAL, 1957. CR 45, I.T.   0262
    (1959) 4947. HARTVIG, MAGNA.

SIVULLINEN. IN MAANPAKO JA VALTAKUNTA, SIVULLINEN, PP. 157FF. 0263
    I.T. (1963) 10390. SEE NO. 305. SALO, KALLE.

I HSIANG YEN. TAIPEI, THE UNITED DAILY NEWS. CR 44, I.T.   0264
    (1960) 5839. TS'UIFENG SHIH.

DER FREMDE. DUSSELDORF, RAUCH, 1957. CR 39, I.T. (1959) 899. 0265
    GOYERT, GEORG. BRENNER, HANS GEORG.

0266 DER FREMDE. ERZÄHLUNG. BAD SALZIG. RAUCH, 1948 CR 37, B.T.A.
      4433 GOYERT, GEORG

0267 THE OUTSIDER. IN THE COLLECTED FICTION OF ALBERT CAMUS. SEE
      NO. 632.

0268 O XENOS. ATHENS, DHAIDHALOS, 1955. CR 49, I.T. (1957) 8146.
      COTSIRAS, GHIORGHIS.

0269 O XENOS ATHENS, SUROPOULOI-KOUMOUNDOUREA, 1960. I.T. (1962),
      11482. PRANGIA, KOULA.

0270 KÖZÖNY. BUDAPEST, MAGVETÖ, 1958 CR 52, I.T. (1959) 9615
      GYERGYAI, ALBERT.

0271 BIDESHI-PATAN, (ORIYA). CUTTACK, PRAFULLA CHANDRA DAS,
      1958. CR 51, I.T. (1960) 11282. RAYA, LALA NAGENDRA
      KUMARA.

0272 AJANABI. DELHI, RAJKAMAL PRAKASAN, 1961. I.T. (1963) 13497.
      YADAV, RAJENDRA.

0273 HA-ZAR. TEL-AVIV, ZOHAR, 1956. CR 50, I.T. (1959) 10938.
      AMIR, A.

0274 HA-ZAR. TEL-AVIV, AM HASEFER, 1962. I.T. (1964) 13435.
      AMIR, AHARON.

0275 LO STRANIERO. MILAN, BOMPIANI, 1947. CR 53, B.P.I. (1948)
      349. ZEVI, ALBERTO.

0276 IHOJIN. TOKYO, SHINCHO-SHA, 1951. CR 55, I.T. (1951-1953)
      9774. KUBOTA, KEISAKU.

0277 IHOJIN, PESUTO. TOKYO, SHINCHO-SHA, 1952. CR 154, I.T.
      (1953) 8379. SEE NO. 246, 522. KUBOTA, KEISAKU.

0278 IHOJIN, TENRAKU. TOKYO, SHINCHO-SHA, 1958. CR 57, I.T.
      (1960) 14287. SEE NO. 138. KUBOTA, KEISAKU.

0279 IHOJIN. TOKYO, SHINCHO-SHA, 1960. I.T. (1962) 15378. SATO,
      SAKU ET AL.

0280 IBANG'IN, PESTEU. SEOUL, JEONGEUMSA, 1960. I.T. (1962) 5963.
      SEE NO. 527. LEE HWI-YEONG AND BANG GON.

0281 DE VREEMDELING. AMSTERDAM, BEZIGE BIJ, 1949. CR 58, I.T.
      (1950) 6370. MORRIËN, ADRIAAN

0282 DE VREEMDELING. AMSTERDAM, BEZIGE BIJ (LITERAIRE POCKETSERIE,
      14), 1958. CR 60, I.T. (1960) 16167.

0283 OBCY. WARSAW, PANSTWOWY INSTYTUT WYDAWNICZY, 1958. CR 61,
      I.T. (1960) 17398. ZENOWICZ, MARIA.

0284 O ESTRANGEIRO. LISBON, LIVROS DO BRASIL, 1954. CR 62, I.T.
      (1956) 16337. QUADROS, ANTÓNIO.

0285 EL EXTRANJERO. MADRID, CID, 1958. CR 48, I.T. (1960) 6996.
      CARRIL, BONIFACIO DEL.

0286 FRÄMLINGEN. STOCKHOLM, BONNIERS (PANACHE-SERIEN), 1946. CR
      63. LINDSTRÖM, SIGFRID.

0287 FRÄMLINGEN. STOCKHOLM, BONNIERS, 1957. CR 65, I.T. (1959)
      19390, I.T. (1962) 21361. LINDSTRÖM, SIGFRID.

DER FREMDE. ROMAN. ZURICH, BÜCHERGILDE GUTENBERG, 1951. CR   0288
     38, I.T. (1952) 14469. HINDERMANN, FRITZ.
YABANCI. ISTANBUL, VARLIK YAYINEVI (YENI MATBAA), 1953. CR   0289
     66, I.T (1958) 21394. GUNTEKIN, RESAT NURIT.
YABANCI. ISTANBUL, VARLIK YAYINEVI, 1958. CR 67, I.T. (1960)   0290
     23740, I.T. (1962) 24480. TIRYAKIOGU, SAMIH.
YABANCI. ISTANBUL, ISTANBUL MATBAASI, 1959. I.T. (1962)   0291
     24479. GUNYOL, VEDAT.
THE OUTSIDER. INTRODUCTION BY CYRIL CONNOLLY. LONDON, H.   0292
     HAMILTON, 1946. CR 40. GILBERT, STUART
THE OUTSIDER. HARMONDSWORTH, PENGUIN, 1961. I.T. (1964)   0293
     22244. GILBERT, STUART.
THE STRANGER. NEW YORK, KNOPF, 1946. CR 42. GILBERT,   0294
     STUART.
THE STRANGER. NEW YORK, VINTAGE BOOKS, 1954. CR 43, I.T.   0295
     (1956) 6575. GILBERT, STUART.
STRANAC. ZAGREB, ZORA, 1951. CR 68, I.T. (1951-1953) 15495.   0296
     SMICIKLAS, DANE.
STRANAC. BELGRADE, NARODNA KNJIGA, 1959. NIKOLIĆ, DRAGAN.   0297

L'EXIL ET LE ROYAUME

0298   L'EXIL ET LE ROYAUME.   PARIS,   GALLIMARD (N.R.F.), 1957.   CR
        258.

0299   L'EXIL ET LE ROYAUME.   NOUVELLES.   ÉDITION RELIÉE D'APRÈS LA
        MAQUETTE DE MARIO PRASSINOS.   PARIS,   GALLIMARD (COLL.
        RELIURES D'ÉDITEUR), 1957.   CR 254, BIBLIO (1957) 150.

0300   L'EXIL ET LE ROYAUME.   NOUVELLES.   PARIS,   GALLIMARD (COLL.
        SOLEIL), 1957.   CR 255, BIBLIO (1955) 150.

0301   L'EXIL ET LE ROYAUME (ÉDITION ILLUSTRÉE PAR ORLANDO PELAYO)
        SEE NO. 618.

0302   L'EXIL ET LE ROYAUME.   ABREGÉE ET ANNOTÉE PAR J. P. VAN DER
        LINDEN ET J. A. G. TANS.   HILVERSUM,   BRAND (SÉRIE JAUNE),
        1962.

0303   EL EXILIO Y EL REINO.   BUENOS AIRES,   LOSADA, 1957.   CR 263,
        I.T. (1960) 2773, (1963) 3743.   BIXIO, ALBERTO L.

0304   EKSIL OG KONGEDOMME.   COPENHAGEN,   GYLDENDAL, 1958.   CR 262.
        ELMQUIST, CARL JOHAN.

0305   MAANPAKO JA VALTAKUNTA (NOVELLEJA), SIVULLINEN.   HELSINKI,
        OTAVA, 1960.   I.T. (1962) 9587, I.T. (1963) 10390.   SEE NO.
        263.   LEHTONEN, MAIJA.

0306   DAS EXIL UND DAS REICH.   ERZÄHLUNGEN.   HAMBURG,   ROWOHLT, 1958.
        CR 259.   MEISTER, GUIDO G.

0307   EXILE AND THE KINGDOM.   IN THE COLLECTED FICTION OF ALBERT
        CAMUS.   SEE NO. 632.

0308   GALUT U-MALCHUT.   IN HA-NEFILA, GALUT U-MALCHUT.   SEE NO. 136,
        298.

0309   L'ESILIO E IL REGNO.   IN LA CADUTA, L'ESILIO E IL REGNO.   SEE
        NO. 137, 298.

0310   TSUIHO.   TOKYO,   SHINCHO-SHA, 1957.   CR 264, I.T. (1959) 13209.
        KUBOTA, KEISAKU.

0311   TSUIHO.   IN URA TO OMOTE.   TSUIHO.   SEE NO. 177.

0312   YUZEOK GWA WANGGUK.   IN HEUKSABYEONG.   YUZEOK GWA WANGGUK.   SEE
        NO. 298, 525.

0313   YU'DONG GWA WANG'GUG.   SEOUL,   HONG'A'CHUL'PAN'SA, 1959.   I.T.
        (1961) 29678.   LEE HANG.

0314   KONINKRIJK EN BALLINGSCHAP.   AMSTERDAM,   BEZIGE BIJ, 1958.
        I.T. (1961) 16032.   PONT, A. EYKMAN-MACLAINE.

0315   KONINKRIJK EN BALLINGSCHAP.   AMSTERDAM,   BEZIGE BIJ
        (REUZENPOCKET 33), 1963.

0316   WYGNANIE I KROLESTWO.   WARSAW,   PANSTWOWY INSTYTUT WYDAWNICZY,
        1958.   CR 265, I.T. (1960) 17399.   GUZE, JOANNA.

0317   O EXÍLIO E O REINO.   LISBON,   LIVROS DO BRASIL, 1958.   CR 266,
        I.T. (1960) 17966.   CABRAL DO NASCIMENTO, JOÃO.

0318   LANDSFLYKTEN OCH RIKET.   STOCKHOLM,   BONNIERS (PANACHE-SERIEN),

1957. CR 267, I.T. (1959) 19391. ALEXANDERSSON, EVA.

DIE EHEBRECHERIN. DER GAST. (EXCERPTS FROM L'EXIL ET LE   0319
    ROYAUME). ZURICH, VERLAG DER ARCHE, 1959. I.T. (1961)
    21178. MEISTER, GUIDO G.

SURGUN VE KRALLIK. ISTANBUL, DUSUN YAYINEVI, 1960. I.T.   0320
    (1962) 24477.

EXILE AND THE KINGDOM. LONDON, H. HAMILTON, 1958. CR 260,   0321
    I.T. (1960) 20275. O'BRIEN, JUSTIN.

IZGNANSTVO I KRALJEVSTVO. BELGRADE, SRPSKA KNJIŽEVNA ZADRUGA,   0322
    1959. I.T. (1962) 30725. JOKIĆ, LJUBICA.

EXILE AND THE KINGDOM. NEW YORK, KNOPF, 1958. CR 261, I.T.   0323
    (1960) 7958. O'BRIEN, JUSTIN.

LA FEMME ADULTÈRE. 12 LITHOGRAPHIES ORIGINALES EN COULEURS DE   0324
    PIERRE-EUGÈNE CLAIRIN. ALGER, ÉDITIONS DE L'EMPIRE (COLL.
    ORIGINALES ILLUSTRÉES), 1954. CR 228, BIBLIO (1954) 128.
    SEE NO. 298.

DIE EHEBRECHERIN. DER GAST. ERZÄHLUNGEN. ZURICH, VERLAG DER   0325
    ARCHE (KLEINE BÜCHER DER ARCHE 287-288) CR 229. SEE NO.
    324, 331. MEISTER, GUIDO G. MEISTER, GERTRUD.

ÄKTENSKAPSBRYTERSKAN. BONNIERS LITTERÄRA MAGASIN, VOL. 25,   0326
    NO. 8 (OCT. 1956), PP. 602-611. SEE NO. 324.

L'HÔTE. RÉALITÉS, FÉMINA-ILLUSTRATION, NO. 136 (MAY 1957),   0327
    PP. 76-77, 113-115. CR 418. SEE NO. 298.

L'HÔTE. IN L'EXIL ET LE ROYAUME, PP. 7-23. SEE NO. 302.   0328

DER GAST. IN KLEINE PROSA, PP. 131-146. SEE NO. 327, 631.   0329
    MEISTER, GUIDO G.

THE GUEST. THE LONDON MAGAZINE, VOL. 5, NO. 3 (MARCH 1958),   0330
    PP. 14-25. CR 430. SEE NO. 327. O'BRIEN, JUSTIN.

DER GAST. IN DIE EHEBRECHERIN, DER GAST. SEE NO. 325, 327.   0331

JONAS OU L'ARTISTE AU TRAVAIL. IN L'EXIL ET LE ROYAUME, PP.   0332
    24-57. SEE NO. 298, 302.

JONAS ODER DER KÜNSTLER BEI DER ARBEIT. WIESBADEN, INSEL   0333
    VERLAG, 1959. I.T. (1962) 1287. SEE NO. 332. MEISTER,
    GUIDO G.

LES MUETS. ÉDITÉ ET ANNOTÉ PAR WERNER LIEBE. FRANKFURT AM   0334
    MAIN, DIESTERWEG (NEUSPRACHLICHE BIBLIOTHEK, 4051), 1959.

LES MUETS. IN L'EXIL ET LE ROYAUME, PP. 58-73. SEE NO. 302.   0335

DIE STUMMEN. IN KLEINE PROSA, PP. 117-130. SEE NO. 334, 631.   0336
    MEISTER, GUIDO G.

LA PIERRE QUI POUSSE. ANNOTÉ PAR P. KLEEREBEZEM. AMSTERDAM,   0337
    MEULENHOFF, 1961. BIBLIO (1962) 163. SEE NO. 298.

DER TREIBENDE STEIN. ERZÄHLUNG. MUNICH, PIPER (PIPERBÜCHEREI   0338
    139), 1959. CR 268, UNESCO I.T. (1962) 1290. MEISTER,
    GUIDO G.

DIE KLIP WAT GROEI. CAPETOWN, NASIONALE BOEKHANDEL, 1961.   0339

I.T. (1963) 21510.   RABIE, JAN.

0340   L'ESPRIT CONFUS (LE RENÉGAT).   NOUVELLE REVUE FRANÇAISE,   VOL.
        4, NO. 42 (JUNE 1, 1956) PP. 961-978.   CR 253.   SEE NO.
        298.

0341   DER ABTRÜNNIGE ODER EIN VERWIRRTER GEIST.   IN KLEINE PROSA, PP.
        99-115.   SEE NO. 340.   MEISTER, GUIDO G.

0342   RENÉGAT - ALBO UMYSL ZMACONY.   TWÓRCZOŚĆ,   VOL. 13, NO. 8 (AUG.
        1957), PP. 9-18.   SEE NO. 340.   GUZE, JOANNA.

0343   THE RENEGADE.   PARTISAN REVIEW,   VOL. 25, NO. 1 (WINTER 1958)
        PP. 11-24.   CR 433   SEE NO. 340.   O'BRIEN, JUSTIN.

L'HOMME RÉVOLTÉ

L'HOMME RÉVOLTÉ. PARIS, GALLIMARD (N.R.F.), 1951. CR 190.   0344

L'HOMME RÉVOLTÉ. ÉDITION ORIGINALE, RELIÉE D'APRÈS LA MAQUETTE   0345
     DE MARIO PRASSINOS. PARIS, GALLIMARD, 1951. CR 189,
     BIBLIO (1951) 125.

L'HOMME RÉVOLTÉ. DANS RÉVOLTE SUR MESURE. PARIS, ÉDITIONS DE   0346
     LA RUE (NUMÉRO SPÉCIAL DE LA RUE), 1952. CR 196.

L'HOMME RÉVOLTÉ. PARIS, GALLIMARD (COLL. SOLEIL), 1958. CR   0347
     198.

EL HOMBRE REBELDE. IN EL MITO DE SISIFO, EL HOMBRE REBELDE   0348
     SEE NO. 438.

THE REBEL. PREFACE BY SIR HERBERT READ. TORONTO, MCCLELLAND   0349
     AND STEWART, 1954. BOWER, ANTHONY.

THE REBEL, AN ESSAY ON MAN IN REVOLT, WITH A FOREWORD BY SIR   0350
     HERBERT READ. TORONTO, MCCLELLAND AND STEWART, 1956.
     BOWER, ANTHONY,

DER MENSCH IN DER REVOLTE. HAMBURG, ROWOHLT, 1953. CR 200.   0351
     STRELLER, JUSTUS.

DER MENSCH IN DER REVOLTE. UNTER MITARBEITUNG VON FRANÇOIS   0352
     BONDY. HAMBURG, ROWOHLT, 1958. CR 201. STRELLER,
     JUSTUS. SCHLOCKER, GEORGES.

L'UOMO IN RIVOLTA. MILAN, BOMPIANI, 1957. CR 207. MAGRINI,   0353
     LILIANA.

HANKOTEKI NINGEN. TOKYO, SHINCHO-SHA, 1956. CR 209, I.T.   0354
     (1958) 12280. SATO, SAKU. SHIRAI, KOJI.

BAN'HANG'JEOG IN'GAN. SEOUL, IL'SIN'SA, 1959. I.T. (1961)   0355
     29514. SIN GUCHEOL.

DE MENS IN OPSTAND. AMSTERDAM, BEZIGE BIJ, 1952. CR 211,   0356
     I.T. (1953) 9606. MEIJERS, J.A.

CZŁOWIEK ZBUNTOWANY. PARIS, INSTYTUT LITERACKI, 1958. BIBLIO   0357
     (1959) 161, I.T. (1961) 8955.

MÄNNISKANS REVOLT. STOCKHOLM, BONNIERS (PANACHE-SERIEN),   0358
     1953. CR 212, I.T. (1954) 14563. BRANDDELL, GUNNAR.

DER MENSCH IN DER REVOLTE. LONDON, BARMERLEA BOOK SALES,   0359
     1952. CR 199. STRELLER, JUSTUS.

THE REBEL. FOREWORD BY SIR HERBERT READ. LONDON, H.   0360
     HAMILTON, 1953. CR 202. BOWER, ANTHONY.

THE REBEL. FOREWORD BY SIR HERBERT READ. LONDON, PENGUIN   0361
     BOOK, 1962. CBI (1961-1962), 415. BOWER, ANTHONY.

THE REBEL. FOREWORD BY SIR HERBERT READ. NEW YORK, KNOPF,   0362
     1954. CR 203, I.T. (1956) 6269. BOWER, ANTHONY.

THE REBEL. FOREWORD BY SIR HERBERT READ. NEW YORK, VINTAGE   0363
     BOOKS, 1956. CR 204, I.T. (1958) 5353. BOWER, ANTHONY.

THE REBEL. PREFACE BY SIR HERBERT READ. TORONTO, MCCLELLAND   0364

AND STEWART, 1956.   CR 204, I.T. (1958) 5353.   BOWER,
ANTHONY.

0365   L'HOMME RÉVOLTÉ (EXCERPT).   LES NOUVELLES LITTÉRAIRES,   NO.
       1573 (OCT. 24, 1957), P. 6.   SEE NO. 464.

0366   NIESPODZIANKI LITERATURY CZYLI AKTUALNOŚĆ SADE'A.   TWÓRCZOŚĆ,
       VOL. 12, NO. 9 (SEP. 1956), PP. 197-202.   BLOŃSKI, JAN.

0367   LES MEURTRIERS DÉLICATS.   LA TABLE RONDE,   NO. 1 (JAN. 1948),
       PP. 42-50.   CR 348.   SEE NO. 344.

0368   THE SENSITIVE MURDERERS.   WORLD REVIEW,   NO. 9 (NOV. 1949), PP.
       30-33.   SEE NO. 367.

0369   LE MEURTRE ET L'ABSURDE.   EMPÉDOCLE,   VOL. 1, NO. 1 (APR.
       1949), PP. 19-27.   CR 358.   SEE NO. 344.

0370   REMARQUE SUR LA RÉVOLTE.   IN EXISTENCE, ESSAIS PAR CAMUS,
       ÉTIENNE GILSON, JEAN GRENIER.   PARIS,   GALLIMARD, 1945.
       SEE NO. 344.

0371   REMARQUE SUR LA RÉVOLTE   IN L'EXISTENCE, PP. 9-23.   SEE NO.
       344, 1887.

0372   ART AND REVOLT.   PARTISAN REVIEW,   VOL. 19, NO. 3 (MAY-JUNE
       1952), 268-281.   CR 368, FR VII 7223.   SEE NO. 344.   FRANK,
       JOSEPH.

0373   REVOLTE OG KUNST.   DANSKE MAGASIN,   VOL. 1 (1953), PP. 221-234.
       SEE NO. 344.

0374   NIETZSCHE ET LE NIHILISME.   LES TEMPS MODERNES,   VOL. 7, NO. 70
       (AUG. 1951), PP. 193-208.   CR 365.   SEE NO. 344.

0375   NIETZSCHE UND DER NIHILISMUS.   MONAT,   VOL. 4, NO. 39 (1951),
       PP. 227-237.   BFZ (1951) P. 946.   SEE NO. 374.

LES JUSTES

LES JUSTES. PIÈCE EN CINQ ACTES. PARIS, GALLIMARD (N.R.F.),   0376
     1950. CR 181, BIBLIO (1950) 121.

LES JUSTES. PIÈCE EN CINQ ACTES. ÉDITION ORIGINALE, RELIÉE   0377
     D'APRÈS LA MAQUETTE DE MARIO PRASSINOS. PARIS,
     GALLIMARD, 1950. CR 180.

LES JUSTES (ÉDITION ILLUSTRÉE PAR TIBOR CSERNUS). IN RÉCITS ET   0378
     THÉÂTRE. SEE NO. 618.

LES JUSTES. PIÈCE EN CINQ ACTES. EDITÉE ET ANNOTÉE PAR PAUL   0379
     SCHMIDT AVEC UNE PRÉFACE DE RICHARD THIEBERGER. STUTTGART,
     ERNST KLETT VERLAG, 1960.

LOS JUSTOS. PIEZA EN CINCO ACTOS. IN TEATRO, PP. 191-241.   0380
     SEE NO. 622. BERNARDEZ, AURORA. TORRE, GUILLERMO DE.

LOS JUSTOS. IN EL MALENTENDIDO. EL ESTADO DE SITIO. LOS   0381
     JUSTOS. SEE NO. 420.

THE JUST ASSASSINS. IN CALIGULA AND THREE OTHER PLAYS. SEE   0382
     NO. 624.

DE RETFÆRDIGE. SKUESPIL I FEM AKTER. COPENHAGEN, GYLDENDAL,   0383
     1961. I.T. (1963) 6837. FRIDBERG, SVEND.

DIE GERECHTEN. IN FRANZÖSISCHES THEATER. SEE NO. 2499.   0384

DIE GERECHTEN. IN DRAMEN, PP. 187-234. SEE NO. 628.   0385

I GIUSTI. DRAMMA IN CINQUE ATTI. IN TEATRO, PP. 159-225. SEE   0386
     NO. 636. OUSSET, FRANÇOIS.

SEIGI NO HITOBITO. TOKYO, SHINCHO-SHA, 1953. CR 186, I.T.   0387
     (1954) 10637. KATO, MICHIO. SHIRAI, KENZABURO.

JEONG-EUI. IN JEONG-EUI, EUI SARAMDEUL. SEE NO. 638.   0388

OS JUSTOS. LISBON, LIVROS DO BRASIL, 1960. I.T. (1962)   0389
     19056. QUADROS, ANTÓNIO.

DE RÄTTFÄRDIGA. IN CALIGULA, MISSFÖRSTÄNDET, DE RÄTTFÄRDIGA.   0390
     SEE NO. 641. THULIN, ELSA.

DENEMELER. ISTANBUL, KUTULMUS MATBAASI, 1960. I.T. (1962)   0391
     24476. EYUBOGLU, SEBAHATTIN. GUNYOL, VEDAT.

THE JUST ASSASSINS. A PLAY IN FIVE ACTS. IN CALIGULA AND   0392
     THREE OTHER PLAYS, PP. 233-302. SEE NO. 643.

THE JUST ASSASSINS. IN CALIGULA AND THREE OTHER PLAYS, PP.   0393
     233-302. SEE NO. 644.

LES JUSTES. (ACTE 1). EMPÉDOCLE, VOL. 2, NO. 8 (FEB. 1950),   0394
     PP. 3-20. CR 359. SEE NO. 376.

LES JUSTES. (SCENE FROM ACT II). CALIBAN, NO. 37 (MARCH   0395
     1950), PP.33-41. SEE NO. 376.

LES JUSTES, EDITED BY E. O. MARSH. LONDON, HARRAP, 1960. KL   0396
     II 391.

LETTRES À UN AMI ALLEMAND

0397   LETTRE À UN AMI ALLEMAND. (PREMIÈRE). REVUE LIBRE,   NO. 2
        (1943).   CR 110.

0398   LETTRE À UN AMI ALLEMAND. (SECONDE). SIGNÉE LOUIS NEUVILLE.
        CAHIERS DE LA LIBÉRATION,   NO. 3 (1944).   CR 110, 320.

0399   LETTRES À UN AMI ALLEMAND.   ÉDITION ORIGINALE.   PARIS,
        GALLIMARD, 1945. CR 110, BIBLIO (1945) 104.

0400   LETTRES À UN AMI ALLEMAND.   LAUSANNE,   MARGUERAT, 1946.   CR
        111.

0401   LETTRES À UN AMI ALLEMAND. NOUVELLE ÉDITION AVEC UNE PRÉFACE
        INÉDITÉ.   PARIS, GALLIMARD, 1948.   CR 113, BIBLIO (1948)
        157, BR.

0402   LETTRES À UN AMI ALLEMAND.   ÉDITÉES PAR RAYMONDE HALFMANN.
        FRANKFURT-AM-MAIN,   DIESTERWEG, 1961.   BIBLIO (1962) P.25.

0403   BRIEVEN AAN EEN DUITSCHEN VRIEND. LITTERAIR PASPOORT, VOL. 1,
        NO. 5 (SEP. 1946), PP. 5-6.   SEE NO. 401.   NORD, MAX.

0404   CARTOS A UN AMIGO ALEMÁN.   SUR,   VOL. 15, NO. 140 (JUNE 1946),
        PP. 7-30.   SEE NO. 399.

0405   BRIEFE AN EINEN DEUTSCHEN FREUND.   IN FRAGEN DER ZEIT, PP.
        7-38.   SEE NO. 401, 630.   MEISTER, GUIDO G.

0406   BRIEFE AN EINEN DEUTSCHEN FREUND.   IN KLEINE PROSA, PP. 77-98.
        SEE NO. 401, 631.   MEISTER, GUIDO G.

0407   LETTERE AD UN AMICO TEDESCO.   IN RIBELLIONE E MORTE, PP. 9-39.
        SEE NO. 401, 634.   DAZZI, MARIA VASTA.

0408   FUJORI TO HANKO.   KYOTO,   JIMBUN SHOIN, 1953.   CR 114, I.T.
        (1954) 10638.   SEE NO. 399.   SATO, SAKU. SHIRAI, KOJI.

0409   LETTERS TO A GERMAN FRIEND.   IN RESISTANCE, REBELLION AND
        DEATH, PP. 1-24.   SEE NO. 401, 633.   O'BRIEN, JUSTIN.

0410   YE'SUL GWA JEO'HANG.   SEOUL,   SIN'TAE'YANG'SA, 1959.   I.T.
        (1961) 29677.   SEE NO. 401.   BAG I-MUN.

0411   LETTERS TO A GERMAN FRIEND.   IN RESISTANCE, REBELLION AND
        DEATH, PP. 1-32.   SEE NO. 401, 647.   O'BRIEN, JUSTIN.

0412   PREMIÈRE LETTRE À UN AMI ALLEMAND IN LA PATRIE SE FAIT TOUS
        LES JOURS, PP. 209-214.   SEE NO. 2684.

0413   DERDE BRIEF UIT DE BRIEVEN AAN EEN DUITSCHEN VRIEND.   LITTERAIR
        PASPOORT,   VOL. 1, NO. 5 (SEP. 1946), PP. 5-6.   CR 324.
        NORD, MAX.

LE MALENTENDU

LE MALENTENDU. PIÈCE EN TROIS ACTES. SUIVI DE CALGULA PIÈCE EN   0414
    QUATRE ACTES. PARIS, GALLIMARD (N.R.F.), 1944. CR 100.
LE MALENTENDU. PIÈCE EN TROIS ACTES. SUIVIE DE CALIGULA PIÈCE   0415
    EN QUATRE ACTES. NOUVELLES VERSIONS. PARIS, GALLIMARD,
    1958. CR 104.
LE MALENTENDU (ÉDITION ILLUSTRÉE PAR FRANCIS TAILLEUR. IN   0416
    RÉCITS ET THÉÂTRE. SEE NO. 618.
LE MALENTENDU. SUIVI DE CALIGULA. PARIS, GALLIMARD, 1961.   0417
LE MALENTENDU. EDITED BY JACQUES HARDRÉ AND GEORGE B. DANIEL.   0418
    NEW YORK, MACMILLAN, 1964.
EL MALENTENDIDO. PIEZA EN TRES ACTOS. IN TEATRO, PP. 7-54.   0419
    SEE NO. 622. BERNÁRDEZ, AURORA. TORRE, GUILLERMO DE.
EL MALENTENDIDO. EL ESTADO DE SITIO. LOS JUSTOS.   0420
    BUENOS AIRES. LOSADO, 1957. CR 106, I.T. (1960) 2774.
    SEE NO. 381. BERNARDEZ, AURORA. TORRE, GUILLERMO DE.
DAS MISSVERSTÄNDNIS. IN DRAMEN, PP. 75-116. SEE NO. 628.   0421
    MEISTER, GUIDO G.
IL MALINTESO. TRAGEDIA IN TRE ATTI. MILAN, BOMPIANI, 1947.   0422
    CR 107. PANDOLFI, VITO.
IL MALINTESO. DRAMMA IN TRE ATTI. IN TEATRO, PP. 9-67.   0423
    B.N.I. (1961) 1953. SEE NO. 422, 636. PANDOLFI, VITO.
GOKAI. IN KARIGYURA. GOKAI. SEE NO. 104.   0424
EUI SARAMDEUL. IN JEONG-EUI EUI SARAMDEUL. SEE NO. 638.   0425
O EQUIVOCO. IN CALIGULA, O EQUIVOCO. SEE NO. 106.   0426
MISSFÖRSTÄNDET. SKÄDESPEL I TRE AKTER. IN CALIGULA,   0427
    MISSFÖRSTÄNDET. SEE NO. 107. MOLIN, NILS. TORSSLOW, STIG.
MISSFÖRSTÄNDET. IN CALIGULA, MISSFÖRSTÄNDET, DE RATTFARDIGA.   0428
    SEE NO. 641. MOLIN, NILS AND STIG TORSSLOW.
YANLISLIK. ISTANBUL, ATAC KITABEVI, 1960. I.T. (1962) 24481.   0429
    EDGU, FERID.
CROSS PURPOSE. IN CALIGULA AND CROSS PURPOSE. SEE NO. 102.   0430
THE MISUNDERSTANDING. A PLAY IN THREE ACTS. IN CALIGULA AND   0431
    THREE OTHER PLAYS, PP. 75-134. SEE NO. 643.
THE MISUNDERSTANDING. IN CALIGULA AND THREE OTHER PLAYS, PP.   0432
    75-134. SEE NO. 644.
THE MISUNDERSTANDING. IN CALIGULA AND THREE OTHER PLAYS. SEE   0433
    NO. 624. GILBERT, STUART.

LE MYTHE DE SISYPHE

0434   LE MYTHE DE SISYPHE. ESSAI SUR L'ABSURDE. ÉDITION ORIGINALE.
        PARIS, GALLIMARD (COLL. LES ESSAIS), 1942. CR 69.

0435   LE MYTHE DE SISYPHE. ESSAI SUR L'ABSURDE. NOUVELLE ÉDITION
        AUGMENTÉE D'UNE ÉTUDE SUR FRANZ KAFKA. PARIS, GALLIMARD
        (COLL. LES ESSAIS), 1948. CR 71.

0436   LE MYTHE DE SISYPHE. ESSAI SUR L'ABSURDE. NOUVELLE ÉDITION
        AUGMENTÉE D'UNE ÉTUDE SUR FRANZ KAFKA. ÉDITION RELIÉE
        D'APRÈS LA MAQUETTE DE MARIO PRASSINOS. PARIS, GALLIMARD,
        1953. CR 72.

0437   LE MYTHE DE SISYPHE. ESSAI SUR L'ABSURDE. PARIS, GALLIMARD
        (COLL. LES IDÉES), 1961.

0438   EL MITO DE SISIFO. EL HOMBRE REBELDE. BUENOS AIRES, LOSADA,
        1955. I.T. (1956) 2132. SEE NO. 348. ECHAVARRI, LUIS

0439   THE MYTH OF SISYPHUS AND OTHER ESSAYS. TORONTO, MCCLELLAND
        AND STEWART, 1956. CBI (1953-1956), 268. SEE NO. 453.
        O'BRIEN, JUSTIN.

0440   MYTH OF SISYPHUS, AND OTHER ESSAYS. TORONTO, MCCLELLAND AND
        STEWART, 1959. CR 82. SEE NO. 453. O'BRIEN, JUSTIN.

0441   SISYFOS-MYTEN. COPENHAGEN, GYLDENDAL, 1960. I.T. (1962)
        6100. LAURIDSEN, HELGA VANG.

0442   DER MYTHOS VON SISYPHOS. EIN VERSUCH ÜBER DAS ABSURDE.
        DUSSELDORF, BAD SALZIG, RAUCH, 1950. CR 75. BRENNER,
        HANS. RASCH, WOLFDIETRICH.

0443   DER MYTHOS VON SISYPHOS. DUSSELDORF, KARL RAUCH, 1956. SEE
        NO. 443. BRENNER, HANS GEORG. RASCH, WOLFDIETRICH.

0444   DER MYTHOS VON SISYPHOS. EIN VERSUCH ÜBER DAS ABSURDE. MIT
        EINEM KOMMENTIERENDEN ESSAY VON LISELOTTE RICHTER. HAM-
        BURG, ROWOHLT (RORORO BUCH), 1959. CR 77. BRENNER, HANS
        GEORG. RASCH, WOLFDIETRICH.

0445   THE MYTH OF SISYPHUS. IN THE MYTH OF SISYPHUS AND OTHER
        ESSAYS, PP. 1-109. CR 78, I.T. (1962) 135. O'BRIEN,
        JUSTIN.

0446   IL MITO DI SISIFO. MILAN, BOMPIANI, 1947. CR 83. BORELLI,
        ATTILIO.

0447   SISYPHE NO SHINWA. TOKYO, SHINCHO-SHA, 1951. CR 84, I.T.
        (1952) 9776, (1956) 12645. YANAIHARA, ISAKU.

0448   SISYPHE NO SHINWA. IN KEKKON, SISYPHE NO SHINWA. SEE NO. 637.
        REPRINT OF NO. 447.

0449   MYTEN OM SISYFOS. OSLO, CAPPELEN, 1953. CR 87, I.T. (1954)
        11390. MARTENS, JOHANNES SKANCKE.

0450   O MITO DE SISIFO. LISBON, LIVROS DO BRASIL, N.D. (1961).
        I.T. (1963) 20298. SEE NO. 444, 2859. TAVARES RODRIGUES,
        URBANO AUGUSTO.

MYTEN OM SISYFOS. STOCKHOLM, BONNIERS, 1947. CR 88.   0451
    BRANDELL, GUNNAR. JOHN, BENGT.
MYTEN OM SISYFOS. STOCKHOLM, BONNIERS, 1957. CR 89, I.T.   0452
    (1959) 19392. BRANDELL, GUNNAR. JOHN, BENGT.
MYTH OF SISYPHUS AND OTHER ESSAYS. NEW YORK, KNOPF, 1955. CR 0453
    79. O'BRIEN, JUSTIN.
MYTH OF SISYPHUS, AND OTHER ESSAYS. NEW YORK, VINTAGE BOOKS, 0454
    1959. CR 82. SEE NO. 453. O'BRIEN, JUSTIN.
THE MYTH OF SISYPHUS, AND OTHER ESSAYS. NEW YORK, VINTAGE   0455
    BOOKS, 1959. I.T. (1961) 7236.   O'BRIEN, JUSTIN.
TWO CHAPTERS FROM LE MYTHE DE SISYPHE. (SISYPHUS, HOPE AND THE 0456
    ABSURD IN THE WORKS OF FRANZ KAFKA). PARTISAN REVIEW,
    VOL. 13, NO. 2 (SPRING 1946), PP. 188-200. SEE NO. 457,
    458.
SISYPHUS. IN TWO CHAPTERS FROM LE MYTHE DE SISYPHE. SEE NO.   0457
    456. SCHWARTZ, DELMORE.
HOPE AND THE ABSURD IN THE WORK OF FRANZ KAFKA. IN TWO CHAPTERS 0458
    FROM LE MYTHE DE SISYPHE. SEE NO. 456. BARRETT, WILLIAM.
SISYPHOS. FÄHRE, VOL. 2, (1947), PP. 43-46. CR 341. WEBER, 0459
    CARL AUGUST.
PHILOSOPHIE ET ROMAN (EXTRAIT DU MYTHE DE SISYPHE). BIBLIO,   0460
    VOL. 8, NO. 10 (DECEMBER 1957), PP. 7-9.
LUOMINEN ILMAN HUOMISPÄIVÄÄ. IN ESSEITÄ (VALIKOIMA), PP.   0461
    133-138. SEE NO. 627.
FILOSOFIA JA ROMAANI. IN ESSEITÄ (VALIKOIMA), PP. 139-150.   0462
    SEE NO. 627.
SISYFOKSEN MYYTTI. IN ESSEITÄ (VALIKOIMA), PP. 102-107. SEE   0463
    NO. 627.
LE MYTHE DE SISYPHE, L'ÉTÉ, LA PESTE, L'HOMME RÉVOLTÉ.   0464
    (EXTRAITS). LES NOUVELLES LITTÉRAIRES, NO. 1573 (OCT. 24,
    1957) P. 6, CR 419. SEE NO. 245, 365, 552.
HOFFNUNG UND WIDERSINN IN FRANZ KAFKAS WERK. EUROPÄISCHE   0465
    RUNDSCHAU, VOL. 1, (1946), PP. 128-130. CR 325.

NOCES

0466   NOCES. ÉDITION ORIGINALE. ALGER,   CHARLOT, 1939.   CR 5.

0467   NOCES. NOUVELLE ÉDITION. ALGER-PARIS, CHARLOT, 1945 CR 7.

0468   NOCES, ESSAIS. PARIS, GALLIMARD (LES ESSAIS), 1947. CR 9.

0469   NOCES. ÉDITION RELIÉE D'APRÈS LA MAQUETTE DE MARIO PRASSINOS.
          PARIS, GALLIMARD, 1947. CR 10.

0470   NOCES. PARIS, CENT FEMMES AMIES DES LIVRES, 1952. CR 16.

0471   NOCES (ÉDITION ILLUSTRÉE PAR C. CAILLARD). IN RÉCITS ET
          THÉÂTRE. SEE NO. 618.

0472   NOCES. ILLUSTRATIONS DE JACQUES HOUPLAIN. PARIS, LUBINEAU,
          1959.

0473   NOCES, SUIVI DE L'ÉTÉ. PARIS, GALLIMARD (SOLEIL), 1959 CR 18.

0474   HOCHZEIT DES LICHTS. IN LITERARISCHE ESSAYS, PP. 75-121. SEE
          NO. 629, 468. REPRINT OF NO. 481. GAN, PETER.

0475   HOCHZEIT DES LICHTS. LONDON, BARMERLEA BOOK SALES, 1954. CR
          20. SEE NO. 468. REPRINT OF NO. 481. GAN, PETER.

0476   NOZZE. IN SAGGI LETTERARI, PP. 59-97. SEE NO. 635, 468.

0477   KEKKON. TOKYO, SHINCHO-SHA, 1952. CR 22, I.T. (1953) 8382.
          SEE NO. 468. KUBOTA, KEISAKU.

0478   KEKKON. IN KEKKON, SISYPHE NO SHINWA. SEE NO. 468, 637.
          REPRINT OF NO. 477.

0479   SOMMER I ALGER, BRYLLUP I TIPASA, VINDEN I DJEMILA, ØRKENEN.
          IN DEN UOVERVINNELIGE SOMMER, PP. 41-86. SEE NO. 468, 639.
          VESTRE, BERNT.

0480   BRÖLLOP. IN SOMMAR, PP. 67-122. SEE NO. 642, 468.

0481   HOCHZEIT DES LICHTS. ZURICH, VERLAG DER ARCHE, 1954. CR 19,
          21, I.T. (1956) 18317. SEE NO. 468. GAN, PETER.

0482   SOMMEREN I ALGIER. IN SOMMER, ESSAYS, PP. 40-57. SEE NO. 626.

0483   ALGERIN KESÄ. IN ESSEITÄ (VALIKOIMA), PP. 30-43. I.T. (1964)
          9399. SEE NO. 627.

0484   SOMMER IN ALGIER. MONAT, VOL. 1, NO. 12 (1949), PP. 81-86.
          BDZ 100-86 (1950).

0485   SUMMER IN ALGIERS. IN THE MYTH OF SISYPHUS AND OTHER ESSAYS,
          PP. 111-122. SEE NO. 645, 466.

0486   FESTEN I TIPASA. IN SOMMER, ESSAYS, PP. 29-39. SEE NO. 626.

0487   HÄÄT TIPASASSA. IN ESSEITÄ (VALIKOIMA), PP. 44-52. I.T.
          (1964) 9399. SEE NO. 627.

0488   DER WIND VON DJEMILA. NEUES EUROPA, VOL. 2 (1947), PP. 26-29.
          CR 343. ZIWUTSCHKA, JOSEPH.

0489   DER WIND IN DJEMILA. ATLANTIS, VOL. 28, NO. 9 (1956), PP.
          392-393. BDZ 113-294 (1956).

LA PESTE

LA PESTE. ÉDITION ORIGINALE. RELIÉE D'APRÈS LA MAQUETTE DE   0490
    MARIO PRASSINOS. PARIS, GALLIMARD, 1947. CR 115.

LA PESTE. PARIS, GALLIMARD, 1947. CR 116.   0491

LA PESTE. PARIS, GALLIMARD (N.R.F.), 1947. CR 117.   0492

LA PESTE. PARIS, GALLIMARD (COLL. POURPRE), 1949. CR 118.   0493

LA PESTE. PARIS, GALLIMARD (LE RAYON D'OR, 2), 1950. CR 120.   0494

LA PESTE. ÉDITION RELIÉE D'APRÈS LA MAQUETTE DE MARIO   0495
    PRASSINOS. PARIS, GALLIMARD, 1951. CR 121.

LA PESTE. PARIS, GALLIMARD, 1952. CR 123.   0496

LA PESTE. PARIS, GALLIMARD (COLL. POURPRE), 1953. CR 124.   0497

LA PESTE. PARIS, LIBRAIRIE GÉNÉRALE FRANÇAISE (COLL. LE LIVRE   0498
    DE POCHE, 132), 1955. CR 125.

LA PESTE. SUIVI D'UN TEXTE INÉDIT. EXHORTATIONS AUX MEDECINS   0499
    DE LA PESTE. PARIS, LE CLUB DU MEILLEUR LIVRE (ROMANS),
    1955. CR 126. SEE NO. 557.

LA PESTE. PARIS, GALLIMARD, 1956. CR 129.   0500

LA PESTE. PARIS, GALLIMARD (COLL. SOLEIL), 1958. CR 131.   0501

LA PESTE (ÉDITION ILLUSTRÉE PAR ORLANDO PELAYO). IN RÉCITS ET   0502
    THÉÂTRE. SEE NO. 618.

LA PESTE. BUENOS AIRES, EDITORIAL NOVA (COLECCIÓN SUR), 1948.   0503
    CR 145, I.T. (1949) 918. CHACEL, ROSA.

DIE PEST. ROMAN. INNSBRUCK, ABENDLANDVERLAG, 1948. CR 134.   0504
    MEISTER, GUIDO G.

PESTEN. COPENHAGEN, SCHULTZ, 1948. CR 143, I.T. (1949) 1581.   0505
    PADE, HENNING.

PESTEN. COPENHAGEN, SCHULTZ, 1957. CR 144, I.T. (1959) 4948.   0506
    PADE, HENNING.

PESTEN. COPENHAGEN, SCHULTZ, 1961. I.T. (1963) 6836. PADE,   0507
    HENNING.

PESTEN. COPENHAGEN, SCHULTZ, 1963. PADE, HENNING.   0508

RUTTO. HELSINKI, OTAVA, 1948. CR 147, I.T. (1949) 2608.   0509
    MANNERKORPI, JUHA.

RUTTO. HELSINKI, OTAVA, 1957. CR 148, I.T. (1959) 7447.   0510
    MANNERKORPI, JUHA.

DIE PEST. ROMAN. BAD SALZIG, RAUCH, 1949. CR 135. MEISTER,   0511
    GUIDO G.

DIE PEST. HAMBURG, ROWOHLT, 1950. CR 137, I.T. (1952) 528.   0512
    MEISTER, GUIDO.

DIE PEST. DUSSELDORF, RAUCH, 1958. CR 138, I.T. (1960)   0513
    1024-1025. MEISTER, GUIDO G.

PLEG. DELHI, RAJKAMAL PRAKASAN, 1961. I.T. (1963) 13499,   0514
    I.T. (1964) 12239. I.N.B. (1962) P. 89. CAUHAN,
    SIVDANSIMA. CAUHAN, VIJAY.

0515   HA-DEVER. TEL-AVIV, AM OVED, 1953. CR 149, I.T. (1956)
        10300. RATOSH, YONATHAN.

0516   HA-DEVER. TEL-AVIV, AM OVED, 1962. I.T. (1964) 13434.
        RATOSH, YONATHAN.

0517   LA PESTE. ROMANZO. LUGANO, GHILDA DEL LIBRO, 1948. CR 151.
        FABBRO, BENIAMINO DAL.

0518   LA PESTE. MILAN, BOMPIANI, 1948. CR 150. FABBRO, BENIAMINO
        DAL.

0519   LA PESTE. MILAN, BOMPIANI, 1964. FABBRO, BENIAMINO DAL.

0520   PESUTO. TOKYO, SOGEN-SHA, 1950. CR 152, I.T. (1951) 7172.
        MIYAZAKI, MINEO.

0521   PESUTO. TOKYO, SOGEN-SHA, 1952. CR 153, I.T. (1953) 8383.
        MIYAZAKI, MINEO.

0522   PESUTO. IN IHOJIN, PESUTO. SEE NO. 277, 492.

0523   PESUTO. TOKYO, SHINCHO-SHA (CHOSAKUSHU, 2), 1958. CR 155,
        I.T. (1960) 14289. MIYAZAKI, MINEO.

0524   PESTE. SEOUL, LEE CHO BU, 1958. CR 141, I.T. (1960) 6016.
        SAMUNSA.

0525   HEUKSABYEONG. YUZEOK GWA WANGGUK. SEOUL, LEE HANG AND LEE
        ZIN KU, 1958. CR 142, I.T. (1960) 6015. SEE NO. 312, 492.
        DONGA CHULPANSA.

0526   HEUG SA BYEONG. SEOUL, LEE-JIN-GU, 1959. I.T. (1961) 29676.
        DONGA CHULPANSA.

0527   PESTEU. IN IBANG'IN, PESTEU. SEE NO. 280.

0528   DE PEST. AMSTERDAM, BEZIGE BIJ, 1948. CR 156. CORSARI,
        WILLY.

0529   PESTEN. OSLO, ASCHEHOUG, 1949. CR 157, I.T. (1950) 5739.
        MARTENS, JOHANNES SKANCKE.

0530   DZUMA. WARSAW, PANSTWOWY INSTYTUT WYDAWNICZY, 1957, CR 158,
        I.T. (1959) 16409, I.T. (1962) 18494. GUZE, JOANNA.

0531   A PESTE. LISBON, LIVROS DO BRASIL, 1955. CR 159, I.T. (1957)
        24121. CARDOSO, ERSÍLIO.

0532   LA PESTE. MADRID, TAURUS, 1957. CR 146, I.T. (1960) 6997.
        CHACEL, ROSA.

0533   LA PESTE. MADRID, CID, 1958. I.T. (1961) 6574.

0534   LA PESTE. MADRID, CID, 1960. I.T. (1963) 8117. CHACEL,
        ROSA.

0535   PESTEN. STOCKHOLM, BONNIERS (PANACHE-SERIEN), 1948. CR 160.
        THULIN, ELSA.

0536   PESTEN. STOCKHOLM, BONNIERS, 1957. CR 161, I.T. (1959)
        19393. THULIN, ELSA.

0537   PESTEN. STOCKHOLM, BONNIERS, 1962. I.T. (1964) 22873.
        THULIN, ELSA.

0538   DIE PEST. ZURICH, BÜCHERGILDE GUTENBERG, 1949. CR 136, I.T.
        (1950) 8416. MEISTER, GUIDO G.

VEBA. ISTANBUL, VARLIK YAYINEVI, 1955. CR 162, I.T. (1958)   0539
   21393, I.T. (1962) 24478. AKBAL, OKTAY.

AL-TA UN. CAIRO, DAR AL-THAQAFAH ALARABIYYAH, 1962. I.T.   0540
   (1964) 20574. KAWTHAR ABD-AL-SALAM.

THE PLAGUE. LONDON, H. HAMILTON, 1948. CR 139. GILBERT,   0541
   STUART.

THE PLAGUE. NEW YORK, MODERN LIBRARY, 1961. GILBERT, STUART.   0542

THE PLAGUE. NEW YORK, KNOPF, 1948. CR 140. GILBERT, STUART.   0543

KUGA. ZAGREB, ZORA, 1952. CR 163, I.T. (1954) 17748.   0544
   HERGEŠIČ, IVO.

KUGA. BELGRADE, PROSUETA, 1956. CR 165, I.T. (1958) 27208.   0545
   MARKOVIĆ-ČIŽEK, JOVANKA.

ČUMA. SKOPJE, KŌCŌ RACIN, 1956. CR 164, I.T. (1958) 27207.   0546
   HRISTOVA, VERA.

LA PESTE. ÉDITION ABRÉGÉE ET ANNOTÉE PAR J.A.G. TANS ET J.P.   0547
   VAN DER LINDEN. BUSSUM, BRAND (SERIE JAUNE, I), 1951. CR
   122, BIBLIO (1951) 125.

LA PESTE. (EXTRAITS). BIELEFELD, VELHAGEN UND HLASING, 1955.   0548
   CR 127.

THE PLAGUE. IN THE COLLECTED FICTION OF ALBERT CAMUS. SEE NO.   0549
   632.

LA PESTE. LONDON, METHUEN, 1959. CR 133, FR VII 23572.   0550

LA PESTE. LONDON, METHUEN, 1962. BIBLIO (1962) P. 14, C.B.I.   0551
   (1961-1962) P. 415.

LA PESTE (EXTRAIT). LES NOUVELLES LITTÉRAIRES, NO. 1573 (OCT.   0552
   24, 1957), P. 6, PORT.

GESELS EN SLACHTOFFERS. (FRAGMENT UIT DE PEST). DE VLAM,   0553
   VOL. 4, NO. 17 (APR. 23, 1948), P. 6, PORT. CR 347,

DIE PEST. (EXTRAIT). DIE UMSCHAU, VOL. 3 (1948), PP. 2-25.   0554
   CR 351. ROLAND, CHARLOTTE.

KUGA.(EXTRAIT). POBJEDA, VOL. 11 (1954), P. 5. CR 375.   0555

DZUMA, TAK TYLKO DOSIEGO SIE DNA... TWÓRCZOŚĆ, VOL. 13, NO. 6   0556
   (JUNE 1957), PP. 147-150. ANDRZEJ, KIJOWSKI.

LES ARCHIVES DE LA PESTE. LES CAHIERS DE LA PLÉIADE, (APR.   0557
   1947), PP. 147-154. CR 328. SEE NO. 499.

EXHORTATIONS AUX MÉDECINS DE LA PESTE. MÉDECINE DE FRANCE,   0558
   NO. 2 (1949), PP. 8-11. CR 355. SEE NO. 499.

UR ARKIV FÖR FRÅGOR RÖRANDE PESTEN. BONNIERS LITTERÄRA   0559
   MAGASIN, NO. 4 (APR. 1948), PP. 272-275. SEE NO. 557.
   BJURSTRÖM, CARL GUSTAF. NYSTRÖM, TUVE AMBJÖRN.

LES EXILÉS DANS LA PESTE. IN DOMAINE FRANÇAIS. (UN MANIFESTO   0560
   DES LETTRES D'AUJOURD'HUI). GENEVA, TROIS COLLINES, 1943.

LES EXILÉS DANS LA PESTE. LA NEF, VOL. 1, NO. 3 (SEP. 1944),   0561
   PP. 20-31. CR 318.

ARTICLES

0562   ANDRÉ GIDE IS 77. THE VOICE OF THE WORLD,   VOL. 1, NO. 1
           (SPRING 1947), PP. 35-36.

0563   ANGST IST EINE TECHNIK. EIN BEITRAG ZUM ERKENNEN UNSERES
           JAHRHUNDERTS. KULTUR, VOL. 1, NO. 2 (OCT. 15, 1952), P.
           4. BDZ 107-129 (1953).

0564   APPEL POUR LES CONDAMNÉS À MORT. ESPRIT, VOL. 20, NO. 189
           (APR. 1952), PP. 725-726. CR 372.

0565   AN APPEAL TO SILENCE FURY AND UNITE MOST ALGERIANS. CHICAGO
           TRIBUNE, VOL. 115, NO. 64 (MARCH 5, 1961), P. 20.

0566   CE QUE JE DOIS À L'ESPAGNE. PREUVES, NO. 85 (MAR. 1958), PP.
           41-43. CR 428.

0567   LO QUE DEBO A ESPAÑA. CUADERNOS (DEL CONGRESO POR LA LIBERTAD
           DE LA CULTURA), NO. 41 (MARCH-APRIL 1960), PP. 58-59.

0568   DOSTOÏEVSKI, PROPHÈTE DU XXE SIÈCLE. SPECTACLES, NO. 1 (MAR.
           1958), P. 5. CR 429,

0569   THE HUMAN CRISIS. TWICE A YEAR, NOS. 14-15 (FALL-WINTER 1946-
           1947), PP. 19-33. ABEL, LIONEL.

0570   ICH HABE EIN STARKES GEFÜHL FÜR ALLES LEBENDIGE... KULTUR,
           VOL. 6, NO. 103 (MAR. 1, 1958), P. 10. BDZ 116-316 (1958).

0571   IL AIDAIT À VIVRE. (À PROPOS DE ROGER MARTIN DU GARD). LE
           FIGARO LITTÉRAIRE, VOL. 13, NO. 645 (AUG. 30, 1958), P. 1,
           COL. 6-7. CR 431.

0572   DE L'INSIGNIFIANCE. CAHIERS DES SAISONS, NO. 15 (WINTER
           1959), PP. 193-196.

0573   L'INTELLIGENCE ET L'ÉCHAFAUD. CONFLUENCES, VOL. 3, NOS. 21-24
           (1943), PP. 218-223. CR 316.

0574   L'INTELLIGENCE ET L'ÉCHAFAUD. LIÈGE, ÉDITIONS DYNAMO (COLL.
           BRIMBORIONS, 59), 1960.

0575   BESCHRÄNKUNG AUF DAS WESENTLICHE. GEDANKEN ÜBER DEN
           FRANZÖSISCHEN ROMAN. MONAT, VOL. 13, NO. 7 (FEB. 1960),
           PP. 9-13. SEE NO. 573.

0576   DIE RATIO UND DAS SCHAFOTT. WORT UND TAT, NO. 6 (SEP. 1947),
           PP. 67-74. CR 340. SCHON, PETER M. SEE NO. 573.

0577   LA TRADICIÓN CLÁSICA DE LA NOVELA FRANCESA. CUADERNOS (DEL
           CONGRESO POR LA LIBERTAD DE LA CULTURA), NO. 43
           (JULY-AUGUST 1960), PP. 89-92. SEE NO. 573.

0578   LA JUSTICE, ELLE AUSSI, A SES PHARISIENS. CALIBAN, NO. 39
           (MAY 1950), PP. 22-24.

0579   KADAR A EU SON JOUR DE PEUR. FRANC-TIREUR, MARCH 18, 1957

0580   KADAR A EU SON JOUR DE PEUR. IN MERAY, TIBOR, BUDAPEST (23
           OCTOBRE 1956), PP. 11-15.

0581   KADAR HAT SEINEN TAG DER ANGST ERLEBT. IN FRAGEN DER ZEIT, PP.
           232-240. (PUBLISHED IN FRANC-TIREUR, MARCH 18, 1957). SEE

NO. 630.

KADAR HAD HIS DAY OF FEAR. IN RESISTANCE, REBELLION AND DEATH,   0582
    PP. 113-118. (PUBLISHED IN FRANC-TIREUR, MARCH 18, 1957).
    SEE NO. 633.

KADAR HAD HIS DAY OF FEAR (HUNGARY). IN RESISTANCE, REBELLION   0583
    AND DEATH, PP. 157-164. (PUBLISHED IN FRANC-TIREUR, MARCH
    18, 1957). SEE NO. 647.

UNE MACUMBA AU BRÉSIL. EXTRAIT INÉDIT D'UN JOURNAL DE VOYAGE.   0584
    LIVRES DE FRANCE, VOL. 2, NO. 9 (NOV. 1951), PP. 5-7. CR
    364.

MADELEINE RENAUD. LE CALIBAN, NO. 24 (1949), PP. 9-11. CR   0585
    357.

MÉDITATIONS SUR LE THÉÂTRE. LIÈGE, DYNAMO, 1961. BIBLIO   0586
    (1961) P. 150.

NOTRE AMI ROBLÈS. SIMOUN, VOL. 8, NO. 30 (1959), P. 3.   0587

UNE PATRIE ALGÉRIENNE, DEUX PEUPLES... ÉTUDES   0588
    MÉDITERRANÉENNES, NO. 7 (SPRING 1960), PP. 19-24.

PLUIES DE NEW YORK. FORMES ET COULEURS, VOL. 9, NO. 6 (1947).   0589
    CR 339.

PORTRAIT D'UN ÉLU. LES CAHIERS DU SUD, VOL. 30, (APR. 1943),   0590
    PP. 306-311. CR 317.

RÉFLEXIONS SUR LA GUILLOTINE. IN RÉFLEXIONS SUR LA PEINE   0591
    CAPITALE. SEE NO. 2196.

RÉFLEXIONS SUR LA GUILLOTINE. (I). LA NOUVELLE NOUVELLE REVUE   0592
    FRANÇAISE, VOL. 5, NO. 54 (JUNE 1957), PP. 961-981. CR
    425.

RÉFLEXIONS SUR LA GUILLOTINE. (II). LA NOUVELLE NOUVELLE   0593
    REVUE FRANÇAISE, VOL. 5, NO. 55 (JULY 1957), PP. 83-102.
    CR 426.

DIE GUILLOTINE. IN FRAGEN DER ZEIT, PP. 113-181. SEE NO. 630,   0594
    591.

REFLECCIONES SOBRE LA GUILLOTINA. IN LA PENA DE MUERTE EN   0595
    FRANCIA. SEE NO. 1176.

LA GHIGLIOTTINA. IN LA PENA DI MORTE IN FRANCIA. SEE NO.   0596
    1174.

GIROCHIN. TOKYO, KINOKUNIYA SHOTEN, 1958. CR 285, I.T.   0597
    (1960) 14285. SEE NO. 591. SUGI, TOSHIO. KAWAMURA,
    KATSUMI.

REFLECTIONS ON THE GUILLOTINE. IN RESISTANCE, REBELLION AND   0598
    DEATH, PP. 127-165. SEE NO. 633.

REFLECTIONS ON THE GUILLOTINE, AN ESSAY ON CAPITAL PUNISHMENT.   0599
    MICHIGAN CITY, INDIANA. FRIDTJOF-KARLA PUBLICATIONS, 1959.
    I.T. (1961) 7237, I.T. (1962) 8398.

REFLECTIONS ON THE GUILLOTINE. EVERGREEN REVIEW, VOL. 4, NO.   0600
    13 (MARCH-APRIL 1960).

0601   REFLECTIONS ON THE GUILLOTINE.   IN RESISTANCE, REBELLION AND
           DEATH, PP. 173-234.   SEE NO. 647.

0602   REMARQUES SUR LA POLITIQUE INTERNATIONALE.   RENAISSANCES,   VOL.
           2, NO. 10 (MAY 1945), PP. 16-20.   CR 323.

0603   RENCONTRES AVEC ANDRÉ GIDE IN HOMMAGES À ANDRÉ GIDE.   LA
           NOUVELLE REVUE FRANÇAISE,   (1951), PP. 223-228.   CR 366.

0604   À PROPOS DE LA REVUE INTERNATIONALE DE THÉÂTRE.   REVUE
           INTERNATIONALE DE THÉÂTRE,   VOL. 1, (OCT-DEC. 1947), P. 14.

0605   EEN SCHRIJVER VAN HET ABSURDE LEVEN.   ELSEVIERS WEEKBLAD,   VOL.
           8, NO. 22 (MAY 31, 1952), P. 4, PORT.   CR 373.

0606   THE SENSITIVE MURDERERS.   WORLD REVIEW,   (1949), PP. 30-33.
           SEE NO. 368.

0607   LE SOCIALISME DES POTENCES.   DEMAIN,   NO. 63 (FEB. 21-27,
           1957), PP. 10-11.   CR 427.

0608   DER SOZIALISMUS DER GALGEN (UNGARN).   IN FRAGEN DER ZEIT, PP.
           241-248.   (PUBLISHED IN DEMAIN, FEB. 21, 1957).   SEE NO.
           630.

0609   SOCIALISM OF THE GALLOWS (HUNGARY).   IN RESISTANCE, REBELLION
           AND DEATH, PP. 119-123.   (PUBLISHED IN DEMAIN, FEB. 21,
           1957).   SEE NO. 633.

0610   SOCIALISM OF THE GALLOWS (HUNGARY).   IN RESISTANCE, REBELLION
           AND DEATH, PP. 165-171.   (PUBLISHED IN DEMAIN, FEB. 21,
           1957).   SEE NO. 647.

0611   TÉMOIGNAGES SUR ANDRÉ GIDE.   FIGARO LITTÉRAIRE,   VOL. 6, NO.
           253 (FEB. 24, 1951), P. 5.

0612   TOUT NE S'ARRANGE PAS.   LES LETTRES FRANÇAISES,   NO. 16 (1944),
           P. 4.   CR 322.

0613   TRÊVE POUR LES CIVILS INNOCENTS.   DEMAIN,   NO. 7 (JAN.
           26-FEB.1, 1956), PP. 10-11.   CR 415.

0614   LA VALLÉE HEUREUSE, PAR JULES ROY.   L'ARCHE,   VOL. 3, NO. 24
           (FEB. 1947), PP. 117-121.   CR 342.

0615   LA VIE D'ARTISTE, MIMODRAME EN DEUX PARTIES.   SIMOUN,   VOL. 2,
           NO. 8 (1953), PP. 14-20.

0616   LES VRAIES TÂCHES.   LES CAHIERS DES SAISONS,   NO. 20 (1960),
           PP. 615-616.

0617   WE TOO ARE MURDERERS.   TWICE A YEAR,   (1948), PP. 74-75.   ABEL,
           LIONEL.

COLLECTIONS

RÉCITS ET THÉÂTRE, ÉDITION RELIÉE, ILLUSTRÉE EN COULEURS, 32   0618
    AQUARELLES. PARIS, GALLIMARD, 1958. CR 276. SEE NO. 97,
    121, 172, 195, 209, 256, 301, 378, 416, 471, 502.

OEUVRES COMPLÈTES RÉALISÉES PAR ANDRÉ SAURET EN SIX TOMES.   0619
    PARIS, IMPRIMERIE NATIONALE, 1962.

THÉÂTRE, RÉCITS, NOUVELLES. PRÉFACE PAR JEAN GRENIER. TEXTES   0620
    ÉTABLIS ET ANNOTÉS PAR ROGER QUILLIOT. PARIS, GALLIMARD
    (BIBLIOTHÈQUE DE LA PLÉIADE), 1962.

ESSAIS. INTRODUCTION PAR R. QUILLIOT, TEXTES ÉTABLIS ET ANNOTÉS   0621
    PAR R. QUILLOT ET L. FAUCON. PARIS, GALLIMARD ET
    CALMANN-LEVY (BIBLIOTHÈQUE DE LA PLÉIADE), 1965.

TEATRO. EL MALENTENDIDO, CALIGULA, EL ESTADO DE SITIO, LOS   0622
    JUSTOS. BUENOS AIRES, LOSADA, 1949. CR 185, I.T. (1963)
    3746. SEE NO. 98, 196, 380, 419.

TEATRO 2. LOS POSEÍDOS. BUENOS AIRES, LOSADA, 1960. SEE NO.   0623
    727. OCAMPO, VICTORIA.

CALIGULA AND THREE OTHER PLAYS. TORONTO, RANDOM HOUSE   0624
    (VINTAGE), 1962. CBI (1961-1962), 415. SEE NO. 99, 197,
    382, 433. GILBERT, STUART.

CIZINEC-PÁD (L'ÉTRANGER-LA CHUTE). PRAGUE, MLADA FRONTA, 1966.   0625
    SEE NO. 126, 261, 2814. ZILINA, MILOSLAV.

SOMMER, ESSAYS. COPENHAGEN, GYLDENDAL, 1961. HANSEN,   0626
    THORKILD.

ESSEITÄ (VALIKOIMA). HELSINKI, HELSINGISSA, 1963. I.T.   0627
    (1964) 9399. SEE NO. 37, 68, 72, 153, 182, 183, 188, 219,
    221, 226, 235, 238, 240, 461, 462, 463, 483, 487, 2290.
    LOFSTEDT, LEENA.

DRAMEN. HAMBURG, ROWOHLT, 1959. I.T. (1961) 850, CR 183.   0628
    SEE NO. 101, 385, 421, 729. MEISTER, GUIDO G.

LITERARISCHE ESSAYS. HAMBURG, ROWOHLT, 1959. SEE NO. 174,   0629
    212, 474.

FRAGEN DER ZEIT. HAMBURG, ROWOHLT, 1960. SEE NO. 8, 11, 15,   0630
    18, 21, 39, 43, 59, 69, 73, 76, 79, 80, 155, 158, 405, 581,
    594, 608, 665, 701. MEISTER, GUIDO G.

KLEINE PROSA. HAMBURG, ROWOHLT, 1961. MEISTER, GUIDO G.   0631

THE COLLECTED FICTION OF ALBERT CAMUS. LONDON. HAMISH   0632
    HAMILTON, 1960. I.T. (1963) 22843. SEE NO. 133, 267, 307,
    549.

RESISTANCE, REBELLION AND DEATH. LONDON, H. HAMILTON, 1961.   0633
    I.T. (1964) 21712. SEE NO. 9, 12, 16, 19, 22, 40, 44, 60,
    70, 74, 77, 82, 83, 167, 409, 582, 598, 609, 666, 702.
    O'BRIEN, JUSTIN.

RIBELLIONE E MORTE. MILAN, BOMPIANI, 1961. DAZZI, MARIA   0634

VASTA. GUGLIELMI, GIUSEPPE. SENSINI, ALBERTO.

0635   SAGGI LETTERARI. IL ROVESCIO E IL DIRITTO, NOZZE, L'ESTATE.
        MILAN, BOMPIANI, 1959. I.T. (1962) 14008. SEE NO. 176,
        215, 476. MORANDO, SERGIO.

0636   TEATRO. IL MALINTESO, CALIGOLA, I GIUSTI, LO STATO D'ASSEDIO.
        MILAN, BOMPIANI, 1960. I.T. (1963) 15502. SEE NO. 103,
        201, 386, 423.

0637   KEKKON. SISYPHE NO SHINWA. TOKYO, SHINCHO-SHA, 1958. CR 23,
        I.T. (1960) 14288. SEE NO. 478, 448.

0638   JEONG-EUI, EUI SARAMDEUL. SEOUL, YANGMUNSA, 1962. I.T.
        (1964) 5450. SEE NO. 388, 425. GON BANG.

0639   DEN UOVERVINNELIGE SOMMER. OSLO, H. ASCHEHOUG AND CO., 1960.
        SEE NO. 35, 57, 81, 160, 184, 189, 227, 230, 242, 3309.
        VESTRE, BERNT.

0640   O AVESSO E O DIREITO. DISCURSO DA SUÉCIA. LISBON, LIVROS DO
        BRASIL (COLL. MINIATURA), N.D. (1959). I.T. (1961) 17702.
        SEE NO. 161, 180. VICTORINO, SOUSA.

0641   CALIGULA, MISSFÖRSTÄNDET, DE RÄTTFÄRDIGA. STOCKHOLM,
        BONNIERS, 1957. I.T. (1959) 19388, CR 187. SEE NO. 108,
        390, 428.

0642   SOMMAR. STOCKHOLM, BONNIERS, 1963. SEE NO. 480. BJURSTROM,
        C. G.

0643   CALIGULA AND THREE OTHER PLAYS. NEW YORK, KNOPF, 1958. SEE
        NO. 109, 203, 392, 431. GILBERT, STUART.

0644   CALIGULA AND THREE OTHER PLAYS. NEW YORK, VINTAGE BOOKS,
        1958. CR 96. SEE NO. 110, 204, 393, 432. GILBERT,
        STUART.

0645   THE MYTH OF SISYPHUS AND OTHER ESSAYS. LONDON, H. HAMILTON,
        1955. CR 78, I.T. (1962) 135. SEE NO. 62, 224, 234, 241,
        445, 485. O'BRIEN, JUSTIN.

0646   THE MYTH OF SISYPHUS AND OTHER ESSAYS. NEW YORK, KNOPF, 1955.
        CR 79. SEE NO. 63. O'BRIEN, JUSTIN.

0647   RESISTANCE, REBELLION AND DEATH. NEW YORK, KNOPF, 1961.
        O'BRIEN, JUSTIN.

0648   RESISTANCE, REBELLION AND DEATH. NEW YORK, MODERN LIBRARY,
        1963. O'BRIEN, JUSTIN.

0649   LE DESERT. IN DESERT VIVANT, PP. 7-9. SEE NO. 1597.

0650   PLUIES ET FLORAISONS. IN DESERT VIVANT, PP. 57-62. SEE NO.
        1597.

0651   LE DESERT. IN DESERT VIVANT, PP. 7-9. SEE NO. 1600, 649.

0652   PLUIES ET FLORAISONS. IN DESERT VIVANT, PP. 57-62. SEE NO.
        1600, 650.

0653   DIE WÜSTE. IN DIE WÜSTE LEBT, PP. 7-9. SEE NO. 1598, 649.

0654   REGEN UND BLÜTENRAUSCH. IN DIE WÜSTE LEBT, PP. 57-62. SEE NO.
        1598, 650.

IL DESERTO.   IN DESERTO CHE VIVE, PP. 7-9.   SEE NO. 1599, 649.   0655
PIOGGE E FIORITURE.   IN DESERTO CHE VIVE, PP. 57-62.   SEE NO.   0656
     1599, 650.

INTERVIEWS

0657   THE OBSTINATE CONFIDENCE OF A PESSIMISTIC MAN. INTERVIEW BY
         JEAN BLOCH-MICHEL. REPORTER, VOL. 17, NO. 9 (NOV. 28,
         1957), PP. 37-39.

0658   ALBERT CAMUS. EIN GESPRÄCH MIT DEM NOBEL-PREISTRÄGER.
         INTERVIEW BY JEAN BLOCH-MICHEL. MONAT, VOL. 10, NO. 3
         (DEC. 1957), PP. 3-9.

0659   ALBERT CAMUS TALKS WITH NICOLA CHIAROMONTE. WORLD REVIEW, NO.
         9 (NOV. 1949), P. 34. FR VII 33993.

0660   A. CAMUS NOUS PARLE DE SON ADAPTATION DES POSSÉDÉS.
         SPECTACLES, NO. 1 (MAR. 1958), P. 6.

0661   CAMUS NOUS PARLE... LE FIGARO LITTÉRAIRE, VOL. 14, NO. 682
         (MAY 16, 1959), PP. 1, 4. CR 434.

0662   A FINAL INTERVIEW (ANSWERS TO QUESTIONS POSED BY ROBERT DONALD
         SPECTOR). VENTURE, VOL. 3, NO. 4 (SPRING-SUMMER, 1960),
         PP. 25-38.

0663   CAMUS' ILLUMINATING ANSWERS TO SEARCHING QUESTIONS. NEW YORK
         HERALD TRIBUNE BOOK REVIEW, VOL. 36, NO. 29 (FEB. 21,
         1960), P. 1.

0664   LE PARI DE NOTRE GENERATION. DEMAIN, NO. 98 (OCT. 24-30,
         1957), PP. 11-13. CR 420, FR V11 16721.

0665   DIE WETTE UNSERER GENERATION. IN FRAGEN DER ZEIT, PP. 250-261.
         SEE NO. 630, 664.

0666   THE WAGER OF OUR GENERATION. IN RESISTANCE, REBELLION AND
         DEATH, PP. 169-175

0667   THE WAGER OF OUR GENERATION IN RESISTANCE, REBELLION AND DEATH
         PP. 237-248.

LETTERS

LETTRE À ROLAND BARTHES, SUR LA PESTE.   CLUB,   (FEB. 1955).   CR   0668
    388 BIS.
LETTRE À BERNANOS.   (WRITTEN AUG. 29, 1945).   BULLETIN DE LA   0669
    SOCIÉTÉ DES AMIS DE GEORGES BERNANOS.   NO. 45 (MARCH 1962).
UNE LETTRE D'ALBERT CAMUS EN REPONSE À ANDRÉ BRETON.   ARTS,   0670
    NO. 329 (OCT. 19, 1951), P. 1.
LETTRE AU JOURNAL ARTS. À PROPOS DU DIALOGUE ENTRE ANDRÉ BRETON   0671
    ET AIMÉ PATRI.   ARTS,   NO. 334 (NOV. 23, 1951), PP. 1-3.
    CR 363, FR VII 13301.
LETTERS.   M. CAMUS AND ALGERIA.   M. CAMUS REPLIES (TO PETER L.   0672
    CARACCIOLO).   ENCOUNTER,   VOL. 8, NO. 45 (JUNE 1957), P.
    68.   CR 1004.
LETTRE AU DIRECTEUR DE LA NEF, À PROPOS DE CALIGULA.   LA NEF,   0673
    VOL. 3, NO. 14 (JAN. 1946), PP. 144-145.   CR 326.
LETTRE A UN AMI ALGÉRIEN.   MODERNA SPRAK,   VOL. 52, NO. 1   0674
    (1958), PP. 49-51.
LETTRE AU DIRECTEUR DES TEMPS MODERNES.   TEMPS MODERNES,   VOL.   0675
    8, NO. 82 (AUG. 1952), PP. 317-333.   CR 370.   SEE NO. 46.
GENDAI,   NO SHUHITSU ENO TEGAMI.   (LETTRE AU DIRECTEUR DES   0676
    TEMPS MODERNES.   ALSO SARTRE-REPONSE À A. CAMUS,
    JEANSON-POUR TOUT VOUS DIRE).   TOKYO, SHINCHO-SHA, 1953.
    I.T. 10640.   SATO, SAKU.   SEE NO. 675.
EXTRAIT D'UNE LETTRE.   FIGARO LITTÉRAIRE,   VOL. 15, NO. 716   0677
    (JAN. 9, 1960), P. 6.   SEE NO. 3302.
LETTER DATED MAY 30, 1951.   THE HARVARD ADVOCATE,   VOL. 135,   0678
    (SEP. 1951), P. 21.
LETTRES D'ALBERT CAMUS À JEAN GILLIBERT.   REVUE D'HISTOIRE DU   0679
    THÉÂTRE,   NO. 4 (1960), PP. 355-359.
LETTRE À MAURICE LIME.   LA RÉVOLUTION PROLÉTARIENNE,   NO. 447   0680
    (FEB. 1960), PP. 26-27.
À PROPOS DES POURSUITES CONTRE M. JEAN DE MAISONSEUL.   MONDE,   0681
    VOL. 9, NO. 397 (MAY 24-30, 1956), P. 1.
LETTRE AU SUJET DU 'PARTI PRIS' DE FRANCIS PONGE.   NOUVELLE   0682
    REVUE FRANÇAISE,   VOL. 8, NO. 45 (SEP. 1956), PP. 386-392.
    CR 408.
LETTRE A L'UNESCO.   PARIS, LE 12 JUIN 1952.   SIMOUN,   VOL. 1,   0683
    NO. 4 (SEP. 1952), PP. 10-12.

PREFACES

0684   PRÉFACE À L'ALLEMAGNE VUE PAR LES ÉCRIVAINS DE LA RÉSISTANCE
         FRANÇAISE DE KONRAD F. BIEBER.   GENEVA,   LIBRAIRIE E. DROZ,
         1954.   CR 302.

0685   PRÉFACE À L'ALLEMAGNE VUE PAR LES ÉCRIVAINS DE LA RÉSISTANCE
         FRANÇAISE DE KONRAD F. BIEBER.   LILLE,   LIBRAIRIE GIARD,
         1954.   CR 302.

0686   PRÉFACE À L'ESPAGNE LIBRE DE JEAN CAMP, ET AL.   PARIS,
         CALMAN-LEVY, 1946. CR 290.

0687   PRÉFACE AUX MAXIMES ET ANECDOTES DE SEBASTIEN-ROCH-NICHOLAS
         CHAMFORT.   MONACO,   DAC (COLL. INCIDENCES, 2), 1944.   CR
         286.

0688   CHAMFORT.   THE SWANEE REVIEW,   VOL. 56, NO. 1 (WINTER 1948),
         PP. 12-23.   CR 345.   TRANSLATION OF NO. 687.   LESAGE,
         LAURENCE.

0689   RENÉ CHAR.   DIE NEUE RUNDSCHAU,   VOL. 64, NO. 3 (1953), PP.
         392-395.

0690   DIX ESTAMPES ORIGINALES DE PIERRE-EUGÈNE CLAIRIN.   PARIS,
         ROMBALDI (LES MAÎTRES DE L'ESTAMPE FRANÇAISE
         CONTEMPORAINE, 3), 1946.   CR 289.

0691   PRÉFACE À REQUIEM POUR UNE NONNE DE WILLIAM FAULKNER.   PARIS,
         GALLIMARD (COLL. DU MONDE ENTIER), 1957. CR 305.

0692   SUR LES ÎLES DE JEAN GRENIER.   PREUVES,   NO. 95 (JAN. 1959),
         PP. 13-15.   CR 305 BIS.

0693   PRÉFACE AUX ÎLES DE JEAN GRENIER.   PARIS,   NOUVELLE REVUE
         FRANÇAISE, 1959.   CR 305 BIS.

0694   SOBRE LAS ISLAS DE JEAN GRENIER.   SUR,   NO. 258 (MAY-JUNE
         1959), PP. 25-28.   CR 305 BIS.

0695   PRÉFACE À LA MAISON DU PEUPLE ET AUX COMPAGNONS DE LOUIS
         GUILLOUX.   PARIS,   BERNARD GRASSET, 1953.   CR 298.

0696   PRÉFACE À LA MAISON DU PEUPLE DE LOUIS GUILLOUX.   PARIS,   CLUB
         FRANCAIS DU LIVRE (COLL. RECITS), 1959.   CR 299.

0697   LETTRE-PRÉFACE À DEVANT LA MORT DE JEANNE HÉON-CANONNE.
         ANGERS,   SIRAUDEAU, 1951.   CR 293.

0698   LETTRE-PRÉFACE À DEVANT LA MORT DE JEANNE HÉON-CANONNE.   PARIS,
         AMIOT-DUMONT, 1953. CR 294.

0699   LETTRE-PRÉFACE, LES HOMMES BLESSÉS À MORT CRIENT DE JEANNE
         HÉON-CANONNE.   PARIS, CHALET, 1966.

0700   PRÉFACE AUX POÉSIES POSTHUMES DE RENÉ LEYNAUD.   PARIS,
         GALLIMARD, 1947. CR 291.

0701   VORWORT ZU DEN GEDICHTEN VON RENÉ LEYNAUD (RENÉ LEYNAUD).   IN
         FRAGEN DER ZEIT, PP. 49-59.   SEE NO. 630, 2. TRANSLATION OF
         NO. 700.

0702   RENÉ LEYNAUD.   IN RESISTANCE, REBELLION AND DEATH, PP. 33-38.

SEE NO. 633, 1. TRANSLATION OF NO. 700.

THE FLESH. IN RESISTANCE, REBELLION AND DEATH, PP. 41-54. SEE   0703
NO. 647, 2. TRANSLATION OF NO. 700.

PRÉFACE AUX OEUVRES COMPLÈTES DE ROGER MARTIN DU GARD. PARIS,   0704
GALLIMARD (BIBLIOTHÈQUE DE LA PLÉIADE), 1955. CR 304.

ROGER MARTIN DU GARD. NOUVELLE REVUE FRANÇAISE, VOL. 3, NO.   0705
34 (OCT. 1955), PP. 641-671. CR 397.

PRÉFACE À CONTRE-AMOUR DE DANIEL MAUROC ET RECIT III DE P.   0706
PONNELLE. PARIS, ÉDITIONS DE MINUIT, 1952. CR 295.

PRÉFACE À LAISSEZ PASSER MON PEUPLE. LA TRAGÉDIE D'UN EXODUS DE   0707
JACQUES MÉRY. PARIS, ÉDITION DU SEUIL (COLL. ESPRIT-
FRONTIÈRE), 1947. CR 292.

PRÉFACE À MOSCOU SOUS LÉNINE. LES ORIGINES DU COMMUNISME   0708
D'ALBERT ROSMER. PARIS, ÉDITIONS DE FLORE (PIERRE HORAY),
1953. CR 300.

A MOSCA AL TEMPO DI LENIN. LE ORIGINI DEL COMUNISMO DI ALFRED   0709
ROSMER. FLORENCE, LA NUOVA ITALIA (COLL. DOCUMENTI DELLA
CRISI CONTEMPORANEA, 10), 1953. CR 301. STELLA, ANTONIO.

PRÉFACE À LA VÉRITÉ SUR L'AFFAIRE NAGY, LES FAITS, LES   0710
DOCUMENTS, LES TÉMOIGNAGES INTERNATIONAUX. PARIS, PLON
(COLL. LES DOCUMENTS DE TRIBUNE LIBRE), 1958. CR 306.

PREFACE TO THE TRUTH ABOUT THE NAGY AFFAIR. FACTS, DOCUMENTS,   0711
COMMENTS. LONDON, SECKER AND WARBURG, 1959.

PREFACE TO THE TRUTH ABOUT THE NAGY AFFAIR. FACTS, DOCUMENTS,   0712
COMMENTS. NEW YORK, PRAEGER, 1959.

LETTRE-PRÉFACE, LE COMBAT SILENCIEUX D'ANDRÉ SALVET. PARIS,   0713
ÉDITIONS FRANCE-EMPIRE (COLL. LE PORTULAN), 1945. CR 287.

L'ENCHANTEMENT DE CORDES DANS CORDES-EN-ALBIGEOIS PAR CLAIRE   0714
TARGUEBAYRE. TOULOUSE. PRIVAT (COLL. SITES DE FRANCE),
1954. CR 303.

L'ARTISTE EN PRISON IN LA BALLADE DE LA GEÔLE DE READING   0715
D'OSCAR WILDE. PARIS. FALAIZE (LES CARNETS OUBLIÉS, 9),
1952. CR 296.

L'ARTISTE EN PRISON, ÉTUDE INÉDITE SUR OSCAR WILDE IN LA   0716
BALLADE DE LA GEÔLE DE READING BY OSCAR WILDE.
ILLUSTRATIONS DE ROBERT FONTA. PARIS, FALAIZE
(BIBLIOPHILES ET GRAVEURS D'AUJOURD'HUI), 1952. CR 297.

L'ARTISTE EN PRISON. ARTS, NO. 390 (DEC. 19-25, 1952), PP. 1,   0717
5. CR 369. SEE NO. 715.

KONSTÄREN I FÄNGELSE. BONNIERS LITTERÄRA MAGASIN, VOL. 21,   0718
NO. 7 (SEP. 1953), PP. 522-525. TRANSLATION OF NO. 715.
ALEXANDERSSON, EVA.

THE ARTIST IN PRISON. ENCOUNTER, NO. 6 (MAR. 1954), PP.   0719
23-29. CR 374. TRANSLATION OF NO. 715. WHITE, ANTONIA.

VORWORT. IN DRAMEN, PP. 9-14. SEE NO. 628.   0720

0721   PRÉFACE À L'ÉTRANGER.   IN L'ÉTRANGER D'ALBERT CAMUS.   SEE NO.
          252, 254.

TRANSLATIONS AND ADAPTATIONS

UN CAS INTÉRESSANT. (TRADUCTION D'UN CASO CLINICO, PIÈCE EN   0722
    DEUX PARTIES ET DEUX TABLEAUX DE DINO BUZZATI).
    L'AVANT-SCÈNE, NO. 105, N.D. (C. 1955), PP. 1-25. CR 311.
LA DÉVOTION À LA CROIX. (TRADUCTION D'UNE PIÈCE EN TROIS   0723
    JOURNÉES DE PEDRO CALDERÓN DE LA BARCA). PARIS,
    GALLIMARD, 1953. CR 309.
LA DÉVOTION À LA CROIX IN 'THÉÂTRE ESPAGNOL'. PARIS. CLUB DES   0724
    LIBRAIRES DE FRANCE, N.D. (1958). CR 314.
LES POSSÉDÉS. (PIÈCE EN TROIS PARTIES, ADAPTÉE DU ROMAN DE   0725
    FEODOR DOSTOIEVSKI). PARIS, GALLIMARD (LE MANTEAU
    D'ARLEQUIN), 1959. CR 315.
LES POSSÉDÉS. PARIS-THÉÂTRE, VOL. 12, NO. 147 (1960), PP.   0726
    9-50.
LOS POSEÍDOS. IN TEATRO 2. SEE NO. 623.   0727
THE POSSESSED, A PLAY IN THREE PARTS. TORONTO, COLLINS AND   0728
    SONS AND CO., 1960. O'BRIEN, JUSTIN.
DIE BESESSENEN. IN DRAMEN, PP. 235-346. SEE NO. 628.   0729
THE POSSESSED, A PLAY IN THREE PARTS. LONDON, HAMILTON, 1960.   0730
    O'BRIEN, JUSTIN.
OS POSSESSOS. LISBON, LIVROS DO BRASIL, 1961. I.T. (1962)   0731
    19057. FERREIRA, ARMANDO.
THE POSSESSED, A PLAY IN THREE PARTS. NEW YORK, KNOPF, 1960.   0732
    O'BRIEN, JUSTIN.
THE POSSESSED, A PLAY IN THREE PARTS. NEW YORK, VINTAGE   0733
    BOOKS, 1964. O'BRIEN, JUSTIN.
REQUIEM POUR UNE NONNE. PIÈCE EN DEUX PARTIES ET SEPT TABLEAUX   0734
    (D'APRÈS LE ROMAN DE WILLIAM FAULKNER). PARIS, GALLIMARD
    (COLL. LE MANTEAU D'ARLEQUIN), 1956. CR 312.
REQUIEM POUR UNE NONNE. PARIS-THÉÂTRE, VOL. 11, NO. 123   0735
    (1957), PP. 19-49.
REQUIEM PARA UNA RECLUSA. BUENOS AIRES, SUR, 1960. I.T.   0736
    (1963) 3745. SEE NO. 734. OCAMPO, VICTORIA.
LES ESPRITS. COMÉDIE. (ADAPTATION EN TROIS ACTES D'UN OUVRAGE   0737
    DE PIERRE DE LARIVEY. PARIS, GALLIMARD, 1953. CR 310.
LE CHEVALIER D'OLMEDO. COMÉDIE DRAMATIQUE EN TROIS JOURNÉES.   0738
    (ADAPTÉE DE LOPE DE VEGA CARPIO). PARIS, GALLIMARD, 1957.
    CR 313.
CHANT SPIRITUEL, COUPE DE SOLEIL. (TRADUCTIONS AVEC PIERRE   0739
    PAGES DES POÈMES DE JOAN MARAGALL). LE CHEVAL DE TROIE,
    NOS. 2-3 (AUG.-SEP. 1947), PP. 243-246. CR 307.
LA DERNIÈRE FLEUR. (TRADUCTION DE THE LAST FLOWER BY JAMES   0740
    THURBER). PARIS, GALLIMARD, 1952. CR 308.
LA RÉVOLTE DANS LES ASTURIES. (4 ACTES). ESSAI DE CRÉATION   0741

COLLECTIVE.   ALGIERS,   CHARLOT,   1936.

WORKS
ABOUT CAMUS

AARNES, ASBJØRN S. GLIMT FRA FRANKRIKE. VINDUET, VOL. 1, NO.   0742
    5 (1947), PP. 374-375. FR VII 28221.

AARNES, ASBJØRN S. MODERNE FRANSK LITTERATUR PA NORSK.   0743
    VINDUET, VOL. 2, NO. 5 (1948), PP. 393-399. FR VII 28424.

AARNES, ASBJØRN S. TANKER OMKRING ALBERT CAMUS. VINDUET, VOL.   0744
    4, NO. 8 (1950), PP. 599-601. FR VII 29349.

AARNES, ASBJØRN S. SISYFOS, DR. RIEUX OG OPPRØREREN. EN LINJE   0745
    I CAMUS' FORFATTERSKAP. VINDUET, VOL. 7, NO. 2 (1953),
    PP. 157-163. FR VII 29348.

ABEL, LIONEL. LETTERS FROM PARIS. IMPRESSIONS AND   0746
    CONVERSATIONS. PARTISAN REVIEW, VOL. 16, NO. 4 (APRIL
    1949), PP. 395-399. BO 260, BR, CR 680 BIS, FR VII 2245.

ABEL, LIONEL. ALBERT CAMUS, MORALIST OF FEELING. COMMENTARY,   0747
    VOL. 31, NO. 2 (FEB. 1961), PP. 172-175. FR VII 29350.

ABRAHAM, CLAUDE K. CALIGULA. DRAMA OF REVOLT OR DRAMA OF   0748
    DECEPTION. MODERN DRAMA, VOL. 5, NO. 4 (FEB. 1963), PP.
    451-453. PMLA 7967 (1964).

ADAMS, J. DONALD. SPEAKING OF BOOKS. (CONCERNS 'THE PLAGUE'.)   0749
    NEW YORK TIMES BOOK REVIEW, VOL. 97, NO. 33090 (AUG. 29,
    1948), SECT. 7, P. 2.

ADAMS, J. DONALD. SPEAKING OF BOOKS, (ACCEPTANCE SPEECH). NEW   0750
    YORK TIMES BOOK REVIEW, MARCH 2, 1958, P. 2.

ADAMS, ROBERT M. ADVENTURER IN MORALITY. NATION, VOL. 188,   0751
    NO. 18 (MAY 2, 1959), PP. 412-413. FR VII 23579.

ADOUM, JORGE ENRIQUE. PREMIO NOBEL. ALBERT CAMUS Y LAS TAREAS   0752
    DE SU GENERACIÓN. LETRAS DEL ECUADOR, VOL. 13, NO. 109
    (JULY-DEC. 1957), P. 16. FR VII 19403.

AHLENIUS, HOLGER. I DIKTENS FRANKRIKE OCH IDEERNAS, STUDIER OCH   0753
    ESSAYER. STOCKHOLM. WAHLSTRÖM AND WIDSTRAND, 1955. CAMUS
    OCH NIHILISMEN, PP. 91-107. CAMUS VID UNGDOMSKÄLLORNA, PP.
    108-122. FR VII 16530.

AIKEN, HENRY DAVID. THE REVOLT AGAINST IDEOLOGY. COMMENTARY,   0754
    VOL. 37, NO. 4 (APRIL 1964), PP. 29-39.

ALBÉRÈS, RENÉ-MARILL. PORTRAIT DE NOTRE HÉROS, ESSAI SUR LE   0755
    ROMAN ACTUEL. PARIS. LE PORTULAN, 1945. PP. 78-79.

0756   ALBÉRÈS, RENÉ-MARILL. ALBERT CAMUS Y LA REBELIÓN DE PROMETEO.
          SUR,   VOL. 15, NO. 142 (AUGUST 1946), PP. 18-28.   BO 183,
          BR, CR 552, FR VII 2694.

0757   ALBÉRÈS, RENÉ-MARILL. LA RÉVOLTE DES ÉCRIVAINS D'AUJOURD'HUI.
          PARIS. CORRÊA, 1949.   ALBERT CAMUS ET LE MYTHE DE
          PROMÉTHÉE, PP. 63-81. BO 197, BR, CR 437, FR VII 2023.

0758   ALBÉRÈS, RENÉ-MARILL. L'AVENTURE INTELLECTUELLE DU XXE SIÈCLE,
          1900-1950. PARIS. LA NOUVELLE ÉDITION, 1950. CF. PP.
          305-309. CR 435.

0759   ALBÉRÈS, RENÉ-MARILL. LES ÉCRIVAINS DE LA RÉVOLTE.   REVUE DE
          PARIS,   VOL. 58, NO. 8 (1951), PP. 61-67. BO 219.

0760   ALBÉRÈS, RENÉ-MARILL. LA RÉVOLTE ABSTRAITE, FIGARO LITTÉRAIRE,
          VOL. 7, NO. 307 (MARCH 8, 1952), PP. 1, 6. FITCH.

0761   ALBÉRÈS, RENÉ-MARILL. LES HOMMES TRAQUÉS. PARIS. LA NOUVELLE
          ÉDITION, 1953. ALBERT CAMUS ET LA NOSTALGIE DE L'ÉDEN, PP.
          187-220. BO 71, CR 436, FR VII 8661.

0762   ALBÉRÈS, RENÉ-MARILL. AMBIGUITÉS DE LA RÉVOLTE. REVUE DE
          PARIS,   VOL. 60, NO. 6 (JUNE 1953), PP. 57-66. BO 228, CR
          844, BFZ 35-240 (1952-53).

0763   ALBÉRÈS, RENÉ-MARILL. L'AVENTURE INTELLECTUELLE DU XXE SIÈCLE,
          PANORAMA DES LITTÉRATURES EUROPÉENNES 1900-1963. TROISIÈME
          ÉDITION, REVUE ET AUGMENTÉE. PARIS. A. MICHEL, 1959.

0764   ALBÉRÈS, RENÉ-MARILL. LE PARI DE VIVRE. NOUVELLES LITTÉRAIRES,
          NO. 1688 (JAN. 7, 1960), PP. 1, 8. FR VII 23580, KL II
          393, PMLA 6807 (1961).

0765   ALBÉRÈS, RENÉ-MARILL. ALBERT CAMUS DANS SON SIÈCLE.   TÉMOIN ET
          ÉTRANGER. TABLE RONDE, NO. 146 (FEB. 1960), PP. 9-15.
          BFZ 46-283, BUL SIGN 15-19-685, 15-19-13752, FR VII 23569,
          KL II 386, PMLA 6808 (1961).

0766   ALBÉRÈS, RENÉ-MARILL. CE QUE FURENT EN 1960 LES LETTRES.
          NOUVELLES LITTÉRAIRES, NO. 1740 (JAN. 5, 1961), PP. 1, 8.

0767   ALBÉRÈS, RENÉ-MARILL. L'ART DE LA MISE EN SCÈNE. NOUVELLES
          LITTÉRAIRES, NO. 1779 (OCT. 5, 1961), PP. 2-3.

0768   ALBÉRÈS, RENÉ-MARILL. BILAN LITTÉRAIRE DU XXE SIÈCLE. PARIS.
          AUBIER, ÉDITIONS MONTAIGNE, 1962. SCATTERED REFERENCES.

0769   ALBÉRÈS, RENÉ-MARILL. HISTOIRE DU ROMAN MODERNE. PARIS. ALBIN
          MICHEL, 1962. SCATTERED REFERENCES.

0770   ALBÉRÈS, RENÉ-MARILL. J. CRUICKSHANK. THE NOVELIST AS
          PHILOSOPHER. TABLE RONDE, NO. 178 (NOV. 1962), PP.
          112-114. FR VII 28486.

0771   ALBÉRÈS, RENÉ-MARILL. CAMUS NOUS JUGE. NOUVELLES LITTÉRAIRES,
          VOL. 41, NO. 1846 (JAN. 17, 1963), P. 5. FR VII 33933.

0772   ALBÉRÈS, RENÉ-MARILL. LE PRIX NOBEL. IN ANONYMOUS, CAMUS, PP.
          217-246. SEE NO. 940.

0773   ALBERT, ALAN. STUDY IN BROWN (II). DE LA MENTALIE (SIC)

COLONIALE. TEMPS MODERNES,   VOL. 18, NO. 195 (AUGUST
1962), PP. 332-346.

ALEXANDER, IAN W. LA PHILOSOPHIE EXISTENTIALISTE EN FRANCE.   0774
FRENCH STUDIES,   VOL. 1, NO. 2 (APRIL 1947), PP. 95-114.

ALEXANDER, IAN W.   ALBERT CAMUS AND THE LITERATURE OF REVOLT   0775
BY JOHN CRUICKSHANK. MODERN LANGUAGE REVIEW, VOL. 56, NO.
1 (JAN. 1961), P. 121.

ALHEINC, RAOUL. LES ANCÊTRES DE 'L'ÉTRANGER' DE CAMUS. SIMOUN,   0776
VOL. 3, NO. 14 (1954), PP. 27-36. BO 310, FR VII 17284.

ALIOTTA, ANTONIO. CRITICA DELL'ESISTENZIALISMO. ROME.   0777
CREMONESE, 1951. IL SATANISMO DI SARTRE E DI CAMUS, PP.
77-85. CAMUS E IL MITO DI SISIFO, PP. 82-85. BO 169.

ALIOTTA, ANTONIO. CRITICA DELL ESISTENZIALISMO. ROME.   0778
CREMONESE, 1957. IL SATANISMO DI SARTRE E DI CAMUS, PP.
93-103. PART 4. CAMUS E IL MITO DI SISIFO, PP. 99-101.
RIVENDICAZIONE DEL VALORE DELLE OPERE UMANE CONTRO IL
CAMUS, PP. 101-103.

ALLEN, LOUIS. ALBERT CAMUS. LA CHUTE. DOWNSIDE REVIEW, VOL.   0779
75, NO. 241 (SUMMER 1957), PP. 259-274. FR VII 19404, KL I
274, MA 180.

ALONSO, JULIO LAGO. ALBERT CAMUS. EN EL TERCER ANIVERSARIO DE   0780
SU MUERTE. ARBOR,   VOL. 54, NO. 206 (FEB. 1963), PP.
95-99, (203-207).

ALTER, ANDRÉ. C'EST AUSSI UN HOMME DE THÉÂTRE. FIGARO   0781
LITTÉRAIRE, VOL. 12, NO. 601 (OCT. 26, 1957), P. 7. CR
979, FR VII 17285, KL I 272.

ALTER, ANDRÉ. DE CALIGULA AUX JUSTES. DE L'ABSURDE À LA   0782
JUSTICE. REVUE D'HISTOIRE DU THÉÂTRE, VOL. 12, NO. 4
(OCT.-DEC. 1960), PP. 321-336. FR VII 23570, PMLA 7350
(1962).

ALTGELT, ERIKA. ABSURDITÄT UND EINVERSTÄNDNIS.   0783
KOMMUNITÄT-VIERTELJAHRESHEFTE DER EVANGELISCHEN AKADEMIE,
VOL. 6, (JAN. 1962), PP. 70-72. BDZ 62

ALTMAN, GEORGES. SUR UN LIVRE D'ALBERT CAMUS (LA CHUTE).   0784
FRANC-TIREUR, (JUNE 8, 1956). FITCH.

ALTMAN, GEORGES. ALBERT CAMUS, NOTRE AMI. FRANC-TIREUR, (OCT.   0785
18, 1957), P. 283. CR 979 BIS.

ALVAREZ, A. THE PARIS SCENE. NEW STATESMAN, VOL. 58, NO. 1497   0786
(NOV. 21, 1959), PP. 704, 706.

ALVAREZ, CARLOS LUIS. UNAMUNO Y CAMUS. ESTAFETA LITERARIA,   0787
NO. 300-301 (SEPT. 12-26, 1964), PP. 29-30.

ALVAREZ, D. LA PICARESCA ESPAÑOLA Y LA LITERATURA   0788
EXISTENCIALISTA. HUMANIDADES, VOL. 10, NO. 21 (1958), PP.
207-212. BUL SIGN 14. 13380.

AMBRIÈRE, F. LA GALÉRIE DRAMATIQUE 1945-1948. LE THÉÂTRE   0789

FRANÇAIS DEPUIS LA LIBÉRATION. PARIS. COLLECTION MISES AU
POINT, 1949. CALIGULA, PP. 86-89. L'ÉTAT DE SIÈGE, PP.
350-354. BO 370.

0790   AMBRIÈRE, FRANCIS. INTRODUCTION À L'HISTOIRE DU THÉÂTRE EN
FRANCE DEPUIS LA LIBÉRATION (SUITE). ÂGE NOUVEAU,   NO. 33
(JAN. 1949), PP. 58-64.

0791   AMER, HENRY. LE MYTHE DE SISYPHE. NOUVELLE REVUE FRANÇAISE,
VOL. 8, NO. 87 (MARCH 1960), PP. 487-490. FR VII 23575, KL
II 391.

0792   AMES, SANFORD. LA CHUTE. FROM SUMMITRY TO SPELEOLOGY. FRENCH
REVIEW, VOL. 39, NO. 4 (FEB. 1966), PP. 559-566.

0793   ANDREUS, HANS. ONZE CORRESPONDENT MELDT. ALBERT CAMUS.
(L'HOMME RÉVOLTÉ). LITTERAIR PASPOORT, NO. 61 (NOV.
1952), PP. 210-211. CR 802.

0794   ANDRIANNE, RENÉ. LE CAS ALBERT CAMUS BY ANNE DURAND. (REVIEW).
LETTRES ROMANES, VOL. 17, NO. 2 (MAY 1, 1963), PP. 193-
194. FR VII 33934.

0795   ANEX, GEORGES. LA PESTE, PAR ALBERT CAMUS. FORMES ET COULEURS,
VOL. 9, NO. 4 (1947), (UNNUMBERED). BO 382, BR, CR 582.

0796   ANEX, GEORGES. ALBERT CAMUS, PRIX NOBEL. GAZETTE LITTÉRAIRE,
(OCT. 20, 1957), CR 979 TER.

0797   ANEX, GEORGES. L'INDIFFÉRENCE. NOUVELLE REVUE FRANÇAISE, VOL.
8, NO. 87 (MARCH 1960), PP. 522-526. FR VII 23575, KL II
388.

0798   ANGIOLETTI, GIOVANNI BATTISTA. L'ANATRA ALLA NORMANNA. MILAN.
FABRI, 1957. LA RIVOLTA DI CAMUS, PP. 130-135.

0799   ANGIOLETTI, GIOVANNI BATTISTA. LA RIVOLTA DI CAMUS. HUMANITAS,
VOL. 15, NO. 1 (JAN. 1960), PP. 60-63. FR VII 23581, KL II
391, PMLA 16531.

0800   ANONYMOUS. L'ÉTRANGER, PAR ALBERT CAMUS. INDICATIONS,   2E
SERIE, FASC. 7, (1944), PP. 1-6. CR 563.

0801   ANONYMOUS. LA PESTE, PAR ALBERT CAMUS. INDICATIONS, 5E SERIE,
FASC. 3, (1947), PP. 1-12. CR 719.

0802   ANONYMOUS. ALBERT CAMUS. L'HOMME RÉVOLTÉ. INDICATIONS, 10E
SERIE, FASC. 2 (1952), PP. 1-13. CR 888.

0803   ANONYMOUS. ALBERT CAMUS. LA CHUTE. INDICATIONS, 14 E SERIE,
FASC. 1, (1956), PP. 1-9. CR 1090.

0804   ANONYMOUS. ALBERT CAMUS. L'EXIL ET LE ROYAUME. INDICATIONS,
15E SERIE, FASC. 2, (1957), PP. 1-5. CR 1097.

0805   ANONYMOUS. LE THÉÂTRE À PARIS. TROIS TRAGÉDIES... (LE
MALENTENDU D'ALBERT CAMUS, PP. 192-194). FRANCE LIBRE,
VOL. 9, NO. 51 (JAN. 15, 1945), PP. 191-195. CR 539.

0806   ANONYMOUS. ALBERT CAMUS. OPÉRA, OCT. 17, 1945. CR 513.

0807   ANONYMOUS. LETTRES À UN AMI ALLEMAND, PAR ALBERT CAMUS
(REVIEW). BULLETIN CRITIQUE DU LIVRE FRANÇAIS,   VOL. 1,

NO. 2 (OCT.-NOV. 1945), P. 10.

ANONYMOUS. VOUS M'EN DIREZ TANT... GAZETTE DES LETTRES, VOL.   0808
    2, NO. 6 (MARCH 2, 1946), P. 4. CR 580.

ANONYMOUS. ABSURDISTE. NEW YORKER, VOL. 22, NO. 10 (APRIL 20,   0809
    1946), PP. 22-23. BO 182.

ANONYMOUS. MAN IN A VACUUM. THE STRANGER. TIME (ATLANTIC   0810
    OVERSEAS EDITION), VOL. 47, NO. 20 (MAY 20, 1946), PP. 92,
    94. BO 299.

ANONYMOUS. ETERNAL ROCK PUSHER. REVIEW OF 'THE STRANGER'.   0811
    NEWSWEEK, VOL. 27, NO. 15 (APRIL 15, 1946), PP. 97-99. BO
    315, MA 188.

ANONYMOUS. ALBERT CAMUS VU PAR LES AMÉRICAINS. GAZETTE DES   0812
    LETTRES, VOL. 2, NO. 13 (JUNE 8, 1946), P. 13. CR 560.

ANONYMOUS. A VICTIM. TIMES LITERARY SUPPLEMENT, VOL. 45, NO.   0813
    2316 (JUNE 22, 1946), P. 293. FR VII 34030.

ANONYMOUS. ÜBER 'CALIGULA'. PRISMA, NO. 7 (MAY 1947), P. 26.   0814
    CR 589.

ANONYMOUS. THE STRANGER. THEATRE ARTS, VOL. 31, NO. 3 (MARCH   0815
    1947), P. 54. BO 302.

ANONYMOUS. LES GRANDS PRIX LITTÉRAIRES. LA PESTE. SOIR, VOL.   0816
    61, NO. 165 (JUNE 15, 1947), P. 2. CR 618.

ANONYMOUS. THE PLAGUE WITHIN US. TIMES LITERARY SUPPLEMENT,   0817
    VOL. 46, NO. 2374 (AUG. 2, 1947), P. 389. FR VII 34020.

ANONYMOUS. LA PESTE. BULLETIN CRITIQUE DU LIVRE FRANÇAIS,   0818
    VOL. 2, NOS. 7-8 (AUG.-SEPT., 1947), P. 5. CR 619.

ANONYMOUS. NOCES, PAR ALBERT CAMUS. BULLETIN CRITIQUE DU LIVRE   0819
    FRANÇAIS, VOL. 2, NO. 10 (NOV. 1947), P. 3. CR 614.

ANONYMOUS. 'CALIGULA', URAUFFÜHRUNG IN STUTTGART, WUPPERTAL.   0820
    BÜHNENKRITIK, NO. 1 (1948), PP. 12-17. BDZ 98 (1948) P.
    181, CR 646.

ANONYMOUS. ALBERT CAMUS, 'CALIGULA'. AUFFÜHRUNG IN CELLE.   0821
    BÜHNENKRITIK, NO. 3 (1948), P. 15. CR 647.

ANONYMOUS. CHRONIQUE THÉÂTRALE. CALIGULA D'ALBERT CAMUS.   0822
    CHANTIERS, VOL. 12, NO. 7 (APRIL 1948), PP. 220-225. CR
    645, FR VII 4408.

ANONYMOUS. PLAYS OF THE MIND. TIMES LITERARY SUPPLEMENT, VOL.   0823
    47, NO. 2420 (JUNE 19, 1948), P. 340. FR VII 34021.

ANONYMOUS. CAMUS THE CLASSICIST. NEWSWEEK, VOL. 32, NO. 5   0824
    (AUG. 2, 1948), PP. 77-78. BO 407.

ANONYMOUS. PLAGUE IN ORAN. ALBERT CAMUS. THE PLAGUE. TIMES   0825
    LITERARY SUPPLEMENT (LONDON), VOL. 47, NO. 2431 (SEPT. 4,
    1948), P. 497. BO 415, FR VII 34019.

ANONYMOUS. ALBERT CAMUS. DE KUNSTENAAR IS DE GETUIGE DER   0826
    VRIJHEID. VLAM, VOL. 5, NO. 5 (JAN. 29, 1949), P. 8. BO
    97.

0827   ANONYMOUS. DAS GESPRACH ZWISCHEN ALBERT CAMUS UND DEN CHRISTEN.
          HERDER-KORRESPONDENZ, VOL. 3, NO. 13 (1949), PP. 557-560.
          BDZ 99-167 (1949), BO 108, CR 699.

0828   ANONYMOUS. L'ÉTAT DE SIÈGE. SPECTACLE EN TROIS PARTIES.
          BULLETIN CRITIQUE DU LIVRE FRANÇAIS, VOL. 4, NO. 3 (MARCH
          1949), P. 160. CR 693.

0829   ANONYMOUS. ALBERT CAMUS. CALIGULA. TIMES (LONDON), NO. 51325
          (MARCH 9, 1949), P. 2. CR 686.

0830   ANONYMOUS. CAMUS ET MARTIN DU GARD ESPOIRS DU SPRINT.
          CARREFOUR, NO. 252 (JULY 13, 1949), P. 9.

0831   ANONYMOUS. ALBERT CAMUS EN ZIJN 'DE VREEMDELING'. NIEUWE EEUW,
          VOL. 24, (SEPT. 1949), PP. BO 303.

0832   ANONYMOUS. ALBERT CAMUS' CALIGULA. VOORTREFFELIJKE VOORSTELLING
          VAN BELANGRIJK STUK. ELSEVIERS WEEKBLAD, VOL. 5, NO. 47
          (NOV. 26, 1949), P. 35. CR 687.

0833   ANONYMOUS. GEDACHTEN VAN CAMUS....IN EEN GESPREK MET NICOLA
          CHIAROMANTE (SIC).... ELSEVIERS WEEKBLAD, VOL. 5, NO. 47
          (NOV. 26, 1949), P. 40. BO 22, CR 697.

0834   ANONYMOUS. LES GONCOURT. C'EST ALBERT CAMUS QU'IL NOUS FAUT.
          CARREFOUR, VOL. 16, NO. 272 (NOV. 29, 1949), P. 1.

0835   ANONYMOUS. EN MARGE DES 'JUSTES'. NOUVELLES LITTÉRAIRES, VOL.
          29, NO. 1168 (JAN. 19, 1950), P. 5. BO 465.

0836   ANONYMOUS. DIE PEST. AUSSPRACHE, NO. 4 (1950), PP. 75-81. BO
          436.

0837   ANONYMOUS. ALBERT CAMUS ALS JOURNALIST. GEISTIGES FRANKREICH,
          VOL. 4, NO. 172 (1950), BO 98.

0838   ANONYMOUS. LES JUSTES. PIÈCE EN CINQ ACTES. BULLETIN CRITIQUE
          DU LIVRE FRANÇAIS, VOL. 5, NO. 6 (JUNE 1950), P. 363. CR
          756.

0839   ANONYMOUS. ACTUELLES. CHRONIQUE 1944-48. BULLETIN CRITIQUE DU
          LIVRE FRANÇAIS, VOL. 5, NO. 11 (NOV. 1950), P. 689. CR
          732.

0840   ANONYMOUS. A MOVEMENT OF RESISTANCE. (REVIEW). TIMES LITERARY
          SUPPLEMENT, NO. 2546 (NOV. 17, 1950), P. 734. FR VII
          34016.

0841   ANONYMOUS. BIBLIOGRAPHIE DES OEUVRES D'ALBERT CAMUS. BIBLIO,
          VOL. 19, NO. 9 (NOV. 1951), P. 9. FR VII 5736.

0842   ANONYMOUS. RÉVOLTE SUR MESURE. PARIS. ÉDITIONS DE LA RUE,
          1952. BO 223.

0843   ANONYMOUS. BRETON CONTRA CAMUS. GEISTIGES FRANKREICH, VOL. 5,
          NO. 235 (1952). BO 259.

0844   ANONYMOUS. L'HOMME RÉVOLTÉ. BULLETIN CRITIQUE DU LIVRE
          FRANÇAIS, VOL. 7, NO. 2 (FEB. 1952), P. 82. CR 820.

0845   ANONYMOUS. L'ÉQUIPE DE ROMAN. ROMAN ET RÉVOLTE. ROMAN, NO. 8
          (JULY 1952), PP. 646-647. BO 224, FR VII 7703.

ANONYMOUS. LA POLÉMIQUE SARTRE-CAMUS. FIGARO LITTÉRAIRE, VOL.   0846
     7, NO. 334 (SEPT. 13, 1952), P. 4.   BO 282, FR VII 8500.

ANONYMOUS. THE CLIMATE OF FICTION. TIMES LITERARY SUPPLEMENT.   0847
     NO. 2668 (MARCH 20, 1953), PP. 10-11.

ANONYMOUS. A PRACTISING REBEL. ALBERT CAMUS' 'THE REBEL'.   0848
     TIMES LITERARY SUPPLEMENT, VOL. 52, NO. 2707 (DEC. 18,
     1953), PP. 809-810. BO 511, FR VII 11238, MA 188.

ANONYMOUS. UNE DÉFENSE DE L'HUMANISME MÉDITERRANÉEN.   L'ÉTÉ,   0849
     PAR ALBERT CAMUS. ARTS, NO. 454 (MARCH 10-16, 1954), P.
     5. BO 537, CR 879, FR VII 13303.

ANONYMOUS. SISYPHOS. KULTURWORT, VOL. 2, NO. 5 (1954), PP.   0850
     7-11. BDZ 109-1434 (1954).

ANONYMOUS. A HOPEFUL FRENCHMAN. NEWSWEEK, VOL. 44, NO. 12   0851
     (1954), PP. 50-51. BO 47.

ANONYMOUS. THE REBEL. NEW YORKER, VOL. 29, NO. 49 (JAN. 23,   0852
     1954), PP. 101-102. BO 530.

ANONYMOUS. ACTUELLES II. CHRONIQUES 1948-53. BULLETIN CRITIQUE   0853
     DU LIVRE FRANÇAIS, VOL. 9, NO. 2 (FEB. 1954), P. 83. CR
     868.

ANONYMOUS. L'ÉTÉ, PAR ALBERT CAMUS. EXPRESS, VOL. 1, NO. 44   0854
     (MARCH 20, 1954), P. 9. CR 880.

ANONYMOUS. ALBERT CAMUS. LJETO (L'ÉTÉ). VJESNIK V SRJIEDU,   0855
     NO. 3 (MARCH 24, 1954), P. 99. CR 894.

ANONYMOUS. ALBERT CAMUS. 'PRAVEDNICI'. (LES JUSTES). POVODOM   0856
     IZVOJENJA RADIO DRAME, 30 MARS 1954. NARODNI LIST, VOL.
     10, (MARCH 30, 1954), P. 2725. CR 901.

ANONYMOUS. 'THE REBEL' BY ALBERT CAMUS. LISTENER. VOL. 51,   0857
     NO. 1312 (APRIL 22, 1954), PP. 705, 707.

ANONYMOUS. 'L'ÉTÉ', PAR A. CAMUS. BULLETIN CRITIQUE DU LIVRE   0858
     FRANÇAIS, VOL. 9, NO. 7 (JULY 1954), P. 498. CR 881.

ANONYMOUS. L'ÉTRANGER. BROADCAST PERFORMANCE REVIEWED   0859
     (RADIO). TIMES (LONDON), NO. 52987 (JULY 19, 1954), P.
     11. CR 882.

ANONYMOUS. HOW GOOD WITHOUT GOD. (ALBERT CAMUS), 'THE MYTH OF   0860
     SISYPHUS'. TIME, VOL. 66, NO. 14 (OCT. 3, 1955), P. 100.
     BFZ 39-279 (1954-56), CR 920.

ANONYMOUS. ALBERT CAMUS. DER WIND IN DJEMILA. ATLANTIS, VOL.   0861
     28, NO. 9 (1956), PP. 392-393. CR 928.

ANONYMOUS. ALBERT CAMUS. HALBSEIDENE TAPFERKEIT. SPIEGEL,   0862
     VOL. 10, NO. 25 (1956), PP. 42-45. BDZ 112-299 (1955), BO
     545, CR 931.

ANONYMOUS. LES JUSTES. TIMES (LONDON), NO. 53529 (MAY 12,   0863
     1956), P. 8. CR 950.

ANONYMOUS. ALBERT CAMUS PRÉPARE REQUIEM POUR UNE NONNE.   0864
     FIGARO, VOL. 130, NO. 3649 (MAY 31, 1956), P. 10.

0865   ANONYMOUS. ALBERT CAMUS: 'IL FAUDRA M'ARRÊTER AUSSI'. DEMAIN,
        NO. 25 (JUNE 1-7, 1956), P. 4. CR 932.

0866   ANONYMOUS. FAULKNER, CAMUS ET SALACROU OUVRIRONT LA SAISON AU
        THÉÂTRE. FIGARO LITTÉRAIRE, VOL. 11, NO. 540 (AUG. 25,
        1956), P. 1. FR VII 15343.

0867   ANONYMOUS. ALBERT CAMUS, 'LA CHUTE'. CAHIERS D'ÉTUDES
        CATHARES, VOL. 7, NO. 26 (SUMMER 1956), PP. 116-117.

0868   ANONYMOUS. ALBERT CAMUS CONVIE LES ÉCRIVAINS ET INTELLECTUELS
        EUROPÉENS À UN RECOURS À L'O.N.U. FIGARO LITTÉRAIRE, VOL.
        11, NO. 552 (NOV. 17, 1956), PP. 1, 4, FR VII 15335.

0869   ANONYMOUS. LITERATUR-NOBELPREIS 1957 AN ALBERT CAMUS. KULTUR,
        VOL. 6, NO. 95 (1957-1958), P. 2. BDZ 115-350 (1958).

0870   ANONYMOUS. ALBERT CAMUS. DER FALL. MERKUR, VOL. 11, NO. 107
        (JAN. 1957), PP. 60-65. BO 549.

0871   ANONYMOUS. M. CAMUS DRAMATIZES FAULKNER NOVEL: 'REQUIEM FOR A
        NUN', IN PARIS. TIMES (LONDON), NO. 53751 (JAN. 29,
        1957), P. 3. CR 1056.

0872   ANONYMOUS. 'REQUIEM POUR UNE NONNE'. PIECE EN 2 PARTIES ET SEPT
        TABLEAUX D'APRÈS WILLIAM FAULKNER, ADAPTATION D'ALBERT
        CAMUS. BULLETIN CRITIQUE DU LIVRE FRANÇAIS, VOL. 12, NO.
        2 (FEB. 1957), P. 106. CR 1057.

0873   ANONYMOUS. NEW FICTION. ALBERT CAMUS. 'THE FALL'. TIMES
        (LONDON), NO. 53765 (FEB. 14, 1957), P. 11. CR 1019.

0874   ANONYMOUS. SOUL IN DESPAIR. 'THE FALL'. TIME (ATLANTIC
        OVERSEAS EDITION), VOL. 69, NO. 7 (FEB. 18, 1957), P. 102.
        BFZ 41-249 (1955-57), CR 1020.

0875   ANONYMOUS. LES DEUX EXTRÊMES. EXPRESS, VOL. 4, NO. 302 (APRIL
        5, 1957), P. 27. CR 1013.

0876   ANONYMOUS. LOPE DE VÉGA AU BOIS DE BOULOGNE. DEMAIN, NO. 79
        (JUNE 13-19, 1957), P. 16. CR 1075.

0877   ANONYMOUS. CONTRE LA PEINE DE MORT. (ARTHUR KOESTLER ET ALBERT
        CAMUS). EXPRESS, VOL. 5, NO. 315 (JULY 5, 1957), PP.
        30-31. CR 1053.

0878   ANONYMOUS. L'EXIL ET LE ROYAUME. BULLETIN CRITIQUE DU LIVRE
        FRANÇAIS, VOL. 12, NOS. 7-8 (JULY-AUG. 1957), P. 532. CR
        1018.

0879   ANONYMOUS. CAMUS, PRIX NOBEL. DEMAIN, VOL. 2, NO. 97 (OCT.
        17-23, 1957), P. 14.

0880   ANONYMOUS. FRENCH AUTHOR HONOURED. NOBEL AWARD FOR M. CAMUS.
        TIMES (LONDON), NO. 53975 (OCT. 18, 1957), P. 8. CR 1000.

0881   ANONYMOUS. ALBERT CAMUS, PRIX NOBEL DE LITTÉRATURE. SOIR,
        VOL. 71, NO. 291 (OCT. 18, 1957), P. 1. CR 999.

0882   ANONYMOUS. ON ATTEND DE STOCKHOLM LE PRIX NOBEL DE LITTÉRATURE.
        FIGARO LITTÉRAIRE, VOL. 12, NO. 600 (OCT. 19, 1957), P. 1.

0883   ANONYMOUS. ALBERT CAMUS, PRIX NOBEL. CAMUS ET SARTRE SE

RECONCILIERONT—ILS? CARREFOUR, VOL. 14, NO. 684 (OCT. 23,
1957), P. 7.

ANONYMOUS. ALBERT CAMUS, PRIX NOBEL. POURQUOI CAMUS?   0884
CARREFOUR, VOL. 14, NO. 684 (OCT. 23, 1957), P. 7.

ANONYMOUS. ÉTAPES D'UNE VIE. NOUVELLES LITTÉRAIRES, NO. 1573   0885
(OCT. 24, 1957), P. 6. CR 1017, FR VII 21387.

ANONYMOUS. ALBERT CAMUS, PRIX NOBEL. UNE OEUVRE EN DEBAT   0886
DEVANT LA NOUVELLE GÉNÉRATION (I). FIGARO LITTÉRAIRE,
VOL. 12, NO. 601 (OCT. 26, 1957), P. 7. CR 1001.

ANONYMOUS. LA VIE ET LES OEUVRES. UNE JEUNESSE EN ALGÉRIE.   0887
FIGARO LITTÉRAIRE, VOL. 12, NO. 601 (OCT. 26, 1957), P. 7.

ANONYMOUS. L'OEUVRE DE CAMUS EN DEBAT DEVANT LA NOUVELLE   0888
GÉNÉRATION (II). FIGARO LITTÉRAIRE, VOL. 12, NO. 602
(NOV. 2, 1957), P. 11. CR 1002.

ANONYMOUS. QUESTING HUMANIST. TIME, VOL. 70, NO. 18 (OCT. 28,   0889
1957), PP. 33-34. BFZ 42-284 (1956-58), CR 1050.

ANONYMOUS. 'RÉFLEXIONS SUR LA PEINE CAPITALE', PAR-ARTHUR   0890
KOESTLER ET ALBERT CAMUS. BULLETIN CRITIQUE DU LIVRE
FRANÇAIS, VOL. 12, NO. 11 (NOV. 1957), P. 803. CR 1054.

ANONYMOUS. 'ALBERT CAMUS, A STUDY OF HIS WORK' BY PHILIP THODY.   0891
LISTENER, VOL. 58, NO. 1495 (NOV. 21, 1957), PP. 849-850.

ANONYMOUS. ALBERT CAMUS. ESSAI DE BIBLIOGRAPHIE. BIBLIO,   0892
VOL. 25, NO. 10 (DEC. 1957), PP. 8-9. FR VII 17283.

ANONYMOUS. ALBERT CAMUS À STOCKHOLM. SOIR, VOL. 71, NO. 345   0893
(DEC. 11, 1957), P. 10. CR 1003.

ANONYMOUS. AUTHORS IN ALGERIA, A. CAMUS, ROGER MARTIN DU GARD,   0894
F. MAURIAC. TIME AND TIDE, VOL. 39, NO. 26 (1958), P.
788. BFZ 45-278 (1958-59).

ANONYMOUS. ALBERT CAMUS À STOCKHOLM. ANNALES (SUPPLEMENT),   0895
VOL. 65, NO. 87 (JAN. 1958), PP. 2-3. CR 1089.

ANONYMOUS. A PROPOS DE 'CAMUS'. NEF, VOL. 15, NO. 13 (JAN.   0896
1958), P. 96. CR 1085.

ANONYMOUS. WESTERN LITERATURE. A NEW APPROACH. EAST EUROPE,   0897
VOL. 7, NO. 1 (JAN. 1958), PP. 3-14. MA 191.

ANONYMOUS. LA VIE LITTÉRAIRE. LITTÉRATURE ET VIE. ALBERT CAMUS.   0898
SOIR, VOL. 72, NO. 21 (JAN. 22, 1958), P. 7. CR 1086.

ANONYMOUS. CAMUS PRODUCES 'CALIGULA'. REVIVAL IN PARIS. TIMES   0899
(LONDON), NO. 54084 (FEB. 25, 1958), P. 3. CR 1084.

ANONYMOUS. À PROPOS D'UNE REPRISE. M. ALBERT CAMUS SOULIGNE LA   0900
PORTÉE DE 'REQUIEM POUR UNE NONNE', DE WILLIAM FAULKNER.
SOIR, VOL. 72, NO. 60 (MARCH 2, 1958), P. 2. CR 1116.

ANONYMOUS. FROM FRANCE. ALBERT CAMUS. 'EXILE AND THE KINGDOM'.   0901
TIMES (LONDON), NO. 54127 (APRIL 17, 1958), P. 15. CR
1098.

ANONYMOUS. L'ENVERS ET L'ENDROIT. BULLETIN CRITIQUE DU LIVRE   0902

FRANÇAIS,   VOL. 13, NO. 6 (JUNE 1958), P. 427.   CR 1096.

0903   ANONYMOUS. DISCOURS DE SUÈDE.   BULLETIN CRITIQUE DU LIVRE
       FRANÇAIS,   VOL. 13, NO. 7 (JULY 1958), P. 517.   CR 1095.

0904   ANONYMOUS. LA SOURCE DE NOS COMMUNS MALHEURS. LETTRE D'UN
       ALGÉRIEN MUSULMAN.   PREUVES,   NO. 91 (SEPT. 1958), PP.
       72-75.   CR 1121.

0905   ANONYMOUS. CAMUS UND BONHOEFFER ALS KRITIKER VON GLAUBE UND
       KIRCHE.   KIRCHENBLATT FÜR DIE REFORMIERTE SCHWEIZ.   VOL.
       115, (1959), PP. 263-264.   BDZ 119-300 (1959).

0906   ANONYMOUS. NECROLOGIE. TIJDSCHRIFT VOOR PHILOSOPHIE,   VOL. 21,
       NO. 4 (DEC. 1959), PP. 784-785.   BFZ 46-284 (1958-60).

0907   ANONYMOUS. DOSTOEVISKY (SIC) VIA CAMUS. 'THE POSSESSED'.   TIME
       (U.S.A.),   VOL. 73, NO. 6 (FEB. 9, 1959), PP. 61-62.   BFZ
       47-280 (1961).

0908   ANONYMOUS. LES PIÈCES DONT ON PARLE. 'LES POSSÉDÉS'.   RÉALITÉS,
       FÉMINA-ILLUSTRATION,   NO. 158 (MARCH 1959), P. 96.   CR
       1146.

0909   ANONYMOUS. DEUIL EN SUÈDE.   FIGARO,   VOL. 134, NO. 4770 (JAN.
       6, 1960), P. 4.   FITCH.

0910   ANONYMOUS. ÉMOTION DANS LE MONDE.   FIGARO,   VOL. 134, NO. 4770
       (JAN. 6, 1960), PP. 1, 4.   FITCH. SEE NO. 3008, 2528.

0911   ANONYMOUS. UN FRANÇAIS D'ALGÉRIE.   CARREFOUR,   VOL. 17, NO. 799
       (JAN. 6, 1960), P. 21.

0912   ANONYMOUS. LES OBSÈQUES D'ALBERT CAMUS ONT ÉTÉ CÉLÉBRÉES À
       LOURMARIN.   JOURNAL DE GENÈVE,   NO. 5 (JAN. 7, 1960), P. 3.

0913   ANONYMOUS. NOTES AND COMMENT.   NEW YORKER,   VOL. 35, NO. 48
       (JAN. 16, 1960), PP. 23-24.   MA 188.

0914   ANONYMOUS. DOOR SHUTS.   NEWSWEEK,   VOL. 55, NO. 3 (JAN. 18,
       1960), P. 32.

0915   ANONYMOUS. GUT, ICH BIN DAGEGEN.   EUROPA,   VOL. 11, NO. 2
       (1960), PP. 33-62.   BDZ 121-321 (1960).

0916   ANONYMOUS. ALBERT CAMUS.   NOUVELLE REVUE FRANÇAISE,   VOL. 8,
       NO. 86 (FEB. 1960), PP. 201-202.

0917   ANONYMOUS. ALBERT CAMUS.   LIBERTÉ 60,   VOL. 2, NO. 1 (JAN.-FEB.
       1960), PP. 47-48.

0918   ANONYMOUS. BROT UND FREIHEIT (ALBERT CAMUS).   FORUM,   VOL. 10,
       (1960-1961), PP. 126-128.   BDZ 122-322 (1961).

0919   ANONYMOUS. ALBERT CAMUS.   SPIEGEL,   VOL. 14, NO. 3 (1960), P.
       46.   BDZ 120-311 (1960).

0920   ANONYMOUS. ALBERT CAMUS.   TIMES LITERARY SUPPLEMENT,   VOL. 59,
       NO. 3019 (JAN. 8, 1960), PP. 13-14.   FR VII 33992, PMLA
       6809 (1961), MA 188.

0921   ANONYMOUS. ALBERT CAMUS.   FIERA LETTERARIA,   VOL. 15, NO. 3
       (JAN. 17, 1960), P. 1.

0922   ANONYMOUS. DEATH OF A REBEL.   NEW REPUBLIC,   VOL. 142, NO. 3

(JAN. 18, 1960), P. 6. FR VII 23607.

ANONYMOUS. THE REBEL. TIME (U.S.A.), VOL. 75, NO. 3 (JAN. 18,   0923
    1960), PP. 28-29. BFZ 48-262 (1962).

ANONYMOUS. COMMENT ON ÉCRIT L'HISTOIRE, OU LE DÉSENGAGEMENT   0924
    D'ALBERT CAMUS. VOICI POURQUOI, NO. 50 (JAN. 21, 1960), P.
    11. FITCH.

ANONYMOUS. NEW PLAY ON BROADWAY. (CALIGULA). TIME (U.S.A.),   0925
    VOL. 75, NO. 9 (FEB. 29, 1960), P. 51. BFZ 48-262 (1962).

ANONYMOUS. ALBERT CAMUS. ANNALES (SUPPLEMENT NO. 54), VOL.   0926
    67, NO. 112 (FEB. 1960), PP. 1-2.

ANONYMOUS. CAMUS, ALBERT (OBITUARY). REVUE PHILOSOPHIQUE DE   0927
    LOUVAIN, VOL. 58, TROISIÈME SERIE NO. 57 (FEB. 1960), PP.
    166-167. BFZ 49-262 (1960-62).

ANONYMOUS. UN DESTIN ACCÉLÉRÉ. UNE 'MÉPRISE' ? BULLETIN DES   0928
    LETTRES, VOL. 22, NO. 216 (MARCH 15, 1960), PP. 92-93.
    FITCH.

ANONYMOUS. ALBERT CAMUS. TEL QUEL, NO. 1 (SPRING 1960), PP.   0929
    92-93. FR VII 26301.

ANONYMOUS. CAMUS, HOMME DE THÉÂTRE. PIÈCES, TRADUCTIONS ET   0930
    ADAPTIONS. REVUE D'HISTOIRE DU THÉÂTRE, VOL. 12, NO. 4
    (OCT.-DEC. 1960), PP. 360-362. KL II 389.

ANONYMOUS. TEATRO DI CAMUS. EUROPA LETTERARIA, VOL. 2, NO. 7   0931
    (FEB. 1961), P. 167. FR VII 26386.

ANONYMOUS. VOICE OF CONSCIENCE. REVIEW. 'THE COLLECTED FICTION   0932
    OF ALBERT CAMUS' AND 'RESISTANCE, REBELLION, AND DEATH'.
    TIMES LITERARY SUPPLEMENT, VOL. 60, NO. 3077 (FEB. 17,
    1961), P. 106. FR VII 26393.

ANONYMOUS. ALBERT CAMUS TALKS WITH ACTORS ON THE OPENING NIGHT   0933
    OF HIS PLAY, 'THE POSSESSED', PARIS, (JAN. 5, 1959). NEW
    YORK TIMES BOOK REVIEW, VOL. 110, NO. 37,724 (MAY 7,
    1961), P. 7.

ANONYMOUS. A CAMUS, SES AMIS DU LIVRE. PARIS. GALLIMARD, 1962.   0934
    PREFACE PAR ROGER GRENIER.

ANONYMOUS. THE OLD NOVEL AND ITS FUTURE. TIMES LITERARY   0935
    SUPPLEMENT, VOL. 61, NO. 3140 (MAY 4, 1962), P. 321.

ANONYMOUS. NOTEBOOKS OF A YOUNG WRITER. TIMES LITERARY   0936
    SUPPLEMENT (LONDON), VOL. 61, NO. 3149 (JULY 6, 1962), P.
    487. FR VII 29395.

ANONYMOUS. CAMUS PLAY IN ARABIC. TIMES (LONDON), NO. 55,677   0937
    (APRIL 17, 1963), P. 14. FR VII 33944.

ANONYMOUS. GUILTY BUT IN STYLE. TIMES LITERARY SUPPLEMENT   0938
    (LONDON), VOL. 62, NO. 3214 (OCT. 4, 1963), P. 788.

ANONYMOUS. DOSTOEVSKY'S CHARACTERS REDUCED IN SCALE. TIMES   0939
    (LONDON), NO. 55,840 (OCT. 24, 1963), P. 15. FR VII
    33947.

0940   ANONYMOUS. CAMUS. PARIS. HACHETTE, 1964. SEE NO. 772, 1211,
       1547, 1816, 2272, 2669, 2873, 2950, 3105.

0941   ANONYMOUS. BIALIK MAKES WAY FOR CAMUS. JEWISH CHRONICLE
       (LONDON), OCT. 2, 1964, P. 22.

0942   ANONYMOUS. CAMUS. POLISH PERSPECTIVES, VOL. 8, NO. 5 (MAY
       1965), PP. 45-46.

0943   ANONYMOUS. PLAYFUL CAMUS. (REVIEW: COLLECTED PLAYS BY ALBERT
       CAMUS). TIMES LITERARY SUPPLEMENT (LONDON), NO. 3327
       (DEC. 2, 1965), P. 1104.

0944   ANTONI, CARLO. LA RIVOLTA DI CAMUS. MONDO, VOL. 4, NO. 42
       (OCT. 18, 1952), P. 6. FR VII 17286.

0945   A(NTONINI), G(IACOMO). ALBERT CAMUS L'AFRICANO. MONDO, VOL.
       1, NO. 41 (NOV. 26, 1949), P. 9. FR VII 17287.

0946   ANTONINI, GIACOMO. PARADIGMA DI CAMUS. FIERA LETTERARIA, VOL.
       11, NO. 24 (JUNE 10, 1956), PP. 1-2. FR VII 15336.

0947   ANTONINI, GIACOMO. CAMUS A CONFRONTO CON I SUOI POSTULATI
       MORALI. L'EXIL ET LE ROYAUME PROVA FELICE. FIERA
       LETTERARIA, VOL. 12, NO. 26 (JUNE 30, 1957), PP. 1, 6. FR
       VII 19405.

0948   ANTONINI, GIACOMO. CAMUS PREMIO NOBEL. FIERA LETTERARIA, VOL.
       12, NO. 49 (DEC. 8, 1957), PP. 1, 2. FR VII 26303.

0949   ANTONINI, GIACOMO. ALBERT CAMUS ET L'ITALIE. NOUVELLE REVUE
       FRANÇAISE, VOL. 8, NO. 87 (MARCH 1960), PP. 563-567. FR
       VII 23575, KL II 392.

0950   ARANGUREN, JOSÉ LUIS. LA MUERTE DE ALBERT CAMUS. PAPELES DE
       SON ARMADANS, VOL. 16, NO. 46 (JAN. 1960), PP. 87-90.

0951   ARBAN, DOMINIQUE. EN ATTENDANT 'REQUIEM POUR UNE NONNE' JE ME
       SUIS COMPLÈTEMENT EFFACÉ DEVANT FAULKNER, AFFIRME ALBERT
       CAMUS. FIGARO LITTÉRAIRE, VOL. 11, NO. 544 (SEPT. 22,
       1956), P. 4. CR 923, KL I 273, FR VII 15337, 17288.

0952   AREND, ALPHONSE. ASPECTS DU ROMAN FRANÇAIS CONTEMPORAIN.
       CAHIERS LUXEMBOURGEOIS, VOL. 23, NOS. 1-2 (1951), PP.
       21-36 (CAMUS REF. P. 32). CR 774.

0953   ARENDT, H(ANNAH). LA PHILOSOPHIE DE L'EXISTENCE. DEUCALION,
       NO. 2 (1947), PP. 214-245. BO 164.

0954   ARENDT, HANNAH. L'EXISTENTIALISME FRANÇAIS VU DE NEW YORK.
       DEUCALION, NO. 2 (1947), PP. 247-252. BO 163.

0955   ARLAND, MARCEL. ALBERT CAMUS ET LA RÉVOLTE. GAZETTE DE
       LAUSANNE, (JAN. 12, 1952), P. 283. CR 802 BIS.

0956   ARLAND, MARCEL. NOUVELLES LETTRES DE FRANCE. PARIS. ALBIN
       MICHEL, 1954. ALBERT CAMUS ET LA RÉVOLTE, PP. 107-113. BO
       234, FR VII 10605.

0957   ARLAND, MARCEL. LA CHUTE. NOUVELLE REVUE FRANÇAISE, VOL. 4,
       NO. 43 (JULY 1956), PP. 123-127. BFZ 44-283, BR, CR 924,
       FR VII 15338, KL I 274.

ARLAND, MARCEL. L'ETRANGER. PARIS. CLUB DES LIBRAIRES DE   0958
    FRANCE, 1957. UN ÉCRIVAIN QUI VIENT. CR 438.

ARMELLINI, RINA ANNA. GENESI ED EVOLUZIONE DELL'ANGOSCIA   0959
    ESISTENZIALISTA. L'UOMO ASSURDO DI ALBERT CAMUS.
    SORGENTE, NUMERO SPECIALE, PP. 39-47. BO 107.

ARNAUD, PIERRE. AFTERMATH-A YOUNG PHILOSOPHER'S VIEW. YALE   0960
    FRENCH STUDIES, NO. 16 (WINTER 1955-56), PP. 106-110.
    TRANSLATED BY DEREK AIKEN.

ARNETT, CARROLL. THE GOOD MEN. MINNESOTA REVIEW, VOL. 4, NO.   0961
    3 (SPRING 1964), P. 353.

ARON, RAYMOND. L'OPIUM DES INTELLECTUELS. PARIS. CALMAN-LEVY,   0962
    1955. RÉVOLTE ET RÉVOLUTION, PP. 62-69.

ARTAUD, ANTONIN. LETTRE À ALBERT CAMUS. NOUVELLE REVUE   0963
    FRANÇAISE, VOL. 8, NO. 89 (MAY 1960), PP. 1012-1020. BFZ
    47-280 (1961), FR VII 23582, KL II 393.

ASENSIO TEIJIDO, J. DATOS CRISTIANOS DE LITERATURA   0964
    CONTEMPORÁNEA. MADRID. ESCUELA CENTRAL DE IDIOMAS, 1960.
    KL II 387.

ASTIER, E. D . ARRACHEZ LA VICTIME AUX BOURREAUX... RÉPONSE À   0965
    ALBERT CAMUS. CALIBAN, (APRIL 1948), PP. 12-17. BO 216,
    CR 635.

ASTORG, BERTRAND D'. ENCORE CAMUS. ESPRIT, VOL. 15, NO. 2   0966
    (1947), PP. 168-170. BO 107.

ASTORG, BERTRAND D'. L'HOMME ENGAGÉ. DE 'LA PESTE' OU D'UN   0967
    NOUVEL HUMANITARISME. ESPRIT, VOL. 16, NO. 10 (OCT. 1947),
    PP. 615-621. BO 383, BR.

ASTORG, BERTRAND D'. ASPECTS DE LA LITTÉRATURE EUROPÉENNE DE-   0968
    PUIS 1945. PARIS. ÉDITIONS DU SEUIL, COLL. PIERRES VIVES,
    1952. DE 'LA PESTE' OU D'UN NOUVEL HUMANISME, PP. 191-208.
    BO 148, CR 439.

AUBARÈDE, GABRIEL D'. RENCONTRE AVEC ALBERT CAMUS. NOUVELLES   0969
    LITTÉRAIRES, VOL. 30, NO. 1236 (MAY 10, 1951), PP. 1, 6.
    BFZ 32-249 (1950-1952), BO 33, CR 775.

AUBERY, PIERRE. ALBERT CAMUS ET LA CLASSE OUVRIÈRE. FRENCH   0970
    REVIEW, VOL. 32, NO. 1 (OCT. 1958), PP. 14-21. KL I 271.

AUDIBERTI, JACQUES. RENCONTRES AU CINÉMA. PARISIENNE, NO. 6   0971
    (JUNE 1953), PP. 813-820. BO 72, FR VII 8747.

AUDISIO, GABRIEL. LE GÉNIE DE L'AFRIQUE DU NORD, DE SAINT   0972
    AUGUSTIN À ALBERT CAMUS. ANNALES DU CENTRE UNIVERSITAIRE
    MÉDITERRANÉEN, VOL. 7 (1953-1954), PP. 151-162. BUL SIGN
    13-2098.

AUDISIO, GABRIEL. L'ALGÉRIEN. NOUVELLE REVUE FRANÇAISE, VOL.   0973
    8, NO. 87 (MARCH 1960), PP. 432-435. FR VII 23575, KL II
    392.

AUDISIO, GABRIEL. FIDÉLITÉ DE CAMUS. SIMOUN, VOL. 8, NO. 31   0974

(JULY 1960), PP. 20-21. FR VII 23573, KL II 393.

0975   AUDRY, COLETTE. ITINÉRAIRE DE CAMUS. EXPRESS, NO. 448 (JAN.
        14, 1960), PP. 27-28. FITCH.

0976   AURY, DOMINIQUE, SEE. PAULHAN, JEAN, NO. 1439.50.

0977   AURY, DOMINIQUE. LA VÉRITÉ COMMUNE. NOUVELLE REVUE FRANÇAISE,
        VOL. 5, NO. 53 (MAY 1957), PP. 890-893. BFZ 42-284, CR
        981, FR VII 17289, KL I 273.

0978   AURY, DOMINIQUE. DEUX PLACES VIDES. NOUVELLE REVUE FRANÇAISE,
        VOL. 8, NO. 87 (MARCH 1960), PP. 449-450. FR VII 23575, KL
        II 393.

0979   AVILÉS, ALEJANDRO. ALBERTO CAMUS. SU TESTIMONIO Y SU GRANDEZA.
        ABSIDE, VOL. 24, NO. 1 (JAN.-MARCH 1960), PP. 96-100. FR
        VII 26304, PMLA 6810 (1961).

0980   AYALA, FRANCISCO. EXPERIENCIA VIVA Y CREACIÓN LITERARIA, LE
        MALENTENDU . SUR, NO. 257 (MARCH-APRIL 1959), PP. 51-53.
        KL II 391.

0981   AYER, A. J. ALBERT CAMUS. HORIZON, VOL. 13, NO. 75 (MARCH
        1946), PP. 155-168. BO 132, CR 553, FR VII 741, MA 180.

0982   AYGUESPARSE, ALBERT. PRÉSENCE DE CAMUS. MARGINALES, VOL. 16,
        NOS. 80-81 (NOV.-DEC. 1961), PP. 53-55. FR VII 26305.

0983   AYRAUD, PIERRE. LA PESTE . GLANES PHILOSOPHIQUES.
        TÉMOIGNAGES, NO. 16 (JAN. 1948), PP. 126-128. BO 404.

0984   B., L. LE THÉÂTRE. CALIGULA . ESSOR, NOUVELLE SÉRIE, VOL. 1,
        NO. 2 (OCT. 6, 1945), P. 6. CR 530.

0985   BÀCCOLO, LUIGI. I 'CARNETS DI CAMUS'. MONDO, VOL. 17, NO. 9
        (MARCH 2, 1965), P. 10.

0986   BAERØE, PER RICHARD. ALBERT CAMUS OG MENNESKETS SITUASJON.
        SAMTIDEN, VOL. 70, NO. 8 (1961), PP. 525-539. PMLA 7351
        (1961).

0987   BAILEY, ANTHONY. THE ISOLATED MAN. COMMONWEAL, VOL. 67, NO. 4
        (OCT. 25, 1957), PP. 91-93. FR VII 21364, MA 180.

0988   BAILLY, RENÉ. LE MOIS THÉÂTRAL. 'L'ÉTAT DE SIÈGE'D'ALBERT
        CAMUS. LAROUSSE MENSUEL, 41ST YEAR, VOL. 12, NO. 412
        (DEC. 1948), P. 194. CR 636.

0989   BAILLY, RENÉ. LE MOIS THÉÂTRAL. 'LES JUSTES', D'ALBERT CAMUS.
        LAROUSSE MENSUEL, 43RD YEAR, VOL. 12, NO. 426 (FEB. 1950),
        P. 418. CR 734.

0990   BAILLY, RENÉ. LE MOIS THÉÂTRAL. 'CALIGULA', D'ALBERT CAMUS.
        LAROUSSE MENSUEL, 43RD YEAR, VOL. 12, NO. 435 (NOV. 1950),
        P. 562. CR 733.

0991   BAILLY, RENÉ. LE MOIS LITTÉRAIRE. 'L'HOMME RÉVOLTÉ', PAR
        ALBERT CAMUS. LAROUSSE MENSUEL, 45TH YEAR, VOL. 13, NO.
        452 (APRIL 1952), P. 65. CR 803.

0992   BAILLY, RENÉ. LE MOIS LITTÉRAIRE. 'ACTUELLES ET L'ÉTÉ', PAR
        ALBERT CAMUS. LAROUSSE MENSUEL, 47TH YEAR, VOL. 13, NO.

481 (SEPT. 1954), P. 530.   CR 869.

BAILLY, RENÉ. LE MOIS LITTÉRAIRE. 'LA CHUTE', PAR ALBERT   0993
    CAMUS. LAROUSSE MENSUEL, 49TH YEAR, VOL. 14, NO. 505
    (SEPT. 1956), P. 145. CR 925.

BAILLY, RENÉ. LE MOIS LITTÉRAIRE. 'L'EXIL ET LE ROYAUME', PAR   0994
    ALBERT CAMUS. LAROUSSE MENSUEL, 51ST YEAR, VOL. 14, NO.
    514 (JUNE 1957), P. 289.   CR 983.

BAILLY, RENÉ. LE MOIS THÉÂTRAL. 'LE CHEVALIER D'OLMEDO', DE   0995
    LOPE DE VEGA. 'CALIGULA', D'ALBERT CAMUS. LAROUSSE
    MENSUEL, 51ST YEAR, VOL. 14, NO. 516 (AUG. 1957), P. 322.
    CR 982.

BAILLY, RENÉ. LE MOIS LITTÉRAIRE. LA VIE LITTÉRAIRE. LE PRIX   0996
    NOBEL DE LITTÉRATURE. LAROUSSE MENSUEL, 51ST YEAR, VOL.
    14, NO. 520 (DEC. 1957), P. 385. CR 984.

BAKKER, REINOUT. ALBERT CAMUS, EINE FRAGE AN DIE KIRCHE.   0997
    ZEITSCHRIFT FUR EVANGELISCHE ETHIK, VOL. 6, NO. 85
    (JAN.-FEB. 1962), PP. 129-140. BDZ 125-310 (1962).

BALACHOVA, TANIA. DES PERSONNALITÉS DU THÉÂTRE... (HOMMAGES À   0998
    CAMUS). FIGARO, VOL. 134, NO. 4770 (JAN. 6, 1960). P. 4.
    FITCH.

B(ALLARD), J(EAN). VARIÉTÉS. COMPAGNIE DES QUATRE VENTS. 'LE   0999
    MALENTENDU' D'ALBERT CAMUS. CAHIERS DU SUD, VOL. 26, NO.
    285 (1947),PP. 2 (UNNUMBERED). CR 602.

B(ALLARD), J(EAN). LE THÉÂTRE. LE GALION D'OR JOUE 'LE   1000
    MALENTENDU' D'ALBERT CAMUS. CAHIERS DU SUD, VOL. 29, NO.
    294 (1949), P. 359. CR 705.

B(ALLARD), J(EAN). ALBERT CAMUS, (NOTICE SUR LA MORT DE CAMUS).   1001
    CAHIERS DU SUD, VOL. 47, NO. 354 (1960), P. 284. KL II
    395.

BALMAS, ENEA. ASPECTS ET PROBLÈMES DE LA LITTÉRATURE   1002
    CONTEMPORAINE. MILAN. LA GOLIARDICA, 1958. FR VII 18917.

BALTES, A. ALBERT CAMUS. 'LA PESTE'. NEUEREN SPRACHEN, VOL.   1003
    7 NO. 9 (SEPT 1958), PP. 435-440. FR VII 19407, KL I 273.

BANTI, ANNA. PSEUDONYM FOR LUCIA LONGHI LOPRESTI. OPINIONI.   1004
    MILAN. SAGGIATORE, 1961.   MORALITÀ DE LA PESTE , PP.
    128-131.

BARENBAUM, SIMON. LE THÉÂTRE D'AVANT-GARDE EN FRANCE,   1005
    1913-1944. BROWN UNIVERSITY (PH. D.), 1957, DISSERTATION
    ABSTRACTS, VOL. 18, NO. 3 (MARCH 1958), P. 1044.

BARISSE, RITA. BOOKS AND BOOKMEN...ABROAD. (REVIEW: LA CHUTE BY   1006
    ALBERT CAMUS). BOOKS AND BOOKMEN, VOL. 1, NO. 10 (JULY
    1956), P. 39.

BARJAVEL, RENÉ. UNE PIÈCE EN MAJUSCULES. LES JUSTES D'ALBERT   1007
    CAMUS, AU THÉÂTRE HÉBERTOT. CARREFOUR, VOL. 16, NO. 275
    (DEC. 20, 1949), P. 11. FITCH.

1008 BARJON, LOUIS. DÉSESPOIR OU DÉPASSEMENT. LES RÉPONSES DE NOS
DRAMATURGES. ÉTUDES, VOL. 83, NO. 264 (MARCH 1950), PP.
289-308. CR 735.

1009 BARJON, LOUIS. LE SILENCE DE DIEU DANS LA LITTÉRATURE
CONTEMPORAINE. 1. SCANDALE DE L'ATHÉE. ÉTUDES, VOL. 87,
NO. 281 (MAY 1954), PP. 178-192. SEE NO. 1010.

1010 BARJON, LOUIS. LE SILENCE DE DIEU DANS LA LITTÉRATURE
CONTEMPORAINE. II TÉMOIGNAGE DU CHRÉTIEN. ÉTUDES, VOL. 87,
NO. 281 (APRIL-MAY-JUNE 1954), PP. 305-322. BR, CR 869
BIS. SEE NO. 1009.

1011 BARJON, LOUIS. ALBERT CAMUS. 'LA CHUTE'. ÉTUDES, VOL. 89,
NO. 291 (OCT.-NOV.-DEC. 1956), PP. 47-59. BFZ 40-252, BUL
SIGN 11-5498, CR 926, FR VII 17290, KL I 273.

1012 BARJON, LOUIS. ALBERT CAMUS' NEUE DIMENSION DES ABSURDEN.
DOKUMENTE, VOL. 13, NO. 1 (1957), PP. 65-70. BDZ 114-301
(1957), CR 985, KL I 273.

1013 BARJON, LOUIS. CAMUS, PRIX NOBEL. ÉTUDES, VOL. 90, NO. 295
(OCT.-NOV.-DEC. 1957), PP. 428-429. BFZ 42-284, CR 986, FR
VII 21365.

1014 BARJON, LOUIS. MONDES D'ÉCRIVAINS--DESTINÉES D'HOMMES. PARIS.
CASTERMANN, 1960. LE MONDE DE L'ABSURDE--ALBERT CAMUS, PP.
195-210. FR VII 22784, KL II 388, PMLA 7151 (1952).

1015 BARJON, (LOUIS), R.P. ALBERT CAMUS. (DEBATS). RECHERCHES ET
DEBATS DU CENTRE CATHOLIQUE DES INTELLECTUELS FRANÇAIS,
NO. 31 (JUNE 1960), PP. 169-192. (BARJON CONTRIBUTION. PP.
176-186). BUL SIGN 15-19-1009.

1016 BARJON, LOUIS. UNE LITTÉRATURE DE 'DÉCOMPOSITION'. ÉTUDES,
94TH YEAR, VOL. 311, NO. 10 (OCT.-NOV.DEC. 1961), PP. 45-60
(CAMUS REF. P. 48). BUL SIGN 16-19-24250.

1017 BARJON, LOUIS. DE BAUDELAIRE À MAURIAC, L'INQUIÉTUDE
CONTEMPORAINE. PARIS. CASTERMAN, 1962.

1018 BARKOVIC, JOSIP. A. CAMUS. STRANAC (L'ÉTRANGER). NAPRYED,
VOL. 19, (SEPT. 19, 1952), P. 39. CR 804.

1019 BARNA-PAULI, EVA. RÉVÉLATION À BUDAPEST. TÉMOINS, VOL. 8, NO.
23 (MAY 1960), PP. 13-15. KL 386.

1020 BARNES, HAZEL E. THE LITERATURE OF POSSIBILITY. LINCOLN,
NEBRASKA. UNIVERSITY OF NEBRASKA PRESS, 1959.

1021 BARNES, HAZEL E. HUMANISM AND ABSURDITY. (REVIEW. ALBERT
CAMUS. A STUDY OF HIS WORK BY PHILIP THODY.) PRAIRIE
SCHOONER, VOL. 34, NO. 2 (SUMMER 1960), PP. 97-99.

1022 BARNES, HAZEL E. MEASURE OF MAGNIFICENCE. PRAIRIE SCHOONER,
VOL. 34, NO. 2 (SUMMER 1960), PP. 115-119.

1023 BARNES, HAZEL E. BALANCE AND TENSION IN THE PHILOSOPHY OF
CAMUS. PERSONALIST, VOL. 41, NO. 4 (OCT. 1960), PP.
433-447. BUL SIGN 15.19, 20061, PMLA 6811 (1961), FR VII

23583, MA 180.

BARNES, HAZEL E. HUMANISTIC EXISTENTIALISM. THE LITERATURE OF   1024
POSSIBILITY. LINCOLN, NEBRASKA. UNIVERSITY OF NEBRASKA
PRESS, 1962. ON CAMUS, SARTRE, AND SIMONE DE BEAUVOIR.
ORIG. PUB. (1959) AS THE LITERATURE OF POSSIBILITY. PMLA
1966 (1963).

BARNES, HAZEL E. MODES OF AESTHETIC CONSCIOUSNESS IN FICTION.   1025
BUCKNELL REVIEW, VOL. 12, NO. 1 (MARCH 1964), PP. 82-93.

BAR-NIR, D. MIABSURD LETIKVAH, LEDARKOH SHEL ALBERT CAMUS (FROM   1026
ABSURDITY TO HOPE, ABOUT ALBERT CAMUS' OUTLOOK). AL
HAMISHMAR, FEB. 19, 1960, PP. 5-7.

BARRA, G. ALBERT CAMUS E I CRISTIANI. CITTÀ DI VITA, NO. 8   1027
(1953), PP. 368-370. BO 117.

BARRAULT, JEAN-LOUIS. NOUVELLES RÉFLEXIONS SUR LE THÉÂTRE.   1028
PARIS. FLAMMARION, 1959.

BARRAULT, JEAN-LOUIS. DES PERSONNALITÉS DU THÉÂTRE... (HOMMAGES   1029
À CAMUS). FIGARO, VOL. 134, NO. 4770 (JAN. 6, 1960), P.
4. FITCH.

BARRAULT, JEAN-LOUIS. SUR 'L' ÉTAT DE SIÈGE'. TABLE RONDE, NO.   1030
146 (FEB. 1960), PP. 67-68. BFZ 46-283, FR VII 23569, KL
II 390.

BARRAULT, JEAN-LOUIS. LE FRÈRE. NOUVELLE REVUE FRANÇAISE,   1031
VOL. 8, NO. 87 (MARCH 1960), PP. 437-439. FR VII 23575, KL
II 393.

BARRAULT, JEAN-LOUIS. THE THEATRE OF JEAN-LOUIS BARRAULT. NEW   1032
YORK. HILL AND WANG, 1961. CAMUS REFERENCE, PP. 15,
19-20. TRANSLATED BY JOSEPH CHIARI, PREFACE BY ARMAND
SALACROU.

BARRETT, MARY L. THE MYTH OF SISYPHUS. LIBRARY JOURNAL, VOL.   1033
80, NO. 14 (AUG. 1955). P. 1679. BO 322.

BARRETT, WILLIAM. THE ABSURD, ENDLESS STRUGGLE. 'THE MYTH OF   1034
SISYPHUS' AND OTHER ESSAYS. NEW YORK TIMES BOOK REVIEW,
SEPT. 18, 1955, P. 34. BO 323.

BARRETT, WILLIAM. VIRTUE IN THE ABSURD. 'THE MYTH OF SISYPHUS'.   1035
SATURDAY REVIEW, VOL. 38, NO. 41 (OCT. 8, 1955), P. 14.
BO 323.

BARRIER, M. G. L'ART DU RÉCIT DANS 'L'ÉTRANGER' D'ALBERT CAMUS.   1036
PARIS. NIZET, 1962. BIBLIO 20-92 (1962).

BARRON, LOUIS. THE REBEL. LIBRARY JOURNAL, VOL. 79, NO. 4   1037
(FEB. 15, 1954), P. 384. BO 515.

BARRY, JOSEPH. FRANCE: THE DECLINE OF AN AMERICAN DREAM. PART   1038
I. EVERGREEN REVIEW, VOL. 6, NO. 23 (MARCH-APRIL 1962),
PP. 48-62 (REFERENCES TO CAMUS, P. 60).

BATAILLE, GEORGES. LA MORALE DU MALHEUR: 'LA PESTE'.   1039
CRITIQUE, VOL. 3, NOS. 13-14 (JUNE-JULY 1947), PP. 3-15.

BO 384, BR, CR 584, FR VII 742.

1040 BATAILLE, GEORGES. LE BONHEUR, LE MALHEUR ET LA MORALE D'ALBERT
CAMUS. 'L'ETAT DE SIEGE'. CRITIQUE, VOL. 5, NO. 33 (FEB.
1949), PP. 184-189. BO 449, CR 681, FR VII 2695.

1041 BATAILLE, GEORGES. LE TEMPS DE LA RÉVOLTE. ALBERT CAMUS:
L'HOMME RÉVOLTE . CRITIQUE, VOL. 7, NO. 55 (DEC. 1951),
PP. 1019-1027. BUL SIGN 7-9630, CR 776.

1042 BATAILLE, GEORGES. LE TEMPS DE LA RÉVOLTE (II). CRITIQUE,
VOL. 8, NO. 56 (JAN. 1952), PP. 29-41. BUL SIGN 8-1020, CR
805.

1043 BATAILLE, GEORGES. L'AFFAIRE DE L'HOMME RÉVOLTÉ. CRITIQUE,
VOL. 8, NO. 67 (DEC. 1952), PP. 1077-1082. CR 806.

1044 BATT, JEAN. THE THEMES OF THE NOVELS AND PLAYS OF ALBERT CAMUS.
JOURNAL OF THE AUSTRALASIAN UNIVERSITIES LANGUAGE AND
LITERATURE ASSOCIATION, NO. 6 (MAY 1957), PP. 47-57. KL I
272, FR VII 21367, MA 180.

1045 BATT, JEAN. ALBERT CAMUS. FROM 'THE MYTH' TO 'THE FALL'.
MEANJIN, VOL. 16, NO. 4 (SUMMER 1957), PP. 411-419. FR
VII 21366.

1046 BATT, JEAN. ALBERT CAMUS: A TRIBUTE. MEANJIN, VOL. 19, NO.
80 (MARCH 1960), PP. 55-58.

1047 BAUER, GÉRARD. LE PRIX NOBEL D'ALBERT CAMUS. JOURNAL D'ALGER,
(OCT. 25, 1957). BR, CR 986 BIS.

1048 BAXTER, K. M. SPEAK WHAT WE FEEL. A CHRISTIAN LOOKS AT THE
CONTEMPORARY THEATRE. LONDON. SCM PRESS, 1964.

1049 BAYON, D. C. CARTA DE PARIS. ALBERT CAMUS. ASOMANTE, VOL. 17,
NO. 1 (JAN.-MARCH 1961), PP. 78-82. BUL SIGN 16-19-2379.

1050 BEATON, CECIL. THE THEATRE. 'CALIGULA'. BY ALBERT CAMUS.
SPECTATOR, VOL. 182, NO. 6299 (MARCH 18, 1949), P. 358.
CR 682.

1051 BEATON, CECIL AND KENNETH TYNAN. PERSONA GRATA. NEW YORK.
PUTNAM, 1954. CF. P. 30. BO 76.

1052 BEAU DE LOMÉNIE, E. LE CAS ALBERT CAMUS. ÉCRITS DE PARIS, NO.
180 (MARCH 1960), PP. 25-32. FR VII 23585.

1053 BEAUJON, EDMOND. LE TRAGIQUE ET L'ABSURDE. JOURNAL DE GENÈVE,
NO. 7 (JAN. 9-10, 1960), P. 1.

1054 BEAUJOUR, MICHEL. L'ANNÉE LITTÉRAIRE 1963-1964. FRENCH REVIEW,
VOL. 38, NO. 3 (JAN. 1965), PP. 303-14.

1055 BEAUJOUR, MICHEL. L'ANNÉE LITTÉRAIRE 1964-65. FRENCH REVIEW,
VOL. 39, NO. 4 (FEB. 1966), PP. 475-490.

1056 BECHTEL, GUY. ALBERT CAMUS, PRIX NOBEL. LES CONTRADICTIONS
D'UN HOMME ENGAGÉ. CARREFOUR, VOL. 14, NO. 684 (OCT. 23,
1957), P. 7.

1057 BECK, THEODORE TOULON. NEO-EXISTENTIALIST FRENCH LITERATURE.
KENTUCKY FOREIGN LANGUAGE QUARTERLY, VOL. 7, NO. 2 (1960),

PP. 64-69.

BECKER, O. E. H. ALBERT CAMUS ALS JOURNALIST. GEISTIGES   1058
    FRANKREICH, VOL. 4, NO. 172 (1950). CR 736.

BECKER, O. E. H. DIE OFFENE TÜR. BEMERKUNGEN ZU EINEM BUCH.   1059
    DER MYTHOS DES SISYPHOS , VON ALBERT CAMUS. KOMMENDEN,
    VOL. 5, NO. 5 (1951), PP. 7-8. BDZ, CR 777.

BECKMANN, HEINZ. RELIGION DER PESTZEIT. CAMUS' WEG AUS DER   1060
    GLEICHGÜLTIGKEIT. MERKUR, VOL. 15, NO. 3 (1960), P. 7.
    BDZ 120-311 (1960).

BECKMANN, HEINZ. CAMUS ODER DIE GLÜHENDEN CHRISTEN. ZEITWENDE,   1061
    VOL. 31, NO. 3 (1960), PP. 183-187. BDZ 121-321, KL II P.
    388.

BECKMANN, HEINZ. LA RELIGION DU TEMPS DE PESTE ET LE   1062
    DÉPASSEMENT DE L'INDIFFÉRENCE CHEZ CAMUS. TABLE RONDE, NO.
    146 (FEB. 1960), PP. 95-98. BUL SIGN 15-19-13765,FR VII
    23569, KL II 387.

BÉDOUIN, JEAN-LOUIS. VINGT ANS DE SURRÉALISME, 1939-1959.   1063
    PARIS. DENOËL, 1961. CHAPTER 15, ALBERT CAMUS DÉMASQUÉ,
    PP. 208-215.

BEEBE, MAURICE. CRITICISM OF ALBERT CAMUS. A SELECTED CHECKLIST   1064
    OF STUDIES IN ENGLISH. MODERN FICTION STUDIES, VOL. 10,
    NO. 3 (AUTUMN 1964), PP. 303-314.

BÉGUIN, ALBERT. ALBERT CAMUS, LA RÉVOLTE ET LE BONHEUR.   1065
    ESPRIT, VOL. 20, NO. 4 (APRIL 1952), PP. 736-746. BO 490,
    BUL SIGN 7-2721, FR VII 7694.

BEHRENS, RALPH. EXISTENTIAL 'CHARACTER-IDEAS' IN CAMUS' THE   1066
    MISUNDERSTANDING. MODERN DRAMA, VOL. 7, NO. 2 (SEPT.
    1964), PP.210-212. PMLA 8606 (1964).

BEIGBEDER, MARC. LE MONDE N'EST PAS ABSURDE. ESPRIT, VOL. 13,   1067
    NO. 3 (FEB. 1945), PP. 415-419. BO 180, BR, CR 509, FR VII
    743.

BEIGBEDER, MARC. LES JUSTES. ESPRIT, VOL. 18, NO. 1 (1950),   1068
    PP. 322-324. BO 459.

BEIGBEDER, MARC. LE THÉÂTRE À L'AGE MÉTAPHYSIQUE. ÂGE NOUVEAU,   1069
    VOL. 9, NO. 85 (JAN. 1954), PP. 30-41. BO 86.

BEIGBEDER, MARC. ALBERT CAMUS DE SOUSSE. NOUVELLE REVUE   1070
    FRANÇAISE, VOL. 8, NO. 87 (MARCH 1960), PP. 587-590. FR
    VII 23575, KL II 393.

BELFIORI, FAUSTO. I 'TACCUINI' DI CAMUS. ITALIA CHE SCRIVE,   1071
    VOL. 46, NOS. 2-3 (FEB.-MARCH 1963), P. 33. FR VII 33935.

BELLE, G. HOMMAGE À CAMUS. TÉMOINS, DEC. 1958, PP. 9-11.   1072
    (FASC. HORS SÉRIE). KL I 271.

BELLE, GEORGES. ALBERT CAMUS EST MORT. TEMPS DES HOMMES, NO.   1073
    9 (JAN.-FEB.-MARCH 1960), PP. 11-14.

BELLE, GEORGES. AIMER CAMUS. TÉMOINS, VOL. 8, NO. 23 (MAY   1074

1960), PP. 20-22.   FITCH.

1075   BELOFF, M. THE REBEL.   MANCHESTER GUARDIAN,   (OCT. 30, 1954),
           P. 4. BO 516.

1076   BEN. L'ÉTAT DE SIÈGE.   NOUVELLES LITTÉRAIRES,   VOL. 27, NO.
           1105 (NOV. 4, 1948), P. 8.   BO 443.

1077   BENAMOU, MICHEL. ROMANTIC COUNTERPOINT: NATURE AND STYLE.
           YALE FRENCH STUDIES,   NO. 25 (SPRING 1960), PP. 44-51.   BUL
           SIGN 17-19-9740,FR VII 23568, KL II 389, MA 180.

1078   BENEDIC, DIRK. BIJ HET DRAMATISCH WERK VAN ALBERT CAMUS.
           VLAAMSE GIDS,   VOL. 39, NO. 2 (FEB. 1955), PP. 114-125.   BO
           89, CR 912.

1079   BENITEZ CLAROS, R. TEATRO EUROPEO DEL EXISTENCIALISMO AL
           ANTITEATRO. REVISTA DE LA UNIVERSIDAD DE MADRID, VOL. 9,
           NO. 33 (1960), PP. 235-254.   FR VII 23162.

1080   BEN-PORAT, Y. LO TIRTSAH (THOU SHALT NOT KILL).   MEVOOTH,   VOL.
           1, (1953-54), PP. 11-12.

1081   BEN-PORAT, Y. BAYN MERED LEMAHPEKHAH (BETWEEN REVOLT AND
           REVOLUTION).   MEVOOTH,   NO. 1 (1953-54), PP. 14-15.

1082   BENTLEY, ERIC. A NOTE ON FRENCH EXISTENTIALISM (WITH LIST OF
           CAMUS   WRITINGS).   BOOKS ABROAD,   VOL. 20, NO. 3 (SUMMER
           1946), PP. 263-264.   CR 554, MA 189.

1083   BENTLEY, ERIC. CALIGULA   AND CROSS PURPOSE. CAMUS: THE
           MELODRAMA OF IDEAS.   NEW YORK TIMES BOOK REVIEW,   AUG. 29,
           1948, P. 4.   BO 355.

1084   BENTLEY, ERIC. JEAN-LOUIS BARRAULT.   KENYON REVIEW,   VOL. 12,
           NO. 2 (SPRING 1950), PP. 224-242.

1085   BENTLY, A. H. THE PLAYWRIGHT AS A THINKER.   NEW YORK.   HARPER,
           1948.

1086   BERGER, F. BRIEF OVER CAMUS.   CAMUS EN ZIJN DUITSE VRIEND.   MET
           NASCHRIFT D. CH. H. WENTINCK.   LIBERTINAGE,   VOL. 2, NO. 6
           (NOV.-DEC. 1949), PP. 458-459.   BO 381, CR 683.   SEE NO.
           3374.

1087   BERGER, MARCEL. LE STYLE AU MICROSCOPE.   'JEUNES GLOIRES'. PAR
           CRITICUS (D. I. MARCEL BERGER).   PARIS.   CALMANN-LEVY,
           1951.   ALBERT CAMUS.   LA PESTE , PP. 43-63.   BO 241, CR
           450 BIS, FR VII 5150.

1088   BERGER, PETER L. CAMUS, BONHOFFER AND THE WORLD COME OF AGE-I.
           CHRISTIAN CENTURY,   VOL. 76, NO. 14 (APRIL 8, 1959), PP.
           417-418.

1089   BERGER, PETER L. CAMUS, BONHOFFER AND THE WORLD COME OF AGE-II.
           CHRISTIAN CENTURY,   VOL. 76, NO. 15 (APRIL 15, 1959), PP.
           450-452.

1090   BERGER, PIERRE. LE THÉÂTRE. 'CALIGULA' D'ALBERT CAMUS.   POÉSIE
           45,   VOL. 16, NO. 28 (OCT.-NOV. 1945), PP. 114-117.   CR
           510.

BERGER, PIERRE. ENTRETIEN AVEC ALBERT CAMUS. GAZETTE DES   1091
    LETTRES,   VOL. 8, NO. 17 (FEB. 15, 1952), PP. 5-12. BO
    491, CR 807, FR VII 7695.

BERGER, PIERRE. CAMUS A-T-IL CESSÉ D'ÊTRE ROMANCIER? ARTS,   1092
    NO. 415 (JUNE 12-18, 1953), P. 12. CR 845.

BERGH, AKE. L'EXIL ET LE ROYAUME. MODERNA SPRÅK, VOL. 54, NO. 1093
    1 (FEB. 1960), PP. 75-76. KL II 391.

BERL, EMMANUEL. LETTRE À ALBERT CAMUS SUR L'IMPOSTURE ET SUR LA 1094
    DISCORDE. TABLE RONDE, NOS. 103-104 (JULY-AUG. 1956), PP.
    301-306. BR, CR 926 BIS, KL I 271.

BERL, EMMANUEL. CAMUS, PRIX NOBEL. TABLE RONDE, NO. 120 (DEC. 1095
    1957), PP. 207-208.

BERL, EMMANUEL. CAMUS. ÉVIDENCES, NO. 81 (JAN.-FEB. 1960),   1096
    PP. 33-34.

BERL, EMMANUEL. FACE À L'ABSURDE. TABLE RONDE, NO. 146 (FEB.   1097
    1960), PP. 163-166. BFZ 46-284, BUL SIGN 685, FR VII
    23569.

BERL, EMMANUEL. LES IMAGES, LA JUSTICE, À L'ÉPREUVE (CAMUS ET   1098
    L'ALGÉRIE). TABLE RONDE, NO. 149 (MAY 1960), PP. 181-183.
    KL II 392.

BERL, EMMANUEL. 'ANCIENS' CONTRE 'MODERNES'. UN MATCH NUL.   1099
    PREUVES, VOL. 16, NO. 184 (JUNE 1966), PP. 73-79.

BERNARD, JEAN-JACQUES. 'CALIGULA', DE M. ALBERT CAMUS.   1100
    FRANCE-ILLUSTRATION, NO. 2 (OCT. 13, 1945), P. 48. BO
    344, CR 511, FR VII 9297.

BERNARD, MARC. LE THÉÂTRE. 'CALIGULA', D'ALBERT CAMUS.   1101
    NOUVELLES LITTÉRAIRES, NO. 1590 (FEB. 20, 1958), P. 10.
    CR 1079.

BERNARD, MARC. LA CONTRADICTION D'ALBERT CAMUS. NOUVELLE REVUE 1102
    FRANÇAISE, VOL. 8, NO. 87 (MARCH 1960), PP. 594-596. FR
    VII 23575.

BERNE-JOFFROY, ANDRÉ. LE SILENCE D'ALBERT CAMUS. NOUVELLE   1103
    REVUE FRANÇAISE, VOL. 8, NO. 87 (MARCH 1960), PP. 597-599.
    FR VII 23575, KL II 393.

BERTELOOT, PIERRE. KRONIEK DER FRANSE LETTEREN. DE   1104
    PHILOSOPHISCHE LITTERATUUR IN FRANKRIJK: OVER ALBERT
    CAMUS. DIETSCHE WARANDE EN BELFORT, NO. 1 (JAN. 1948),
    PP. 46-50. BO 60, CR 637.

BERTHE, LOUIS. ENTRETIEN SUR CAMUS ENTRE LOUIS BERTHE, JACQUES   1105
    CHARPIER, OLIVIER DE MAGNY. LETTRES NOUVELLES, VOL. 4,
    NO. 2 (SEPT. 1956), PP. 357-363. FR VII 15342, KL I 271.
    SEE NO. 1416, 2390.

BERTOCCI, ANGELO P. CAMUS' 'LA PESTE' AND THE ABSURD. ROMANIC   1106
    REVIEW, VOL. 49, NO. 1 (FEB. 1958), PP. 33-41. BFZ
    43-294, BUL SIGN 15-19-6315, CR 1080, KL I 273, MA 180.

1107   BESPALOFF, RACHEL. RÉFLEXIONS SUR L'ESPRIT DE LA TRAGÉDIE.
         DEUCALION,   NO. 2 (1947), PP. 171-193.   BO 249, FR VII
         9298.

1108   BESPALOFF, RACHEL. LES CARREFOURS DE CAMUS,   LE MONDE DU
         CONDAMNÉ À MORT. ESPRIT, VOL. 18, NO. 1 (JAN. 1950), PP.
         1-26.   BFZ 30 P. 185 (1949-1950), BO 201, BUL SIGN 6-7510,
         CR 737, FR VII 11217, 4409.

1109   BESPALOFF, RACHEL. THE WORLD OF MAN CONDEMNED TO DEATH.   IN.
         BRÉE, GERMAINE,   CAMUS, A COLLECTION OF CRITICAL ESSAYS,
         PP. 92-107. FR VII 29338. SEE NO. 1293. TRANSLATION OF NO.
         1108.

1110   BESSIE, S. M. THE EXILE AND THE KINGDOM.   AMERICAN SCHOLAR,
         VOL. 28, NO. 1 (WINTER 1958-59), PP. 120-122.

1111   BIANCHINI, ANGELA. ALBERT CAMUS: VITA INCOMPIUTA D'ARTISTA.
         EUROPA LETTERARIA,   VOL. 4, NO. 19 (FEB. 1963), P. 183.   FR
         VII 33937.

1112   BIEBER, KONRAD F. L'ALLEMAGNE VUE PAR LES ÉCRIVAINS DE LA
         RÉSISTANCE FRANÇAISE. GENEVA.   E. DROZ, 1954.   PRÉFACE,
         ALBERT CAMUS. ALBERT CAMUS ET LE REFUS DE LA HAINE, PP.
         102-122.   BO 103, FR VII 12725.

1113   BIEBER, KONRAD F. THE REBELLION OF A HUMANIST.   'THE REBEL.   AN
         ESSAY ON MAN IN REVOLT', BY ALBERT CAMUS. YALE REVIEW,
         VOL. 43, NO. 3 (MARCH 1954), PP. 473-475.   BO 517, CR 870.

1114   BIEBER, KONRAD F. THE TRANSLATOR--FRIEND OR FOE.   FRENCH
         REVIEW,   VOL. 28, NO. 6 (MAY 1955), PP. 493-497.   BO 518,
         FR VII 13296.

1115   BIEBER, KONRAD. ENGAGEMENT AS A PROFESSIONAL RISK.   YALE FRENCH
         STUDIES,   NO. 16 (WINTER 1955-56), PP. 29-39.   BO 105, CR
         913, FR VII 12618, KL I 272, MA 180.

1116   BIEŃKOWSKI, ZBIGNIEW. CAMUS--LAUREAT NOBLA.   TWÓRCZOŚĆ,   VOL.
         13, NO. 12 (DEC. 1957), PP. 176-178.

1117   BIEŃKOWSKI, ZBIGNIEW. CAMUS.   TWÓRCZOŚĆ,   VOL. 16, NO. 3 (MARCH
         1960), PP. 99-107.   BUL SIGN 15-19-20056.

1118   BILLY, ANDRÉ.'L'HOMME RÉVOLTÉ', D'ALBERT CAMUS.   BIBLIO,   VOL.
         19, NO. 9 (NOV. 1951), P. 8.   BO 482, FR VII 5737.

1119   BILLY, ANDRÉ. 'L'HOMME RÉVOLTÉ', D'ALBERT CAMUS.   LIVRES DE
         FRANCE,   VOL. 2, NO. 9 (NOV. 1951), P. 8.   CR 778.

1120   BILLY, ANDRÉ. 'L'HOMME RÉVOLTÉ', D'ALBERT CAMUS.   LIVRES DE
         FRANCE,   VOL. 2, NO. 9 (NOV. 1951), P. 8.   CR 808.

1121   BILLY, ANDRÉ. LA CHUTE, C'EST CELLE DE L'HOMME MODERNE.
         FIGARO,   VOL. 130, NO. 3649 (MAY 31, 1956), P. 14.

1122   BINNENDIJK, D. A. M. FRANSCHE LETTEREN.   KRONIEK VAN KUNST EN
         KULTUUR,   VOL. 7, NO. 1 (NOV. 1, 1945), PP. 31-32.   BO 3.

1123   BINNENDIJK, D. A. M. EEN KNAP DEBUUT (L'ÉTRANGER).   LITTERAIR
         PASPOORT,   VOL. 1, NO. 1 (JAN. 1946), P. 15.   CR 555.

BISHOP, THOMAS. PIRANDELLO AND THE FRENCH THEATER. NEW YORK.   1124
   NEW YORK UNIVERSITY PRESS, 1960. CF. PP. 121, 122,
   127-129.

BISMUTH, MAURICE. CAMUS PLAY OPENS IN PARIS. (STATE OF SIEGE).   1125
   THEATRE NEWSLETTER, VOL. 3, NO. 60 (NOV. 27, 1948), P. 3.
   FR VII 33996.

BISTRITSKY, N. MERED UMAHPEKHAH (REBELLION AND REVOLUTION). AL   1126
   HAMISHMAR, SEPT. 2, 1960, PP. 5-6.

BITTNER, WILLIAM. THE DEATH OF CAMUS. ATLANTIC MONTHLY, VOL.   1127
   207, NO. 2 (FEB. 1961), PP. 85-88. FR VII 26308.

BIZET, RENÉ, LE THÉÂTRE. NOTES DE SPECTACLE. CALIGULA   1128
   D'ALBERT CAMUS. REVUE HOMMES ET MONDES, VOL. 1, NO. 1
   (JULY 1946), P. 213. CR 556.

BJURSTRÖM, CARL GUSTAF. BREV FRÅN PARIS. BONNIERS LITTERÄRA   1129
   MAGASIN, VOL. 16, NO. 8 (OCT. 1947), PP. 652-658.

BJURSTRÖM, CARL GUSTAF. TEATERBREV FRÅN PARIS. BONNIERS   1130
   LITTERÄRA MAGASIN, VOL. 18, NO. 1 (JAN. 1949), PP. 77-79.
   FR VII 28727.

BJURSTRÖM, C. G. TEATERBREV FRÅN PARIS. BONNIERS LITTERÄRA   1131
   MAGASIN, VOL. 19, NO. 2 (FEB. 1950), PP. 134-136. FR VII
   28728.

BJURSTRÖM, C. G. I STÄLLET FÖR EN TRO. BREV FRÅN PARIS.   1132
   BONNIERS LITTERÄRA MAGASIN, VOL. 23, NO. 9 (NOV. 1954),
   PP. 720-727. FR VII 25256.

BJURSTRÖM, C. G. VÅRSTIDS HJÄLTE. DAGENS NYHETER, JUNE 28,   1133
   1956.

BJURSTRÖM, C. G. ALBERT CAMUS. FRÅN FRÄMLINGSKAP TILL   1134
   LANDSFLYKT. STOCKHOLM. BONNIERS, 1957. KL I 271.

BJURSTRÖM, C. G. CAMUS OCH HANS ROMANER. BONNIERS LITTERÄRA   1135
   MAGASIN, VOL. 26, NO. 10 (1957), PP. 853-858. FR VII
   26309, KL I 272.

BJURSTRÖM, C. G. DEN UNGE CAMUS. DAGENS NYHETER, JUNE 23,   1136
   1958.

BLAISE, M.-C. ALBERT CAMUS. LIBERTÉ, VOL. 2, NO. 1 (JAN.-FEB.   1137
   1960), PP. 47-53. FR VII 23609.

BLAJOT, JORGE, S. J. ALBERT CAMUS HA MUERTO. RAZON Y FE, VOL.   1138
   161, NO. 745 (1960), PP. 195-198. FR VII 26310.

BLAMIRES, HENRY. THE TYRANNY OF TIME. NEW YORK. MOREHOUSE,   1139
   1965.

BLANC-DUFFOUR, A. CHRONIQUES. ESSAIS ET VARIÉTÉS. ACTUELLES   1140
   PAR ALBERT CAMUS. CAHIERS DU SUD, 37TH YEAR, VOL. 2, NO.
   303 (1950), P. 346. CR 738.

BLANC-DUFFOUR, A. L'HOMME RÉVOLTÉ DE CAMUS. CAHIERS DU SUD,   1141
   38TH YEAR, VOL. 34, NO. 309 (1951), PP. 325-327. BO 483,
   FR VII 7696.

1142   BLANC-ROOS, RENÉ. CALIGULA. CROSS PURPOSE. THE PLAGUE. NATICN,
          VOL. 167, NO. 15 (OCT. 9, 1948), PP. 404-406. BO 356.

1143   BLANCHAR, PIERRE. DES PERSONNALITÉS DU THÉÂTRE... (HOMMAGES À
          CAMUS). FIGARO, VOL. 134, NO. 4770 (JAN. 6, 1960). P. 4.
          FITCH.

1144   BLANCHAR, PIERRE. ALBERT CAMUS, ARTISAN DE THÉÂTRE. SIMOUN,
          VOL. 8, NO. 31 (JULY 1960), PP. 58-68. FR VII 23573, KL II
          389.

1145   BLANCHARD, MICHEL. LES IDÉES ET LES HOMMES. ALBERT CAMUS,
          SOLITAIRE OU SOLIDAIRE. REVUE FRANÇAISE DE L'ÉLITE
          EUROPÉENNE, NO. 125 (JAN. 1961), P. 34.

1146   BLANCHARD, MICHEL. DE L'IMMORALISTE À L'ETRANGER. MEURSAULT
          EST-IL LE FILS DE MICHEL? REVUE FRANÇAISE, NO. 141 (JUNE
          1962), PP. 58-59. FR VII 33938, FITCH.

1147   BLANCHET, ANDRÉ. L'HOMME RÉVOLTÉ D'ALBERT CAMUS. ÉTUDES,
          VOL. 85, NO. 272 (JAN.-FEB.-MARCH 1952), PP. 48-60. BFZ
          32-249 (1950-52), BO 492, BUL SIGN 8-5118, CR 809, KL II
          391.

1148   BLANCHET, ANDRÉ. LA VIE LITTÉRAIRE. LA QUERELLE SARTRE-CAMUS.
          ÉTUDES, VOL. 85, NO. 275 (OCT.-NOV.-DEC. 1952), PP.
          238-246. BFZ 35-984 (1952-53), BO 270, BUL SIGN 8-220, CR
          810, FR VII 8482.

1149   BLANCHET, ANDRÉ. ZUR FEHDE SARTRE-CAMUS. DOKUMENTE, VOL. 9,
          NO. 1 (1953), PP. 65-74. CR 846.

1150   BLANCHET, ANDRÉ. LES ENFANTS DU DEMI-SIÈCLE. ÉTUDES, VOL. 89,
          NO. 289 (APRIL-MAY-JUNE 1956), PP. 364-377. KL I 231.

1151   BLANCHET, ANDRÉ. LA LITTÉRATURE ET LE SPIRITUEL. I. PARIS.
          AUBIER, 1959. L'HOMME RÉVOLTÉ , PP. 233-249, LA QUERELLE
          SARTRE-CAMUS , PP. 267-279. FR VII 20651, KL II 391.

1152   BLANCHET, ANDRÉ. ALBERT CAMUS' WETTE. (I). DOKUMENTE, VOL.
          16, NO. 3 (JUNE 1960), PP. 187-198. BDZ 120-311 (1960-PT
          I), BDZ 121-321 (1960-PT I), KL II 387.

1153   BLANCHET, ANDRÉ. ALBERT CAMUS' WETTE. (II). DOKUMENTE, VOL.
          16, NO. 4 (AUGUST 1960), PP. 273-282. BDZ 120-311 (1960-PT
          I), BDZ 121-321 (1960-PT I), KL II 387.

1154   BLANCHET, ANDRÉ. LE PARI D'ALBERT CAMUS. (PART 1). ÉTUDES,
          VOL. 305, NO. 305 (MAY 1960), PP. 183-199, 330-344. BFZ
          46-283, FR VII 23586, KL II 387, PMLA 6813 (1961).

1155   BLANCHET, ANDRÉ. LE PARI D'ALBERT CAMUS. (PART II). ÉTUDES,
          VOL. 305, NO. 306 (JUNE 1960), PP. 183-199. BFZ 46-283, FR
          VII 23586, KL II 387, PMLA 6813 (1961).

1156   BLANCHET, ANDRÉ. LA LITTÉRATURE ET LE SPIRITUEL. III.CLASSIQUES
          D'HIER ET D'AUJOURD'HUI. PARIS. AUBIER, 1961. LE PARI
          D'ALBERT CAMUS ALBERT CAMUS , PP. 193-229. FR VII 25217.

1157   BLANCHOT, MAURICE. FAUX PAS. PARIS. GALLIMARD, 1943. LE

MYTHE DE SISYPHE ET LE ROMAN DE L'ÉTRANGER. BR, BO 57, CR
440.

BLANCHOT, MAURICE. RÉFLEXIONS SUR L'ENFER (I). NOUVELLE REVUE   1158
FRANÇAISE, VOL. 2, NO. 16 (APRIL 1, 1954), PP. 677-686.
BFZ 37-266 (1953-55), CR 871.

BLANCHOT, MAURICE. RÉFLEXIONS SUR LE NIHILISME (II). NOUVELLE   1159
REVUE FRANÇAISE, VOL. 2, NO. 17 (MAY 1, 1954), PP.
850-859. BO 211, CR 872.

BLANCHOT, MAURICE. TU PEUX TUER CET HOMME (III). NOUVELLE   1160
REVUE FRANÇAISE, VOL. 2, NO. 18 (JUNE 1, 1954), PP.
1059-1069. BFZ 37-266 (1953-55), CR 873.

BLANCHOT, MAURICE. LA CONFESSION DÉDAIGNEUSE, NOUVELLE REVUE   1161
FRANÇAISE, VOL. 4, NO. 48 (DEC. 1956), PP. 1050-1056. BFZ
41-249, BR, CR 956 TER, FR VII 23587, KL I 273.

BLANCHOT, MAURICE. ALBERT CAMUS. NOUVELLE REVUE FRANÇAISE,   1162
VOL. 8, NO. 87 (MARCH 1960), PP. 403-404. FR VII 23575, KL
II 395, PMLA 6815 (1961).

BLANCHOT, MAURICE. LE DÉTOUR VERS LA SIMPLICITÉ. NOUVELLE   1163
REVUE FRANÇAISE, VOL. 8, NO. 89 (MAY 1960), PP. 925-937.
BFZ 47-280 (1961), BUL SIGN 15-19-1929, FR VII 23588, KL II
388, PMLA 6814 (1961).

BLANCO AMOR, JOSÉ. L'EXPÉRIENCE TRAGIQUE D'ALBERT CAMUS.   1164
SYNTHÈSES, VOL. 5, NO. 55 (DEC. 1950), PP. 61-67. FR VII
11220.

BLANCO AMOR, JOSÉ. ALBERT CAMUS. 'EL MITO DE SISIFO'. 'EL   1165
HOMBRE REBELDE'. SUR, NO. 229 (JULY-AUG. 1954), PP.
92-94. BO 321, FR VII 11219.

BLANK, J. DER BEKÜMMERTE ATHEIST. SEELE, VOL. 36, (1960), PP.   1166
85-87. BDZ 124-304 (1962).

BLANZAT, JEAN. PREMIÈRE RENCONTRE. NOUVELLE REVUE FRANÇAISE,   1167
VOL. 8, NO. 87 (MARCH 1960), PP. 427-431. FR VII 23575, KL
II 386.

BLETSCHACHER, R. M. J. DIE EINFLÜSSE DER EXISTENZPHILOSOPHIE   1168
AUF DIE FRANZÖSISCHE DRAMATIK DER GEGENWART. DISSERTATION,
WIEN, 1958.

BLIN, GEORGES. ALBERT CAMUS OU LE SENS DE L'ABSURDE. FONTAINE,   1169
VOL. 5, NO. 30 (1943), PP. 553-561. BO 179, BR, CR 494.

BLIN, GEORGES. ALBERT CAMUS ET L'IDÉE DE RÉVOLTE. FONTAINE,   1170
VOL. 10, NO. 53 (JUNE 1946), PP. 109-117. BO 214, CR 554,
FR VII 744.

BLOCH-MICHEL, JEAN. SOLITAIRE OU SOLIDAIRE. DEMAIN, NO. 68   1171
(MARCH 28-APRIL 3, 1957), P. 16. CR 990.

BLOCH-MICHEL, JEAN. MISÈRES ET GLOIRES D'UN FESTIVAL. DEMAIN,   1172
NO. 82 (JULY 4-10, 1957), P. 17. CR 989.

BLOCH-MICHEL, JEAN. CAMUS, IL 'NOBEL' E L'ALGERIA. TEMPO   1173

PRESENTE,   VOL. 2, NO. 12 (DEC. 1957), PP. 975-977.   FR VII
21370.

1174   BLOCH-MICHEL, JEAN. LA PENA DI MORTE IN FRANCIA. MILAN,
LONGANESI, 1958.   SEE NO. 596. TRANSLATION OF NO. 2196.
LILITH, MARIA.

1175   BLOCH-MICHEL, JEAN. ALBERT CAMUS Y SUS CRÍTICOS.   CUADERNOS
(DEL CONGRESO POR LA LIBERTAD DE LA CULTURA),   NO. 28
(JAN.-FEB. 1958), PP. 4-9.   FR VII 19408, KL II 388.

1176   BLOCH-MICHEL, JEAN.   IN COLLABORATION WITH ARTHUR KOESTLER   AND
ALBERT CAMUS. LA PENA DE MUERTE IN FRANCIA.   BUENOS AIRES,
EMECE, 1960.   I.T. (1963) 3583.   SEE NO. 595. TRANSLATION
OF NO. 2196.   PEYROU, MANUEL.

1177   BLOCH-MICHEL, JEAN. ALBERT CAMUS ET LA NOSTALGIE DE
L'INNOCENCE. PREUVES, NO. 110 (APRIL 1960), PP. 3-9. FR
VII 23589, KL II 393, PMLA 7352 (1962).

1178   BLOCH-MICHEL, JEAN. LE PRÉSENT DE L'INDICATIF. ESSAI SUR LE
NOUVEAU ROMAN. PARIS. GALLIMARD, 1963. LA CHUTE, PP. 50-54
AND SCATTERED REFERENCES.   FR VII 31672.

1179   BLOCH-MICHEL, JEAN. LES INTERMITTENCES DE LA MÉMOIRE (SIMONE DE
BEAUVOIR. LA FORCE DES CHOSES). PREUVES,   NO. 155 (JAN.
1964), PP. 66-70.

1180   BLOCH-MICHEL, JEAN. CAMUS ET LA CRITIQUE.   PREUVES,   VOL. 15,
NO. 168 (FEB. 1965), PP. 86-88.

1181   BLOCK, HASKELL M. ALBERT CAMUS.   TOWARDS A DEFINITION OF
TRAGEDY. UNIVERSITY OF TORONTO QUARTERLY, VOL. 119, NO. 4
(JULY 1950), PP. 354-360.   BO 252, FR VII 17291, MA 180.

1182   BLOCK, HASKELL M. 'CAMUS' BY GERMAINE BRÉE.   CRITICISM,   VOL.
2, NO. 1 (WINTER 1960), PP. 94-96.

1183   BLÖCKER, GÜNTER. DIE NEUEN WIRKLICHKEITEN. LINIEN UND PROFILE
DER MODERNEN LITERATUR.   BERLIN.   ARGON, 1957.   ALBERT
CAMUS, PP. 267-276.   BDZ 115-350 (1958), CR 441, FR VII
20653, KL I 272.

1184   BLÖCKER, GÜNTER. KONFLIKTE UNSERER ZEIT.   DAS BEISPIELHAFTE
LEBEN DES ALBERT CAMUS.   ZEIT, VOL. 16, NO. 9 (1961), P.
11.   BDZ 122-322 (1961).

1185   BLÖCKER, GÜNTER. KRITISCHES LESEBUCH. LITERATUR UNSERER ZEIT IN
PROBE UND BERICHT.   HAMBURG. LEIBNIZ-VERLAG, 1962.   ALBERT
CAMUS. LITERARISCHE ESSAYS, PP. 361-366.

1186   BO, CARLO. SULL OPERA DI CAMUS.   HUMANITAS,   VOL. 3, NO. 9
(SEPT. 1948), PP. 897-912.   BO 18, CR 638, FR VII 7698.

1187   BO, CARLO. DELLA LETTURA E ALTRI SAGGI.   FLORENCE.   VALLECCHI,
1953.   SCATTERED REFERENCES.   FR VII 14778.

1188   BOASSO, FERNANDO. ALBERT CAMUS.   ESTUDIOS,   VOL. 87, NO. 462
(MAY-JUNE 1954), PP. 214-223.   BO 45, FR VII 13297.

1189   BODIN, PAUL. UNE GRANDE BATAILLE SE POURSUIT. UNE POLÉMIQUE QUI

NOUS EST FINALEMENT DESTINÉE. ARTS,   NO. 378 (SEPT.
26-OCT. 2, 1952), PP. 1, 5.   CR 811.

BOER, JO. AANTEEKENINGEN OVER HET HEDENDAAGSCHE FRANSCHE   1190
TOONEEL. ÉRASME,   VOL. 1, NOS. 1-2 (JAN.-FEB. 1946), PP.
38-52. BO 82, CR 558, FR VII 2418.

BOER, JO. DE CULTUREELE VESTING VAN FRANKRIJK. MAURIAC, CAMUS,   1191
SARTRE. ÉRASME,   VOL. 1, NOS. 3-4 (MARCH-APRIL 1946), PP.
115-119. BO 58.

BOER, MINNE G. DE. NARRATEUR ET NARRATION DANS L'ÉTRANGER   1192
D'ALBERT CAMUS. BULLETIN DES JEUNES ROMANISTES, NO. 3 (MAY
1961), P. 46.

BOISDEFFRE, PIERRE DE. ALBERT CAMUS. L'INSUFFISANTE NOBLESSE.   1193
CARREFOUR, VOL. 6, NO. 309 (AUG. 15, 1950), PP. 7-8. BO
122, FR VII 13298.

BOISDEFFRE, PIERRE DE. ALBERT CAMUS OU L'EXPÉRIENCE TRAGIQUE.   1194
ÉTUDES, VOL. 267, NO. 12 (DEC. 1950), PP. 303-325. BFZ
30-185 (1949-50), BO 202, BR, CR 739, FR VII 5756.

BOISDEFFRE, PIERRE DE. L'EXPÉRIENCE TRAGIQUE D'ALBERT CAMUS.   1195
SYNTHÈSES, VOL. 5, NO. 55 (DEC. 1950), PP. 61-67. BO 203,
CR 740.

BOISDEFFRE, PIERRE DE. MÉTAMORPHOSES DE LA LITTÉRATURE DE   1196
PROUST À SARTRE. PARIS. ÉDITIONS ALSATIA, 1951. ALBERT
CAMUS OU L'EXPÉRIENCE TRAGIQUE , PP. 259-308. BO 202, CR
443, FR VII 5143.

BOISDEFFRE, PIERRE DE. LA FIN D'UNE AMITIÉ. SARTRE CONTRE   1197
CAMUS. REVUE LIBRE, NO. 3 (DEC. 1952), PP. 51-57. BO 271,
FR VII 12353.

BOISDEFFRE, PIERRE DE. RÉFLEXIONS SUR LA RÉVOLTE À PROPOS DE   1198
L'HOMME RÉVOLTÉ D'ALBERT CAMUS. SIMOUN, VOL. 2, NO. 8
(1953), PP. 120-122.

BOISDEFFRE, PIERRE DE, ÉTIENNE BORNE, AND R. P. DUBARLE.   1199
L'HOMME REVOLTÉ DE CAMUS. RECHERCHES ET DEBATS DU CENTRE
CATHOLIQUE DES INTELLECTUELS FRANÇAIS, CAHIER NO. 3.
PSYCHOLOGIE MODERNE ET RÉFLEXION CHRÉTIENNE , JAN. 1953,
PP. 215-236. FITCH.

BOISDEFFRE, PIERRE DE. UNA FILOSOFÍA DE LA REBELIÓN. A   1200
PROPOSITO DE LA OBRA DE ALBERT CAMUS. CRITERIO (BUENOS
AIRES), VOL. 25, NO. 1179 (JAN. 8, 1953), PP. 13-14. BO
229.

BOISDEFFRE, PIERRE DE. DES VIVANTS ET DES MORTS. PARIS.   1201
ÉDITIONS UNIVERSITAIRES, 1954. ALBERT CAMUS OU L'EX-
PÉRIENCE DE LA RÉVOLTE , PP. 187-218. BO 235, CR 444.

BOISDEFFRE, PIERRE DE. REGARDS SUR L'OEUVRE D'ALBERT CAMUS.   1202
COMBAT, (MAY 2, 1957). BR, CR 990 TER.

BOISDEFFRE, PIERRE DE. L'ÉVOLUTION SPIRITUELLE D'ALBERT CAMUS.   1203

ECCLESIA,   NO. 101 (AUG. 1957), PP. 107-112. BR, CR 990
BIS.

1204   BOISDEFFRE, PIERRE DE. UNE HISTOIRE VIVANTE DE LA LITTÉRATURE
       D'AUJOURD'HUI, 1938-1958. PARIS. LE LIVRE CONTEMPORAIN,
       1958. APPARITION DE CAMUS, PP. 121-126, L'EXPÉRIENCE
       THÉÂTRALE D'ALBERT CAMUS, PP. 631-635. CR 442.

1205   BOISDEFFRE, PIERRE DE. ALBERT CAMUS. REVUE DES DEUX MONDES,
       NO. 3 (FEB. 1, 1960), PP. 398-414. BFZ 48-262 (1962), FR
       VII 23590, KL II 395.

1206   BOISDEFFRE, PIERRE DE. CAMUS S'ÉLOIGNE. REVUE DE PARIS, VOL.
       67, NO. 5 (MAY 1960), PP. 165-166. KL 368.

1207   BOISDEFFRE, PIERRE DE. UN ROMAN SANS ROMANESQUE. REVUE DES
       DEUX MONDES, NO. 19 (OCT. 1, 1960), PP. 420-437.

1208   BOISDEFFRE, PIERRE DE. OU VA LE ROMAN? PARIS. ÉDITIONS
       MONDIALES, 1962. L'EXPÉRIENCE DE LA RÉVOLTE. UNE PRÉFACE
       AU NOUVEAU ROMAN, L'ÉTRANGER D'ALBERT CAMUS, PP. 165-174
       ET PASSIM.

1209   BOISDEFFRE, PIERRE DE. LE LIVRE DE LA SEMAINE. ALBERT CAMUS,
       CARNETS . NOUVELLES LITTÉRAIRES, VOL. 40, NO. 1810 (MAY
       10, 1962), P. 2.

1210   BOISDEFFRE, PIERRE DE. LES PAYSAGES D'ALBERT CAMUS. REVUE DES
       DEUX MONDES, NO. 17 (SEPT. 1, 1963), PP. 81-91. FR VII
       33939.

1211   BOISDEFFRE, PIERRE DE. CAMUS ET SON DESTIN. IN ANONYMOUS,
       CAMUS, PP. 265-278. SEE NO. 940.

1212   BOIS-RABOT, GÉRARD. LE DIEU DE CAMUS, SARTRE ET MALRAUX.
       RÉSURRECTION, NO. 15, PP. 113-122. FR VII 29352.

1213   BOITOUZET, LUCIEN. ALBERT CAMUS TUÉ EN AUTOMOBILE PRÈS DE
       VILLEBLEVIN. FIGARO, VOL. 134, NO. 4770 (JAN. 6, 1960),
       P. 4. FITCH.

1214   BOLLNOW, OTTO FRIEDRICH. EXISTENTIALISMUS. SAMMLUNG, VOL. 2,
       NO. 11 (NOV. 1947), PP. 654-666. BO 316.

1215   BOLLNOW, OTTO FRIEDRICH. ALBERT CAMUS 'DIE PEST'. SAMMLUNG,
       VOL. 3, (1948), PP. 103-113. BDZ 98-181 (1948), BO 405, CR
       639.

1216   BOLLNOW, OTTO FRIEDRICH. VON DER ABSURDEN WELT ZUM MITTEL-
       MEERISCHEN GEDANKEN. BEMERKUNGEN ZU CAMUS' NEUEM BUCH 'DER
       MENSCH IN DER REVOLTE'. ANTARES, VOL. 2, NO. 1 (1954),
       PP. 3-13. BDZ 108-306 (1954), BO 519, CR 874.

1217   BOLLNOW, OTTO F. DU MONDE ABSURDE À LA PENSÉE DE MIDI. REVUE
       DES LETTRES MODERNES, NOS. 90-93 (WINTER 1963), PP. 41-72.
       PMLA 8608 (1964). TRANSLATION OF NO. 1216. SEE NO. 3207.
       TRANSLATED BY M. PIERRE OSMO.

1218   BOLLONGIER, RENÉE. ALBERT CAMUS, HOMME DE THÉÂTRE. DIPLÔME
       D'ÉTUDES SUPÉRIEURES DE LETTRES CLASSIQUES, FACULTÉ DES

LETTRES D'AIX-MARSEILLE. PRÉSENTÉ SOUS LA DIRECTION DE
MONSIEUR LE PROFESSEUR RUFF, OCTOBER 1961.

BOMHOFF, J. G. OVER DE GODDELOZE HELDHAFTIGHEID. WENDING ('S   1219
GRAVENHAGE), VOL. 3, NO. 11 (JAN. 1949), PP. 668-673. BO
429, CR 684.

BONDY, FRANÇOIS. ALBERT CAMUS UND DIE WELT DES ABSURDEN.   1220
SCHWEIZER ANNALEN, VOL. 3, NO. 3 (1946), PP. 150-159. BO
184, BR, CR 559, FR VII 745.

BONDY, FRANÇOIS. EIN TRIUMPHLIED DES LEBENS: 'LA PESTE'.   1221
WELTWOCHE (ZURICH), VOL. 15, NO. 713 (1947), P. 5. BO
385, CR 585.

BONDY, FRANÇOIS. DER AUFSTAND ALS MASS UND ALS MYTHOS. EIN   1222
BLICK AUF DAS WERK VON ALBERT CAMUS AUS ANLASS VON 'L'HOMME
RÉVOLTÉ' MONAT, VOL. 6, NO. 61 (OCT. 1953), PP. 87-96.
BO 506, CR 847.

BONDY, FRANÇOIS. ALBERT CAMUS' MEISTERWERK, ZU SEINER ERZÄHLUNG   1223
LA CHUTE . MONAT, VOL. 8, NO. 94 (JULY 1956), PP. 67-71.
CR 927, FR VII 15339.

BONDY, FRANÇOIS. ALBERT CAMUS ZUM GEDENKEN. MONAT, VOL. 12,   1224
NO. 137 (FEB. 1960), PP. 7-8. BDZ 120-311 (1960), FR VII
23592, KL II 393.

BONDY, FRANÇOIS. ALBERT CAMUS. CUADERNOS (DEL CONGRESO POR LA   1225
LIBERTAD DE LA CULTURA), NO. 41 (MARCH-APRIL 1960), PP.
55-57. FR VII 23591.

BONDY, FRANÇOIS. SARTRE'S REFUSAL. ATLAS, VOL. 9, NO. 1 (JAN.   1226
1965), PP. 51-52.

BONET, LAUREANO. CAMUS VISTO Y NO VISTO ESTAFETA LITERARIA,   1227
NO. 279 (NOV. 23, 1963), P. 5.

BONNEVILLE, GEORGES. L'EUROPE EST ELLE ENCORE LITTÉRAIRE ?   1228
REVUE DES DEUX MONDES, NO. 18 (SEPT. 15, 1961), PP.
245-259. FR VII 25331.

BONNIER, HENRY. ALBERT CAMUS OU LA FORCE D'ÊTRE. LYON. E.   1229
VITTE, 1959. CR 445, FR VII 21359, KL II 386.

BONORA, ETTORE. GLI IPOCRITI DE MALEBOLGE E ALTRI SAGGI DI   1230
LETTERATURA ITALIANA E FRANCESE. MILAN. R. RICCIARDI,
1953.   CAMUS E LA VOCAZIONE AL ROMANZO , PP. 148-158. BO
73, FR VII 12593.

BONSANTI, ALESSANDRO. LO SPECCHIO DI CAMUS. MONDO, VOL. 14,   1231
NO. 28 (JULY 10, 1962), P. 13. PMLA 7967 (1963).

BOOTH, WAYNE C. THE RHETORIC OF FICTION. CHICAGO. UNIVERSITY   1232
OF CHICAGO PRESS, 1961. PP. 294-297.

BOREL, JACQUES. NATURE ET HISTOIRE CHEZ ALBERT CAMUS.   1233
CRITIQUE, VOL. 17, NO. 169 (JUNE 1961), PP. 507-521. BUL
SIGN 16-19-109, FR VII 26311, PMLA 7353 (1962).

BORELIUS, A. ABSURDITÄT UM ALBERT CAMUS. SIE, VOL. 3, NO. 24   1234

(1948), P. 7.   BO 193, CR 641.

1235   BORGAL, CLÉMENT. CAMUS PAR LUI-MÊME BY MORVAN LEBESQUE.
       (REVIEW). TABLE RONDE, NO. 191 (DEC. 1963), PP. 131-132.
       FR VII 33940.

1236   BORNE, ÉTIENNE. DIEU N'EST PAS MORT. (ESSAI SUR L'ATHÉISME
       CONTEMPORAIN). PARIS. FAYARD, 1956. SCATTERED
       REFERENCES.

1237   BORNE, ÉTIENNE. ALBERT CAMUS (DEBAT). RECHERCHES ET DEBATS DU
       CENTRE CATHOLIQUE DES INTELLECTUELS FRANÇAIS, NO. 31 (JUNE
       1960), PP. 169-192. BORNE, ETIENNE. PP. 186-192. BUL SIGN
       15.19, 1009, 15.19.20058.

1238   BORNE, ÉTIENNE. L'HOMME RÉVOLTÉ DE CAMUS. SEE NO. 1199.

1239   BORRELLO, ORESTE. L'ESTETICA DELL ESISTENZIALISMO. MESSINA.
       G. D'ANNA, 1956. FR VII 22837, KL I 231.

1240   BORTOLASO, GIOVANNI. UMANISMO ATEO. CIVILTÀ CATTOLICA, VOL.
       113, PART II, NO. 2688 (JUNE 16, 1962), PP. 535-544. FR
       VII 28584.

1241   BOSQUET, ALAIN. L'ABSURDE DEVIENT-IL DÉCADENT? COMBAT, (MAY
       31, 1950). BR, CR 740 BIS.

1242   BOSQUET, ALAIN. CLASSICISME D'ALBERT CAMUS. COMBAT,   APRIL 1,
       1954. BR, CR 874 BIS.

1243   BOSQUET, ALAIN. RÉFLEXIONS SUR UN PRIX NOBEL. COMBAT,   (OCT.
       24, 1957). BR, CR 990 QUARTO.

1244   BOSQUET, ALAIN. UNE CONSCIENCE CONTRE LE CHAOS. COMBAT, (MAY
       1, 1960).

1245   BOUDOT, M. L'ABSURDE ET LE BONHEUR DANS L'OEUVRE D'ALBERT
       CAMUS. CAHIERS DU SUD,   VOL. 39, NO. 315 (1952), PP.
       291-305. BO 209, BUL SIGN 8-1021, CR 812,FR VII 9299.

1246   BOULLAYE, X. DE LA. 'LES JUSTES' D'ALBERT CAMUS. TÉMOIGNAGES,
       NO. 32 (JAN. 1952), PP. 40-49. BO 470.

1247   BOURDET, CLAUDE. CAMUS ET LA RÉVOLTE DE SISYPHE. OBSERVATEUR,
       (DEC. 13-20, 1951). BR, CR 778 BIS.

1248   BOURDET, CLAUDE, AND GILLES MARTINET. ALBERT CAMUS ET LE
       JOURNALISME. FRANCE OBSERVATEUR,   VOL. 6, NO. 263 (MAY 26,
       1955), PP. 19-20. FR VII 17294.

1249   BOURDET, CLAUDE. LE 'VRAI DEBAT' DE CAMUS. FRANCE OBSERVATEUR,
       VOL. 6, NO. 265 (JUNE 1955), PP. 6-7. FR VII 17293.

1250   BOURDET, CLAUDE. CAMUS OU LES MAINS PROPRES. FRANCE
       OBSERVATEUR,   VOL. 11, NO. 505 (JAN. 7, 1960), P. 18.
       FITCH.

1251   BOURDIN, ANDRÉ. JOUR DE GLOIRE. CAMUS, PRIX NOBEL. NOUVELLES
       LITTERAIRES,   NO. 1573 (OCT. 24, 1957), P. 1. CR 991.

1252   BOURG, TONY. ALBERT CAMUS OU LE SENS DE LA VIE PERDU ET
       RETROUVÉ. CAHIERS LUXEMBOURGEOIS,   VOL. 23, NO. 5 (1951),
       PP. 273-279. CR 779.

BOURG, TONY. CHRONIQUES. LES LIVRES. ALBERT CAMUS. 'L'ÉTÉ'.   1253
    CAHIERS LUXEMBOURGEOIS,   VOL. 26, NOS. 1-2 (1954), PP.
    95-96. CR 875.

BORGEAUD, GEORGES. UNE OEUVRE EN DÉBAT DEVANT LA NOUVELLE   1254
    GÉNÉRATION. IL ME DONNE UN EXEMPLE DE LOYAUTÉ. FIGARO
    LITTÉRAIRE, VOL. 12, NO. 601 (OCT. 26, 1957), P. 7.
    FITCH. SEE NO. 3251.

BOURGET-PAILLERON, ROBERT. REVUE DRAMATIQUE. 'L'ÉTAT DE SIÈGE'   1255
    PIÈCE EN TROIS ACTES D'ALBERT CAMUS. REVUE DES DEUX
    MONDES, NO. 23 (DEC. 1, 1948), PP. 557-560. CR 642.

BOURGET-PAILLERON, ROBERT. REVUE DRAMATIQUE. 'LES JUSTES',   1256
    PIÈCE EN CINQ ACTES D'ALBERT CAMUS. REVUE DES DEUX MONDES,
    NO. 3 (FEB. 1, 1950), PP. 552-555. CR 741.

BOURGET-PAILLERON, ROBERT. REVUE DRAMATIQUE. 'REQUIEM POUR UNE   1257
    NONNE', PIÈCE EN DEUX PARTIES ET SEPT TABLEAUX DE WILLIAM
    FAULKNER, ADAPTATION D'ALBERT CAMUS. REVUE DES DEUX
    MONDES, NO. 20 (OCT. 15, 1956), PP. 736-739. CR 929.

BOURGET-PAILLERON, ROBERT. REVUE DRAMATIQUE. THÉÂTRE ANTOINE.   1258
    LES POSSÉDÉS , PIÈCE EN TROIS PARTIES D'ALBERT CAMUS,
    D'APRÈS LE ROMAN DE DOSTOÏEVSKI. REVUE DES DEUX MONDES,
    NO. 4 (FEB. 15, 1959), PP. 712-714. CR 1131, KL II 392.

BOUTANG, PIERRE. LA PESTE D'ALBERT CAMUS. ASPECTS DE LA FRANCE   1259
    ET DU MONDE, SEPT. 1947, P. 9. BO 386, CR 586.

BOYE, MAURICE-PIERRE. ALBERT CAMUS. 'L'HOMME RÉVOLTÉ'. FICHES   1260
    BIBLIOGRAPHIQUES, (1951). CR 780.

BOYE, MAURICE-PIERRE. ALBERT CAMUS. 'L'ÉTÉ'. FICHES   1261
    BIBLIOGRAPHIQUES, (1954). CR 876.

BOYE, MAURICE-PIERRE. ALBERT CAMUS. ACTUELLES III. CHRONIQUE   1262
    ALGÉRIENNE. FICHES BIBLIOGRAPHIQUES, (1958). CR 1081.

BOYE, MAURICE-PIERRE. ALBERT CAMUS.   L'ENVERS ET L'ENDROIT.   1263
    FICHES BIBLIOGRAPHIQUES, (1958). CR 1082.

BRAAMBEEK, RALF VAN. ALBERT CAMUS. LITTERAIR PASPOORT, VOL.   1264
    2, NO. 7 (JAN. 1947), PP. 7-8. BO 13, CR 587.

BRACE, RICHARD M. ESSAYS ILLUMINE HEART AND MIND OF CAMUS.   1265
    CHICAGO SUNDAY TRIBUNE MAGAZINE OF BOOKS, VOL. 115, NO. 43
    (FEB. 12, 1961), PART IV, PP. 1-2.

BRADBROOK, FRANK W. LETTERS TO THE EDITOR. CAMUS AND LAWRENCE.   1266
    TIMES LITERARY SUPPLEMENT, VOL. 61, NO. 3151 (JULY 20,
    1962), P. 525.

BRAGANÇA, NUNO DE. ALBERT CAMUS.   SEE NO. 3295.   1267

BRASPART, M. CALIGULA. RÉFORME, VOL. 1, NO. 29 (OCT. 1945),   1268
    P. 5. CR 512.

BRATSCHI, GEORGES. ESSAI SUR ALBERT CAMUS. TRIBUNE DE GENÈVE,   1269
    (SEPT. 1, 1956). BR, CR 929 BIS.

BRAUN, HANNS. DIE PEST AUF DER BÜHNE. MÜNCHENER KAMMERSPIELE.   1270

ZEIT,   VOL. 5, NO. 26 (1950), P. 3.   BO 452, CR 743.

1271   BRAUN, HANNS. ALLEGORIE DES WIDERSTANDS. ALBERT CAMUS.
BELAGERUNGSZUSTAND , IN MÜNCHEN. RHEINISCHER MERKUR, VOL.
5, NO. 27 (1950), P. 6.   BO 451, CR 742.

1272   BRAUN, HERMANN. NOBELPREIS FÜR LITERATUR. RUPERTO-CAROLA,
VOL. 10, NO. 23 (1958), PP. 8-9. BDZ 117-307 (1958).

1273   BREARLEY, KATHERINE. THE THEME OF ISOLATION IN CAMUS. KENTUCKY
FOREIGN LANGUAGE QUARTERLY, VOL. 9, NO. 3 (1962), PP.
117-122. PMLA 7968 (1963).

1274   BRÉE, GERMAINE. A. CAMUS ET LE THÉÂTRE DE L'ÉQUIPE. FRENCH
REVIEW, VOL. 22, NO. 3 (JAN. 1949), PP. 225-229. BO 96,
CR 685, FR VII 2696.

1275   BRÉE, GERMAINE. INTRODUCTION TO ALBERT CAMUS. FRENCH STUDIES,
VOL. 4, NO. 1 (JAN. 1950), PP. 27-37. BFZ 32-249
(1950-52), BO 27, CR 744, MA 181.

1276   BRÉE, GERMAINE. ALBERT CAMUS AND THE PLAGUE. YALE FRENCH
STUDIES, NO. 8 (1951), PP. 93-100. BO 437, BR, CR 780, MA
181.

1277   BRÉE, GERMAINE AND MARGARET GUITON. AN AGE OF FICTION. THE
FRENCH NOVEL FROM GIDE TO CAMUS. NEW BRUNSWICK. RUTGERS
UNIVERSITY PRESS, 1957.   ALBERT CAMUS. THE TWO SIDES OF
THE COIN , PP. 218-233. BUL SIGN 15-19-14336, CR 446,FR
VII 16585, KL I 272.

1278   BRÉE, GERMAINE. ALBERT CAMUS: A WRITER AND HIS TIMES.
AMERICAN SOCIETY LEGION OF HONOR MAGAZINE, VOL. 28, NO. 1
(SPRING 1957), PP. 43-52. FR VII 17295, KL I 272, MA 181.

1279   BRÉE, GERMAINE. CAMUS' 'CALIGULA'. EVOLUTION OF A PLAY.
SYMPOSIUM, VOL. 12, NOS. 1-2 (SPRING-FALL, 1958), PP.
43-51. BUL SIGN 14-9009, FR VII 19409, KL II 390, MA 181.

1280   BRÉE, GERMAINE. IN SEARCH OF SELF. 'ALBERT CAMUS' BY PHILIP
THODY AND 'THE THOUGHT AND ART OF ALBERT CAMUS' BY THOMAS
HANNA. NEW YORK TIMES BOOK REVIEW, APRIL 13, 1958, P.10.

1281   BRÉE, GERMAINE. CAMUS. NEW BRUNSWICK. RUTGERS UNIVERSITY
PRESS, 1959. CR 447, FR VII 21360, KL II 386.

1282   BRÉE, GERMAINE. ALBERT CAMUS. GESTALT UND WERK. HAMBURG.
ROWOHLT, 1960. FR VII 26289.

1283   BRÉE, GERMAINE. ALBERT CAMUS: AN ESSAY IN APPRECIATION. NEW
YORK TIMES BOOK REVIEW, VOL. 65, NO. 4 (JAN. 24, 1960).
PP. 5, 14. FR VII 26312, PMLA 6816 (1961), MA 181.

1284   BRÉE, GERMAINE. A GRAIN OF SALT. YALE FRENCH STUDIES, NO. 25
(SPRING 1960), PP. 41-43. BUL SIGN 16-19-9739, FR VII
23568, KL II 389, MA 181.

1285   BRÉE, GERMAINE. CAMUS. FRENCH REVIEW, VOL. 33, NO. 6 (MAY
1960), PP. 541-544. FR VII 23593, PMLA 6817 (1961), MA
181.

BRÉE, GERMAINE. NOTICE SUR LA MORT DE CAMUS. PUBLICATIONS OF   1286
    THE MODERN LANGUAGE ASSOCIATION, VOL. 75, NO. 2 (MAY
    1960), PP. I-II. KL II 395.

BRÉE, GERMAINE. A POSTSCRIPT (TO 'A FINAL INTERVIEW').   1287
    VENTURE, VOL. 3, NO. 4 (SPRING-SUMMER 1960), P. 39.

BRÉE, GERMAINE. ALBERT CAMUS, 1913-1960. ASOMANTE, VOL. 17,   1288
    NO. 1 (JAN.-MARCH 1961), PP. 10-18. FR VII 26313.

BRÉE, GERMAINE. EACH AND EVERY MAN BUILDS FOR ALL,   1289
    RESISTANCE, REBELLION, AND DEATH. NEW YORK TIMES BOOK
    REVIEW, FEB. 12, 1961, P. 5.

BRÉE, GERMAINE. THE GENESIS OF THE STRANGER. SHENANDOAH, VOL.   1290
    12, NO. 3 (SPRING 1961), PP. 3-10. FR VII 29355.

BRÉE, GERMAINE. CAMUS. NEW BRUNSWICK. RUTGERS UNIVERSITY   1291
    PRESS, 1961. FR VII 26290.

BRÉE, GERMAINE. RESISTANCE, REBELLION, AND DEATH. BOOK OF THE   1292
    MONTH CLUB NEWS, (JUNE 1961), PP. 5-6.

BRÉE, GERMAINE (EDITOR). CAMUS, A COLLECTION OF CRITICAL   1293
    ESSAYS. ENGLEWOOD CLIFFS, N. J.. PRENTICEHALL, 1962.
    INTRODUCTION, PP. 1-10. FR VII 29338.

BRÉE, GERMAINE. THE WRITER AND OUR TIME. MALRAUX, SARTRE,   1294
    CAMUS. IN BURNSHAW, STANLEY, VARIETIES OF LITERARY
    EXPERIENCE. EIGHTEEN ESSAYS IN WORLD LITERATURE, PP. 75-94.
    SEE NO. 1349.

BRÉE, GERMAINE. FRAGMENTS BEFORE FAME. NOTEBOOKS. 1935-1942, BY   1295
    ALBERT CAMUS. NEW YORK TIMES BOOK REVIEW, JULY 28, 1963,
    PP. 5, 12.

BRÉE, GERMAINE. ALBERT CAMUS. NEW YORK. COLUMBIA UNIVERSITY   1296
    PRESS(COLUMBIA ESSAYS ON MODERN WRITERS, NO. 1), 1964.

B(RÉHIER), É. ALBERT CAMUS. L'HOMME RÉVOLTÉ. REVUE   1297
    PHILOSOPHIQUE, VOL. 143, NOS. 1-3 (JAN.-MARCH 1953), PP.
    125-127. CR 853, FR VII 11216.

BREISACH, ERNST. INTRODUCTION TO MODERN EXISTENTIALISM. NEW   1298
    YORK. GROVE PRESS INC., 1962. FR VII 32395.

BRENNER, JACQUES. L'HOMME DU SOUTERRAIN. TABLE RONDE, NO. 146   1299
    (FEB. 1960), PP. 99-102. BUL SIGN 15-19-13762, FR VII
    23569, KL II 393.

BRENNER, JACQUES. LA MORT D'ALBERT CAMUS, CAHIERS DES SAISONS,   1300
    NO. 20, (NUMERO SPÉCIAL 1960), PP. 622-627. FITCH.

BRETON, ANDRÉ. SUCRE JAUNE--À PROPOS DE LAUTRÉAMONT. ANDRÉ   1301
    BRETON RÉPOND À ALBERT CAMUS. ARTS, NO. 328 (OCT. 12,
    1951), PP. 1, 3. BO 265, CR 781, FR VII 13912.

BRETON, ANDRÉ. LA CLÉ DES CHAMPS. PARIS. ÉDITIONS DU   1302
    SAGITTAIRE, 1953. SUCRE JAUNE, PP. 250-253.

BRETON, ANDRÉ. POÉSIE & AUTRE. PARIS. GALLIMARD, 1960. SUCRE   1303
    JAUNE, PP. 293-296.

1304   BRETON, ANDRÉ AND AIMÉ PATRIE. DIALOGUE ENTRE ANDRÉ BRETON ET
        AIMÉ PATRI À PROPOS DE L'HOMME RÉVOLTÉ D'ALBERT CAMUS.
        ARTS, NO. 333 (NOV. 16, 1951), PP. 1, 3. BO 484, CR 782,
        FR VII 13304.

1305   BRETON, ANDRÉ. LETTRES À ARTS (DIRIGÉE À LOUIS PAUWELS). ARTS,
        NO. 335 (NOV. 30, 1951), P. 7. BO 63, FR VII 13299.

1306   BRIFFAULT, HERMA. LITERATURE AND ART IN OCCUPIED PARIS.
        LISTENER, VOL. 34, NO. 882 (DEC. 6, 1945), PP. 664-665.
        FR VII 32063

1307   BRIGHOUSE, H. THE PLAGUE. MANCHESTER GUARDIAN, NO. 31,785
        (AUG. 27, 1948), P. 3. BO 406.

1308   BRINDEAU, SERGE. APRÈS LE PRIX NOBEL. UNE MAUVAISE ACTION.
        REVUE SOCIALISTE, NO. 114 (FEB. 1958), PP. 169-173. KL I
        274.

1309   BRINDEAU, SERGE. LA MER ET LES PRISONS. ALBERT CAMUS.
        MARGINALES, VOL. 13, NOS. 62-63 (DEC. 1958), PP. 1-7. CR
        1083, KL II 388.

1310   BRION, MARCEL. AU THÉÂTRE DES NATIONS.   REQUIEM POUR UNE NONNE
        DE WILLIAM FAULKNER. ADAPTATION PAR ALBERT CAMUS. REVUE
        DES DEUX MONDES, NO. 11 (JUNE 1, 1957), PP. 509-512. CR
        992.

1311   BRISSAUD, ANDRÉ. MAÎTRE DE LA JEUNESSE? CARREFOUR, NO. 799
        (JAN. 6, 1960), P. 21. FR VII 23594.

1312   BRISVILLE, J.-C. CALIGULA, SAINT-JUST. ÂGE D'OR, NOS. 5-6
        (DEC. 1946-JAN. 1947), PP. 25-30.

1313   BRISVILLE, JEAN-CLAUDE. GAZETTE DE LA LIBRAIRIE. 'ACTUELLES'.
        GAZETTE DES LETTRES, VOL. 6, NO. 123 (SEPT. 16, 1950), P.
        6. CR 745.

1314   BRISVILLE, JEAN-CLAUDE. HOMMAGE À ALBERT CAMUS. NOTES POUR UN
        PORTRAIT (PRIX NOBEL 1957). FIGARO LITTÉRAIRE, VOL. 12,
        NO. 601 (OCT. 26, 1957), P. 5. CR 993, FR VII 17296, KL I
        271.

1315   BRISVILLE, JEAN-CLAUDE. CAMUS. PARIS. GALLIMARD, 1959. CR
        448, FR VII 21361, KL II 386.

1316   BRISVILLE, JEAN-CLAUDE. LE SOURIRE ET LA VOIX. NOUVELLE REVUE
        FRANÇAISE, VOL. 8, NO. 87 (MARCH 1960), PP. 422-424. FR
        VII 23575, KL II 387.

1317   BRISVILLE, JEAN-CLAUDE. ALBERT CAMUS. NOUVELLES LITTÉRAIRES,
        VOL. 40, NO. 1809 (MAY 3, 1962), PP. 6-7. PMLA 7969
        (1963).

1318   BROCKMANN, CHARLES B. RESISTANCE, REBELLION, AND DEATH, ALBERT
        CAMUS, TRANSLATED BY JUSTIN O'BRIEN. SHENANDOAH, VOL. 12,
        NO. 3 (SPRING 1961), PP. 46-49.

1319   BROCKMANN, CHARLES B. METAMORPHOSES OF HELL. THE SPIRITUAL
        QUANDARY IN 'LA CHUTE'. FRENCH REVIEW, VOL. 35, NO. 4

(FEB. 1962), PP. 361-368. PMLA 7970 (1963).

BRODIN, PIERRE. PRÉSENCES CONTEMPORAINES. I. PARIS. ÉDITIONS   1320
    DEBRESSE, 1954. ALBERT CAMUS, PP. 443-460. BO 46, BR, CR
    449, FR VII 10611.

BRODIN, PIERRE. PRÉSENCES CONTEMPORAINES, III. PARIS. ÉDITIONS   1321
    DEBRESSE, 1957. SCATTERED REFERENCES.

BRODIN, PIERRE. LITTERATURE I. PARIS. NOUVELLES ÉDITIONS   1322
    DEBRESSE, 1958. CAMUS. PP. 443-462. KL I 271.

BROMBERT, VICTOR. CAMUS AND THE NOVEL OF THE 'ABSURD'. YALE   1323
    FRENCH STUDIES, VOL. 1, NO. 1 (SPRING-SUMMER 1948), PP.
    119-123. BO 194, BR, CR 643, FR VII 4411, MA 181.

BROMBERT, VICTOR. THE RENEGADE OR THE TERROR OF THE ABSOLUTE.   1324
    YALE FRENCH STUDIES, NO. 25 (SPRING 1960), PP. 81-84. FR
    VII 23568, KL II 391, MA 181.

BROMBERT, VICTOR. THE INTELLECTUEL HERO, STUDIES IN THE FRENCH   1325
    NOVEL, 1880-1955. PHILADELPHIA. LIPPINCOTT, 1961.   CAMUS
    'LE RENÉGAT' OR THE TERROR OF THE ABSOLUTE , PP. 227-231.
    FR VII 25478.

BROWN, JOHN L. ALBERT CAMUS, APOSTLE OF POSTLIBERATION FRANCE.   1326
    NEW YORK TIMES BOOK REVIEW, APRIL 7, 1946, PP. 4, 36.

BRUA, EDMOND. MOMENT. (A POEM OF THREE QUATRAINS ON CAMUS).   1327
    SIMOUN, VOL. 8, NO. 31 (JULY 1960), P. 44. FR VII 23573.

B(RÜCK), M(AX) V(ON). ALBERT CAMUS. DER GESUNDE MENSCHENVER-   1328
    STAND. ('DIE PEST'). GEGENWART, VOL. 3, NO. 20 (OCT. 15,
    1948), PP. 20-21. BDZ 99-167 (1949), CR 666.

BRÜCK, MAX VON. DER MENSCH IN DER REVOLTE. GEGENWART, VOL. 8,   1329
    NO. 5 (NO. 176) (FEB. 28, 1953), PP. 145-148.

BRUCKBERGER, R(AYMOND)-L(ÉOPOLD). CHRONIQUE LITTÉRAIRE. 'LA   1330
    PESTE', D'ALBERT CAMUS. CHEVAL DE TROIE, NO. 2
    (AUG.-SEPT. 1947), PP. 368-376. BO 387, BR, CR 588, FR VII
    11221.

BRUCKBERGER, RAYMOND-LÉOPOLD. THE SPIRITUAL AGONY OF EUROPE.   1331
    RENASCENCE, VOL. 7, NO. 2 (WINTER 1954), PP. 70-80. BO
    520, FR VII 13182, MA 189.

BRUCKBERGER, RAYMOND-LÉOPOLD. KUNST UND LEBEN. BEGEGNUNG MIT   1332
    ALBERT CAMUS. MERKUR, VOL. 13, NO. 18 (1958), P. 7. BDZ
    119-300 (1959).

BRUCKBERGER, RAYMOND-LÉOPOLD. UNE IMAGE RADIEUSE. NOUVELLE   1333
    REVUE FRANÇAISE, VOL. 8, NO. 87 (MARCH 1960), PP. 515-521.
    FR VII 23575, KL II 388.

BRUCKBERGER, (RAYMOND-LÉOPOLD), RVDO. P. UNA IMAGEN RADIANTE.   1334
    CUADERNOS (DEL CONGRESO POR LA LIBERTAD DE LA CULTURA),
    NO. 43 (JULY-AUG. 1960), PP. 86-88. FR VII 23595.

BRUÉZIÈRE, MAURICE, GUY MICHAUD, AND EMMANUÈLE WAGNER. UN   1335
    TEXTE DE CAMUS. FRANÇAIS DANS LE MONDE, VOL. 3, NO. 20

(OCT.-NOV. 1963), PP. 25-29.   FR VII 33936.

1336   BRULE, CLAUDE. OÙ EN SONT NOS MANDARINS?   RÉALITES,   NO. 137
        (JUNE 1957), PP. 47-49.   CR 994.

1337   BRULEZ, RAYMOND. ALLEN SCHULDIG?...ALBERT CAMUS: 'LA CHUTE'.
        HET BOEK VAN NU,   VOL. 10, NO. 1 (SEPT. 1956), P. 8.   CR
        930.

1338   BRUNE, JEAN. ALBERT CAMUS ENTRE LES MYTHES DE SON TEMPS ET LA
        SAGESSE DE LA MÉDITERRANÉE.   NATION FRANÇAISE,   NO. 223
        (JAN. 13, 1960), PP. 3, 15.   FITCH.

1339   BRUNEAU, CHARLES. LA PROSE LITTÉRAIRE DE PROUST À CAMUS.
        OXFORD.   CLARENDON PRESS, 1953.   BO 74, FR VII 8728.

1340   BRUNER, C. PIETÀ E AMORE DEGLI UOMINI DI CAMUS.   STUDIUM,   VOL.
        55, NO. 3 (MARCH 1959), PP. 171-177.   BUL SIGN 14-18201, KL
        II 389.

1341   BRUNO, F. REVIEW OF ALBERT CAMUS   L'UOMO IN RIVOLTA.   AUSONIA,
        VOL. 12 NO. 4 (SEPT.-OCT. 1957), P. 82.

1342   BRUSTEIN, ROBERT. NIHILISM ON BROADWAY.   NEW REPUBLIC,   VOL.
        142, NO. 9 (FEB. 29, 1960), PP. 21-22.   FR VII 23596.

1343   BRUZZI, AMELIA. IL REGNO DELL ASSURDO E LA MORALE DELLA RIVOLTA
        NELL OPERA DI ALBERTO CAMUS.   CONVIVIUM,   NO. 3 (MAY-JUNE
        1950), PP. 333-366.   BFZ 32-249 (1950-52), BO 204, CR 746,
        FR VII 5738.

1344   BRYDEN, RONALD. ABSURDS.   NEW STATESMAN,   VOL. 67, NO. 1727
        (APRIL 17, 1964), P. 616.

1345   BURGERT, HELMUTH. CAMUS ODER DER LÄUTERNDE ATHEISMUS.   ZEICHEN
        DER ZEIT,   VOL. 15, NO. 3 (1961), PP. 114-115.   BDZ 122-322
        (1961).

1346   BURKE, EDWARD L. CAMUS AND THE PURSUIT OF HAPPINESS.   THOUGHT,
        VOL. 37, NO. 146 (FALL 1962), PP. 391-409.   PMLA 7971
        (1962).

1347   BURKE, KATHLEEN. THE REBEL AND THE RIGHT. DOES CAMUS HOLD A
        MESSAGE FOR CONSERVATIVES?   OPTIMATE,   VOL. 3, NO. 3 (JAN.
        1965), PP. 8-10, 12.

1348   BURNHAM, JAMES. THE PLAGUE BY ALBERT CAMUS.   PARTISAN REVIEW,
        VOL. 15, NO.9 (SEPT. 1948), PP. 1022-1024.   CR 644, MA 181.

1349   BURNSHAW, STANLEY (EDITOR). VARIETIES OF LITERARY EXPERIENCE.
        EIGHTEEN ESSAYS IN WORLD LITERATURE. NEW YORK. NEW YORK
        UNIVERSITY PRESS, 1962.   SEE NO. 1294.

1350   BURUCOA, CHRISTIANE. RENCONTRE DE DEUX POINTS DE VUE:
        RÉFLEXIONS SUR L'ART CHEZ CAMUS ET CHEZ MALRAUX.   SIMOUN,
        VOL. 2, NO. 8 (1953), PP. 116-119.   FITCH.

1351   BURUCOA, CHRISTIANE. ALBERT CAMUS PRIX NOBEL DE LITTÉRATURE.
        SIMOUN,   VOL. 7, NOS. 28-29 (FEB. 1958), PP. 137-139.   FR
        VII 23597, KL II 386.

1352   BUSST, A.J.L. A NOTE ON THE ECCENTRIC CHRISTOLOGY OF CAMUS.

FRENCH STUDIES, VOL. 16, NO. 1 (JAN. 1962), PP. 45-50.
BFZ 262-49 (1960-62), PMLA 7972 (1962), MA 181.

C., J. PLUMES ET FLÈCHES. ALBERT CAMUS. DEMAIN, NO. 23 (MAY   1353
17-23, 1956), P. 15. CR 948.

C., M. REPRISE CHEZ HÉBERTOT. CALIGULA BLESSÉ ET SCIPION   1354
RAJEUNI. FIGARO LITTÉRAIRE, VOL. 5, NO. 233 (OCT. 7,
1950), P. 8. CR 761.

CABRIES, JEAN. ALBERT CAMUS, PRIX NOBEL 1957. REFORME, VOL.   1355
13, NO. 658 (OCT. 26, 1957), P. 6. CR 996.

CAILLET, GÉRARD. LA RELÈVE LITTÉRAIRE. JEAN DUTOURD, ALBERT   1356
CAMUS, FRANÇOIS-RÉGIS BASTIDE, JACQUES NELS. HOMMES ET
MONDES, VOL. 6, NO. 60 (JULY 1951), PP. 265-270. BO 34,
CR 783, FR VII 5189, 5739.

CAILLET, GÉRARD. SARTRE CONTRE CAMUS. FRANCE-ILLUSTRATION,   1357
VOL. 8, NO. 362 (SEPT. 20, 1952), P. 280. BO 272, CR 813,
FR VII 9300.

CAIN, ALEX MATHESON. STORMS OF THE SOUL. TABLET, VOL. 217,   1358
NO. 6441 (NOV. 2, 1963), P. 1181. FR VII 33941.

CALENDOLI, GIOVANNI. LA TRAGEDIA DELL'INTELLIGENZA NEL   1359
CALIGOLA DI CAMUS. FIERA LETTERARIA, VOL. 16, NO. 14
(OCT. 11, 1959), P. 6. FR VII 21371.

CANTONI, REMO. L'UOMO ASSURDO DI ALBERT CAMUS. STUDI   1360
FILOSOFICI, VOL. 9, NO. 1 (JAN.-APRIL 1948), PP. 72-87.
BO 195, FR VII 5740.

CANTONI, R. LA COSCIENZA INQUIETA. MILAN. MONDADORI, 1949.   1361
L'UOMO ASSURDO DI ALBERT CAMUS , PP. 401-415. FR VII 5740.

CAPPE, JEANNE. CAMUS ET LE DÉSERT DU PESSIMISME 'LA CHUTE'.   1362
REVUE GÉNÉRALE BELGE, VOL. 92, (JULY 15, 1956), PP.
1589-1591. KL II 390.

CARACCIOLO, PETER L. LETTERS. M. CAMUS AND ALGERIA. ENCOUNTER   1363
(LONDON), VOL. 8, NO. 6, ISSUE NO. 45 (JUNE 1957), P. 68.
CR 1004.

CARAT, JACQUES. LA RUPTURE CAMUS-SARTRE. PREUVES, VOL. 4, NO.   1364
20 (OCT. 1952), PP. 53-56. FITCH.

CARAT, JACQUES. LE THÉÂTRE. UN CAS INTÉRESSANT DE DINO   1365
BUZZATI. PREUVES, NO. 51 (MAY 1955), PP. 73-74. CR 914.

CARAT, JACQUES. CAMUS EN ÉTAT DE SIÈGE. PREUVES, NO. 82 (DEC.   1366
1957), PP. 59-62. BR, BUL SIGN 14-2180, CR 1005, FR VII
17297, KL I 271.

CARAZZOLO, MARIA. L'ETICA DI ALBERT CAMUS. HUMANITAS   1367
(BRESCIA), VOL. 5, NO. 12 (DEC. 1950), PP. 1198-1203. BO
123, FR VII 9301.

CARAZZOLO, MARIA. LA CRISE DE LA PENSÉE DE CAMUS DANS LA CHUTE.   1368
COMPRENDRE, NOS. 17-18 (1957), PP. 216-220. KL II 390.
BELLEME, LAURENCE.

1369   CARILE, PAOLO. A PROPOSITO DI UNA RECENSIONE SPAGNOLA ALLA
       CHRONIQUE ALGÉRIENNE DI ALBERT CAMUS. CONVIVIUM, VOL. 30,
       NO. 6 (NOV.-DEC. 1962), PP. 729-730. FR VII 33945.

1370   CARLINI, ARMANDO. UOMINI E PROBLEMI. PISA. GIARDINI, 1960.
       A. CAMUS, DALL ASSURDO ALLA VITTORIA , PP. 29-35. PMLA
       8779 (1962).

1371   CARLSON, ERIC W. THOMAS HANNA: THE THOUGHT AND ART OF ALBERT
       CAMUS. ROMANIC REVIEW, VOL. 49, NO. 3 (OCT. 1958),PP.
       236-237. FR VII 19412, KL I 272.

1372   CARLSON, ERIC W. THE HUMANISM OF ALBERT CAMUS, PLUS A REVIEW OF
       FIVE CRITQUES OF CAMUS. HUMANIST (OHIO),   VOL. 20, NO. 5
       (SEPT.-OCT. 1960), PP. 298-315. BUL SIGN 15-13771, PMLA
       7355 (1961).

1373   CARMEL, J. HIRHURIM IM KERIAT HAMAHAZEH TAUTH LE-ALBERT CAMUS
       (REFLECTIONS ABOUT ALBERT CAMUS' PLAY LE MALENTENDU). AL
       HAMISHMAR, APRIL 24, 1959, PP. 5-6.

1374   CARON, ALEXIS ADELBERT. THE TREATMENT AND EVOLUTION OF THE
       JEUNE FILLE AS A DRAMATIC CHARACTER IN THE CONTEMPORARY
       FRENCH DRAMA (1918-1953) AS PORTRAYED BY REPRESENTATIVE
       FRENCH PLAYWRIGHTS. UNIVERSITY OF MINNESOTA (PH. D.),
       1958. DISSERTATION ABSTRACTS, VOL. 19, NO. 6 (DEC. 1958),
       P. 1378.

1375   CARPEAUX, OTTO MARIA. PRESENÇAS. RIO DE JANEIRO. MINISTÉRIO
       DA EDICAÇÃO E CULTURA, INSTITUTO NACIONAL DO LIVRO, 1958.
       A QUEDA DE CAMUS , PP. 45-49.

1376   CARR, MAURICE. ALBERT CAMUS. AN APPRAISAL. JERUSALEM POST,
       (NOV. 8, 1957). P. 5. BR, CR 1005 BIS.

1377   CARRION O., ENRIQUE. CAMUS. PREMIO NOBEL DE LITERATURA.
       MERCURIO PERUANO, 33RD YEAR, VOL. 39, NO. 372 (APRIL
       1958), PP. 153-157. FR VII 19413, KL II 386.

1378   CARROUGES, MICHEL. PHILOSOPHIE DE 'LA PESTE'. VIE
       INTELLECTUELLE, VOL. 15, NO. 7 (JULY 1947), PP. 136-141.
       BO 388, BR, CR 590, FR VII 5741.

1379   CARRUTH, HAYDEN. THE DRY HEART OF MODESTY. VIRGINIA QUARTERLY
       REVIEW, VOL. 39, NO. 4 (AUTUMN 1963), PP. 670-673.

1380   CARSANIGA, G. ALBERT CAMUS O IL MITO DI PROMETEO.
       PROTESTANTESIMO, VOL. 15, NO. 3 (1960), PP. 152-160. BUL
       SIGN 16-19-9742.

1381   CARTER, SYDNEY. ONZE CORRESPONDENT MELDT. ALBERT CAMUS.
       L'EXIL ET LE ROYAUME . LITTERAIR PASPOORT, VOL. 12, NO.
       105 (APRIL 1957), P. 90. CR 1006.

1382   CASNATI, F. UN PASCAL SENZA CRISTO. HUMANITAS, VOL. 15, NO. 1
       (JAN. 1960), PP. 63-64. FR VII 23601, KL II 388.

1383   CASSA SALVI, ELVIRA. L'HOMME RÉVOLTÉ DI ALBERT CAMUS.
       HUMANITAS, VOL. 7, NO. 7 (JULY 1952), PP. 737-746. BO

503, FR VII 7714.

CASSA SALVI, ELVIRA. LA CADUTA ORIGINALE DI ALBERT CAMUS.   1384
    HUMANITAS, VOL. 12, NO. 5 (MAY 1957), PP. 378-387. FR VII
    17298, KL I 273.

CASSIAN, N. SCRISOARE DESCHISĂ LUI CAMUS. STIMATE DOMNULE   1385
    CAMUS. VIATA ROMANEASCĂ, VOL. 11, NO. 5 (MAY 1959), PP.
    7-10. KL II 393.

CASSOT, MARC. DES PERSONNALITÉS DU THÉÂTRE... (HOMMAGES À   1386
    CAMUS). FIGARO, VOL. 134, NO. 4770 (JAN. 6, 1960), P. 4.
    FITCH.

CASTELLI, FERDINANDO. E UNA COSA BUFFA LA VITA! DINO BUZZATI.   1387
    CIVILTÀ CATTOLICA, 112TH YEAR, VOL. 1, NO. 2656 (FEB. 18,
    1961), PP. 391-404. BUL SIGN 16-19-9732.

CASTELLO, G. C. I GIUSTI DI ALBERT CAMUS. SIPARIO, VOL. 5,   1388
    NO. 49 (MAY 1950), PP. 27-28. BO 460, FR VII 5742.

CASTEX,PIERRE-GEORGES. CAMUS ET VIGNY. INFORMATION LITTÉRAIRE,   1389
    VOL. 17, NO. 4 (SEPT.-OCT., 1965), PP. 145-151.

CASTEX, PIERRE-GEORGES. ALBERT CAMUS ET 'L'ÉTRANGER'. PARIS.   1390
    JOSÉ CORTI, 1965. P. 127.

CASTEX, PIERRE-GEORGES. LES CONTRADICTIONS D'ALBERT CAMUS.   1391
    FRANÇAIS DANS LE MONDE, VOL. 5, NO. 43 (SEPT. 1966), PP.
    6-10.

CATESSON, JEAN. À PROPOS DU 'MALENTENDU'. CAHIERS DU SUD,   1392
    VOL. 32, NO. 271 (1945), PP. 343-347. BO 334, CR 514, FR
    VII 746.

CATESSON, JEAN. À PROPOS DE 'LA PESTE'. CAHIERS DU SUD,   35TH   1393
    YEAR, VOL. 27, NO. 287 (SEMESTER 1, 1948), PP. 144-149. BO
    408, CR 648.

CAYROL, JEAN. UNE OEUVRE EN DÉBAT DEVANT LA NOUVELLE   1394
    GÉNÉRATION. JE PRENDS LE RÊVE POUR LA RÉALITÉ. FIGARO
    LITTÉRAIRE, VOL. 12, NO. 601 (OCT. 26, 1957), P. 7.
    FITCH. SEE NO. 3251.

CAYROL, JEAN. DES ÉCRIVAINS NOUS DISENT. (HOMMAGES À CAMUS).   1395
    FIGARO, VOL. 134, NO. 4770 (JAN. 6, 1960), P. 4. FR VII
    23649.

CELA, CAMILO JOSÉ. ESCRITO EN LA MUERTE DE ALBERT CAMUS Y LA   1396
    LUZ DE SU ANTORCHA. PAPELES DE SON ARMADANS, VOL. 16, NO.
    46 (JAN. 1960), PP. 3-6.

CELA, CAMILO JOSÉ. ÉCRIT SUR LA MORT D'ALBERT CAMUS ET À LA   1397
    LUMIÈRE DE SON FLAMBEAU. NOUVELLE REVUE FRANÇAISE, VOL.
    8, NO. 87 (MARCH 1960), PP. 556-558. FR VII 23575.
    TRANSLATION OF NO. 1396. REILLE, J.-F.

CÉZAN, CLAUDE. AVANT 'REQUIEM POUR UNE NONNE'. NOUVELLES   1398
    LITTÉRAIRES, NO. 1516 (SEPT. 20, 1956), P. 10.

CHACEL, ROSA. BREVE EXÉGESIS DE 'LA PESTE'. SUR, VOL. 16, NO.   1399

169 (NOV. 1948), PP. 65-82.   BO 409, CR 649, FR VII 4412.

1400   CHAIGNE, LOUIS. VIES ET OEUVRES D'ÉCRIVAINS, II.   PARIS.
       ÉDITIONS LANORE, 1957. BR, FR VII 18813, KL I 272.

1401   CHAMPIGNY, ROBERT. EXISTENTIALISM IN THE MODERN FRENCH NOVEL.
       THOUGHT,   VOL. 31, NO. 122 (FALL 1956), PP. 365-384.   FR
       VII 14814, KL I 231, KL I 274.

1402   CHAMPIGNY, ROBERT. CAMUS' FICTIONAL WORKS: THE PLIGHT OF
       INNOCENCE.   AMERICAN SOCIETY LEGION OF HONOR MAGAZINE,
       VOL. 28, NO. 2 (SUMMER 1957), PP. 173-182.   FR VII 17299,
       KL I 272.

1403   CHAMPIGNY, ROBERT. SUR UN HÉROS PAÏEN.   PARIS.   GALLIMARD,
       1959.   CR 450, FR VII 21362, KL II 390.

1404   CHAMPIGNY, ROBERT. THE COMEDY OF ETHICS.   YALE FRENCH STUDIES,
       NO. 25 (SPRING 1960), PP. 72-74.   FR VII 23568, KL II 388.

1405   CHAMPIGNY, ROBERT. ETHICS AND AESTHETICS IN THE STRANGER.   IN
       BRÉE, GERMAINE, CAMUS, A COLLECTION OF CRITICAL ESSAYS,
       PP. 122-131. FR VII 29338. SEE NO. 1293.

1406   CHAMPIGNY, ROBERT. LE GENRE ROMANESQUE.   MONTE-CARLO.   REGAIN,
       1963.   MULTIPLE REFERENCES.   FR VII 31673.

1407   CHAMPROMIS, PIERRE. DE LA RÉVOLTE À LA FRATERNITÉ. ALBERT
       CAMUS.   GAVROCHE,   NO. 15 (DEC. 7, 1944).   BO 212, CR 499,
       FR VII 2697.

1408   CHAPELAN, MAURICE. MAURICE CHAPELAN A AIMÉ...LES CARNETS
       D'ALBERT CAMUS. FIGARO LITTÉRAIRE, VOL. 19, NO. 976 (DEC.
       31, 1964 -JAN. 6, 1965), P. 5.

1409   CHAR, RENÉ. JE VEUX PARLER D'UN AMI. FIGARO LITTÉRAIRE, VOL.
       12, NO. 601 (OCT. 26, 1957), P. 5.   BR, CR 1007, FR VII
       17300.

1410   CHAR, RENÉ. L'ÉTERNITÉ À LOURMARIN.   TÉMOINS,   VOL. 8, NO. 23
       (MAY 1960), P. 3.

1411   CHAR, RENÉ. L'ÉTERNITÉ À LOURMARIN. (POEM).   REVUE D'HISTOIRE
       DU THÉÂTRE,   VOL. 12, NO. 4 (OCT.-DEC. 1960), PP. 319-320.
       FR VII 23570.

1412   CHARLENT, J.-M. UN NOUVEL AGE D'OR.   KOESTLER, CAMUS, MALRAUX.
       CHANTIERS,   VOL. 16, NO. 2 (DEC. 1951), PP. 15-19.   CR 784.

1413   CHARLTON, D. G. ALBERT CAMUS AND THE LITERATURE OF REVOLT, BY
       JOHN CRUICKSHANK.   CRITICAL QUARTERLY,   VOL. 1, NO. 4
       (WINTER 1959), PP. 358-359.   FR VII 33999.

1414   CHARNEY, HANNA. LE HÉROS ANONYME.   DE MONSIEUR TESTE AUX
       MANDARINS . ROMANIC REVIEW, VOL. 50, NO. 4 (DEC. 1959),
       PP. 268-275. CR 1132, FR VII 20741.

1415   CHARNEY, HANNA. INTERPRETATIONEN DRAMATISCHER DICHTUNGEN, I,
       ALBERT CAMUS, 'LES JUSTES' JEAN-PAUL SARTRE, 'LES
       SÉQUESTRÉS D'ALTONA'. VON HEINRICH LAUSBERG. ROMANTIC
       REVIEW,   VOL. 56, NO. 4 (DEC. 1965), P. 315.

CHARPIER, J. ENTRETIEN SUR CAMUS ENTRE L. BERTHE, J. CHARPIER,   1416
    O. DE MAGNY. LETTRES NOUVELLES, VOL. 4, NO. 2 (1956), PP.
    357-363. KL I 271.

CHARTRAND, G.-A. DE L'ABSURDE À LA DÉCOUVERTE DE LA CHARITÉ.   1417
    BULLETIN DE L'ASSOCIATION DES BIBLIOTHECAIRES DE LA LANGUE
    FRANÇAISE, VOL. 6, NO. 1 (1960), PP. 4-9. KL II 388.

CHAUVEAU, P. CALIGULA. NOUVELLES LITTÉRAIRES, VOL. 24, NO.   1418
    948 (1945), P. 8. BO 345, CR 515.

CHAVARDES, MAURICE. LES ÉCRIVAINS RÉVOLTÉS. CONSTRUIRE, VOL.   1419
    8, NO. 11 (NOV. 1953), PP. 578-584. CR 850.

CHAVARDES, MAURICE. LE PURGATOIRE D'ALBERT CAMUS. SIGNES DU   1420
    TEMPS, N.S. NO. 17 (FEB. 1965), PP. 23-24.

CHERKI, M. POLÉMIQUE OU HAINE. NEF, VOL. 14, NO. 12 (DEC.   1421
    1957), P. 96. CR 1008.

CHEVALIER, JACQUES. UNE AURORE SE LÈVE. C'EST-A-DIRE. NO. 28   1422
    (MARCH-APRIL 1960), PP. 51-52.

CHIAROMONTE, NICOLA. ALBERT CAMUS. NEW REPUBLIC, VOL. 114,   1423
    NO. 17 (APRIL 29, 1946), PP. 630-633. BO 7, FR VII 21373.

CHIAROMONTE, NICOLA. ALBERT CAMUS AND MODERATION. PARTISAN   1424
    REVIEW, VOL. 15, NO. 10 (OCT. 1948), PP. 1142-1145. BO
    93, BR, CR 650, FR VII 2698.

CHIAROMONTE, NICOLA. PARIS LETTER. PARTISAN REVIEW, VOL. 17,   1425
    NO. 7 (SEPT.-OCT. 1950), PP. 710-714. CR 747.

CHIAROMONTE, NICOLA. IL MILITANTE ALBERT CAMUS. MONDO, VOL.   1426
    2, NO. 45 (NOV. 11, 1950), PP. 5-6. FR VII 17301.

CHIAROMONTE, NICOLA. SARTRE VERSUS CAMUS: A POLITICAL QUARREL.   1427
    PARTISAN REVIEW, VOL. 19, NO. 6 (NOV.-DEC. 1952), PP.
    680-686. BO 273, CR 814, FR VII 7700.

CHIAROMONTE, NICOLA. SARTRE VERSUS CAMUS: A POLITICAL QUAR-   1428
    REL. IN BRÉE, GERMAINE, CAMUS, A COLLECTION OF CRITICAL
    ESSAYS, PP. 31-37. SEE NO. 1293. REPRINT OF NO. 1427.

CHIAROMONTE, NICOLA. CAMUS E LA RIVOLTA DELL INDIVIDUO. TEMPO   1429
    PRESENTE, VOL. 1, NO. 4 (JULY 1956), PP. 317-319. BR, CR
    932 BIS, FR VII 21376.

CHIAROMONTE, NICOLA. CAMUS E FAULKNER. MONDO, VOL. 9, NO. 2   1430
    (JAN. 8, 1957), P. 14. FR VII 26319.

CHIAROMONTE, NICOLA. ALBERT CAMUS E LA COSCIENZA GELOSA.   1431
    MONDO, VOL. 9, NO. 44 (OCT. 29, 1957), P. 9. BR, CR 1008
    BIS.

CHIAROMONTE, NICOLA. CAMUS E LA POLITICA. TEMPO PRESENTE,   1432
    VOL. 2, NO. 11 (NOV. 1957), PP. 889-891. FR VII 21375.

CHIAROMONTE, NICOLA. CAMUS E L'ALGERIA. TEMPO PRESENTE, VOL.   1433
    3, NO. 7 (JULY 1958), PP. 597-598. FR VII 21374.

CHIAROMONTE, NICOLA. CAMUS E STAVROGHIN. MONDO, VOL. 11, NO.   1434
    8 (FEB. 24, 1959), P. 15. FR VII 26320.

1435   CHIAROMONTE, NICOLA. ALBERT CAMUS. MERKUR, VOL. 14, NO. 3
          (MARCH 1960), PP. 296-300. BDZ 120-311 (1960), KL II 395.
1436   CHIAROMONTE, NICOLA. ALBERT CAMUS. TEMPO PRESENTE, VOL. 5,
          NO. 1 (JAN. 1960), PP. 1-4. FR VII 26317, PMLA 6818
          (1961).
1437   CHIAROMONTE, NICOLA. LA RÉSISTANCE À L'HISTOIRE. PREUVES, NO.
          110 (APRIL 1960), PP. 17-20. FR VII 23602, KL II 387, PMLA
          7356 (1962).
1438   CHIAROMONTE, NICOLA. ALBERT CAMUS. IN MEMORIAM. DISSENT,
          VOL. 7, NO. 3 (SUMMER 1960), PP. 266-270. FR VII 29338.
1439   CHIAROMONTE, NICOLA. ALBERT CAMUS. IN MEMORIAM. IN BRÉE,
          GERMAINE, CAMUS, A COLLECTION OF CRITICAL ESSAYS, PP.
          11-15. FR VII 29338. SEE NO. 1293. REPRINT OF NO. 1438.
1440   CHIAROMONTE, NICOLA. CAMUS DRAMATURGE. MONDO, VOL. 17, NO. 11
          (MARCH 16, 1965), PP. 15-16.
1441   CHISHOLM, A. R. WAS CAMUS A PLAGIARIST? MEANJIN, VOL. 9, NO.
          2 (WINTER 1950), PP. 131-133. BO 256, FR VII 5743.
1442   CHONEZ, CLAUDINE. PORTRAIT D'ALBERT CAMUS. PARU, NO. 47 (OCT.
          1948), PP. 7-13. BO 19, BR, CR 651, FR VII 2699.
1443   CHONEZ, CLAUDINE. EIN INTERVIEW MIT ALBERT CAMUS, PARIS 1950.
          EUROPAS GEHEIMNIS: ES LIEBT DAS LEBEN NICHT. HAMBURG.
          INTERNAT. COPYRIGHT AGENTUR. BO 28.
1444   CHRAÏBI, DRISS. SUR CAMUS. PARISIENNE, NO. 48 (NOV.-DEC.
          1957), PP. 1069-1072. CR 1047 TER, KL I 272.
1445   CHRAÏBI, DRISS. CAMUS UND ALGERIEN. DOKUMENTE, VOL. 15, NO. 1
          (1959), PP. 70-74. BDZ 118-290 (1959), CR 1133, FR VII
          21377, KL II 392.
1446   CHRIST, E. DIE PEST. WELTSTIMMEN (STUTTGART), VOL. 18, NO. 8
          (1949), PP. 8-13. BDZ 99-167 (1949), BO 430, CR 689.
1447   CHRISTENSEN, NAOMI. 'L'ETRANGER': THE UNHEROIC HERO. COLLEGE
          ENGLISH, VOL. 24, NO. 3 (DEC. 1962), PP. 235-236.
1448   CHRISTINI, GIOVANNI. CAMUS E IL 'BIGLIETTO D'INGRESSO'.
          HUMANITAS, NUOVA SERIE VOL. 15, NO. 1 (JAN. 1960), PP.
          64-67. KL II 393.
1449   CHRISTOFIDES, C. G. FOUR RECENT CAMUS STUDIES. SYMPOSIUM,
          VOL. 14, NO. 1 (SPRING 1960), PP. 60-64. FR VII 23603, KL
          386.
1450   CHRISTOPHE, LUCIEN. (NOTICE). REVUE GÉNÉRALE BELGE, VOL. 93
          (NOV. 1957), PP. 23-24. KL I 272.
1451   CHRISTOPHE, LUCIEN. LE COMBAT D'ALBERT CAMUS. REVUE GÉNÉRALE
          BELGE, VOL. 96, NO. 1 (JAN. 1960), PP. 132-139. FR VII
          26321, KL II 387, PMLA 6819 (1961).
1452   CINTIOLI, GIUSEPPE. LA GHIGLIOTTINA DE CAMUS. MONDO, VOL. 10,
          NO. 36 (SEPT. 9, 1958), P. 8. FR VII 26322.
1453   CLANCY, JAMES H. BEYOND DESPAIR. A NEW DRAMA OF IDEAS.

EDUCATIONAL THEATRE JOURNAL,   VOL. 13, NO. 3 (OCT. 1961),
PP. 157-166.

CLAPS, MANUEL ARTURO. ALBERT CAMUS Y LA REBELIÓN. NUMERO,   VOL.   1454
4, NO. 21 (OCT.-DEC. 1952), PP. 379-382. FR VII 34000.

CLAVEL, MAURICE. SUR CAMUS. PARISIENNE,   NO. 48 (NOV.-DEC.   1455
1957), P. 1072. CR 1047 TER.

CLAVEL, MAURICE. UNE RENCONTRE DANS LA RÉSISTANCE. FIGARO   1456
LITTÉRAIRE,   VOL. 15, NO. 716 (JAN. 9, 1960), P. 7. FR VII
26323, KL II 386.

CLAVEL, MAURICE. LE MEILLEUR DES NOTRES. COMBAT,   (MAY 1,   1457
1960).

CLAYTON, ALAN J. NOTE SUR CAMUS ET SUÉTONE. LA SOURCE ANCIENNE   1458
DE DEUX PASSAGES DES 'CARNETS'. FRENCH STUDIES,   VOL. 20,
NO. 2 (APRIL 1966), PP. 164-168.

CLÉBERT, JEAN-PAUL. LA MORT DE CAMUS. ARC, VOL. 3, NO. 10   1459
(APRIL 1960), PP. 91-92. KL II 393.

CLÉMENT, A. RÉVOLTE ET VALEUR. POESIE 44,   VOL. 5, NO. 21   1460
(1944), PP. 107-113. BO 231, CR 500.

CLERGERIE, B. LE MAL ET LA NOSTALGIE DE L'ÊTRE CHEZ CAMUS.   1461
REVUE DU CAIRE,   VOL. 44, NO. 237 (MAY 1960), PP. 375-392.
FR VII 23604. SEE NO. 3259.

CLOT, RENÉ-JEAN. CAMUS. SIMOUN,   VOL. 8, NO. 31 (JULY 1960),   1462
PP. 29-33. FR VII 23573, KL II 395.

CLOUGH, WILSON O. CAMUS 'THE PLAGUE'. COLORADO QUARTERLY,   1463
VOL. 7, NO. 4 (SPRING 1959), PP. 389-404. FR VII 21379, KL
II 391.

CLOUTIER, CÉCILE. CAMUS ROMANCIER. HUMANITIES ASSOCIATION OF   1464
CANADA BULLETIN,   NO. 31 (NOV. 1960), PP. 11-12. FR VII
26324.

CLURMAN, HAROLD. PLAYS FROM PARIS. 'CALIGULA', 'CROSS PURPOSE'.   1465
NEW REPUBLIC,   VOL. 119, NO. 7 (AUG. 16, 1948), PP.
25-26. BO 364.

CLURMAN, HAROLD. LIES LIKE TRUTH. NEW YORK. MACMILLAN, 1958.   1466

CLURMAN, HAROLD. THE MORALIST ON STAGE, 'CALIGULA AND THREE   1467
OTHER PLAYS' BY ALBERT CAMUS. NEW YORK TIMES BOOK REVIEW,
SEPT. 14, 1958, P. 12.

CLURMAN, HAROLD. ALBERT CAMUS. NATION,   VOL. 190, NO. 3 (JAN.   1468
16, 1960), P. 43.

CLURMAN, HAROLD. THEATRE (CALIGULA). NATION,   VOL. 190, NO. 10   1469
(MARCH 5, 1960), P. 213-214.

CLURMAN, HAROLD. THE SUBSTANCE OF SPIRIT. NATION,   VOL. 201,   1470
NO. 14 (NOV. 1, 1965), PP. 310-311.

COCKING, J. M. THE IDEA OF PROMETHEAN REVOLT. LISTENER,   VOL.   1471
48, NO. 1219 (JULY 10, 1952), PP. 63-64. FR VII 34001.

COCKING, J. M. 'CAMUS' BY GERMAINE BRÉE (REVIEW). MODERN   1472

LANGUAGE REVIEW, VOL. 57, NO. 2 (APRIL 1962), PP. 265-267.

1473   COGNIAT, RAYMOND. RÉOUVERTURES. 'CALIGULA' D'ALBERT CAMUS.
        ARTS, NO. 35 (SEPT. 28, 1945), P. 4. CR 516.

1474   COHN, ROBERT GREER. SARTRE-CAMUS RESARTUS. YALE FRENCH
        STUDIES, NO. 30 (FALL-WINTER 1962-1963), PP. 73-77. FR
        VII 36776.

1475   COHN, ROBERT GREER. FROM CHRÉTIEN TO CAMUS: PLUMES AND PRISONS.
        MODERN LANGUAGE NOTES, VOL. 80, NO. 5 (DEC. 1965), PP.
        601-609.

1476   COHN, RUBY. THE ABSURDLY ABSURD. AVATARS OF GODOT. COMPARATIVE
        LITERATURE STUDIES, VOL. 2, NO. 3 (1965), PP. 233-240
        (CAMUS REF. PP. 233-234).

1477   COLIN, PIERRE. ATHÉISME ET RÉVOLTE CHEZ CAMUS. VIE
        INTELLECTUELLE, VOL. 24, NO. 7 (JULY 1952), PP. 30-51. BO
        112, BUL SIGN 8-221, CR 815.

1478   COLLIN, CLAUDE. À PROPOS D'ALBERT CAMUS. RÉFORME, VOL. 1, NO.
        13 (JUNE 16, 1945), P. 7. BO 6, CR 517, FR VII 2700.

1479   COLOMBO, ACHILLE. ALBERT CAMUS NELLA SUA OPERA TEATRALE.
        LETTURE, VOL. 13 NO. 1 (JAN. 1958), PP. 49-54. FR VII
        21380.

1480   COMFORT, ALEX. CAMUS AND THE PROBLEM OF REVOLT. WORLD REVIEW,
        NEW SERIES NO. 9 (NOV. 1949), PP. 35-37. FR VII 34002.

1481   CONDON, ST. D. CAMUS' STYLE IN FICTION AND ESSAY. YALE, 1958.
        (THESIS). KL I 272.

1482   CONILH, JEAN. ALBERT CAMUS, L'EXIL SANS ROYAUME (I). LE PAYSAGE
        DE L'ABSURDE. ESPRIT, VOL. 26, NO. 4 (260) (APRIL 1958),
        PP. 529-543. BFZ 44-283, BR, CR 1091, FR VII 19414.

1483   CONILH, JEAN. ALBERT CAMUS, L'EXIL SANS ROYAUME (II). À LA
        POURSUITE DU ROYAUME. ESPRIT, VOL. 26, NO. 5 (261) (MAY
        1958), PP.673-692. BFZ 44-283, BR, CR 1092.

1484   CONNOLLY, CYRIL. INTRODUCTION TO 'THE OUTSIDER'. SEE NO. 292.

1485   CONNOLLY, CYRIL. INTRODUCTION TO 'THE OUTSIDER'. IN MAJORITY
        1931-1952, LONDON. HAMISH HAMILTON, 1952. PP. 809-812.
        PP. 673-692. FR VII 31512.

1486   CONNOLLY, CYRIL. IDEAS AND PLACES. LONDON. WEIDENFELD AND
        NICOLSON, 1953. SCATTERED REFERENCES. FR VII 31501.

1487   COPLESTON, FREDERICK C. EXISTENTIALISM AND RELIGION. DUBLIN
        REVIEW, VOL. 220, NO. 440 (SPRING 1947), PP. 50-63. BO
        165, BR, CR 589 BIS, FR VII 2120.

1488   COPLESTON, F. C. EXISTENTIALISM AND MODERN MAN. (A PAPER READ
        TO THE AQUINAS SOCIETY OF LONDON ON THE 14TH APRIL 1948).
        LONDON. BLACKFRIARS PUBLICATIONS, 1953. BO 175, FR VII
        10651.

1489   COPLESTON, F. C. CONTEMPORARY PHILOSOPHY, STUDIES IN LOGICAL
        POSITIVISM AND EXISTENTIALISM. LONDON-WESTMINSTER. BURNS

AND OATES, 1956. KL I 231.

CORMEAU, NELLY. REVUE DES LIVRES. ALBERT CAMUS: 'LA PESTE'.   1490
    SYNTHÈSES, VOL. 2, NO. 6 (1947), PP. 367-372. CR 591.

CORMEAU, NELLY. ROMANCIERS-MORALISTES. SYNTHÈSES, VOL. 6, NO.   1491
    63 (1951), PP. 419-427. BUL SIGN 6-7601.

CORMEAU, NELLY. L'ÉTHIQUE D'ALBERT CAMUS. SYNTHÈSES, VOL. 14,   1492
    NOS. 160-162 (SEPT.-NOV. 1959), PP. 325-351. CR 1134, KL
    II 387.

CORTE, ANTONIO. ALBERT CAMUS: 'CARNETS'. PONTE, VOL. 18, NO.   1493
    11 (NOV. 1962), P. 1557. FR VII 29361.

COSMAN, MAX. ALBERT CAMUS: 'THE FALL'. NEW MEXICO QUARTERLY,   1494
    VOL. 27, NOS. 1-2 (1957), PP. 129-131. FR VII 19415, KL II
    390.

COSTA, JOHN. 'LA PESTE' D'ALBERT CAMUS DANS L'ESPRIT   1495
    CATHOLIQUE. REVUE DE L'UNIVERSITÉ LAVAL, VOL. 19, NO. 5
    (JAN. 1965), PP. 459-468.

COTÉ, NICOLAS-M. ALBERT CAMUS ET L'EXISTENCE DE DIEU. CULTURE,   1496
    VOL. 20, NO. 3 (SEPT. 1959), PP. 268-281. FR VII 21381, KL
    II 388.

COUCH, JOHN PHILIP. ALBERT CAMUS' DRAMATIC ADAPTATIONS AND   1497
    TRANSLATIONS. FRENCH REVIEW, VOL. 33, NO. 1 (OCT. 1959),
    PP. 27-36. BUL SIGN 15-19-8647, FR VII 21382, KL II 389.

COUCH, JOHN PHILIP. CAMUS AND FAULKNER. THE SEARCH FOR THE   1498
    LANGUAGE OF MODERN TRAGEDY. YALE FRENCH STUDIES, NO. 25
    (SPRING 1960), PP. 120-125. BUL SIGN 16-19-10098, FR VII
    23568, KL II 392.

COX, HARVEY. THE SECULAR CITY. NEW YORK. MACMILLAN COMPANY,   1499
    1965. ALBERT CAMUS AND PROFANITY, PP. 70-78.

CRANSTON, MAURICE. 'THE REBEL' BY ALBERT CAMUS, 'SARTRE' BY   1500
    IRIS MURDOCH. LONDON MAGAZINE, VOL. 1, NO. 1 (FEB. 1954),
    P. 99-100, 102.

CRANSTON, MAURICE. CORRESPONDENCE. LONDON MAGAZINE, VOL. 1,   1501
    NO. 3 (APRIL 1954), P. 73. SEE NO. 3403, 1500.

CRANSTON, MAURICE. THE MYTH OF SISYPHUS. MANCHESTER GUARDIAN,   1502
    NO. 34,032 (NOV. 25, 1955), P. 14. BO 325.

CRANSTON, MAURICE. SARTRE. NEW YORK. BARNES AND NOBLE, 1966.   1503
    SCATTERED REFERENCES.

CRANSTON, MAURICE. ALBERT CAMUS. ENCOUNTER, VOL. 28, NO. 2   1504
    (FEB. 1967), PP. 43-55.

CRASTRE, VICTOR. CHRONIQUES. LES ESSAIS. ACTUELLES II, PAR   1505
    ALBERT CAMUS. CAHIERS DU SUD, 40TH YEAR, VOL. 38, NO. 322
    (MARCH 1954), PP. 502-503.

CREMIEUX, FRANCIS. LE THÉÂTRE. CALIGULA D'ALBERT CAMUS.   1506
    EUROPE, VOL. 24, NO. 1 (JAN. 1946), PP. 106-110. CR 561.

CRÉPIN, SIMONE. ALBERT CAMUS, ESSAI DE BIBLIOGRAPHIE. MÉMOIRE   1507

PRÉSENTÉ À L'ÉCOLE PROVINCIALE DES BIBLIOTHECAIRES DU
BRABANT, SESSION 1959. BRUSSELS. COMMISSION BELGE DE
BIBLIOGRAPHIE, 1960. FR VII 26292.

1508   CRISTINI, GIOVANNI. CAMUS E IL 'BIGLIETTO D'INGRESSO'.
HUMANITAS, VOL. 15, NO. 1 (JAN. 1960), PP. 64-67. FR VII
23605.

1509   CRITICUS. LE STYLE AU MICROSCOPE. (TOME II). SEE NO. 1087.

1510   CROO, H. DE. CAMUS. LETTRES, VOL. 55, NOS. 5-6 (FEB. 1956),
PP. 5-10. KL II 388.

1511   CROSS, LESLIE. THE CAMUS DIGGINGS ARE STILL RICH. MILWAUKEE
JOURNAL, VOL. 81 (JULY 28, 1963), PART V, P. 4.

1512   CROSSMAN, R. H. S. A FRUSTRATED INTELLECTUAL. THE REBEL. NEW
STATESMAN AND NATION, VOL. 47, NO. 1193 (JAN. 16, 1954),
PP. 72, 74. BO 521.

1513   CRUICKSHANK, JOHN. CAMUS AND LANGUAGE. LETTERATURE MODERNE,
VOL. 6, NO. 2 (MARCH-APRIL 1956), PP. 197-202. BFZ 40-252,
CR 933, FR VII 15340, KL I 272.

1514   CRUICKSHANK, JOHN. CAMUS'S TECHNIQUE IN 'L'ETRANGER'. FRENCH
STUDIES, VOL. 10, NO. 3 (JULY 1956), PP. 241-253. BFZ
40-252, CR 934, FR VII 17303, KL I 273.

1515   CRUICKSHANK, JOHN. LA TECHNIQUE DE CAMUS DANS 'L'ETRANGER'.
REVUE DES LETTRES MODERNES, VOL. 8, NOS. 64-66 (FALL
1961), PP. 387-406 (ALT. PP. 83-102). FR VII 26288.
TRANSLATION OF NO. 1514.

1516   CRUICKSHANK, JOHN. THE ART OF ALLEGORY IN 'LA PESTE'.
SYMPOSIUM, VOL. 11, NO. 1 (SPRING 1957), PP. 61-74. BUL
SIGN 14-2182, CR 1009, FR VII 17302, KL I 273.

1517   CRUICKSHANK, JOHN. EXISTENTIALISM AFTER 12 YEARS. AN
EVALUATION. DUBLIN REVIEW, VOL. 23, NO. 473 (SUMMER 1957),
PP. 52-65. KL I 231.

1518   CRUICKSHANK, JOHN. ALBERT CAMUS AND THE LITERATURE OF REVOLT.
LONDON. OXFORD UNIVERSITY PRESS, 1959. CR 451, FR VII
21363, KL II 386.

1519   CRUICKSHANK, JOHN. ALBERT CAMUS AND THE LITERATURE OF REVOLT.
NEW YORK. OXFORD UNIVERSITY PRESS, 1960. A TRIBUTE TO A.
CAMUS . FR VII 23574.

1520   CRUICKSHANK, JOHN. ALBERT CAMUS AND THE LITERATURE OF REVOLT.
LONDON. GALAXY BOOKS (NO. 43). OXFORD UNIVERSITY PRESS,
1960.

1521   CRUICKSHANK, JOHN. TRIBUTE TO ALBERT CAMUS. TWENTIETH CENTURY,
VOL. 167, NO. 998 (APRIL 1960), PP. 316-327. BFZ 46-284,
FR VII 23606, KL II 393.

1522   CRUICKSHANK, JOHN. LITERATURE CONSIDERED AS PHILOSOPHY. THE
LITERATURE OF POSSIBILITY. A STUDY IN HUMANISTIC
EXISTENTIALISM BY HAZEL E.BARNES. (REVIEW). CHICAGO

REVIEW, VOL. 14, NO. 2 (SUMMER 1960), PP. 114-122.

CRUICKSHANK, JOHN. SARTRE AND CAMUS. REVOLUTION AND REVOLT.   1523
NEW LEADER, VOL. 43, NO. 37 (SEPT. 26, 1960), PP. 14-15.

CRUICKSHANK, JOHN. ALBERT CAMUS. 'LA PESTE'. FRENCH STUDIES,   1524
VOL. 14, NO. 4 (OCT. 1960), PP. 376-377.

CRUICKSHANK, JOHN. ALBERT CAMUS. PARIS. LIBR. M. J. MINARD,   1525
1961. LA TECHNIQUE DE CAMUS DANS L'ETRANGER , PP. 5-191.
FR VII 26288.

CRUICKSHANK, JOHN. CAMUS: A RE-APPRAISAL. TIME AND TIDE,   1526
VOL. 42, NO. 8 (FEB. 24, 1961), PP. 280-281. BFZ 48-262
(1962).

CRUICKSHANK, JOHN, (EDITOR). THE NOVELIST AS PHILOSOPHER,   1527
STUDIES IN FRENCH FICTION, 1935-1960. LONDON. OXFORD
UNIVERSITY PRESS, 1962. 'ALBERT CAMUS' BY JOHN
CRUICKSHANK, PP. 206-229. FR VII 28199.

CUADRA, PABLO ANTONIO. ALBERTO CAMUS. EL MENSAJE DE UN   1528
REBELDE. ABSIDE, VOL. 24, NO. 1 (JAN.-MARCH 1960), PP.
100-103. FR VII 26325, PMLA 6820 (1961).

CURNIER, PIERRE. PAGES COMMENTÉES D'AUTEURS CONTEMPORAINS, I.   1529
PARIS. LAROUSSE, 1962. CAMUS, PP. 187-210, 277-279. FR
VII 32021.

CURTIS, ANTHONY. NEW DEVELOPMENTS IN THE FRENCH THEATRE, A   1530
CRITICAL INTRODUCTION TO THE PLAYS OF JEAN-PAUL SARTRE,
SIMONE DE BEAUVOIR, ALBERT CAMUS AND JEAN ANOUILH. LONDON.
CURTAIN PRESS, 1948. CHAPTER IV, PP. 19-32. BO 84, BR, CR
452, FR VII 2398.

CURTIS, ANTHONY. THREE FOREIGN DRAMATISTS. REVIEW. CALIGULA.   1531
CROSS PURPOSE. NEW STATESMAN AND NATION, VOL. 36, NO. 913
(SEPT. 4, 1948), P. 198. BO 365, FR VII 32736.

DABADIE, JEAN-LOUP. CAMUS ET LA JEUNESSE. FRANCE-OBSERVATEUR,   1532
VOL. 11, NO. 505 (JAN. 7, 1960), P. 20. FITCH.

DADOUN, ROGER. ALBERT CAMUS LE MÉDITERRANÉEN. LE RÊVE DE   1533
LUMIÈRE ET LE COMPLEXE DU CLOS-OBSCUR. SIMOUN, VOL. 1,
NO. 3 (JUNE 1952), PP. 42-47. BO 38, FR VII 26326, 7702.

DAIX, PIERRE. RÉFLEXIONS SUR LA MÉTHODE DE ROGER MARTIN DU GARD   1534
SUIVI DE LETTRE À MAURICE NADEAU ET AUTRES ESSAIS. PARIS.
FRANÇAIS RÉUNIS, 1957. ALBERT CAMUS, PRIX NOBEL, PP.
352-358. UN QUART DE VÉRITÉ SELON CAMUS, PP. 359-362. FR
VII 18816, KL I 272.

DAIX, PIERRE. ALBERT CAMUS PRIX NOBEL. LETTRES FRANÇAISES,   1535
NO. 693 (OCT. 24-30, 1957), PP. 1, 5. BR, CR 1010, FR VII
17304.

DAIX, PIERRE. UN QUART DE VÉRITÉ SELON CAMUS. NOUVELLE   1536
CRITIQUE, VOL. 9, NO. 91 (DEC. 1957), PP. 144-146. FR VII
17305, KL I 272.

1537   DAIX, PIERRE. CAMUS POUR NOUS. LETTRES FRANÇAISES, NO. 926
            (MAY 10-16, 1962), PP. 1, 5. FR VII 29362.

1538   DALLONTANO, E. R. CAMUS UND SARTRE. RHEINISCHER MERKUR, VOL.
            7, NO. 52 (1952), P. 3. BO 274.

1539   DAMIENS, CLAUDE. ALBERT CAMUS OU LE THÉÂTRE ABSURDE.
            PARIS-THEATRE, VOL. 12, NO. 147 (1959), PP. 2-4. FR VII
            21383.

1540   DAN, J. HANOKHREE VEHAMANDAREEN. CAMUS, SARTRE, DE BEAUVOIR
            (THE STRANGER AND THE MANDARIN. CAMUS, SARTRE, DE
            BEAUVOIR). MOLAD, NO. 16 (1958), PP. 61-68.

1541   DANIEL, JEAN. UN CAS INTÉRESSANT DE DINO BUZZATI, ADAPTATION
            D'ALBERT CAMUS... THÉÂTRE POPULAIRE, NO. 12 (MARCH-APRIL
            1955), PP. 92-93.

1542   DANIEL, JEAN. ALBERT CAMUS L'ALGÉRIEN. ACTION, (OCT. 21,
            1957). BR, CR 1010 BIS.

1543   DANIEL, JEAN. ALBERT CAMUS--WIE ER WAR UND WAS ER SEIN WIRD.
            KULTUR, VOL. 8, NO. 147 (1959-60), P. 3. BDZ 120-311
            (1960).

1544   DANIEL, JEAN. ALBERT CAMUS. PARLONS DE LUI... EXPRESS, NO.
            447 (JAN. 7, 1960), PP. 27-29. FITCH.

1545   DANIEL, JEAN. UNE PATRIE ALGÉRIENNE, DEUX PEUPLES... ÉTUDES
            MÉDITERRANÉENNES, NO. 7. (SPRING 1960), PP. 19-24. FITCH.

1546   DANIEL, JEAN. CAMUS OU LE MAL ENTENDU. FIGARO LITTÉRAIRE, NO.
            897 (JUNE 29, 1963), PP. 1, 7. FR VII 33946.

1547   DANIEL, JEAN. LE COMBAT POUR 'COMBAT'. IN ANONYMOUS, CAMUS,
            PP. 77-106. SEE NO. 940.

1548   DARD, FRÉDÉRIC. 'LES JUSTES' D'ALBERT CAMUS. CAHIERS DE LA
            PENSÉE NOUVELLE, NO. 2 (JAN. 28, 1950). BO 461, FR VII
            5744.

1549   DARZINS, JOHN. TRANSPARENCE IN CAMUS AND KAFKA. YALE FRENCH
            STUDIES, NO. 25 (SPRING 1960), PP. 98-103. BUL SIGN
            16-19-9746 (1962), FR VII 23568, KL II 392.

1550   DAVIES, ROBERTSON. WHAT ABOUT A SHOW OF COURAGE? SATURDAY
            NIGHT, VOL. 72, NO. 6 (3283) (MARCH 16, 1957), PP. 20-21.
            DEPTULA.

1551   DAVY, MARIE MADELEINE. CAMUS ET SIMONE WEIL. TABLE RONDE, NO.
            146 (FEB. 1960), PP. 137-143. BFZ 46-284, BUL SIGN
            15-19-13776.

1552   DAX, JEAN. ALBERT CAMUS, 'LA CHUTE'. STREVEN, KATHOLIEK
            CULTUREEL TIJDSCHRIFT, VOL. 10, NO. 7 (APRIL 1957), PP.
            668-669. CR 1011.

1553   DAX, JEAN. CAMUS EN DE MENS. STREVEN, KATHOLIEK CULTUREEL
            TIJDSCHRIFT, (1957-58). PP. 201-207. KL II 387.

1554   DEBÈCHE, DJAMILA. NOTRE FRÈRE ALBERT CAMUS. SIMOUN, VOL. 8,
            NO. 31 (JULY 1960), PP. 38-43. FR VII 23573, KL II 393.

DEBENEDETTI, GIACOMO. SAGGI CRITICI, TERZA SERIE. MILAN. IL   1555
    SAGGIATORE, 1959. L'AVVENTURA DELL'UOMO D'OCCIDENTE , PP.
    117-135. FR VII 22795, KL II 387.

D(EBIDOUR), V.-H. ALBERT CAMUS. -- L'ÉTAT DE SIÈGE. BULLETIN   1556
    DES LETTRES, VOL. 11, NO. 105 (FEB. 15, 1949), PP. 74-75.
    CR 690.

DEBIDOUR, V.-H. ALBERT CAMUS. -- ACTUELLES. BULLETIN DES   1557
    LETTRES, VOL. 12, NO. 122 (NOV. 15, 1950), P. 383. CR
    748.

DEBIDOUR, V.-H. L'HOMME RÉVOLTÉ PAR ALBERT CAMUS. BULLETIN DES   1558
    LETTRES, VOL. 14, NO. 135 (FEB. 15, 1952), PP. 56-59. CR
    816.

DEBIDOUR, V.-H. ALBERT CAMUS. -- ACTUELLES II. BULLETIN DES   1559
    LETTRES, VOL. 15, NO. 153 (DEC. 15, 1953), P. 450. CR
    848.

DEBRAY, PIERRE. TERREUR ET ESPÉRANCE. DIEU VIVANT, NO. 8   1560
    (1947), PP. 115-122. FR VII 16557.

DEBRAY, PIERRE. SUR LA MORT D'ALBERT CAMUS. ASPECTS DE LA   1561
    FRANCE, VOL. 13, NO. 591 (JAN. 7, 1960), P. 2. FITCH.

DEBRAY, PIERRE. ALBERT CAMUS, PIED NOIR. ASPECTS DE LA FRANCE,   1562
    (JAN. 12, 1961). FR VII 29365.

D(ÉCAUDIN), M(ICHEL). A TRAVERS LES LIVRES. PIERRE-GEORGES   1563
    CASTEX, ALBERT CAMUS ET 'L'ETRANGER'. INFORMATION
    LITTÉRAIRE, VOL. 18, NO.4 (SEPT.-OCT., 1966), P. 164.

DEDMON, EMMETT. THE PLAGUE. CHICAGO SUN BOOK WEEK, VOL. 1,   1564
    NO. 44 (AUG. 1, 1948), P. 8X. BO 410.

DELEDALLE, GÉRARD. L'EXISTENTIEL, PHILOSOPHIES ET LITTÉRATURES   1565
    DE L'EXISTENCE. PARIS. RENÉE LACOSTE, 1949. CF. PP.
    43-44. BO 167, CR 453, FR VII 4092.

DELFOSSE, JEAN. ALBERT CAMUS, ACTUELLES III, CHRONIQUE   1566
    ALGÉRIENNE 1939-1958. REVUE NOUVELLE, 14TH YEAR, VOL. 28,
    NO. 10 (OCT. 1958), PP. 358-359. CR 1093.

DELGADO, F. PENSAMIENTO Y ESTILO DE ALBERT CAMUS. RAZÓN Y FE,   1567
    VOL. 157, NO. 721 (FEB. 1958), PP. 151-172. FR VII 21384,
    19416, KL II 390.

DELGADO, F. PENSAMIENTO Y ESTILO DE ALBERT CAMUS, PART II.   1568
    RAZÓN Y FE, VOL. 157, NO. 725 (JUNE 1958), PP. 589-610.
    FR VII 21384, 19416, KL II 390.

DELIBES, MIGUEL. ALBERT CAMUS. NOUVELLE REVUE FRANÇAISE, VOL.   1569
    8, NO. 87 (MARCH 1960), P. 562. FR VII 23575, KL II 393.

DELMAS, C. CHRONIQUES DES ESSAIS. ALBERT CAMUS. ACTUELLES.   1570
    SYNTHÈSES, VOL. 6, NO. 63 (1951), PP. 430-440. BO 472,
    BUL SIGN 7-132.

DELPECH, JEANINE. 'NON, JE NE SUIS PAS EXISTENTIALISTE', NOUS   1571
    DIT ALBERT CAMUS. NOUVELLES LITTÉRAIRES, NO. 954 (NOV.

15, 1945), P. 1. BO 159, CR 518, FR VII 165.

1572   DEMISCH, H. DÄMONIE UND FREIHEIT. GEDANKEN ZU DEM SCHAUSPIEL
       BELAGERUNGSZUSTAND VON A. CAMUS. KOMMENDEN, VOL. 8, NO. 4
       (1954), PP. 5-6. BDZ 108-306, BO 455, CR 877.

1573   DEMOREST, J.-J. ON THE DEATH OF ALBERT CAMUS. AMERICAN SOCIETY
       LEGION OF HONOR MAGAZINE, VOL. 31, NO. 1 (1960), PP.
       11-14. FR VII 23608, KL II 393.

1574   DENNIS, WILLIAM D. MEURSAULT: CONSISTENT OR NONCONSISTENT.
       COLLEGE LANGUAGE ASSOCIATION JOURNAL, VOL. 6, NO. 1 (SEPT.
       1962), PP. 23-27. PMLA 7973 (1963).

1575   DENNIS, WILLIAM D. JEAN-BAPTISTE CLAMENCE-A RESURRECTED
       MEURSAULT? COLLEGE LANGUAGE ASSOCIATION JOURNAL, VOL. 8,
       NO. 1 (SEPT. 1964), PP. 81-87. PMLA 8609 (1964).

1576   DERMENGHEM, EMILE. CHRONIQUES. LES LIVRES. L'ENVERS ET
       L'ENDROIT, PAR ALBERT CAMUS. CAHIERS DU SUD, VOL. 24 (OCT.
       1937), P. 604. CR 490.

1577   DESCAVES, PIERRE. CAMUS EN DE MENSELIJKE WAARDIGHEID. VLAM,
       VOL. 4, NO. 17 (APRIL 23, 1948), P. 7. BO 120, CR 652.

1578   DESCAVES, PIERRE. ALBERT CAMUS ET LE ROMAN. TABLE RONDE, NO.
       146 (FEB. 1960), PP. 47-60. BFZ 46-283, BUL SIGN
       15-19-14339, FR VII 23569, KL II 388.

1579   DESGRAUPES, PIERRE. CHAMFORT ET A. CAMUS. ARCHE. VOL. 2, NO.
       8 (AUG. 1945), PP. 131-132. CR 519.

1580   DESGRAUPES, PIERRE. GÉOGRAPHIE DU DESERT. CONFLUENCES, VOL.
       5, NO. 7 (SEPT. 1945), PP. 790-791. CR 520.

1581   DESGRAUPES, PIERRE. SUR ALBERT CAMUS. POÉSIE 47, VOL. 8, NO.
       37 (JAN.-FEB. 1947), PP. 115-125. BO 14, CR 592, FR VII
       2701, 747.

1582   DESMEDT, CL. GRANDEUR D'ALBERT CAMUS. CHANTIERS, VOL. 24, NO.
       3 (JAN. 1960), PP. 24-26.

1583   DESNUES, R.-M. LITTÉRATURE THÉÂTRE ESSAIS. REQUIEM POUR UNE
       NONNE (FAULKNER CAMUS). LIVRES ET LECTURES, (JAN. 1957),
       PP. 27-28. CR 1012.

1584   DESROSIERS, L. P. ALBERT CAMUS. LIBERTÉ, VOL. 2, NO. 1
       (JAN.-FEB. 1960), PP. 47-53. FR VII 23609.

1585   DEVISMES, M. LA JUSTICE SELON CAMUS. COUR D'APPEL DE CAEN.
       SÉANCE SOLENNELLE DE RENTRÉE DU 16 SEPT. 1959. MELUN,
       IMPR. ADMINISTRATIVE, 1959. FR VII 26293, KL II 389.

1586   DHOMME, SYLVAIN. THÉÂTRE. REQUIEM POUR UNE NONNE, D'ALBERT
       CAMUS ET WILLIAM FAULKNER. DEMAIN, NO. .42 (SEPT. 27-OCT.
       3, 1956), P. 14. CR 935.

1587   DHOTEL, ANDRÉ. LE SOLEIL ET LA PRISON. NOUVELLE REVUE
       FRANÇAISE, VOL. 8, NO. 87 (MARCH 1960), PP. 605-607. FR
       VII 23575, KL II 393.

1588   DIB, MOHAMMED. DANS UN MONDE EN RUINES. SIMOUN, VOL. 8, NO.

31 (JULY 1960), P. 57.   FR VII 23573, KL II 393.

DIÉGUEZ, MANUEL DE. DE L'ABSURDE, PRÉCÉDÉ D'UNE LETTRE À ALBERT   1589
    CAMUS.   PARIS.   ÉDITIONS DU TRIOLET, 1948.   BO 196, FR VII
    5203.

DIÉGUEZ, MANUEL DE. IDÉES, SITUATION ET POSTÉRITÉ D'ALBERT   1590
    CAMUS.   COMBAT, (JULY 1, 1960).

DIELS, G. LE MYTHE DE SISYPHE.   WOORD,   VOL. 2 (AUTUMN 1947),   1591
    PP. 45-56.   BO 317, CR 593.

DIERICKX, LOUIS. CLICHÉS À PROPOS D'ALBERT CAMUS.   CHANTIERS,   1592
    VOL. 20, NO. 1 (OCT.-NOV. 1955), PP. 17-19.   CR 915.

DIETRICH, MARGRET. DAS MODERNE DRAMA.   STUTTGART.   ALFRED KRÖNER   1593
    VERLAG, 1961.   ALBERT CAMUS, PP. 292-302.   FR VII 32687.

D(INIZ), M(ARIA) E(MÍLIA). SPELLED DINIS IN INDEX.   ALBERT   1594
    CAMUS.   OCIDENTE,   VOL. 54, NO. 237 (JAN. 1958), PP. 3-5.
    BFZ 43-294 (1957-59).

DINIZ, MARIA EMÍLIA. EM TORNO DO CONCEITO DE HOMEM REVOLTADO.   1595
    OCIDENTE,   VOL. 54, NO. 237 (JAN. 1958), PP. 13-16.   CR
    1094.

DIRKS, J. EDWARDS. THE EDITOR'S PREFACE.   CHRISTIAN SCHOLAR,   1596
    VOL. 42, NO. 4 (DEC. 1959), PP. 243-247.

DISNEY, WALT (EDITOR). DÉSERT VIVANT.   PRÉFACE DE WALT DISNEY,   1597
    TEXTES D'ALBERT CAMUS, MARCEL AYMÉ, HENRY DE MONTHERLANT,
    ANDRÉ MAUROIS, FRANÇOIS MAURIAC, JULIAN HUXLEY, LOUIS
    BROMFIELD. PARIS.   SOCIÉTÉ FRANÇAISE DU LIVRE (COLL. C'EST
    LA VIE), 1954.   ALBERT CAMUS, LE DÉSERT, PP. 7-9, PLUIES ET
    FLORAISON, PP. 57-62.   SEE NO. 649, 650.

DISNEY, WALT (EDITOR). DIE WÜSTE LEBT.   MUNICH.   GABLER, 1954.   1598
    CR 282.   SEE NO. 653, 654.   MONTGELAS, MARGARETE.

DISNEY, WALT (EDITOR). DESERTO CHE VIVE.   FLORENCE.   A.   1599
    VALLECHI, 1954.   CR 283.   SEE NO. 655, 656.   NANNETTI,
    VIERI.

DISNEY, WALT (EDITOR). DÉSERT VIVANT. UMANA. LAUSANNE.   PAYOT,   1600
    1956.   SEE NO. 651, 652.

DOMBASLE, JACQUES. LA JEUNE LITTÉRATURE FRANÇAISE ET L'AFRIQUE   1601
    DU NORD.   ÉRASME,   VOL. 1, NOS. 5-6 (MAY-JUNE 1946), PP.
    173-176.   CR 562.

DOMENACH, JEAN-MARIE. CAMUS-SARTRE DEBATE.   REBELLION VS.   1602
    REVOLUTION. NATION, VOL. 176, NO. 10 (MARCH 7, 1953), PP.
    202-203.   BO 275.

DOMENACH, JEAN-MARIE. ALBERT CAMUS.   ESPRIT,   VOL. 28, NO. 281   1603
    (FEB. 1960), PP. 280-283.   FR VII 23610.

DORT, BERNARD. FESTIVAL D'ANGERS.   LA DÉVOTION À LA CROIX, DE   1604
    CALDERON DE LA BARCA.   CAHIERS DU SUD,   43RD YEAR, VOL. 1,
    NO. 318 (1953), PP. 173-176.   CR 849.

DORT, BERNARD. REQUIEM POUR UNE NONNE, DE WILLIAM FAULKNER,   1605

ADAPTATION ET MISE EN SCÈNE D'ALBERT CAMUS, DÉCORS DE
LÉONOR FINI, AU THÉÂTRE DES MATHURINS. THÉÂTRE POPULAIRE,
NO. 21 (NOV. 1, 1956), PP. 97-100.

1606   DORT, BERNARD. REQUIEM POUR UNE NONNE, DE WILLIAM FAULKNER,
        TRADUCTION ALLEMANDE DE ROBERT SCHNORR... THÉÂTRE
        POPULAIRE, NO. 25 (JULY 1957), PP. 90-92.

1607   DOUBROVSKY, SERGE. SARTRE AND CAMUS. A STUDY IN INCARCERATION.
        YALE FRENCH STUDIES, NO. 25 (SPRING 1960), PP. 85-92. BUL
        SIGN 16-19-9718 (1962), FR VII 23568, KL II 392.

1608   DOUBROVSKY, SERGE. LA MORALE D'ALBERT CAMUS. PREUVES, NO. 116
        (OCT. 1960), PP. 39-49. FR VII 23611, KL II 387, PMLA 6823
        (1961).

1609   DOUBROVSKY, SERGE. THE ETHICS OF ALBERT CAMUS. IN   BRÉE,
        GERMAINE, CAMUS, A COLLECTION OF CRITICAL ESSAYS, PP.
        71-84. SEE NO. 1293. TRANSLATION OF NO. 1608.

1610   DOUBROVSKY, SERGE. THE MORALITY OF ALBERT CAMUS. QUEST, NO.
        30 (SUMMER 1961), PP. 45-56. TRANSLATION OF NO. 1608.

1611   DOUBROVSKY, SERGE. CAMUS ET L'AMÉRIQUE. NOUVELLE REVUE
        FRANÇAISE, VOL. 98 (FEB. 1, 1961), PP. 292-296. FR VII
        29338.

1612   DOUBROVSKY, SERGE. CAMUS IN AMERICA. IN   BRÉE, GERMAINE,
        CAMUS, A COLLECTION OF CRITICAL ESSAYS, PP. 16-19. FR VII
        29338. SEE NO. 1293. TRANSLATION OF NO. 1611.

1613   DOUBROVSKY, SERGE. CAMUS EMBAUMÉ OU LIBRE ET NU. 'ESSAIS' PAR
        ALBERT CAMUS. EXPRESS, NO. 768 (MARCH 7-13, 1966), PP.
        95-97.

1614   DOWDEN, GEORGE. FOR ALBERT CAMUS (POEM). VENTURE, VOL. 3, NO.
        4 (SPRING-SUMMER 1960), P. 40.

1615   DRESDEN, S. ALBERT CAMUS EN DE PROBLEMATIEK VAN HET ABSURDE.
        CRITERIUM, NOS. 3-4 (DEC. 1945-JAN. 1946), PP. 168-182.
        BO 185, CR 521.

1616   DRESDEN, SAMUEL. BEZONKEN AVONTUREN. AMSTERDAM. J. M.
        MEULENHOFF, 1949. ALBERT CAMUS EN DE PROBLEMATIEK HET
        ABSURDE , PP. 161-181. CR 455.

1617   DRIVER, TOM F. SUPERIOR SUICIDE. CHRISTIAN CENTURY, VOL. 77,
        NO. 12 (MARCH 23, 1960), PP. 352-354.

1618   DRUON, MAURICE. LE[PRIX NOBEL D'ALBERT CAMUS. LE] RESPECT QU'ON
        DOIT À L'ESPRIT. NEF, VOL. 14, NO. 12 (DEC. 1957), P. 94.
        CR 1014, FR VII 17306.

1619   DUBARLE, R. P. L'HOMME RÉVOLTÉ DE CAMUS. SEE NO. 1199.

1620   DUBOIS, PIERRE H. EEN HOUDING IN DE TIJD. AMSTERDAM. J. M.
        MEULENHOFF, 1950. ALBERT CAMUS, ONZEKERHEID ALS MORAAL,
        PP. 103-114. CR 456.

1621   DUBOIS, PIERRE H. ZONDER MENSELIJKE PATHTIEK. 'LES JUSTES'.
        LITTERAIR PASPOORT, VOL. 5, NO. 37 (MAY 1950), P. 110. BO

462, CR 749.

DUBOIS, PIERRE H. UNZEITGEMÄSSE BETRACHTUNGEN, VAN ALBERT   1622
    CAMUS. (ACTUELLES, L'HOMME RÉVOLTÉ.) LITTERAIR PASPOORT,
    NO. 53 (JAN. 1952), PP. 12-14. CR 817.

DUBOIS, PIERRE H. UIT VELERLEI PEN. ALBERT CAMUS: KONINKRIJK   1623
    EN BALLINGSCHAP. HET BOEK VAN NU, VOL. 12, NO. 6 (FEB.
    1959), P. 119. CR 1135.

DUCHÉ, JEAN. DU ROCHER DE SISYPHE AU ROCHER DE BRIGHTON. TABLE   1624
    RONDE, NO. 2 (FEB. 1948), PP. 306-308. BO 262, BR, CR
    653.

DUCHÉ, JEAN. GRANDEURS ET SERVITUDES DU PRIX NOBEL DE   1625
    LITTÉRATURE. FIGARO LITTERAIRE, VOL. 12, NO. 609 (DEC.
    21, 1957), PP. 1,4. CR 1015, FR VII 21385, KL I 274.

DUCHET, MICHÈLE AND CLAUDE. INACTUELLES III, OU LE JUSTE ET   1626
    L'ALGÉRIE. NOUVELLE CRITIQUE, VOL. 10, NO. 99 (SEPT.-OCT.
    1958), PP. 143-153. FR VII 29368.

DUHRSSEN, ALFRED. SOME FRENCH HEGELIANS. REVIEW OF   1627
    METAPHYSICS, VOL. 7, NO. 2, ISSUE NO. 26 (DEC. 1953), PP.
    323-337. BO 155, FR VII 14960.

DUMUR, GUY. PORTRAIT D'ALBERT CAMUS. CONFLUENCES, VOL. 4, NO.   1628
    33 (JULY 1944), PP. 65-68. BR, CR 501, FR VII 748.

DUMUR, GUY. LES SILENCES D'ALBERT CAMUS. MÉDECINE DE FRANCE,   1629
    NO. 1 (1948), P. 37. CR 654.

DUMUR, GUY. LES JUSTES. TABLE RONDE, NO. 26 (FEB. 1950), PP.   1630
    152-155. FITCH.

DUMUR, GUY. LE THÉÂTRE DANS LE THÉÂTRE (CALIGULA). TABLE   1631
    RONDE, NO. 35 (NOV. 1950), PP. 163-165. CR 750.

DUMUR, GUY. UNE BOUTEILLE À LA MER (À PROPOS DE 'L'HOMME   1632
    REVOLTE', D'ALBERT CAMUS). CAHIERS DU SUD, VOL. 35, NO.
    311 (1952), PP. 154-160. CR 818.

DUMUR, GUY. LA DÉVOTION À LA CROIX DE CALDERÓN. TRADUCTION   1633
    D'ALBERT CAMUS. MISE EN SCÈNE DE MARCEL HERRAND. FESTIVAL
    ANGERS, JUIN 1953. THÉÂTRE POPULAIRE, NO. 1 (MAY-JUNE
    1953), PP. 81-82.

DUMUR, GUY. LE THÉÂTRE. LA DÉVOTION À LA CROIX, DE CALDERÓN DE 1634
    LA BARCA. (ADAPTATION ET TRADUCTION D'ALBERT CAMUS).
    TABLE RONDE, NO. 68 (AUG. 1953), PP. 139-140. CR 852.

DUMUR, GUY. LES LETTRES. ALBERT CAMUS ET LA SOLITUDE. DEMAIN, 1635
    NO. 14 (MARCH 15-21, 1956), P. 15. CR 936.

DUMUR, GUY. ALBERT CAMUS, PRIX NOBEL. MÉDECINE DE FRANCE, NO. 1636
    88 (1957), PP. 43-44. CR 1016.

DUMUR, GUY. ALBERT CAMUS ET LE THÉÂTRE. PARIS-THÉÂTRE, VOL.   1637
    11, NO. 123 (1957), PP. 6-10. FR VII 17307.

DUMUR, GUY. DIX ANS DE LITTÉRATURE EN FRANCE. MÉDECINE DE   1638
    FRANCE, NO. 100, (1959), PP. 69-91. CR 1136.

1639   DUMUR, GUY. HOMME D'UNE GÉNÉRATION D'ESPOIRS ET DE SOUFFRANCES.
       FIGARO LITTÉRAIRE,   VOL. 15, NO. 716 (JAN. 9, 1960), P. 5.
       FR VII 26327, KL II 393.

1640   DUMUR, GUY. UNE GÉNÉRATION TRAHIE.   NOUVELLE REVUE FRANÇAISE,
       VOL. 8, NO. 87 (MARCH 1960), PP. 568-574.   FR VII 23575, KL
       II 393.

1641   DUMUR, GUY. UNE ABSENCE DÉFINITIVE.   FRANCE OBSERVATEUR,   VOL.
       12, NO. 557 (JAN. 5, 1961), P. 16.   SEE NO. 3253.

1642   DUPUY, AIMÉ. L'ALGÉRIE DANS LES LETTRES D'EXPRESSION FRANÇAISE.
       PARIS. ÉDITIONS UNIVERSITAIRES, 1956. CHAPTER IV.
       DEPUIS 1935, OU L'ALGÉRIANISME DÉPASSÉ. I. ALBERT CAMUS,
       PP. 125-136.

1643   DURÁN, MANUEL. ALBERT CAMUS O LA FIDELIDAD.   REVISTA DE LA
       UNIVERSIDAD VERACRUZANA,   VOL. 23, NO. 3 (JULY-SEPT. 1957),
       PP. 71-75. BR, CR 1016 BIS.

1644   DURÁN, MANUEL. LUCRECIO Y ALBERT CAMUS. VIDAS PARALELAS.
       TORRE,   NO. 28 (OCT.-DEC. 1959), PP. 177-192. FR VII
       23612.

1645   DURÁN, MANUEL. CAMUS AND THE SPANISH THEATRE. YALE FRENCH
       STUDIES,   NO. 25 (SPRING 1960), PP. 126-131. BUL SIGN
       16-19-10097, FR VII 23568, KL II 389.

1646   DURAND, ANNE. LE CAS ALBERT CAMUS, L'ÉPOQUE CAMUSIENNE. PARIS.
       ÉDITIONS FISCHBACHER, 1961. PMLA 7974 (1962).

1647   DURFEE, HAROLD A. CAMUS CHALLENGE TO MODERN ART. JOURNAL OF
       AESTHETICS AND ART CRITICISM,   VOL. 14, NO. 2 (DEC. 1955),
       PP. 201-205. BO 239, FR VII 15341, KL I 272.

1648   DURFEE, HAROLD A. ALBERT CAMUS AND THE ETHICS OF REBELLION.
       JOURNAL OF RELIGION,   VOL. 38, NO. 1 (JAN. 1958), PP.
       29-45. FR VII 21386, KL II 387.

1649   DURON, JACQUES-ROBERT. UN NOUVEAU MAL DU SIÈCLE. RENAISSANCES,
       NO. 16 (NOV. 25, 1945), PP. 62-68. BO 160, CR 522, FR VII
       749.

1650   DU ROSTU, JEAN. UN PASCAL SANS CHRIST, ALBERT CAMUS. ÉTUDES,
       78TH YEAR, VOL. 247 (OCT. 1945), PP. 48-65. BO 181, FR VII
       750.

1651   DURTAL, ANGE. REQUIEM POUR UNE NONNE. ESPRIT,   VOL. 25, NO.
       246 (JAN. 1957), PP. 96-98. FR VII 17308.

1652   DUSE, GASTONE. LA FELICITÀ DI SISIFO. FIERA LITTERARIA,   VOL.
       40, NO. 36 (SEPT. 19, 1965), P. 6.

1653   DUSSANE, BÉATRIX. THÉÂTRE. L'ÉTAT DE SIÈGE, D'ALBERT CAMUS.
       MERCURE DE FRANCE,   VOL. 305, NO. 1025 (JAN. 1949), PP.
       135-137. CR 691.

1654   DUSSANE, BÉATRIX. MERCURIALE. THÉÂTRE. LES JUSTES, PIÈCE EN 3
       ACTES, D'ALBERT CAMUS. MERCURE DE FRANCE,   VOL. 308, NO.
       1038 (FEB. 1950), PP. 318-321. CR 751.

DUSSANE, BÉATRIX. NOTES DE THÉÂTRE 1940-1950. LYON.   1655
    LARDANCHET, 1951. TRAGIQUES CONTEMPORAINES ET ROMANTIQUES
    ACTUELS , PP. 113-206. BO 85.

DUSSANE, BÉATRIX. CAMUS ET LA MER. SAMEDI-SOIR, (SEPT. 3,   1656
    1953). BO 44, FR VII 13305.

DUSSANE, BÉATRIX. MERCURIALE. THÉÂTRE. REQUIEM POUR UNE   1657
    NONNE, DE WILLIAM FAULKNER, ADAPTATION D'ALBERT CAMUS.
    MERCURE DE FRANCE, VOL. 328 NO. 1119 (NOV. 1956), PP.
    512-513. CR 938.

DUSSANE, (BÉATRIX). ALBERT CAMUS ET LE THÉÂTRE. MERCURE DE   1658
    FRANCE, VOL. 338, NO. 1159 (MARCH 1960), PP. 497-499. BUL
    SIGN 14-18317, FR VII 23613, KL II 389.

DUTOIT, ERNEST. DOMAINES, LES IDÉES ET LES MOTS. AVANT-PROPOS   1659
    D'ANDRÉ ROUSSEAUX. FRIBOURG. ÉDITIONS UNIVERSITAIRES,
    1960. SCATTERED REFERENCES.

DUTOURD, JEAN. UN PETIT MAL DU SIÈCLE. NOUVELLES LITTÉRAIRES,   1660
    NO. 1782 (OCT. 26, 1961), P. 1.

DUVIGNAUD, JEAN. CALDERÓN: LA DÉVOTION À LA CROIX. PIÈCE EN   1661
    TROIS JOURNÉES. TEXTE FRANÇAIS D'ALBERT CAMUS. LARIVEY:
    LES ESPRITS. ADAPTATION D'ALBERT CAMUS. NOUVELLE REVUE
    FRANÇAISE, VOL. 2, NO. 19 (JULY 1954), PP. 141-142. FR
    VII 1222.

DUVIGNAUD, JEAN. L'OEUVRE DE CAMUS EN DÉBAT DEVANT LA NOUVELLE   1662
    GÉNÉRATION. PLUTÔT QU'UN MAÎTRE, UNE SORTE DE GRAND FRÈRE.
    FIGARO LITTÉRAIRE, VOL. 12, NO. 602 (NOV. 2, 1957), P. 11.
    FITCH. SEE NO. 3252.

EATON, WALTER PRITCHARD. CALIGULA. CROSS PURPOSE. NEW YORK   1663
    HERALD TRIBUNE BOOK REVIEW, VOL. 24, NO. 52 (AUG. 15,
    1948), P. 13. BO 366.

ECKSTEIN, P. 'DIE PEST' IST ANSTECKEND. ZEIT, VOL. 4, NO. 6   1664
    (1949), P. 3. BDZ 99-167 (1949), BO 257, CR 692.

EDMAN, IRWIN. THE REBEL. NEW YORK HERALD TRIBUNE BOOK REVIEW,   1665
    VOL. 30, NO. 21 (JAN. 10, 1954), P. 6. BO 522.

EHRET, H. LE SOLEIL DE CAMUS. KWARTALNIK NEOFILOLOGICZNY,   1666
    VOL. 7, NO. 3 (1960), PP. 169-179. FR VII 23614, KL II
    393.

EHRMANN, JACQUES. CAMUS AND THE EXISTENTIALIST ADVENTURE. YALE   1667
    FRENCH STUDIES, NO. 25 (SPRING 1960), PP. 93-97. BUL SIGN
    16-19-9747, FR VII 23568, KL II 387.

EKELÖF, GUNNAR. VAD ÄR SANNING.(REVIEW OF CAMUS' 'FRÄMLINGEN'.   1668
    ÖVERSÄTTNING AV SIGFRID LINDSTRÖM. BONNIERS 1946.) BONNIERS
    LITTERÄRA MAGASIN, VOL. 15, NO. 6 (JULY-AUG. 1946), PP.
    510-511.

ÉLIE, R. ALBERT CAMUS. LIBERTÉ, VOL. 2, NO. 1 (JAN.-FEB.   1669
    1960). FR VII 23609.

1670   ELMEN, PAUL. TWICE-BLESSED ENAMEL FLOWERS. REALITY IN
         CONTEMPORARY FICTION.   IN   SCOTT, NATHAN A., JR., THE
         CLIMATE OF FAITH IN MODERN LITERATURE, PP. 84-101 (CAMUS
         REF. PP. 88, 93, 97).   SEE NO. 3044.

1671   ELSEN, CLAUDE. ALBERT CAMUS EST-IL   TABOU ? ÉCRITS DE PARIS,
         NO. 155 (DEC. 1957), PP. 100-103.   KL II 387.

1672   EMBLER, W. METAPHOR AND SOCIAL BELIEF.   ETC.   A REVIEW OF
         GENERAL SEMANTICS,   VOL. 8, NO. 2 (1951), PP. 83-93.   BUL
         SIGN 6-1526, BO 242.

1673   EMBLER, WELLER. FIVE METAPHORS FROM THE MODERN REPERTORY.
         ETC.,   VOL. 19, NO. 4 (FEB. 1963), PP. 403-426.

1674   EMMENS, J. ALBERT CAMUS EN ZIJN 'LA PESTE'. CRITERIUM,   VOL.
         8, NO. 7 (1947), PP. 751-754.   BO 389.

1675   EMMENS, JAN. EEN CONSERVATIEVE REACTIE. (A. CAMUS, 'LA PESTE').
         CRITERIUM,   NO. 12 (DEC. 1947), PP. 751-754.   CR 594.

1676   EMMERY, E. K.   WHEN 'LA PESTE' BECOMES THE'PLAGUE'.   MEANJIN,
         VOL. 9, NO. 41 (WINTER 1950), PP. 134-138.   FR VII 29370.

1677   ENG, H. MENNESKET I ALBERT CAMUS' FILOSOFI.   SAMTIDEN,   VOL.
         63, NO. 6 (1954), PP. 381-400.   FR VII 23615.

1678   ENGLER, WINFRIED. ACENTOS DE LA MORALÍSTICA FRANCESA DESDE
         MONTAIGNE HASTA CAMUS.   FILOLOGÍA MODERNA,   VOL. 3, NO. 9
         (OCT. 1962), PP. 17-39.   FR VII 32036.

1679   ENGUIDANOS, MIGUEL. ENTRAÑA ESPAÑOLA DE CAMUS.   ASOMANTE,   VOL.
         17, NO. 1 (JAN.-MAR. 1961), PP. 62-69.   BUL SIGN 16-19-109,
         16-19-2383, FR VII 26328.

1680   ENZENSBERGER, HANS MAGNUS. KRITIK NOCH VOR DEM PREIS.
         FRANKFURTER HEFTE,   VOL. 12, NO. 11 (NOV. 1957), PP.
         807-809.   KL I 274.

1681   ESPIAU DE LA MAÉSTRE, A. ALBERT CAMUS UND DAS CHRISTENTUM ODER
         DAS DRAMA DES   ATHEISTISCH EN ILUMANISMUS . ENTSCHLUSS,
         VOL. 14, (NOV. 1958), PP. 80-85.   BDZ 118-290 (1958).

1682   ESPIAU DE LA MAÉSTRE, A. ALBERT CAMUS UND DAS CHRISTENTUM ODER
         DAS DRAMA DES   ATHEISTISCHE EN ILUMANISMUS . ENTSCHLUSS,
         VOL. 14, (DEC. 1958), PP. 125-129.   BDZ 118-290 (1958).

1683   ESPIAU DE LA MAÉSTRE, A. DIE REVOLTE DES CAMUS.   ZUM TOD DES
         DICHTERS UND DENKERS EINES ATHEISTISCHEN HUMANISMUS. WELT
         UND WORT,   VOL. 15, NO. 1 (JAN.-MARCH 1960), PP. 279-291.
         BDZ 122-322 (1961), FR VII 26330, KL II 393.

1684   ESPIAU DE LA MAÉSTRE, ANDRE. DER SINN UND DAS ABSURDE.
         SALZBURG. OTTO MÜLLER VERLAG, 1961.   ALBERT CAMUS, PP.
         49-86.

1685   ESPIAU DE LA MAÉSTRE, A. ALBERT CAMUS, PÈLERIN DE L'ABSOLU.
         LETTRES ROMANES,   VOL. 15, NO. 1 (FEB. 1, 1961), PP. 3-22.
         BFZ 48-262 (1962), FR VII 26329, PMLA 7359.

1686   ESSLIN, MARTIN. THE THEATRE OF THE ABSURD.   GARDEN CITY, N. Y..

ANCHOR BOOKS, 1961.

ESTALL, H. M. THE EXISTENTIALISTS. QUEEN'S QUARTERLY, VOL.   1687
    63, NO. 2 (SUMMER 1956), PP. 302-304.

ESTANG, LUC. ALBERT CAMUS, PRIX NOBEL. CROIX, (OCT. 20,   1688
    1957). BR, CR 1016 TER.

ETCHEVERRY, AUGUSTE. LA POLÉMIQUE SARTRE-CAMUS. LES RAISONS   1689
    D'UNE RUPTURE. REVISTA UNIVERSITARIA, NO. 3 (1953), PP.
    1-2. BO 276, FR VII 14534.

ETCHEVERRY, (AUGUSTE), R.P. LA POLÉMIQUE SARTRE-CAMUS. LES   1690
    RAISONS D'UNE RUPTURE. CHRONIQUE DE L'INSTITUT CATHOLIQUE
    DE TOULOUSE, NO. 3 (JULY 1953), PP. 1-2. BFZ 34-872
    (1951-53).

ETCHEVERRY, AUGUSTE. LE CONFLIT ACTUEL DES HUMANISMES. PARIS.   1691
    PRESSES UNIVERSITAIRES DE FRANCE, 1955.

ÉTIEMBLE, R. L'ETRANGER, PAR ALBERT CAMUS. FRANCE LIBRE, VOL.   1692
    2, NO. 61 (NOV. 15, 1945), PP. 76-79. BO 298, BR, CR 523.

É(TIEMBLE, R.). LE MALENTENDU ET CALIGULA . VALEURS, NOS.   1693
    7-8 (OCT. 1946-JAN. 1947), PP. 167-168. BO 338.

ÉTIEMBLE, R. PESTE OU PÉCHÉ? TEMPS MODERNES, VOL. 3, NO. 26   1694
    (NOV. 1947), PP. 911-920. BO 390, BR, CR 595, FR VII 751.

ÉTIEMBLE, R. CHRONIQUE LITTÉRAIRE. UN TRAVAIL DE SISYPHE.   1695
    TEMPS MODERNES, VOL. 3, NO. 28 (JAN. 1948), PP. 1268-1274.
    CR 655.

ÉTIEMBLE, R. MICHEL GALLIMARD A-T-IL TUÉ ALBERT CAMUS? LETTRES   1696
    FRANÇAISES, NO. 808 (JAN. 21-27, 1960), PP. 1, 4. FR VII
    23616, KL II 392.

ÉTIEMBLE, R. D'UNE AMITIÉ. NOUVELLE REVUE FRANÇAISE, VOL. 8,   1697
    NO. 87 (MARCH 1960), PP. 461-465. FR VII 23575, KL II 392.

EUBÉ, CHARLES. HUMANISME D'AUJOURD'HUI. LES LIVRES DE LA   1698
    NOUVELLE JUNGLE. POÉSIE 47, VOL. 8, NO. 40 (AUG.-SEPT.
    1947), PP. 130-134. BO 391, FR VII 8778.

EVERSOLE, FINLEY. A QUESTIONING VOICE IS STILLED. CHRISTIAN   1699
    CENTURY, VOL. 77, NO. 3 (JAN. 20, 1960), PP. 67-68.

FABRE, EUGÈNE. L'HOMME DE THÉÂTRE. JOURNAL DE GENÈVE, NO. 3   1700
    (JAN. 5, 1960), PP. 1, 3.

FABRÈGUES, JEAN DE. IL Y A UN AN, ALBERT CAMUS MOURAIT...   1701
    POURQUOI LES JEUNES FRANÇAIS LUI RESTENT-ILS FIDÈLES?
    FRANCE CATHOLIQUE, (JAN. 13, 1961). FR VII 29371.

FAGONE, VIRGILIO, S.I. A. CAMUS E L'OPERA D'ARTE ASSURDA.   1702
    CIVILTÀ CATTOLICA, 109TH YEAR, VOL. 1, NO. 2582 (JAN. 18,
    1958), PP. 134-150. BFZ 42-284, BUL SIGN 12-15524, FR VII
    19417, KL II 387.

FAGONE, VIRGILIO, S.I. L'UMANESIMO PROMETEICO DI ALBERT CAMUS.   1703
    CIVILTÀ CATTOLICA, 109TH YEAR, VOL. 1, NO. 2585 (MARCH 1,
    1958), PP. 475-489. BFZ 42-284, FR VII 19418, KL II 387.

1704   FALCONI, CARLO. APPUNTI PER UN DISCORSO SUL TEATRO
            ESISTENZIALISTA FRANCESE. HUMANITAS, VOL. 2, NO. 11 (NOV.
            1947), PP. 1107-1122.   BO 83, FR VII 7477.

1705   FANIZZA, FRANCO. LA RIVOLTA MORALE E IL 'MORALISMO' IN CAMUS.
            AUT AUT, NO. 53 (SEPT. 1959), PP. 303-317.   FR VII 26331.

1706   FARABET, RENÉ. ALBERT CAMUS À L'AVANT-SCENE.   REVUE D'HISTOIRE
            DU THÉÂTRE,   VOL. 12, NO. 4 (OCT.-DEC. 1960), PP. 350-354.
            FR VII 23570, PMLA 7360 (1962).

1707   FARABET, RENÉ. LETTRES D'ALBERT CAMUS À JEAN GILLIBERT.   REVUE
            D'HISTOIRE DU THÉÂTRE,   VOL. 12, NO. 4 (OCT.-DEC. 1960),
            PP. 355-359. FR VII 23570.

1708   FARBER, M. L'ACTIVITÉ PHILOSOPHIQUE CONTEMPORAINE EN FRANCE ET
            AUX ETATS-UNIS, ETUDES. VOL. II. LA PHILOSOPHIE FRANÇAISE.
            PARIS. PRESSES UNIVERSITAIRES DE FRANCE, 1950. SCATTERED
            REFERENCES.

1709   FARLEY, CLIVE. ALBERT CAMUS 'THE FALL'. LISTENER, VOL. 71,
            NO. 1824 (MARCH 12, 1964), P. 436.

1710   FARRINGTON, MARY MARGARET. IL FAUT VIVRE AVEC NOS MAUX. (A
            COMMENTARY ON THE WORKS OF ALBERT CAMUS). MASTER OF ARTS
            DISSERTATION, MONTANA STATE UNIVERSITY, 1950. BO 29, FR
            VII 7704.

1711   FAUCONNIER, R. L. FRENCH NOVELISTS IN REVOLT. QUEEN'S
            QUARTERLY, VOL. 43, NO. 4 (WINTER 1957), PP. 608-619. FR
            VII 20883.

1712   FAUCON, LOUIS. NAISSANCE DE LA PESTE. NOUVELLES LITTÉRAIRES,
            VOL. 41, NO. 1848 (JAN. 31, 1963), P. 3.

1713   FAULKNER, WILLIAM. L'ÂME QUI S'INTERROGE. NOUVELLE REVUE
            FRANÇAISE, VOL. 8, NO. 87 (MARCH 1960), PP. 537-538. FR
            VII 23575, KL II 393.

1714   FAUVE, JACQUES. A DRAMA OF ESSENCE. SALACROU AND OTHERS. YALE
            FRENCH STUDIES, NO. 14 (WINTER 1954-55), PP. 30-40. BO
            87.

1715   FAVATI, GUIDO. IN MARGINE ALL' ÉTRANGER DI ALBERT CAMUS.
            COINCIDENZE CON LUIGI PIRANDELLO. RIVISTA DI LETTERATURE
            MODERNE E COMPARATE, VOL. 17, NO. 1 (MARCH 1964), PP. 136-
            149. PMLA 8610 (1964).

1716   FECHTER, PAUL. DAS EUROPÄISCHE DRAMA. GEIST UND KULTUR IM
            SPIEGEL DES THEATERS. VOL. III. VOM EXPRESSIONISMUS ZUR
            GEGENWART. MANNHEIM. BIBLIOGRAPHISCHES INSTITUT, 1958.
            BELAGERUNGSZUSTAND, PP. 332-335. FR VII 19078.

1717   FEIBLEMAN, JAMES K. CAMUS AND THE PASSION OF HUMANISM. KENYON
            REVIEW, VOL. 25, NO. 2 (SPRING 1963), PP. 281-292.

1718   FELLMANN, HANS. DIE FRAGE NACH DER GEWISSHEIT IN DER NEUEREN
            DICHTUNG. DEUTSCHUNTERRICHT, VOL. 7, NO. 1 (1955), PP.
            65-78. BO 157.

FERAOUN, MOULOUD. LE DERNIER MESSAGE. PREUVES, NO. 110 (APRIL   1719
    1960), PP. 21-24. FR VII 23617, KL II 393, PMLA 7363
    (1962).

FERAOUN, MOULOUD. AU-DESSUS DES HAINES. SIMOUN, VOL. 8, NO.   1720
    31 (JULY 1960), PP. 18-19. FR VII 23573, KL II 393.

FERAOUN, MOULOUD. TEXTES SUR L'ALGÉRIE. PREUVES, NO. 139   1721
    (SEPT. 1962), SUPPLEMENT. PMLA 7985 (1963).

FERMAUD, JACQUES. HUMANISM IN CONTEMPORARY FRENCH FICTION.   1722
    AMERICAN SOCIETY LEGION OF HONOR MAGAZINE, VOL. 22, NO. 4
    (WINTER 1951), PP. 341-353. BO 64, FR VII 5333.

FERNÁNDEZ, G. LA MUERTE DE CAMUS. REVISTA DE FILOSOFÍA DE LA   1723
    UNIVERSIDAD DE COSTA RICA. VOL. 2, NO. 7 (JAN. -JUNE
    1960), PP. 306-307. FR VII 26332, KL II 393.

FERNANDEZ-SANTOS, FRANCISCO. UN HUMANISMO 'PROVISIONAL', LA   1724
    EDAD DE LOS DESILUSIONADOS. INDICE DE ARTES Y LETRAS,
    VOL. 11, NO. 107 (DEC. 1957), PP. 7-8.

FERNANDEZ-SANTOS, FRANCISCO. REQUIEM POR UN HOMBRE. INDICE DE   1725
    ARTES Y LETRAS, VOL. 14, NO. 133 (FEB. 1960), PP. 3-4. FR
    VII 26333.

FERRATER MORA, JOSÉ. MAN AT THE CROSSROADS. BOSTON. BEACON   1726
    PRESS, 1957.

FEUERLICHT, IGNACE. CAMUS'S L'ETRANGER RECONSIDERED.   1727
    PUBLICATIONS OF THE MODERN LANGUAGE ASSOCIATION, VOL. 78,
    NO. 5 (DEC. 1963), PP. 606-621.

FIEDLER, LESLIE A. THE POPE AND THE PROPHET. COMMENTARY, VOL.   1728
    21, NO. 2 (FEB. 1956), PP. 190-195. BO 331, FR VII 21388.

FIESCHI. L'ÉTRANGER, PAR ALBERT CAMUS. NOUVELLE REVUE   1729
    FRANÇAISE, VOL. 30, NO. 343 (SEPT. 1942), PP. 368-374. BO
    292, BR, CR 491.

FIEUW, ROGER. DE MODERNE DRAMATURGIE. BAND, VOL. 17, (1958),   1730
    PP. 103-110.

FITCH, BRIAN T. REVUE DES REVUES. ALBERT CAMUS. BULLETIN DES   1731
    JEUNES ROMANISTES, NO. 1 (JUNE 1960), PP. 33-34. FITCH.

FITCH, BRIAN T. NARRATEUR ET NARRATION DANS 'L'ETRANGER'   1732
    D'ALBERT CAMUS. ARCHIVES DES LETTRES MODERNES, VOL. 3, NO.
    34 (1960), PP. 3-48. FR VII 26294, PMLA 7362 (1962).

FITCH, BRIAN T. AESTHETIC DISTANCE AND INNER SPACE IN THE   1733
    NOVELS OF CAMUS. MODERN FICTION STUDIES, VOL. 10, NO. 3
    (AUTUMN 1964), PP. 279-292.

FITZSIMONS, M. A. INGENIOUS TO THE POINT OF ECCENTRICITY.   1734
    REVIEW. THE REBEL. CHICAGO SUNDAY TRIBUNE MAGAZINE OF
    BOOKS, PART IV (JAN. 10, 1954), P. 4. BO 523.

FLAM, L. HET EXISTENTIALISME UITDRUKKING VAN DE MORELE CRISIS   1735
    VAN ONZE TIJD. NIEUW VLAAMS TIJDSCHRIFT, VOL. 10, NO. 4
    (APRIL 1956), PP. 419-428. KL I 231.

1736   FLAM, L. DE OPSTAND VAN ALBERT CAMUS. NIEUW VLAAMS
            TIJDSCHRIFT, VOL. 11, NO. 11 (NOV. 1957), PP. 1121-1137.
            KL I 273, FR VII 21389.

1737   FLAM, L. DE DROEFHEID EN DE OPSTAND VAN CAMUS. NIEUW VLAAMS
            TIJSCHRIFT, VOL. 13, NO. 10 (OCT. 1959), PP. 1150-1162.
            FR VII 26334, KL II 391, PMLA 6824 (1961).

1738   FLAM, L. DE VREEMDELING IN HET WERK VAN ALBERT CAMUS.
            TIJDSCHRIFT VAN DE VRIJE UNIVERSITEIT VAN BRUSSEL, VOL. 1,
            NO. 1 (1959), PP. 4-19. FR VII 23618, KL II 390.

1739   FLEISCHMAN, J. MAHALOKET CAMUS VE-SARTRE VEHA EXISTENTIALISM
            (THE DISPUTE BETWEEN CAMUS AND SARTRE AND EXISTENTIALISM).
            BEHINOT, NO. 4 (1953), PP. 14-23.

1740   FLETCHER, VIRGINIA. ALBERT CAMUS, PRIX NOBEL. COMPTES RENDUS
            DE L'ATHENÉE LOUISIANAIS, (MARCH 1960). FR VII 26335, KL
            II 386.

1741   FLICK, M. CARITÀ SENZA SPERANZA. STUDIUM, VOL. 45, NOS. 11-12
            (1949), PP. 492-495. BO 198, BUL SIGN 6-7349.

1742   FLORENNE, YVES. LE THÉÂTRE. REQUIEM POUR UNE NONNE, DE WILLIAM
            FAULKNER, ADAPTATION PAR A. CAMUS. REVUE FRANÇAISE, NO.
            86 (FEB. 1957), P. 37. CR 1021.

1743   FLORENNE, YVES. FESTIVALS, AN XII. DRAMATURGIE À CIEL OUVERT,
            ENQUÊTE. SEPT METTEURS EN SCÈNE PLAIDENT POUR LE PLEIN
            AIR (VILAR, MARCHAT, CAMUS, ETC). SPECTACLES, VOL. 1, NO.
            2 (JUNE 1958), PP. 17-24. FR VII 25762.

1744   FOLLIET, JOSEPH. INVENTAIRE APRÈS DÉCÈS. CHRONIQUE SOCIALE DE
            FRANCE, VOL. 68, NO. 4 (JUNE 30, 1960), PP. 285-289. FR
            VII 26336.

1745   FONDA, CARLO. LES ACCUSATIONS DE PLAGIAT CONTRE CAMUS À PROPOS
            DE 'LA PESTE'. CULTURE, VOL. 27, NO. 1 (MARCH 1966), P.
            3-8.

1746   FONTAN, ANTONIO. CAMUS ENTRE LE PAGANISME ET LE CHRISTIANISME.
            TABLE RONDE, NO. 146 (FEB. 1960), PP. 114-119. BFZ
            46-283, BUL SIGN 15-19-13770, FR VII 23569, KL II 387.

1747   FONTENIS, GEORGES. LE RÉVOLTÉ DE CAMUS EST-IL DES NÔTRES?
            LIBERTAIRE, VOL. 57, NO. 296 (JAN. 4, 1952), P. 3. FITCH.

1748   FONTINELL, EUGENE. A TRIBUTE TO CAMUS. RECENT STUDIES OF HIS
            WORK. CROSS CURRENTS, VOL. 10, NO. 3 (SUMMER 1960), PP.
            283-289. FR VII 23619.

1749   FORT, KEITH. BEYOND DESPAIR. A COMPARATIVE STUDY OF FOUR
            NOVELS. DISSERTATION ABSTRACTS, VOL. 25, NO. 4 (OCT.
            1964), P. 2511. PMLA 988 (1964).

1750   FORTON, JEAN. CAMUS. NOUVELLE REVUE FRANÇAISE, VOL. 8, NO. 87
            (MARCH 1960), PP. 581-582. FR VII 23575, KL II 395.

1751   FOSS, MARTIN. DEATH, SACRIFICE, AND TRAGEDY. LINCOLN.
            UNIVERSITY OF NEBRASKA PRESS, 1966. CHAPTER IV, THE

SCIENTIFIC SYSTEM AND ITS FAILURE. THE ABSURD, PP. 21-29.
CHAPTER V, THE EVASIVE EXPERIENCE OF DEATH AND ITS
SUBSTITUTES, PP. 30-37.

FOUCHET, MAX-POL. CONSÉCRATION. CAMUS DANS LA PLÉIADE.   1752
EXPRESS, NO. 614 (MARCH 21, 1963), PP. 27-28. FR VII
33950.

FOUCHET, MAX-POL. LA MORALE TUE. 'CARNETS, JANVIER 1942-MARS   1753
1951''PAR ALBERT CAMUS. EXPRESS, NO. 706 (DEC. 28,
1964-JAN. 3, 1965), PP. 49-51.

FOURAS, HUGUES. L'APRÈS-DERNIER CHAPITRE DE 'LA PESTE', PRÊTÉ À 1754
ALBERT CAMUS. GAZETTE DES LETTRES, VOL. 4, NO. 68 (AUG.
7, 1948), PP. 11-12. CR 656.

FOURAS, HUGUES. CE LUNDI 4 JANVIER 1960 . FIGARO LITTERAIRE,   1755
VOL. 15, NO. 716 (JAN. 9, 1960), P. 7. FR VII 26337, KL II
393.

FOWLIE, WALLACE. THE FRENCH LITERARY MIND. ACCENT, VOL. 8,   1756
NO. 2 (WINTER 1948), PP. 67-81. BO 61, BR, CR 657, FR VII
2247.

FOWLIE, WALLACE. THE FRENCH LITERARY SCENE. COMMONWEAL, VOL. 1757
56, NO. 8 (1952), PP. 201-202. BO 493.

FOWLIE, WALLACE. DIONYSUS IN PARIS, A GUIDE TO CONTEMPORARY   1758
FRENCH THEATER. NEW YORK. MERIDIAN BOOKS, 1960. FR VII
23139.

FRAISSE, SIMONE. DE LUCRÈCE À CAMUS OU LES CONTRADICTIONS DE LA 1759
RÉVOLTE. ESPRIT, VOL. 27, NO. 271 (MARCH 1959), PP.
437-453. BUL SIGN 41-2327, CR 1137, FR VII 19419, 21390,
KL II 392.

FRANK, BERNARD. UNE BONNE OEUVRE. NEF, VOL. 14, NO. 11 (NOV.   1760
1957), PP. 61-63. CR 1022, FR VII 17309.

FRANK, BERNARD. SUR CAMUS. PARISIENNE, NO. 48 (NOV.-DEC.   1761
1957), PP. 1072-1075. CR 1047 TER, KL I 272.

FRANK, RACHEL. UNAMUNO. EXISTENTIALISM AND THE SPANISH NOVEL. 1762
ACCENT, VOL. 9, NO. 2 (WINTER 1949), PP. 80-88. CR 694,
FR VII 2124.

FRANK, WALDO. THAT EUROPE MAY LIVE... THE REBEL. NEW REPUBLIC, 1763
VOL. 130, NO. 3 (JAN. 18, 1954), PP. 19-20. BO 524.

FRANK, WALDO. LIFE IN THE FACE OF ABSURDITY. NEW REPUBLIC,   1764
VOL. 133, NO. 12 (SEPT. 19, 1955), PP. 18-20. BO 326.

FRANZEN, ERICH. FORMEN DES MODERNEN DRAMAS. VON DER   1765
ILLUSIONSBÜHNE ZUM ANTITHEATER. MÜNCHEN. C. H. BECK,
1961. FR VII 28696.

FREEDLEY, GEORGE. CALIGULA. CROSS PURPOSE. LIBRARY JOURNAL,   1766
VOL. 73 (JULY 1948), P. 1029. BO 367.

FREMANTLE, ANNE. THE PLAGUE AND ITS CURE. COMMONWEAL, VOL.   1767
48, NO. 26 (OCT. 8, 1948), PP. 619-621. BO 411.

1768   FRÉMINVILLE, CL(AUDE) DE. LE THÉÂTRE. CALIGULA AU THÉÂTRE
          HÉBERTOT. RENAISSANCES, NO. 15 (OCT. 25, 1945), PP.
          157-160.   BO 346, CR 524, FR VII 13306.

1769   FRÉMINVILLE, CLAUDE DE. SYMBOLIQUE DE TIPASA.   POPULAIRE,
          (APRIL 6, 1954).   BR, CR 882 BIS.

1770   FRÉMINVILLE, CLAUDE DE. CAMUS ET LE SECRET.   SIMOUN,   VOL. 8,
          NO. 31 (JULY 1960), PP. 54-56.   FR VII 23573, KL II 393.

1771   FREMONT, LAURENT. ALBERT CAMUS, PROMÉTHÉE ET LE BONHEUR.   REVUE
          DE L'UNIVERSITÉ LAVAL,   VOL. 19, NO. 6 (FEB. 1965), PP.
          551-563.

1772   FRESCAROLI, ANTONIO. SEI RACCONTI DI CAMUS.   VITA E PENSIERO,
          VOL. 41 (MAY 1958), PP. 360-362.   FR VII 19420.

1773   FRESCAROLI, ANTONIO. LA MORTE DI UN TESTIMONE.   VITA E
          PENSIERO,   VOL. 43, NO. 2 (FEB. 1960), PP. 127-128.   FR VII
          23620, KL II 393.

1774   FREUND, JOHN B. MARTYRS, PILGRIMS AND THE MEMORY OF CAMUS.
          MINNESOTA REVIEW,   VOL. 4, NO. 3 (SPRING 1964), PP. 483-
          485.

1775   FREYER, GRATTAN. THE NOVELS OF ALBERT CAMUS.   ENVOY,   VOL. 3,
          NO. 11 (OCT. 1950), PP. 19-35.   BO 307, FR VII 5745.

1776   FRIAR, KIMON. REVOLT AGAINST ABSURDITY.   SATURDAY REVIEW,   VOL.
          44, NO. 6 (FEB. 11, 1961), PP. 57, 68.

1777   FRIEDMAN, MAURICE. PROBLEMATIC REBEL. AN IMAGE OF MODERN MAN.
          NEW YORK. RANDOM HOUSE, 1963.   PASSIM.

1778   FRIEDMAN, MELVIN J. CAMUS' LAST.   PROGRESSIVE, VOL. 24, NO. 8
          (AUG. 1960), PP. 33-35.

1779   FRITZ, WALTER HELMUT. ALBERT CAMUS.   DEUTSCHE RUNDSCHAU,   VOL.
          86, NO. 2 (FEB. 1960), PP. 174-177.   KL II 395.

1780   FROHOCK, W. M. CAMUS.   IMAGE, INFLUENCE AND SENSIBILITY.   YALE
          FRENCH STUDIES,   VOL. 2, NO. 2, ISSUE NO. 4 (FALLWINTER
          1949), PP. 91-99.   BO 261, BR, CR 695, FR VII 4413.

1781   FUGAZY, IRENE MERCEDES. THE POSITIVE VALUES IN THE WORK OF
          ALBERT CAMUS. DISSERTATION ABSTRACTS, VOL. 26, NO. 4 (OCT.
          1965), P. 2210.

1782   FUZIER, CLAUDE. UN HOMME LIBRE.   POPULAIRE DE PARIS,   VOL. 39,
          NO. 10,948 (JAN. 6, 1960), P. 1.   FITCH.

1783   G., CL. EN MARGE DES 'JUSTES'.   NOUVELLES LITTÉRAIRES,   VOL.
          29, NO. 1168 (JAN. 19, 1950), P. 5.   FR VII 4414.

1784   G., M. SPOR CAMUS-SARTRE.   NAŠI RAZGLEDI,   VOL. 1, NO. 19
          (1952), PP. 15-16.   CR 828.

1785   GABEL, JOSEPH. DIE VERDINGLICHUNG IN CAMUS''ÉTRANGER'.
          JAHRBUCH FÜR PSYCHOLOGIE UND PSYCHOTHERAPIE,   VOL. 5, NOS.
          1-2 (1957), PP. 123-140.   BDZ 116-316 (1958).

1786   GADOUREK, CARINA. LES INNOCENTS ET LES COUPABLES. ESSAI
          D'EXÉGÈSE DE L'OEUVRE D'ALBERT CAMUS. THE HAGUE. MOUTON,

1963. FR VII 33924.

GAILLARD, POL. CHRONIQUE THÉÂTRALE. PIÈCES NOIRES. PENSÉE,   1787
NOUVELLE SERIE NO. 1 (OCT.-NOV.-DEC. 1944), PP. 108-117.
BO 332, CR 502, FR VII 2426, PMLA

GAILLARD, POL. PIÈCES FAUSSES ET PIÈCES VRAIES. PENSÉE, NO. 5   1788
(OCT.-NOV.-DEC. 1945), PP. 97-107. BO 347, FR VII 5506.

GAILLARD, POL. L'OTTIMISMO DI J.-P. SARTRE, FILOSOFIA DELL   1789
ASSURDO E MORALE DELLA SINCERITA IN A. CAMUS. SOCIALISMO,
VOL. 1, NO. 5(1946). BO 186.

GAILLARD, POL. CHRONIQUE THÉÂTRALE. CAMUS ET CLAUDEL CHEZ   1790
JEAN-LOUIS BARRAULT. 'L'ÉTAT DE SIÈGE'. PENSÉE, NO. 23
(MARCH-APRIL 1949), PP. 86-90. BFZ 30-134 (1949-50), BO
450, FR VII 5746.

GALAND, RENE. FOUR FRENCH ATTITUDES ON LIFE. MONTHERLANT,   1791
MALRAUX, SARTRE, CAMUS. NEW ENGLAND MODERN LANGUAGE
ASSOCIATION BULLETIN, VOL. 15, NO. 1 (FEB. 1953), PP.
9-15. BO 151, FR VII 8702.

GALL, MICHEL. CAMUS À 100 EXEMPLAIRES. EXPRESS, NO. 298   1792
(MARCH 8, 1957), P. 29. CR 1023.

GALLOWAY, DAVID D. THE ABSURD MAN AS PICARO. THE NOVELS OF SAUL 1793
BELLOW. TEXAS STUDIES IN LITERATURE AND LANGUAGE, VOL. 6,
NO. 2 (SUMMER 1964), PP. 226-254.

GALLOWAY, DAVID D. THE LOVE STANCE. RICHARD E. KIM'S THE   1794
MARTYRED (REVIEW). CRITIQUE, VOL. 7, NO. 2 (WINTER
1964-65), PP. 163-171.

GALLOWAY, DAVID D. THE ABSURD MAN AS TRAGIC HERO. THE NOVELS OF 1795
WILLIAM STYRON. TEXAS STUDIES IN LITERATURE AND LANGUAGE,
VOL. 6, NO. 4 (WINTER 1965), PP. 512-534.

GALMACHE, JOSÉ. ALBERT CAMUS. FLAMBEAU, VOL. 43, NOS. 1-2   1796
(JAN.-FEB. 1960), PP. 28-40. FR VII 23621, KL II 395.

GALPIN, ALFRED. ITALIAN ECHOES IN ALBERT CAMUS. TWO NOTES ON   1797
LA CHUTE , I. DANTE IN AMSTERDAM, II. 'E DUE'-VARIATIONS
ON A THEME BY PIRANDELLO. SYMPOSIUM, VOL. 12, NOS. 1-2
(SPRING-FALL, 1958), PP. 65-79. BUL SIGN 14-9011, FR VII
19421, KL II 390.

GAMBRA, RAFAEL. LA ÚLTIMA POSICIÓN DE CAMUS. ARBOR, VOL. 27,   1798
NO. 98 (FEB. 1954), PP. 224-232. BFZ 36-234 (1953-54), BO
525, BUL SIGN 13661, CR 883, FR VII 11223.

GAMBRA, RAFAEL. LA REBELIÓN CAMBIA DE CAMPO. INDICE DE ARTES Y   1799
LETRAS, VOL. 11, NO. 107 (DEC. 1957), PP. 5-6. BR, CR
1025 BIS.

GAMBRA, RAFAEL. REBELIÓN Y REVOLUCIÓN EN LA OBRA DE CAMUS.   1800
NUESTRO TIEMPO, 7TH YR., VOL. 12, NO. 69 (MARCH 1960), PP.
281-290. KL II 389.

GANDON, YVES. LE THÉÂTRE. ALBERT CAMUS, PAUL FÉVAL.   1801

FRANCE-ILLUSTRATION, VOL. 6, NO. 221 (JAN. 7, 1950), P. 23. BO 464, CR 752, FR VII 9302.

1802   GANDON, YVES. DEN FRANSKE LITTERATUR ETTER KRIGEN. VINDUET, VOL. 6, NO. 2 (1952), PP. 121-129. FR VII 28385.

1803   GANDON, YVES. LE DÉMON DU STYLE. PARIS. PLON, 1960. ALBERT CAMUS OU LE STYLE RÉVOLTÉ , PP. 233-253. KL II 390.

1804   GANDREY-RETY, JEAN. FLAMMES ET CENDRES. LES JUSTES D'ALBERT CAMUS. ARTS, NO. 243 (DEC. 30, 1949), P. 7. BO 456, CR 696, FR VII 11224.

1805   GANNE, GILBERT. LES PREMIÈRES ARMES DE CAMUS, ANIMATEUR ET MAQUILLEUR DU THÉÂTRE DE L'ÉQUIPE. ESSOR, NO. 33 (MAY 16, 1946), P. 7. CR 564.

1806   GANNE, GILBERT. INTERVIEWS IMPUBLIABLES. PARIS. A. BONNE, 1952. BO 66, FR VII 8667.

1807   GARAGORRI, PAULINO. ALBERT CAMUS Y SU GENERACIÓN. CUADERNOS (DEL CONGRESO POR LA LIBERTAD DE LA CULTURA), NO. 43 (JULY-AUG. 1960), PP. 81-85. FR VII 23622.

1808   GARAUDY, ROGER. NYE TRAEK I FRANSK LITTERATUR. DIALOG, VOL. 4, NO. 7 (NOV. 1954), PP. 18-23. FR VII 28523.

1809   GARCÍA BACCA, JUAN D. CAMUS Y LA FILOSOFÍA CONTEMPORÁNEA. CUADERNOS AMERICANOS, 17TH YEAR, VOL. 99, NO. 3 (MAY-JUNE 1958), PP. 124-131. FR VII 19422, KL I 274.

1810   GARGAN, EDWARD T. REVOLUTION AND MORALE IN THE FORMATIVE THOUGHT OF ALBERT CAMUS. REVIEW OF POLITICS, VOL. 25, NO. 4 (OCT. 1963), PP. 483-496.

1811   GARNER, HARRY H. AND ROBERT F. JEANS. CONFRONTATION TECHNIQUE IN PSYCHOTHERAPY: SOME EXISTENTIAL IMPLICATIONS. JOURNAL OF EXISTENTIAL PSYCHIATRY, VOL. 2, NO. 8 (SPRING 1962), PP. 393-408.

1812   GARRETT, JOHN. PLAYS THAT MISFIRE. REVIEW. CALIGULA. CROSS PURPOSE, ET AL. SPECTATOR, VOL. 181, NO. 6267 (AUG. 6, 1948), PP. 187-188. BO 368.

1813   GARRIC, DANIEL. L'UNE DES PLUS NOBLES EXPRESSIONS DE LA LITTÉRATURE. FIGARO, VOL. 134, NO. 4771 (JAN. 7, 1960), P. 9.

1814   GÄRTNER, FRITZ-LUDWIG. ALBERT CAMUS. BÜHNENWERKE: 'LE MALENTENDU' UND 'L'ÉTAT DE SIÈGE'. KOMMENDEN, VOL. 5, NO. 21 (1951), P. 6. BDZ 104-308, BO 342, CR 785.

1815   GARVIN, HARRY R. CAMUS AND THE AMERICAN NOVEL. COMPARATIVE LITERATURE, VOL. 8, NO. 3 (SUMMER 1956), PP. 194-204. BFZ 40-252, CR 939, FR VII 15344, KL I 274.

1816   GASCAR, PIERRE. LE DERNIER VISAGE DE CAMUS. IN ANONYMOUS, CAMUS, PP. 247-264. SEE NO. 940.

1817   GASCHT, ANDRÉ. ALBERT CAMUS, PRIX NOBEL 1957. THYRSE, VOL. 59, NO. 11 (NOV. 1957), PP. 435-436. CR 1024, KL II 386.

GASCOIGNE, BAMBER. THE QUALITY OF JUSTICE. SPECTATOR, VOL.   1818
    209, NO. 7013 (NOV. 23, 1962), P. 794.

GASSNER, JOHN. MASTERS OF THE DRAMA. NEW YORK. DOVER   1819
    PUBLICATIONS, 1954. BO 88, FR VII 10909.

GASSNER, JOHN. FORMS OF MODERN DRAMA. COMPARATIVE LITERATURE, 1820
    VOL. 7, NO. 2 (SPRING 1955), PP. 129-142. BO 90, FR VII
    12940.

GASTER, BERYL. ALBERT CAMUS. CONTEMPORARY REVIEW, VOL. 197,   1821
    NO. 1130 (MARCH 1960), PP. 148-149. BFZ 46, FR VII 23623,
    KL II 395.

GAUTIER, JEAN-JACQUES. THÉÂTRE. REQUIEM POUR UNE NONNE.   1822
    REALITES, NO. 130 (NOV. 1956), P. 118. FITCH.

GAUTIER, J. M. REVIEW OF RICHARD THIEBERGER: 'ALBERT CAMUS,   1823
    EINE EINFUHRUNG IN SEIN DICHTERISCHES WERK'. ROMANISCHE
    FORSCHUNGEN, VOL. 74, NOS. 3-4 (1962), PP. 439-440.

GENÊT. LETTER FROM PARIS. NEW YORKER, VOL. 29, NO. 15   1824
    (MAY 30, 1953), PP. 82-87. BO 507.

GENEVOIX, MAURICE. DES ÉCRIVAINS NOUS DISENT. (HOMMAGES À   1825
    CAMUS). FIGARO, VOL. 134, NO. 4770 (JAN. 6, 1960), P.4.
    FR VII 23649.

GENNEP, FREDERIK ONSLOW VAN. ALBERT CAMUS. EEN STUDIE VAN ZIJN 1826
    ETHISCHE DENKEN. AMSTERDAM. POLAK AND VAN GENNEP, 1962.
    PMLA 8611 (1964).

GEORGESCU, PAUL. INSEMNARI DESPRE ALBERT CAMUS (I). GAZETA   1827
    LITERARA, VOL. 11, NO. 26 (JUNE 25, 1964) PP. 1, 8. PMLA
    8612 (1964).

GEORGESCU, PAUL. INSEMNĂRI DESPRE ALBERT CAMUS (II). GAZETA   1828
    LITERÁRA, VOL. 11, NO. 27 (JULY 2, 1964), P. 8. PMLA 8612
    (1964).

GEORGIADES, NIKI. WHAT IS EXISTENTIALISM. WORLD REVIEW, JUNE 1829
    1946, PP. 14-19.

GEORGIN, RENÉ. JEUX DE MOTS, DE L'ORTHOGRAPHIE AU STYLE.   1830
    PARIS. ANDRÉ BONNE, 1957. COMME ILS ÉCRIVENT : ALBERT
    CAMUS, PP. 238-240. FR VII 22867, KL II 390.

GEORGIN, RENÉ. LA LANGUE FRANÇAISE. CAMUS: 'L'EXIL ET LE   1831
    ROYAUME'. DU GRAND ART CLASSIQUE. ARTS, NO. 637 (SEPT.
    25-OCT. 1, 1957), P. 2. CR 1025.

GÉRALD (GÉRALD GASSIOT-TALABOT). LE MOIS À PARIS. LE THÉÂTRE. 1832
    LES POSSÉDÉS . ANNALES, VOL. 66 NO. 101 (MARCH 1959), PP.
    50-52. CR 1138.

GERHARD, ROBERTO. THE PLAGUE. LISTENER, VOL. 71, NO. 1826   1833
    (MARCH 26, 1964), P. 533.

GERSHMAN, HERBERT S. ON 'L'ETRANGER'. FRENCH REVIEW, VOL. 29, 1834
    NO. 4 (FEB. 1956), PP. 299-305. BUL SIGN 12-15852, FR VII
    15345, KL I 273.

1835   GERSHMAN, H. S. REPLY TO L. S. ROUDIEZ'S CRITICISM OF HIS
            ARTICLE. FRENCH REVIEW, VOL. 29, NO. 6 (MAY 1956), PP.
            491-493. SEE NO. 1834.

1836   GIBSON, A. BOYCE. EXISTENTIALISM. AN INTERIM REPORT. MEANJIN,
            VOL. 7, NO. 1 (FALL 1948), PP. 41-52. FR VII 25303.

1837   GIGNOUX, HUBERT. CHRONIQUE DU THÉÂTRE. (L'ÉTAT DE SIÈGE ,
            D'ALBERT CAMUS). ÉTUDES, VOL. 81, NO. 259 (OCT.-NOV.-DEC.
            1948), PP. 395-396. CR 658.

1838   GILLON, ADAM. THE ABSURD IN 'LES VALEURS IDÉALES' IN CONRAD,
            KAFKA, AND CAMUS. POLISH REVIEW, VOL. 6, NO. 3 (SUMMER
            1961), PP. 3-10.

1839   GILMAN, RICHARD. TWO VOICES OF CAMUS. COMMONWEAL, VOL. 73,
            NO. 22 (FEB. 24, 1961), PP. 552-553. FR VII 26338, PMLA
            7364 (1962).

1840   GIMÉNEZ ARNAU, J. EL TEATRO DE CAMUS. CON DOS OPINIOÑES SOBRE
            EL ESTUDIO DE FR. JOSÉ QUÍLEZ.. Y DE D. LUIS HORNO LIRIA.
            ZARAGOZA. IMP. ZARAGOZA DEPORTIVA, 1958. KL II 389.

1841   GINGRAS, GEORGE E. THE CATEGORIES FOR TRAGEDY IN THE
            CONTEMPORARY FRENCH DRAMA (THE THEATRE OF 1918-1950).
            CATHOLIC UNIVERSITY OF AMERICA (PH. D.), 1962.
            DISSERTATION ABSTRACTS, VOL. 23, NO. 9 (MARCH 1963), P.
            3373.

1842   GIRARD, MARCEL. GUIDE ILLUSTRÉ DE LA LITTÉRATURE FRANÇAISE
            MODERNE, DE 1918 À 1949. PARIS. PIERRE SEGHERS, 1949.
            CF. PP. 199-200, 212, 221. CR 457.

1843   GIRARD, RENÉ. CAMUS'S STRANGER RETRIED. PUBLICATIONS OF THE
            MODERN LANGUAGE ASSOCIATION OF AMERICA, VOL. 79, NO. 5
            (DEC. 1964), PP. 519-533. PMLA 8613 (1964).

1844   GIROLAMO, NICOLA DI. CAMUS UNO ET DUE. SIENA. MAIA, 1959. FR
            VII 26295, KL II 387.

1845   GIZZI, CARLO. A. CAMUS. L'UOMO IN RIVOLTA. FILOSOFIA, VOL. 9,
            NO. 2 (1958), PP. 347-350. BUL SIGN 14-2181.

1846   GLAESER, ERNST. ALBERT CAMUS. BOGEN, VOL. 2, NOS. 2-3 (1947),
            P. 29. BO 250, CR 596.

1847   GLAESER, ERNST, AND HANS H. HAUSER. CALIGULAS SELBSTMORD
            HÖHEREN GRADES. PRISMA, NO. 7 (MAY 1947), PP. 27-29. CR
            597.

1848   GLICKSBERG, CHARLES I. THE NOVEL AND THE PLAGUE. UNIVERSITY OF
            KANSAS CITY REVIEW, VOL. 21, NO. 1 (FALL 1954), PP. 55-62.
            BO 440, FR VII 15346.

1849   GLICKSBERG, CHARLES I. THE LITERATURE OF ABSURDITY. WESTERN
            HUMANITIES REVIEW, VOL. 12, NO. 1 (WINTER 1958), PP.
            29-38. FR VII 21391.

1850   GLICKSBERG, CHARLES I. CAMUS'S QUEST FOR GOD. SOUTHWEST
            REVIEW, VOL. 44, NO. 3 (SUMMER 1959), PP. 241-250. BUL

SIGN 14-9003, KL II 388.

GLICKSBERG, CHARLES I. LITERATURE AND RELIGION, A STUDY IN   1851
CONFLICT. DALLAS. SOUTHERN METHODIST UNIVERSITY PRESS,
1960. CAMUS'S QUEST FOR GOD, PP. 212-222. KL II 388.

GLICKSBERG, CHARLES I. TO BE OR NOT TO BE. THE LITERATURE OF   1852
SUICIDE. QUEEN'S QUARTERLY, VOL. 68, NO. 3 (FALL 1960),
PP. 384-395. FR VII 22888.

GLICKSBERG, CHARLES I. FORMS OF MADNESS IN LITERATURE. ARIZONA   1853
QUARTERLY, VOL. 17, NO. 1 (SPRING 1961), PP. 43-53.

GLICKSBERG, CHARLES IRVING. THE TRAGIC VISION IN   1854
TWENTIETH-CENTURY LITERATURE. CARBONDALE, ILLINOIS.
SOUTHERN ILLINOIS UNIVERSITY PRESS, 1963. CAMUS AND THE
REVOLT AGAINST THE ABSURD, PP. 51-63. FR VII 31592.

GLOTON, R. ALBERT CAMUS MORALISTE. LECTURES CULTURELLES,   1855
(JAN.-FEB. 1958). BR, CR 1098 BIS.

GOBIN, P. B. ALBERT CAMUS. QUEEN'S QUARTERLY, VOL. 67, NO. 1   1856
(SPRING 1960), PP. 117-124. BFZ 46-283, KL 386.

GOLDBERG, HARVEY. THE VIOLENCE OF VIRTUE. 'THE FALL' BY ALBERT   1857
CAMUS. NATION, VOL. 184, NO. 13 (MARCH 30, 1957), P.
278-280.

GOLDBERG, L. HIRHUREEM AL PERAS NOBEL LESIFRUT (REFLECTIONS   1858
ABOUT THE NOBEL PRIZE FOR LITERATURE). AL HAMISHMAR, NOV.
1, 1957, P. 5.

GOLDBERG, M.A. CHRONOLOGY, CHARACTER AND THE HUMAN CONDITION. A   1859
REAPPRAISAL OF THE MODERN NOVEL. CRITICISM, VOL. 5, NO. 1
(WINTER 1963), PP. 1-12.

GOLDSMITH, J. H. PARIS LETTER. THE NEW FRENCH SENSE OF REALITY.   1860
PARTISAN REVIEW, VOL. 23, NO. 1 (WINTER 1956-57), PP.
81-89. KL I 231.

GOLDSTEIN, LEON J. THE EMPEROR OF CHINA AS THE EMPEROR OF ROME.   1861
PERSONALIST, VOL. 43, NO. 4 (FALL 1962), PP. 515-526.
PMLA 7975 (1963).

GOLLIET, PIERRE. UN AN APRÈS SA MORT LE PROBLÈME D'ALBERT CAMUS   1862
RESTE OUVERT. MONDE, VOL. 14, NO. 638 (JAN. 5-11, 1961),
P. 7. DEPTULA.

GÓMEZ, PAZ JULIETA. ALGUNAS FIGURAS DEL TEATRO DE CAMUS.   1863
REALIDAD (BUENOS AIRES), VOL. 6, NOS. 17-18 (SEPT.-DEC.
1949), PP. 295-300. BO 251.

GOOSSENS, F. RENARD, SIMONE, ET JEAN GUERITTE. LE CHRETIEN   1864
DEVANT LE MAL. PARIS. EDITIONS ST. PAUL, 1949.
PRESENTATIONS DE LA PESTE D ALBERTCAMUS. BO 431.

GORE, KEITH O. A WRITER'S NOTEBOOKS. ALBERT CAMUS. BOOKS   1865
ABROAD, VOL. 39, NO. 4 (AUTUMN 1965), P. 403-404.

GOTH, MAJA. FRANZ KAFKA ET LES LETTRES FRANÇAISES 1928-1955.   1866
PARIS. LIBRAIRIE J. CORTI, 1956. LA CONCEPTION DE L'AB-

SURDE CHEZ ALBERT CAMUS ET FRANZ KAFKA , PP. 123-135. FR
VII 16675, KL I 53, KL I 241.

1867   GOTHOT, CLAUDINE. LES ESSAIS MÉDITERRANÉENS D'ALBERT
CAMUS--ÉTUDES DE THÈMES. (I). MARCHE ROMANE, VOL. 9, NO. 2
(APRIL-JUNE 1959), PP. 59-74. FR VII 26339, KL 388, PMLA
6825 (1961).

1868   GOTHOT, CLAUDINE. LES ESSAIS MÉDITERRANÉENS D'ALBERT
CAMUS--ÉTUDES DE THÈMES (II). MARCHE ROMANE, VOL. 9, NO. 3
(JULY-SEPT. 1959), PP. 113-132. FR VII 26339, KL II 388,
PMLA 6825 (1961).

1869   GOUHIER, HENRI. LE MALENTENDU. VIE INTELLECTUELLE, VOL. 13,
NO. 1 (OCT. 1945), PP. 131-132. BO 335, CR 526.

1870   GOUHIER, HENRI. THÉÂTRE. CALIGULA D'ALBERT CAMUS. VIE
INTELLECTUELLE, VOL. 13, NO. 9 (OCT. 1945), PP. 146-148.
CR 525.

1871   GOUHIER, HENRI. TRAGEDY AND TRANSCENDENCE, FREEDOM AND POETRY.
CROSS CURRENTS, VOL. 10, NO. 3 (WINTER 1960), PP. 15-28.
FR VII 23076.

1872   GOUHIER, HENRI. ALBERT CAMUS ET LE THÉÂTRE. TABLE RONDE, NO.
146 (FEB. 1960), PP. 61-66. BFZ 46-283, BUL SIGN
15-19-14604, FR VII 23569, KL II 389.

1873   GOURFINKEL, NINA. LES POSSÉDÉS. REVUE D'HISTOIRE DU THÉÂTRE,
VOL. 12, NO. 4 (OCT.-DEC. 1960), PP. 337-342. FR VII
23570, PMLA 7365 (1962).

1874   GOVAARTS, TH. ALBERT CAMUS EN ZIJN 'DE MENS IN OPSTAND'.
NIEUWE EEUW, VOL. 30, NO. 14 (APRIL 3, 1954), P. 10. BO
526, CR 884.

1875   GOZZINI, MARIO. CAMUS, L'UOMO E 'LA PESTE'. ULTIMA, VOL. 30,
NO. 26 (FEB. 25, 1948), PP. 21-28. BO 412.

1876   GRAEF, HILDA. MODERN GLOOM AND CHRISTIAN HOPE. CHICAGO. HENRY
REGNERY COMPANY, 1959. ALBERT CAMUS, PP. 16-19.

1877   GRAZZINI, GIOVANNI. ALBERT CAMUS, LA RIVOLTA. NAZIONE
ITALIANA, (AUG. 13, 1957). BR, CR 1025 TER.

1878   GREACEN, ROBERT. ALBERT CAMUS. ATHEIST AND REBEL. HUMANIST
(LONDON), VOL. 74, NO. 6 (JUNE 1959), PP. 18-19. FR VII
34006.

1879   GREEN, JULIEN. PAGES DE JOURNAL. 1946. TABLE RONDE, NO. 14
(FEB. 1949), PP. 181-197.

1880   GREENE, MAXINE. A RETURN TO HEROIC MAN. SATURDAY REVIEW, VOL.
42, NO. 34 (AUG. 22, 1959), PP. 10-11, 35-36.

1881   GREENE, NORMAN. JEAN-PAUL SARTRE. THE EXISTENTIALIST ETHIC.
ANN ARBOR. UNIVERSITY OF MICHIGAN PRESS, 1960.

1882   GREENE, THEODORE M. ANXIETY AND THE SEARCH FOR MEANING. TEXAS
QUARTERLY, VOL. 1, NO. 3 (SUMMER-AUTUMN 1958), PP.
172-191.

GREENMAN, MARTIN A. THE THOUGHT AND ART OF ALBERT CAMUS BY   1883
    THOMAS HANNA. (REVIEW). PHILOSOPHY AND PHENOMENOLOGICAL
    RESEARCH, VOL. 20, NO. 2 (DEC. 1959), PP. 278-279.

GREGOR, JOSEPH. DER SCHAUSPIELFÜHRER. STUTTGART. HIERSEMANN,   1884
    1957. RÉSUMÉS OF CAMUS   BELAGERUNGSZUSTAND (L'ÉTAT DE
    SIÈGE, 1946), PP. 106-107. CALIGULA (1945), PP. 98-99.
    DER IRRTUM (LE MALENTENDU, 1944), PP. 99-100.

GRENAUD, PIERRE. 'LA CHUTE', PAR ALBERT CAMUS. REVUE DE LA   1885
    MÉDITERRANÉE, VOL. 17, NO. 80 (JULY-AUG. 1957), PP.
    447-449. CR 1026.

GRENIER, JEAN. UNE OEUVRE, UN HOMME. CAHIERS DU SUD, VOL. 30,   1886
    NO. 253 (FEB. 1943), PP. 224-228. BO 2, CR 495, FR VII
    752.

GRENIER, JEAN (EDITOR). L'EXISTENCE, ESSAIS PAR ALBERT CAMUS,   1887
    BENJAMIN FONDANE, M. DE GANDILLAC, ETIENNE GILSON, JEAN
    GRENIER, LOUIS LAVELLE, RENÉ LE SENNE, BRICE PARAIN, A. DE
    WAELHENS. PARIS. GALLIMARD (COLL. METAPHYSIQUE), 1945 CR
    278, FR VII 125. SEE NO. 371.

GRENIER, JEAN. UN OUI, UN NON, UNE LIGNE DROITE. FIGARO   1888
    LITTERAIRE, VOL. 12, NO. 601 (OCT. 26, 1957), PP. 1, 5.
    BR, CR 1027, FR VII 17310.

GRENIER, JEAN. IL ME SERAIT IMPOSSIBLE... NOUVELLE REVUE   1889
    FRANCAISE, VOL. 8, NO. 87 (MARCH 1960), P. 409. FR VII
    23575, KL II 393.

GRENIER, JEAN. PRÉFACE AUX OEUVRES COMPLÈTES D'ALBERT CAMUS.   1890
    PARIS. IMPRIMERIE NATIONALE, ANDRÉ SAURET, EDITEUR, 1962.

GRENIER, ROGER. LES LIVRES. 'LA CHUTE' RÉVÈLE UN NOUVEAU   1891
    CAMUS. RÉALITÉS, NO. 27 (JULY-AUG. 1956), P. 3. CR 941.

GRENIER, ROGER. JE N'AI JAMAIS RENCONTRÉ PERSONNE QUI FASSE   1892
    COMME LUI CONFIANCE À UN INCONNU. FIGARO LITTÉRAIRE, VOL.
    15, NO. 716 (JAN. 9, 1960), P. 6. FR VII 26340, KL II 393.

GRENIER, ROGER. À 'COMBAT'. NOUVELLE REVUE FRANÇAISE, VOL. 8,   1893
    NO. 87 (MARCH 1960), PP. 472-475. FR VII 23575, KL II 389.

GRENIER, ROGER. PRÉFACE À A. CAMUS, SES AMIS DU LIVRE. SEE NO.   1894
    934.

GRENZMANN, WILHELM. WELTDICHTUNG DER GEGENWART, PROBLÈME UND   1895
    GESTALTEN. BONN. ATHENAUM-VERLAG, 1955. ALBERT CAMUS,
    PP. 271-292. BDZ 112-229 (1956), BO 79, CR 458.

GRENZMANN, WILHELM. WELTDICHTUNG DER GEGENWART. PROBLEME UND   1896
    GESTALTEN. FRANKFURT AM MAIN. ATHENAUM VERL., 1961. FR
    VII 25229.

GRIL, LUCIEN. RÉPONSE À M. ALBERT CAMUS. ÂGE NOUVEAU, NO. 97   1897
    (JULY 1956), PP. 21-26. CR 942.

GRISOLI, CHRISTIAN. ENTRETIEN AVEC JEAN-PAUL SARTRE. PARU,   1898
    NO. 13 (DEC. 1945), PP. 5-10.

1899   GRIVA, DOMENICO PERETTI. PREFAZIONE IN LA GHIGLIOTTINA DI
        ALBERTO CAMUS. MILAN. LONGANESI, 1958.

1900   GROBE, EDWIN P. THE PSYCHOLOGICAL STRUCTURE OF CAMUS'S
        'L'HÔTE'. FRENCH REVIEW, VOL. 40, NO. 3 (DEC. 1966), PP.
        357-367.

1901   GROBE, EDWIN P. TARROU'S CONFESSION. THE ETHICAL FORCE OF THE
        PAST DEFINITE. FRENCH REVIEW, VOL. 39, NO. 4 (FEB. 1966),
        PP. 550-558.

1902   GROS, L.-G. CHRONIQUES. PERMANENCE DE LA GRÈCE. CAHIERS DU
        SUD, 36TH YEAR, VOL. 30, NO. 297 (2ND SEMESTER 1949), PP.
        344-346. CR 700.

1903   GROSJEAN, JEAN. MICHEL GALLIMARD. NOUVELLE REVUE FRANÇAISE,
        VOL. 8, NO. 87 (MARCH 1960), PP. 466-468.

1904   GRUBBS, HENRY A. ALBERT CAMUS AND GRAHAM GREENE. MODERN
        LANGUAGE QUARTERLY, VOL. 10, NO. 1 (MARCH 1949), PP.
        33-42. BO 263, CR 701.

1905   GUÉHENNO, JEAN. MAIS NON, LA VIE N'EST PAS ABSURDE. FIGARO
        LITTÉRAIRE, VOL. 6, NO. 292 (NOV. 24, 1951), PP. 1, 6. BO
        207, BR, CR 786, FR VII 5747.

1906   GUÉHENNO, JEAN. UNE PURETÉ ÉCLATANTE. FIGARO LITTÉRAIRE, VOL.
        15, NO. 716 (JAN. 9, 1960), PP. 1, 7. FR VII 26341, KL II
        393.

1907   GUÉHENNO, JEAN. TOUT MON ROYAUME EST DE CE MONDE. ÉDUCATION
        NATIONALE, NO. 2 (JAN. 14, 1960), PP. 16-17. FR VII
        23624.

1908   GUÉHENNO, JEAN. CE MONDE DE PAUVRETÉ ET DE LUMIÈRE. TABLE
        RONDE, NO. 146 (FEB. 1960), PP. 167-168. BFZ 46-284, BUL
        SIGN 15-19-13756, FR VII 23569, KL II 393.

1909   GUÉRARD, ALBERT J. ALBERT CAMUS. FOREGROUND, VOL. 1, NO. 1
        (WINTER 1946), PP. 45-59. BO 8, BR, CR 564 BIS.

1910   GUÉRARD, ALBERT. ALBERT CAMUS. 'L'ETRANGER'. BOOKS ABROAD,
        VOL. 21, NO. 2 (SPRING 1947), P. 178. CR 598.

1911   GUÉRARD, ALBERT, SR. ALBERT CAMUS. 'LA PESTE'. BOOKS ABROAD,
        VOL. 22, NO. 1 (WINTER 1948), P. 44. CR 659.

1912   GUÉRARD, ALBERT. ALBERT CAMUS. ACTUELLES. CHRONIQUES,
        1944-1948 . BOOKS ABROAD, VOL. 25, NO. 2 (SPRING 1951), P.
        128. CR 787.

1913   GUÉRARD, CATHERINE. THÉÂTRE: 'REQUIEM POUR UNE NONNE'.
        FEMINA-ILLUSTRATION, NO. 30 (NOV. 1956), P. 5. CR 943.

1914   GUÉRIN, RAYMOND. L'INIMITABLE, LE JONGLEUR ET LE NOVICE.
        PARISIENNE, NO. 18 (JUNE 1954), PP. 686-696. BO 77, FR
        VII 10794.

1915   GUERNY, YVES DU. ALBERT CAMUS À STOCKHOLM. UNE CONFÉRENCE DU
        PRIX NOBEL. SOIR, VOL. 71, NO. 347 (DEC. 13, 1957), P. 5.
        CR 1028.

GUEZ, GILBERT. ALBERT CAMUS RÉPOND... PARIS-THÉÂTRE, VOL. 11,   1916
    NO. 125 (1957), PP. 12-14. FR VII 17311.

GUGLIELMI, GUIDO. IL ROMANZO DI ALBERT CAMUS. PARAGONE, VOL.   1917
    9, NO. 116 (AUG. 1959), PP. 27-42. FR VII 21392, KL II
    388.

GUIBERT, ARMAND. ALBERT CAMUS. 'L'ÉTÉ'. MONDE NOUVEAU-PARU,   1918
    VOL. 10, NO. 85 (JAN. 1955), PP. 123-124. CR 916.

GUIBERT, ARMAND. LIMPIDE ET RAVAGÉ... TABLE RONDE, NO. 146   1919
    (FEB. 1960), PP. 26-29. BFZ 46-283, BUL SIGN 15-19-13755,
    FR VII 23569, KL II 393.

GUICHARNAUD, JACQUES. THOSE YEARS. EXISTENTIALISM 1943-1945.   1920
    YALE FRENCH STUDIES, NO. 16 (WINTER 1955-1956), PP.
    127-145. BO 178. TRANSLATED BY KEVIN NEILSON.

GUICHARNAUD, JACQUES. MODERN FRENCH THEATRE FROM GIRAUDOUX TO   1921
    BECKETT. NEW HAVEN. YALE UNIVERSITY PRESS, 1961. CHAPTER
    VI. MAN AND HIS ACTS. JEAN-PAUL SARTRE AND ALBERT CAMUS ,
    PP. 131-152.

GUIDO, BEATRIZ. LOS DOS ALBERTOS EN LA NOVELA CONTEMPORANEA.   1922
    ARGENTINA. ROSARIO, 1950. BO 267, FR VII 7689.

GUIGUET, JEAN. DEUX ROMANS EXISTENTIALISTES: LA NAUSÉE ET   1923
    L'ETRANGER . FRENCH REVIEW, VOL. 23, NO. 2 (DEC. 1949),
    PP. 86-91. BO 304, CR 702, FR VII 4108.

GUILLET, H. 'LA CHUTE', PAR ALBERT CAMUS. LIVRES ET LECTURES,   1924
    (JULY-AUG. 1956), PP. 407-408. CR 944, KL I 274.

GUILLET, H. KOESTLER ET CAMUS. RÉFLEXIONS SUR LA PEINE   1925
    CAPITALE. LIVRES ET LECTURES, (1957), P. 550. CR 1029.

GUILLORÉ, RAYMOND. ALBERT CAMUS ET NOUS. LA RÉVOLUTION   1926
    PROLÉTARIENNE, NO. 447 (FEB. 1960), PP.25-26.

GUIRAUD, PIERRE, ET AL. STYLE ET LITTERATURE. LA HAYE, VAN   1927
    GOOR ZONEN, 1962. SEE NO. 3180.

GUISAN, GILBERT M. ESQUISSE STYLISTIQUE DE LA PESTE. CAHIERS   1928
    DE L'ASSOCIATION INTERNATIONALE DES ÉTUDES FRANÇAISES, NO.
    16 (MARCH 1964), PP. 31-41. PMLA 8614 (1964).

GUISSARD, FIRMAIN. ALBERT CAMUS. 'LA PESTE'. FICHES   1929
    BIBLIOGRAPHIQUES, (1947). CR 599.

GUISSARD, LUCIEN. ALBERT CAMUS OU L'HUMANISME TRAGIQUE. LIVRES   1930
    ET LECTURES, NO. 73 (DEC. 1953), PP. 499-502. CR 854.

GUISSARD, LUCIEN. ALBERT CAMUS ET NOUS. CROIX, VOL. 81, NO.   1931
    23,421 (JAN. 6, 1960), PP. 1, 4. FITCH.

GUISSARD, LUCIEN. ÉCRITS EN NOTRE TEMPS. PARIS. FAYARD, 1961.   1932
    CHAPTER VIII.   ALBERT CAMUS, À LA RECHERCHE D'UNE
    LÉGITIMITÉ , PP. 267-282. FR VII 25231, PMLA 7171 (1962).

GUITON, MARGARET. AN AGE OF FICTION. SEE NO. 1277.   1933

GUITTON, JEAN. EXTRAITS D'UN JOURNAL. TABLE RONDE, NO. 146   1934
    (FEB. 1960), PP. 169-173. BUL SIGN 15-19-13758, FR VII

23569, KL II 394.

1935   GULLICHSEN, HARALD. PASCAL OG CAMUS. VINDUET, VOL. 9, NO. 1
        (1955), PP. 71-77. FR VII 29374.

1936   GULLÓN, RICARDO. LOS MITOS DE CAMUS. INSULA, VOL. 8, NO. 96
        (DEC. 15, 1953), PP. 3, 5, 11. BO 244, FR VII 11225.

1937   GULLON, RICARDO. ALBERT CAMUS, PREMIO NOBEL. INSULA, VOL. 12,
        NO. 132 (NOV. 1957), PP. 1, 8. FR VII 21393.

1938   GÜRSTER, EUGEN. SCHULD OHNE RICHTER. HOCHLAND, VOL. 49, NO. 2
        (DEC. 1956), PP. 188-191. BDZ 114-301 (1957), CR 940, KL I
        273.

1939   GUTIERREZ, FELIX. PASTICHE. MAINSTREAM, VOL. 13, NO. 5 (MAY
        1960), PP. 62-63. FR VII 36342.

1940   GUY, ROBERT. CAMUS, UNE TENTATIVE DE JUSTIFICATION DE L'HOMME.
        REVUE DOMINICAINE, VOL. 2, NO. 64 (JULY-AUG. 1958), PP.
        15-25. FR VII 21394.

1941   GUYARD, MARIUS-FRANÇOIS. ALBERT CAMUS. PRIX NOBEL DE
        LITTERATURE. CLASSE DE FRANÇAIS, VOL. 7, NO. 6 (NOV.-DEC.
        1957), PP. 321-325. KL I 274.

1942   GUYOT, CHARLY. ALBERT CAMUS, DRAMATURGE. LABYRINTHE, NO. 5
        (FEB. 15, 1945), P. 2. BO 248, CR 527.

1943   GUYOT, C. L'HUMANISME D'ALBERT CAMUS. CAHIERS PROTESTANTS,
        NO. 36 (1952), PP. 54-65. BFZ 32-249 (1950-52), BO 149, CR
        819.

1944   H., M. A. MORE DIM VIEWS. SATURDAY NIGHT, VOL. 73, NO. 14
        (3317) (JULY 5, 1958), P. 23.

1945   H., W. OP ZOEK NAAR DE MORAAL. NIEUWE ROMAN VAN CAMUS. NIEUWE
        EEUW, VOL. 30, NO. 242 (SEPT. 24, 1949), P. 7. CR 726.

1946   HAAS, WILLY. NOBELPREISTRÄGER DER LITERATUR. EIN KAPITEL
        WELTLITERATUR DES ZWANZIGSTEN JAHRHUNDERTS. HEIDELBERG,
        HEINZ MOOS, 1962. CAMUS. REDE IN STOCKHOLM ZUR VERLEIHUNG
        DES NOBELPREISES AM 10. DEZEMBER 1957, PP. 31-35. FR VII
        32120.

1947   HADGOPOULOS, SARALYN POOLE. ODYSSEUS' CHOICE. A COMPARISON AND
        CONTRAST OF WORKS BY ALBERT CAMUS AND NIKOS KAZANTZAKIS.
        DISSERTATION ABSTRACTS. VOL. 27, NO. 1 (JULY 1966), PP.
        204A205A.

1948   HAEDENS, K. 'LA CHUTE'. PARIS-PRESSE, (JUNE 1956). BO 546.

1949   HAESE, BERTHA. ALBERT CAMUS. LEBT ALS OB! KATHOLISCHE
        FRAUENBILDUNG, VOL. 62, (1961), PP. 655-666. BDZ 123-307
        (1961).

1950   HAGGIS, DONALD R. ALBERT CAMUS. 'LA PESTE'. LONDON. EDWARD
        ARNOLD, 1962. PMLA 7976 (1963).

1951   HAGGIS, DONALD R. 'CARNETS 1935-1942' BY ALBERT CAMUS. MODERN
        LANGUAGE REVIEW, VOL. 60, NO. 1 (JAN. 1965), P. 125-126.

1952   HAGGIS, DONALD R. ALBERT CAMUS. LA PESTE. FRANÇAIS DANS LE

MONDE. NO. 38, (JAN.-FEB. 1966), PP. 29-33.

HAHN, K. J. ALBERT CAMUS' LAATSTE ROMAN. LINIE, VOL. 11, NO.   1953
    546 (SEPT. 15, 1956),P. 9. BR, CR 944 BIS.

HALL, H. GASTON. ASPECTS OF THE ABSURD. YALE FRENCH STUDIES,   1954
    NO. 25 (SPRING 1960), PP. 26-32. BUL SIGN 16-19-9736, FR
    VII 23568, KL II 389.

HALLIE, PHILIP. CAMUS AND THE LITERATURE OF REVOLT. COLLEGE   1955
    ENGLISH, VOL. 16, NO. 1 (OCT. 1954), PP. 25-32, 83. BFZ
    37-266 (1953-55), BO 236, CR 885, FR VII 19423.

HALLIER, JEAN-EDERN. ALBERT CAMUS: 'L'ETE'. TABLE RONDE, NO.   1956
    77 (MAY 1954), PP. 117-118. BFZ 36-234 (1953-54), BO 538,
    CR 886.

HAMBRO, CARL. NOEN FRANSKE FORMULERINGER AV MODERNE PROBLEMER.   1957
    VINDUET, VOL. 1, NO. 2 (1947), PP. 133-138. FR VII 28242.

HAMBRO, CARL. TEATERBREV FRA PARIS. VINDUET, VOL. 3, NO. 5   1958
    (1949), PP. 276-382. FR VII 28767.

HAMILTON, WILLIAM. THE CHRISTIAN, THE SAINT, AND THE REBEL.   1959
    ALBERT CAMUS. IN SCOTT, NATHAN A., JR., FORMS OF
    EXTREMITY IN THE MODERN NOVEL, PP. 55-74. SEE NO. 3045.

HAMELIN, JEAN. MONTREAL, THE FRENCH THEATRE. TAMARACK REVIEW,   1960
    NO. 25 (AUTUMN 1962), PP. 69-75. FR VII 28768.

HAMMELRATH, WILLI. DIE 'PEST' VON CAMUS IN DER   1961
    ARBEITERHOCHSCHULE. KULTURARBEIT, VOL. 5, NO. 1 (JAN. 5,
    1953), P. 19. BO 439, CR 855.

HAMMELRATH, WILLI. VOLKSBILDUNG, ARBEITERBILDUNG. NUREMBERG.   1962
    GLOCK UND LUTZ, 1954. EIN BEISPIEL: 'DIE PEST' VON CAMUS
    MIT ARBEITERN GELESEN , PP. 108-112. BO 441. REPRINT OF
    NO. 1961.

HAMMER, LOUIS Z. IMPOSSIBLE FREEDOM IN CAMUS' 'CALIGULA'   1963
    PERSONALIST, VOL. 44, NO. 3 (SUMMER 1963), PP. 322-336.

HAMPSHIRE, STUART. THE FACTS OF CONSCIOUSNESS. REVIEW OF THE   1964
    ENGLISH TRANSLATION OF 'THE MYTH OF SISYPHUS'. LISTENER,
    VOL. 54, NO. 1396 (DEC. 1, 1955), P. 957. FR VII 29375.

HAMPSHIRE, STUART. PHILOSOPHY IN FRANCE. REVIEW. ALBERT CAMUS   1965
    BY PHILIP THODY. NEW STATESMAN, VOL. 55, NO. 1402 (JAN.
    25, 1958), PP. 109-110. FR VII 33695.

HANNA, THOMAS L. ALBERT CAMUS AND THE CHRISTIAN FAITH. JOURNAL   1966
    OF RELIGION, COLLECTION OF CRITICAL ESSAYS, VOL. 36, NO. 4
    (OCT. 1956), PP. 224-233. BUL SIGN 11-9221, FR VII 19424,
    KL I 272.

HANNA, THOMAS L. ALBERT CAMUS AND THE CHRISTIAN FAITH. IN   1967
    BRÉE, GERMAINE, CAMUS, A COLLECTION OF CRITICAL ESSAYS .
    PP. 48-58. SEE NO. 1293. REPRINT OF NO. 1966.

HANNA, THOMAS. THE THOUGHT AND ART OF ALBERT CAMUS. CHICAGO.   1968
    H. REGNERY CO., 1958. BR, CR 458 BIS, FR VII 19399, KL I

272.

1969   HANNA, THOMAS. THE LYRICAL EXISTENTIALISTS. NEW YORK.
        ATHENEUM, 1962. FR VII 28274.

1970   HANNEDOUCHE, S. LE PROBLÈME DU MAL CHEZ QUELQUES ÉCRIVAINS
        CONTEMPORAINS. CAHIERS D'ÉTUDES CATHARES, VOL. 8, NO. 30
        (SUMMER 1957), PP. 67-74. KL I 241.

1971   HANSEN, THORKILD. ALBERT CAMUS: SOMMER, ESSAYS. COPENHAGEN.
        GYLDENDAL, 1961. FORORD, PP. 5-22, EFTERSKRIFT, PP.
        156-158.

1972   HARDRÉ, JACQUES. CAMUS DANS LA RÉSISTANCE. FRENCH REVIEW,
        VOL. 37, NO. 6 (MAY 1964), PP. 646-650.

1973   HARLASS, GERALD. REVOLTE OHNE HOFFNUNG. IN MEMORIAM ALBERT
        CAMUS. WELT UND WORT, VOL. 25, NO. 2, (FEB. 1960), PP.
        35-36. FR VII 23625, KL II 394, PMLA 6826 (1961).

1974   HAROUTUNIAN, LULU. ALBERT CAMUS AND THE WHITE PLAGUE. MODERN
        LANGUAGE NOTES, VOL. 79, NO. 3 (MAY 1964), PP. 311-315.
        PMLA 8615 (1964).

1975   HARPER, RALPH. THE DARK NIGHT OF SISYPHUS. IN SCOTT, NATHAN
        A., JR., THE CLIMATE OF FAITH IN MODERN LITERATURE, PP.
        65-83. SEE NO. 3044.

1976   HARRINGTON, CATHERINE STETA. SOUTHERN FICTION AND THE QUEST FOR
        IDENTITY. DISSERTATION ABSTRACTS, VOL. 25, NO. 2 (AUGUST
        1964), PP. 1210-1211. PMLA 6552 (1964).

1977   HARRINGTON, MICHAEL. ETHICS OF REBELLION. COMMONWEAL, VOL.
        59, NO. 17 (JAN. 29, 1954), PP. 428-431. BO 527.

1978   HARRINGTON, MICHAEL. THE DESPAIR AND HOPE OF MODERN MAN.
        COMMONWEAL, VOL. 63, NO. 2 (OCT. 14, 1955), PP. 44-45. BO
        327, FR VII 15347.

1979   HARTLEY, ANTHONY. A TRIBUTE TO ALBERT CAMUS. LISTENER, VOL.
        53, NO. 1607 (JAN. 14, 1960), P. 59. FR VII 29376.

1980   HARTLEY, ANTHONY. A WORLD OF PAIN AND SUNLIGHT. 'CARNETS
        1942-1951' BY ALBERT CAMUS. NEW SOCIETY, VOL. 7, NO. 178
        (FEB. 24, 1966), P. 24-25.

1981   HARTMAN, GEOFFREY, H. THE FULNESS AND NOTHINGESS OF LITERATURE.
        YALE FRENCH STUDIES, NO. 16 (WINTER 1955-56), PP. 63-78.

1982   HARTMAN, GEOFFREY H. CAMUS AND MALRAUX. THE COMMON GROUND.
        YALE FRENCH STUDIES, NO. 25 (SPRING 1960), PP. 104-110.
        BUL SIGN 16-19-9749 (1962),FR VII 23568, KL II 392.

1983   HARTSOCK, MILDRED. CAMUS' 'THE FALL'. DIALOGUE OF ONE. MODERN
        FICTION STUDIES, VOL. 7, NO. 4 (WINTER 1961-62), PP.
        357-364. PMLA 7977 (1962).

1984   HARTSOCK, MILDRED E. THE DIZZYING CREST. STRETHER AS MORAL MAN.
        MODERN LANGUAGE QUARTERLY, VOL. 26, NO. 3 (SEPT. 1965),
        PP. 414-425.

1985   HARTT, J. N. BEYOND EXISTENTIALISM. YALE REVIEW, VOL. 45, NO.

3 (MARCH 1956), PP. 444-451. FR VII 15348, KL I 273.

HARTT, JULIAN N. ALBERT CAMUS. AN APPRECIATION. CHRISTIANITY   1986
     AND CRISIS, VOL. 20, NO. 1 (FEB. 8, 1960), PP. 7-8.

HARTT, JULIAN N. THE LOST IMAGE OF MAN. BATON ROUGE. LOUISIANA   1987
     STATE UNIVERSITY PRESS, 1963. PMLA 1301 (1964).

HARTUNG, R. VOM TRAUM DER VERBANNTEN. NEUE DEUTSCHE HEFTE,   1988
     NO. 47 (JUNE 1958), PP. 268-269. KL II 391.

HASSAN, IHAB. THE DISMEMBERMENT OF ORPHEUS. REFLECTIONS ON   1989
     MODERN CULTURE, LANGUAGE AND LITERATURE. AMERICAN SCHOLAR,
     VOL. 32, NO. 3 (SUMMER 1963), PP. 463FF. (CAMUS REF. PP.
     468, 470).

HASSAN, IHAB. THE NOVEL OF OUTRAGE. A MINORITY VOICE IN POSTWAR   1990
     AMERICAN FICTION. AMERICAN SCHOLAR, VOL. 34, NO. 2
     (SPRING 1965), PP. 239-253 (CAMUS REF. PP. 240-241, 246).

HATZFELD, HELMUT. INITIATION À L'EXPLICATION DE TEXTES   1991
     FRANÇAIS. MÜNCHEN. M. HUEBER, 1957. ALBERT CAMUS, PP.
     181-190. FR VII 16586.

HATZFELD, HELMUT. TRENDS AND STYLES IN TWENTIETH CENTURY FRENCH   1992
     LITERATURE. WASHINGTON, D. C.. CATHOLIC UNIVERSITY PRESS,
     1957.

HAUPTMANN, FRANZ. ALBERT CAMUS: 'DER FALL'. ANTARES, VOL. 5,   1993
     NO. 3 (MAY 1957), P. 79.

HAUSER, HANS H. CALIGULAS SELBSTMORD HÖHEREN GRADES. PRISMA,   1994
     NO. 7 (MAY 1947), PP. 27-29. CR 597. SEE NO. 1847.

HÉBERTOT, JACQUES. DES PERSONNALITÉS DU THÉÂTRE... (HOMMAGES À   1995
     CAMUS). FIGARO, VOL. 134, NO. 4770 (JAN. 6, 1960). P. 4.
     FITCH.

HEIDELBERGER, ERNST. SCHWARZES THEATER. UMSCHAU, VOL. 2, NO.   1996
     4 (1947), PP. 442-449. BO 340.

HEINEMANN, F. H. EXISTENTIALISM AND THE MODERN PREDICAMENT.   1997
     NEW YORK. HARPER, 1953. KL I 231.

HEIST, W. ALBERT CAMUS UND DER NACHFASCHISMUS. FRANKFURTER   1998
     HEFTE, VOL. 8, NO. 4 (1953), PP. 296-303. BO 101, CR 856.

HEIST, WALTER. DIE TRAGÖDIE CAMUS. VOM KURZEN ATEM EINES   1999
     MORALISTEN. LA CHUTE. DEUTSCHE UNIVERSITÄTSZEITUNG, VOL.
     11, NOS. 15-16 (1956), PP. 26-27. CR 945.

HEIST, WALTER. DAS FRAGWÜRDIGE AN ALBERT CAMUS, ÜBER DEN   2000
     POLITISCHEN ASPEKT SEINES WERKES. FRANKFURTER HEFTE, VOL.
     18, NO. 1 (JAN. 1963), PP. 19-29. PMLA 7972 (1964), FR VII
     33954.

HEIST, WALTER. L'ÉQUIVOQUE POLITIQUE. REVUE DES LETTRES   2001
     MODERNES, NOS. 90-93 (WINTER 1963), PP. 125-144. PMLA
     8608 (1964). SEE NO. 3207. TRANSLATION OF NO. 2000.
     TRANSLATED BY BERNARD LORTHOLARY.

HELL, HENRI. DEUX RÉCITS. FONTAINE, NO. 21 (MAY 1942), PP.   2002

352-355.

2003   HELL, HENRI. 'LA CHUTE'. TABLE RONDE,   NO. 106 (OCT. 1956),
        PP. 109-112. KL I 274.

2004   HELL, HENRI. ALBERT CAMUS: 'L'EXIL ET LE ROYAUME'. TABLE
        RONDE,   NO. 114 (JUNE 1957), PP. 202-205. BFZ 42-284, CR
        1030, FR VII 17312, KL I 273.

2005   HELL, HENRI. GIDE ET CAMUS. TABLE RONDE,   NO. 146 (FEB. 1960),
        PP. 22-25. BFZ 46-583, BUL SIGN 15-19-13775, FR VII 23569,
        KL II 392.

2006   HELLENS, FRANZ. LE MYTHE CHEZ ALBERT CAMUS.   NOUVELLE REVUE
        FRANCAISE,   VOL. 8, NO. 87 (MARCH 1960), PP. 480-486.   FR
        VII 23575, KL II 389.

2007   HELWIG, W. L. ALBERT CAMUS EN HET ZUIDEN. NIEUWE EEUW,   VOL.
        36, NO. 2 (JAN. 8, 1955), P. 7. CR 917.

2008   HELWIG, W. L. ALBERT CAMUS EN ZIJN ESSAYS 'L'ETE'. NIEUWE
        EEUW,   VOL. 36, NO. 2 (JAN. 8, 1955), P. 7.   BO 543, CR
        917.

2009   HELWIG, W. L. DE CRISIS VAN HET MODERNE LEVENSGEVOEL. ALBERT
        CAMUS.   LA CHUTE . NIEUWE EEUW, VOL. 37, NO. 42 (OCT.
        27, 1956), P. 7.   CR 946.

2010   HEMINGWAY, ERNEST. DES ÉCRIVAINS NOUS DISENT. (HOMMAGES À
        CAMUS.) FIGARO, VOL. 134, NO. 4770 (JAN. 6, 1960), P. 4.
        FR VII 23649.

2011   HEMPEL, HANS PETER. ALBERT CAMUS. DER MENSCH IN DER REVOLTE.
        DEUTSCHE RUNDSCHAU,   VOL. 88, NO. 7 (JULY 1962), PP.
        627-634. BDZ 310-125 (62), FR VII 29378.

2012   HENDEL, J. ALBERT CAMUS, BAAL PERAS NOBEL LESIFRUT 1957 (ALBERT
        CAMUS.   THE WINNER OF THE 1957 NOBEL PRIZE FOR LITERATURE).
        DAVAR,   OCT. 25, 1957, P. 5.

2013   HENDERICKX, PAUL. COMMENT LES PERSONNAGES DE LA PESTE FONT-ILS
        VIVRE LA PENSÉE DE CAMUS? REVUE DES LANGUES VIVANTES
        (BRUXELLES),   VOL. 30, NO. 2 (MARCH-APRIL 1964), PP.
        99-120. PMLA 8616 (1964).

2014   HENEIN, GEORGES. CAMUS OU LES MAINS PROPRES. ÉTUDES
        MÉDITERRANÉENNES,   NO. 7 (SPRING 1960), PP. 10-14.   FITCH.

2015   HENEIN, G. NOTES SUR QUELQUES ATTITUDES DE CAMUS. REVUE DU
        CAIRE,   VOL. 44, NO. 237 (MAY 1960), PP. 371-374.   FR VII
        23626. SEE NO. 3259.

2016   HENN, T(HOMAS) R(ICE). THE HARVEST OF TRAGEDY. LONDON.
        METHUEN, 1956. THE TRANSMIGRATION OF THE GREEK, PP.
        233-243. FR VII 32689.

2017   HENRICHS, H. DIE LOGIK DES ABSURDEN AUF DER BÜHNE. DIE
        GRUNDGEDANKEN DER STUTTGARTER INSZENIERUNG DES 'CALIGULA'
        VON ALBERT CAMUS. QUELLE, VOL. 2, NO. 5 (1948), PP.
        37-41. BDZ 98-181 (48), BO 369, CR 660.

HENRIOT, ÉMILE. 'LA CHUTE', D'ALBERT CAMUS. MONDE, VOL. 9,   2018
    NO. 398 (MAY 31-JUNE 6, 1956), P. 4. BO 547.

HENRIOT, ÉMILE. L'EXIL ET LE ROYAUME D'ALBERT CAMUS. MONDE,   2019
    VOL. 10, NO. 446 (MAY 2-8, 1957), P. 4.

HENRIOT, ÉMILE. ALBERT CAMUS, PRIX NOBEL DE LITTERATURE.   2020
    MONDE, VOL. 10, NO. 470 (OCT. 17-23, 1957), PP. 1-4. BR,
    CR 1030 BIS.

HENRIOT, ÉMILE. ALBERT CAMUS. PRIX NOBEL DE LITTÉRATURE.   2021
    BIBLIO, VOL. 25, NO. 10 (DEC. 1957), PP. 3-6. CR 1032, FR
    VII 17313.

HENRIOT, ÉMILE. ALBERT CAMUS. PRIX NOBEL DE LITTÉRATURE.   2022
    LIVRES DE FRANCE, VOL. 8, NO. 10 (DEC. 1957), PP. 3-6. FR
    VII 21395, KL I 274.

HENRIOT, ÉMILE. LE MORALISTE DE L'ABSURDE. MONDE, VOL. 13,   2023
    NO. 585 (DEC. 31, 1959-JAN. 6, 1960), P. 1. FR VII 23627.

HENRIQUEZ UREÑA, MAX. DE RIMBAUD A PASTERNAK Y QUASIMODO,   2024
    ENSAYOS SOBRE LITERATURAS CONTEMPORÁNEAS. MEXICO.
    TEZONTLE, 1960. ALBERT CAMUS, PREMIO NOBEL, PP. 95-106.

HEPPENSTALL, RAYNER. NEW NOVELS (REVIEW: 'THE OUTSIDER'). NEW   2025
    STATESMAN AND NATION, VOL. 31, NO. 801 (JUNE 29, 1946), P.
    474.

HEPPENSTALL, RAYNER. ALBERT CAMUS AND THE ROMANTIC PROTEST.   2026
    PENGUIN NEW WRITING, NO. 34 (1948), PP. 104-116. FR VII
    19425.

HEPPENSTALL, RAYNER. TWO BEST-SELLERS. NEW STATESMAN AND   2027
    NATION, VOL. 52, NO. 1329 (SEPT. 1, 1956), P. 256.

HEPPENSTALL, RAYNER. THE FOURFOLD TRADITION. LONDON. BARRIE   2028
    AND ROCKLIFF, 1961. THE SURVIVOR , PP. 187-210. FR VII
    25375.

HEPPENSTALL, RAYNER. BORED WITH CONSCIENCE. 'CARNETS 1942-   2029
    1951' BY ALBERT CAMUS. LISTENER, VOL. 75, NO. 1926 (FEB.
    24, 1966), P. 287.

HERBART, PIERRE. PAS DE TEMPS À PERDRE. NOUVELLE REVUE   2030
    FRANÇAISE, VOL. 8, NO. 87 (MARCH 1960), PP. 469-471. FR
    VII 23575, KL II 389.

HÉRIAT, PHILIPPE. LA CHALEUR HUMAINE. NOUVELLE REVUE   2031
    FRANÇAISE, VOL. 8, NO. 87 (MARCH 1960), PP. 425-426. FR
    VII 23575, KL II 394.

HERLING, GUSTAV. TWO SANCTITIES. GREENE AND CAMUS. ADAM   2032
    INTERNATIONAL REVIEW, VOL. 17, NO. 201 (DEC. 1949), PP.
    10-19. FR VII 23628.

HERLING-GRUDZIŃSKI, GUSTAW. SAD OSTATECZNY, CAMUS I KAFKA.   2033
    KULTURA, NO. 115 (MAY 1957), PP. 33-44. FR VII 17314, KL
    I 274.

HERMANS, W. F. ALBERT CAMUS. DE MOED TOT HET ABSURDE.   2034

LITTERAIR PASPOORT,   VOL. 2, NO. 8 (MARCH 1947), PP. 14-15.
BO 15.

2035   HERRERO, JAVIER. CAMUS Y LA REBELIÓN.   ALCALA,   NO. 17 (SEPT.
25, 1952), P. 1 (UNNUMBERED).   BO 221, FR VII 7705.

2036   HERTEL, LEO. ALBERT CAMUS, ET AL.   'OFFENER HORIZONT,
FESTSCHRIFT FÜR KARL JASPERS'.   BOOKS ABROAD,   VOL. 28, NO.
2 (SPRING 1954), P. 184.   CR 887.

2037   HERVÉ, PIERRE. LA RÉVOLTE CAMUSE. REVIEW OF 'L'HOMME RÉVOLTÉ'.
NOUVELLE CRITIQUE,   VOL. 4, NO. 35 (APRIL 1952), PP. 66-76.
FR VII 29379.

2038   HEUGTEN, J. V. 'CALIGULA'.   STREVEN, KATHOLIEK CULTUREEL
TIJDSCHRIFT, VOL. 3, (1950), PP. 376-380. BO 374, CR 753.

2039   HEURGON, JACQUES. JEUNESSE DE LA MÉDITERRANÉE.   TABLE RONDE,
NO. 146 (FEB. 1960), PP. 16-21.   BFZ 46-283, BUL SIGN
15-19-13759, FR VII 23569, KL II 394.

2040   HICKS, GRANVILLE. THE SEARCH FOR THE IDEAL ABSURDITY.   SATURDAY
REVIEW,   VOL. 49, NO. 36 (SEPT. 3, 1966), PP. 21-22.

2041   HIGHET, GILBERT. THE CLASSICAL TRADITION, GREEK AND ROMAN
INFLUENCES ON WESTERN LITERATURE.   OXFORD.   CLARENDON
PRESS, 1949.   SCATTERED REFERENCES.   FR VII 7284.

2042   HILL, CHARLES G. CAMUS AND VIGNY.   PUBLICATIONS OF THE MODERN
LANGUAGE ASSOCIATION,   VOL. 77, NO. 1 (MARCH 1962), PP.
156-167.   BFZ 262-49 (60-62), PMLA 7978 (1963).

2043   HOCHBERG, HERBERT. ALBERT CAMUS AND THE ETHIC OF ABSURDITY.
ETHICS,   VOL. 75, NO. 2 (JANUARY 1965), PP. 87-102.

2044   HOEVEN, P. V. D. DE VREEMDELING OP WEG.   WAAGSCHAAL,   (JULY 6,
1951),   BO 309, CR 704.

2045   HOEVEN, P. V. D. ALBERT CAMUS ALS MORALIST.   WENDING ('S
GRAVENHAGE),   VOL. 8, NO. 7 (SEPT. 1953), PP. 469-480   BO
127, CR 857.

2046   HOEVEN, P. V. D. ALBERT CAMUS EN ZIJN 'L'HOMME RÉVOLTÉ'.
WAAGSCHAAL,   (MAY 21, 1955),   BO 535, CR 918.

2047   HOFFMAN, FREDERICK J. CAMUS AND AMERICA.   SYMPOSIUM,   VOL. 12,
NOS. 1-2 (SPRING-FALL 1958), PP. 36-42.   BUL SIGN 14-9006,
FR VII 19426, KL II 392.

2048   HOFFMAN, STANLEY. HOMAGE TO CAMUS.   MASSACHUSETTS REVIEW,   VOL.
1, NO. 2 (FEB. 1960), PP. 212-214.

2049   HOLDHEIM, WILLIAM W. GIDE'S 'PALUDES'. THE HUMOR OF FALSITY.
FRENCH REVIEW,   VOL. 32, NO. 5 (APRIL 1959), PP. 401-409.

2050   HOLDHEIM, WILLIAM W. GIDE'S CAVES DU VATICAN AND THE
ILLUSIONISM OF THE NOVEL. MODERN LANGUAGE NOTES, VOL. 77,
NO. 3 (MAY 1962), PP. 292-304 (CAMUS REF. P. 295).

2051   HOLMQUIST, BENGT. REVOLT OCH FÖRVIRRING.   REVIEW OF 'L'HOMME
RÉVOLTÉ' (MANNISKANS REVOLT, TRANSLATED BY GUNNAR BRANDELL,
BONNIERS, 1953.)   BONNIERS LITTERÄRA MAGASIN,   VOL. 22, NO.

5 (MAY-JUNE 1953), PP. 385-387.

HOLSTEIN. L'HOMME RÉVOLTÉ . FACULTÉS CATHOLIQUES DE L'OUEST,   2052
NO. 2 (1953), PP. 27-30. BO 508.

HOLZ, H. H. LEIDEN UND RETTUNG DES SISYPHOS. BEMERKUNGEN ZUM   2053
LITERARISCHEN WERK VON ALBERT CAMUS. PANORAMA, VOL. 1,
(NOV. 1957), P. 4. BDZ 123-307 (1961).

HOLZ, H. H. DER FRANZÖSISCHE EXISTENZIALISMUS, THEORIE UND   2054
AKTUALITÄT. SPEYER-MUNCHEN. O. DOBBECK, 1958. CHAPTER
II. LEIDEN UND RETTUNG DES SISYPHUS , PP. 65-91. KL I
231.

HOPE-WALLACE, PHILIP. THE POSSESSED AT THE MERMAID. MANCHESTER   2055
GUARDIAN, NO. 36,485 (OCT. 24, 1963), P. 9. FR VII 33955.

HOPPER, STANLEY R. IRONY, THE PATHOS OF THE MIDDLE. CROSS   2056
CURRENTS, VOL. 12, NO. 1 (WINTER 1962), PP. 31-40. FR VII
28331.

HORIA, VINTILA. ALBERT CAMUS O LA LUCHA CONTRA LA ABSTRACCIÓN.   2057
CUADERNOS HISPANOAMERICANOS, NO. 122 (FEB. 1960), PP.
230-234. FR VII 23630.

HORST, AGATHE. ALBERT CAMUS UND DAS PROBLEM DER SCHULD.   2058
DORNACH. GOETHEANUM (DAS WOCHENBLATT FUR ANTHROPOSOPHIE),
1958. BDZ 119-300 (1959).

HORST, E. BEKENNTNIS ZUM MENSCHEN. NEUE DEUTSCHE HEFTE, NO.   2059
73 (AUG. 1960), PP. 462-463. FR VII 23631, KL II 390.

HOSKINS, KATHERINE. A NOVELIST OF THE ABSURD. (REVIEW.   2060
L'ETRANGER .) PARTISAN REVIEW, VOL. 13, NO. 1 (WINTER
1946), PP. 121-123.

HOURDIN, GEORGES. CAMUS LE JUSTE. PARIS. EDITIONS DU CERF,   2061
1960. FR VII 23576.

HOUWENS POST, HENRIQUE. L'AUTEUR BRÉSILIEN MACHADO DE ASSIS ET   2062
LE MYTHE DE SISYPHE . ANNALI DELL'ISTITUTO UNIVERSITARIO
ORIENTALE, VOL. 2, NO. 2 (1961), PP. 1-15. KL II 391.

HOWE, IRVING. THE WEIGHT OF DAYS. NEW REPUBLIC, VOL. 136, NO.   2063
10 (MARCH 11, 1957), PP. 16-17. FR VII 17315.

HOWE, IRVING. BETWEEN FACT AND FABLE. 'EXILE AND THE KINGDOM'   2064
BY ALBERT CAMUS. NEW REPUBLIC, VOL. 138, NO. 13 (MARCH
31, 1958), P. 17-18.

HOWLETT, J. ÉCRIVAINS D'AUJOURD HUI. PARIS, 1960. CAMUS, PP.   2065
159-168. KL II 388.

HOY, TERRY. ALBERT CAMUS. THE NATURE OF POLITICAL REBELLION.   2066
WESTERN POLITICAL QUARTERLY, VOL. 13, NO. 3 (SEPT. 1960),
PP. 573-580. FR VII 26343, PMLA 6829 (1961).

HUBBLE, THOMAS NEWMAN. THE ACT ITSELF AND THE WORD. A STUDY OF   2067
ABSTRACTION VERSUS THE CONCRETE IN THE WORK OF ALBERT
CAMUS. DISSERTATION ABSTRACTS, VOL. 23, NO. 7 (JAN.
1963), P. 2528.

2068   HÜBSCHER, ARTHUR. CAMUS-MARCEL-SARTRE. WELT UND WORT, NO. 11
       (NOV. 1949), PP. 404-406. BDZ 99-167 (49), CR 703, FR VII
       18870.

2069   HÜBSCHER, ARTHUR. PHILOSOPHEN DER GEGENWART, FUNFZIG BILDNISSE.
       MUNCHEN. R. PIPER, 1949. ALBERT CAMUS, PP. 43-45.

2070   HÜBSCHER, ARTHUR. ALBERT CAMUS. WELT UND WORT, VOL. 4,
       (1949), PP. 404-406. BO 139, CR 460.

2071   HÜBSCHER, ARTHUR. DENKER UNSERER ZEIT. I. MÜNCHEN. R. PIPER,
       1956. ALBERT CAMUS, PP. 256-259. BO 158.

2072   HUDER, WALTHER. ALBERT CAMUS UND DAS ABSURDE WUNDER DER
       FREIHEIT. ECKART JAHRBUCH, (1961-62), PP. 36-46. PMLA
       7979 (1963).

2073   HUDON, LOUIS. 'THE STRANGER' AND THE CRITICS. YALE FRENCH
       STUDIES, NO. 25 (SPRING 1960), PP. 59-64. BUL SIGN
       16-19-9949, FR VII 23568, KL II 390.

2074   HUGHES, H. STUART. METAPHYSICAL REBELLION. 'THE REBEL' BY
       ALBERT CAMUS. COMMENTARY, VOL. 17, NO. 3 (MARCH 1954), PP.
       306-308.

2075   HUGUET, JEAN. 'LA CHUTE' D'ALBERT CAMUS. J'AI LU, NO. 18
       (JULY-AUG. 1956), P. 4. CR 947.

2076   HUGUET, JEAN. CAMUS OU LE SENS ET LE GOÛT DU BONHEUR... ÂGE
       NOUVEAU, NO. 109 (APRIL-JUNE 1960), PP. 118-120. KL II
       394.

2077   IBERT, JEAN-CLAUDE. SUR CAMUS. PARISIENNE, NO. 48 (NOV.-DEC.
       1957), PP. 1075-1076. CR 1047 TER.

2078   IBERT, JEAN-CLAUDE. A PROPÓSITO DE LOS CARNETS DE ALBERT CAMUS.
       INSULA, VOL. 17, NO. 192 (NOV. 1962), P. 7. FR VII 29381.

2079   IDRISS, YOUSSEF. HOMMAGE À ALBERT CAMUS DES ÉCRIVAINS ARABES.
       SEE NO. 3047.

2080   IENS, WALTER. EUROPÄER CAMUS. ZEIT, VOL. 13, NO. 14 (1958),
       P. 9. BDZ 116-316 (1958).

2081   IHERING, H. 'CALIGULA' ODER DER SELBSTMORD EUROPAS. THEATER
       DER ZEIT, VOL. 2, NO. 4 (1947), P. 16. BO 353, CR 601.

2082   IKOR, ROGER. UNE OEUVRE EN DÉBAT DEVANT LA NOUVELLE GÉNÉRATION.
       CONFIANCE À L'HOMME, À L'ÉNERGIE, À LA LOYAUTÉ. FIGARO
       LITTÉRAIRE, VOL. 12, NO. 601 (OCT. 26, 1957), P. 7. FR
       VII 17316. SEE NO. 3251.

2083   IONESCU, GHITA. ABOUT ALBERT CAMUS. NEW LEADER, VOL. 40, NO.
       46 (NOV. 18, 1957), PP. 22-23.

2084   IONESCU, GHITA. THE LIFE AND WORK OF ALBERT CAMUS. THOUGHT,
       VOL. 12, NO. 5 (JAN. 30, 1960), PP. 11-12. FR VII 23632.

2085   ITTERBEEK, EUGÈNE VAN. FRANSE LETTEREN. SCHLUMBERGER EN CAMUS.
       DIETSCHE WARANDE EN BELFORT, NO. 2 (FEB. 1957), PP.
       111-119. CR 1033, KL I 274.

2086   JACKSON, ESTHER MERLE. THE AMERICAN NEGRO AND THE IMAGE OF THE

ABSURD. PHYLON, THE ATLANTA UNIVERSITY REVIEW OF RACE AND
CULTURE,   FOURTH QUARTER, 1962, PP. 359-371.

JACKSON, NAOMI C. POT-BOUND. CAMUS' CARNETS. MODERN FICTION   2087
STUDIES,   VOL. 10, NO. 3 (AUTUMN 1964), PP. 274-278.

JACOB, ARMAND. ALBERT CAMUS ALS JOURNALIST. 'ACTUELLES' VON   2088
ALBERT CAMUS. GEISTIGES FRANKREICH,   VOL. 4, NO. 172
(SEPT. 18, 1950), PP. 1-4.

JAENSSON, KNUT. PESTEN. BONNIERS LITTERÄRA MAGASIN,   VOL. 17,   2089
NO. 5 (MAY-JUNE 1948), PP. 363-367.

JAFFE, O. B. ALBERT CAMUS, HATAN PERAS NOBEL LESIFRUT 1957   2090
(ALBERT CAMUS. THE WINNER OF THE 1957 NOBEL PRIZE FOR
LITERATURE). AL HAMISHMAR, OCT. 25, 1957, P. 5.

JAFFE, O. B. MERIDAH UMASHMAUTAH (A REBELLION AND ITS   2091
SIGNIFICANCE). AL HAMISHMAR,   NOV. 1, 1957, PP. 5-6.

JAGGER, GEORGES. CAMUS' 'LA PESTE'. YALE FRENCH STUDIES,   VOL.   2092
1, NO. 1 (SPRING-SUMMER 1948), PP. 124-127. BO 413, BR, CR
661, FR VII 4415.

JAKEL, WERNER. ANTIKE STOFFE IN EINIGEN DRAMEN DER GEGENWART.   2093
SAMMLUNG,   NO. 13 (1958), PP. 178-195. FR VII 21035.

JALOUX, EDMOND. ALBERT CAMUS. PSYCHÉ,   VOL. 3, NO. 16 (FEB.   2094
1948), PP. 223-232. BO 20, CR 602 BIS, CR 662, FR VII
5748.

JANON, RENÉ. SES COMPAGNONS ET LES JEUNES D'ALGÉRIE PLEURENT   2095
L'ÉCRIVAIN ET L'HOMME. FIGARO,   VOL. 134, NO. 4770 (JAN.
6, 1960), P. 4. FITCH.

JANS, ADRIEN. LA VIE LITTÉRAIRE. LES GRANDS PRIX LITTÉRAIRES   2096
DE L'ACADÉMIE. (ALBERT CAMUS). SOIR,   VOL. 61, NO. 171
(JUNE 21, 1947), P. 5. CR 603.

JANS, ADRIEN. LA VIE LITTÉRAIRE. ACTUELLES D'ALBERT CAMUS.   2097
SOIR,   VOL. 64, NO. 188 (JULY 8, 1950), P. 7. CR 754.

JANS, ADRIEN. LA VIE LITTÉRAIRE. CETTE SEMAINE... 'L'HOMME   2098
RÉVOLTÉ'. SOIR,   VOL. 65, NO. 334 (DEC. 1, 1951), P. 7.
CR 790.

JANS, ADRIEN. LA VIE LITTÉRAIRE. ALBERT CAMUS. 'L'ÉTÉ'. SOIR,   2099
VOL. 68, NO. 106 (APRIL 17, 1954), P. 7. CR 889.

JANS, ADRIEN. LA VIE LITTÉRAIRE. ALBERT CAMUS. 'LA CHUTE'.   2100
SOIR,   VOL. 70, NO. 150 (MAY 30, 1956), P. 8. CR 949.

JANS, ADRIEN. LA VIE LITTÉRAIRE. ALBERT CAMUS. 'L'EXIL ET LE   2101
ROYAUME'. SOIR,   VOL. 71, NO. 86 (MARCH 27, 1957), P. 7.
CR 1034.

JANS, ADRIEN. LA VIE LITTÉRAIRE. ALBERT CAMUS, PRIX NOBEL DE   2102
LITTÉRATURE. SOIR,   VOL. 71, NO. 296 (OCT. 23, 1957), P.
8. CR 1035.

JARRETT-KERR, MARTIN. THE SECULAR PROMISE, CHRISTIAN PRESENCE   2103
AMID CONTEMPORARY HUMANISM. LONDON. SCM PRESS, 1964. THE

ARTIST AGAINST SOCIETY, PP. 157-165 ET PASSIM.

2104   JEAN-DAROUY, LUCIENNE. CONTAGION DE LA PESTE. GAZETTE DES
        LETTRES, VOL. 5, NO. 80 (JAN. 22, 1949), P. 13. CR 706.

2105   JEAN-NESMY, DOM CLAUDE. L'IMAGE ET LE SACRÉ DANS LA LITTÉRATURE
        CONTEMPORAINE. TABLE RONDE, NO. 142 (OCT. 1959), PP.
        77-90. FR VII 20752.

2106   JEANS, ROBERT F. CONFRONTATION TECHNIQUE IN PSYCHOTHERAPY. SOME
        EXISTENTIAL IMPLICATIONS. SEE NO. 1811.

2107   JEANSON, FRANCIS. ALBERT CAMUS OU LE MENSONGE DE L'ABSURDE.
        REVUE DOMINICAINE, VOL. 1, NO. 53 (FEB. 1947), PP.
        104-107. FR VII 17317.

2108   JEANSON, FRANCIS. UNE ÉVOLUTION DANS LA PENSÉE DE CAMUS.
        ÉRASME, VOL. 2, NOS. 22-24 (OCT.-DEC. 1947), PP. 437-440.
        CR 604., FR VII 2703.

2109   JEANSON, FRANCIS. UNE ÉVOLUTION DANS LA PENSÉE DE CAMUS. REVUE
        DOMINICAINE, VOL. 2, NO. 54 (NOV. 1948), PP. 223-226. BO
        133, FR VII 17318.

2110   JEANSON, FRANCIS. PIRANDELLO ET CAMUS, À TRAVERS 'HENRI IV' ET
        'CALIGULA'. TEMPS MODERNES, VOL. 6, NO. 61 (NOV. 1950), PP.
        944-953. BFZ 31-675 (1949-51), BO 269, CR 755.

2111   JEANSON, FRANCIS. ALBERT CAMUS OU L'ÂME RÉVOLTÉE. TEMPS
        MODERNES, VOL. 7, NO. 79 (MAY 1952), PP. 2070-2090. BFZ
        36-234 (1953-55), BO 222, CR 821, FR VII 7706.

2112   JEANSON, FRANCIS. POUR TOUT VOUS DIRE. TEMPS MODERNES, VOL.
        8, NO. 82 (AUGUST 1952), PP. 354-383. BO 277, CR 822, FR
        VII 7707.

2113   JENS, WALTER. L'EXIL ET LE ROYAUME (REZENSION). DIE ZEIT,
        VOL. 3, NO. 4 (1958).

2114   JENS, WALTER. CAMUS L'EUROPÉEN. REVUE DES LETTRES MODERNES,
        NOS. 90-93 (WINTER 1963), PP. 145-149. PMLA 1964 (8608).
        TRANSLATION OF NO. 2080. SEE NO. 3207. TRANSLATED BY
        BERNARD LORTHOLARY.

2115   JESCHKE, HANS. ALBERT CAMUS--BILD EINER GEISTIGEN EXISTENZ.
        NEUEREN SPRACHEN, VOL. 1, NO. 2 (1952), PP. 459-473. BO
        39, CR 823.

2116   JESCHKE, HANS. ALBERT CAMUS. RITRATTO DI UN'ESISTENZA
        SPIRITUALE. LETTERATURA, VOL. 1, NOS. 5-6 (SEPT.-DEC.
        1953), PP. 55-68. FR VII 15349.

2117   JOHN, S. THE CHARACTERS OF ALBERT CAMUS. UNIVERSITY OF TORONTO
        QUARTERLY, VOL. 23, NO. 4 (JULY 1954), PP. 362-379. BO
        245, BUL SIGN 9-12048, FR VII 17320.

2118   JOHN, S. ALBERT CAMUS. MODERN LANGUAGES, VOL. 36, NO. 1 (DEC.
        1954), PP. 13-18. BFZ 37-266 (1953-1955), BO 48, CR 890.

2119   JOHN, S. BEYNON. ALBERT CAMUS. A BRITISH VIEW. IN   BRÉE,
        GERMAINE, CAMUS, A COLLECTION OF CRITICAL ESSAYS, PP.

85-91. FR VII 29338. SEE NO. 1293. REPRINT OF NO. 2118.

JOHN, S. BEYNON. ALBERT CAMUS. IN   KOSTELANETZ, RICHARD, ON   2120
CONTEMPORARY LITERATURE, PP. 306-314. SEE NO. 2204.
REPRINT OF NO. 2118.

JOHN, S. IMAGE AND SYMBOL IN THE WORK OF ALBERT CAMUS. FRENCH   2121
STUDIES, VOL. 9, NO. 1 (JAN. 1955), PP. 42-53. BFZ 37-266
(1953-55), BO 247, CR 919, FR VII 13307.

JOHN, S. BEYNON. IMAGE AND SYMBOL IN THE WORK OF ALBERT CAMUS.   2122
IN   BRÉE, GERMAINE, CAMUS, A COLLECTION OF CRITICAL
ESSAYS, PP. 132-144. FR VII 29338. SEE NO. 1293. REPRINT
OF NO. 2121.

JOHNSON, GERALD W. GOVERNMENT AS A CREATIVE ACT. NEW REPUBLIC,   2123
VOL. 138, NO. 22 (JUNE 2, 1958), PP. 16-17. FR VII 21397.

JOLIVET, PHILIPPE. LE MOTIF DE LA PESTE CHEZ ALBERT CAMUS.   2124
ORBIS LITTERARUM, VOL. 13, NOS. 3-4 (1958), PP. 163-168.
BFZ 45-278, FR VII 21396, KL II 391.

JOLIVET, REGIS. EL DIÁLOGO ENTRE J. P. SARTRE Y ALBERTO CAMUS.   2125
SAPIENTIA, VOL. 9, NO. 32 (APRIL-JUNE 1954), PP. 119-123.
BFZ 38-1197 (1954-55), BO 278.

JONES, C. HAMLET'S QUESTION AND ABSURD TIME. THOUGHT, VOL.   2126
12, NO. 26 (JUNE 25, 1960), PP. 10-11. FR VII 23633.

JONES, MARIAN. CAMUS' REBELS. WESTERN HUMANITIES REVIEW, VOL.   2127
12, NO. 1 (WINTER 1958), PP. 51-56. FR VII 21398.

JONES, ROBERT EMMET. CALIGULA, THE ABSURD, AND TRAGEDY.   2128
KENTUCKY FOREIGN LANGUAGE QUARTERLY, VOL. 5, NO. 3 (1958),
PP. 123-127. FR VII 19427, KL II 390.

JONES, ROBERT EMMET. THE ALIENATED HERO IN MODERN FRENCH DRAMA.   2129
ATHENS. UNIVERSITY OF GEORGIA PRESS, 1962. FR VII 28699.

JONG, PIETER DE. CAMUS AND BONHOEFFER ON THE FALL. CANADIAN   2130
JOURNAL OF THEOLOGY, VOL. 7, NO. 4 (OCT. 1961), PP.
245-257.

JOTTERAND, FRANK. ENTRETIEN AVEC ALBERT CAMUS. GAZETTE DE   2131
LAUSANNE, (MARCH 28, 1954). BR, CR 890 BIS.

JOTTERAND, FRANK. 'LA CHUTE', D'ALBERT CAMUS. GAZETTE DE   2132
LAUSANNE, (JUNE 23, 1956). BR, CR 949 BIS.

JOTTERAND, FRANCK. SUR LE THÉÂTRE D'ALBERT CAMUS. NOUVELLE   2133
REVUE FRANÇAISE, VOL. 8, NO. 87 (MARCH 1960), PP. 509-514.
FR VII 23575, KL II 389.

JOYAUX, GEORGES J. LA LITTÉRATURE FRANÇAISE D'AFRIQUE DU NORD.   2134
FRENCH REVIEW, VOL. 32, NO. 5 (APRIL 1959), PP. 410-418.
BUL SIGN 15-19-7962.

JOYAUX, GEORGES J. DRISS CHRAÏBI, MOHAMMED DIB, KATEB YACINE,   2135
AND INDIGENOUS NORTH AFRICAN LITERATURE. YALE FRENCH
STUDIES, NO. 24 (SUMMER 1959), PP. 30-40. BUL SIGN
16-19-9952 (1962).

2136   JOYAUX, GEORGES J. THE FRENCH-LANGUAGE NORTH AFRICAN
            LITERATURE. CENTENNIAL REVIEW, VOL. 3, NO. 1 (WINTER
            1959), PP. 35-50.

2137   JOYAUX, GEORGES J. 'CAMUS' BY GERMAINE BRÉE. FRENCH REVIEW,
            VOL. 33, NO. 2 (DEC. 1959), PP. 202-203.

2138   JOYAUX, GEORGES J. THE FRENCH LITERARY CLIMATE. KENTUCKY
            FOREIGN LANGUAGE QUARTERLY, VOL. 7, NO. 1 (1960), PP.
            8-18.

2139   JOYAUX, GEORGES J. ALBERT CAMUS AND NORTH AFRICA. YALE FRENCH
            STUDIES, NO. 25 (SPRING 1960), PP. 10-19. BUL SIGN
            16-19-9743 (1962), KL II 392.

2140   JOYAUX, GEORGES J. EMMANUEL ROBLÈS ET LE THÈME DE L'HONNEUR.
            KENTUCKY FOREIGN LANGUAGE QUARTERLY, VOL. 11, NO. 3
            (1964), PP. 134-141.

2141   JUDRIN, ROGER. SISYPHE ET LE VENT. NOUVELLE REVUE FRANÇAISE,
            VOL. 8, NO. 87 (MARCH 1960), PP. 600-604. FR VII 23575, KL
            II 394.

2142   JUN, ISHIKAWA. SUR UN SILENCE D'ALBERT CAMUS. FRANCE-ASIE,
            VOL. 17, NO. 165 (JAN.-FEB. 1961), PP. 1711-1714. FR VII
            26344.

2143   KAHLER, ERICH. THE TRANSFORMATION OF MODERN FICTION.
            COMPARATIVE LITERATURE, VOL. 7, NO. 2 (SPRING 1955), PP.
            121-128. BO 80, FR VII 12691.

2144   KAIL, ANDRÉE. THE TRANSFORMATION OF CAMUS' HEROES FROM THE
            NOVEL TO THE STAGE. EDUCATIONAL THEATRE JOURNAL, VOL. 13,
            NO. 3 (OCT. 1961), PP. 201-206. PMLA 7366 (1962).

2145   KAISER, JOACHIM. WIE KOMMT ES ZUM SPRUNG? FRANKFURTER HEFTE,
            VOL. 13, NO. 9 (SEPT. 1958), PP. 654-656. KL I 272.

2146   KAMBER, GERALD. THE ALLEGORY OF THE NAMES IN 'L'ETRANGER'.
            MODERN LANGUAGE QUARTERLY, VOL. 22, NO. 3 (SEPT. 1961),
            PP. 292-301. BFZ 49-262 (1960-62), FR VII 26345, PMLA 7367
            (1962).

2147   KANTERS, ROBERT. CHRONIQUES. LE THÉÂTRE. CALIGULA, D'ALBERT
            CAMUS. AU THÉÂTRE HÉBERTOI. CAHIERS DU SUD, 32ND YEAR,
            VOL. 23, NO. 274 (2ND SEMESTER 1945), PP. 850-853. CR 528.

2148   KANTERS, ROBERT. L'HOMME MALADE DE LA PESTE. GAZETTE DES
            LETTRES, VOL. 3, NO. 39 (JUNE 28, 1947), PP. 4-5. CR 605.

2149   KANTERS, ROBERT. DES ÉCRIVAINS ET DES HOMMES. PARIS. R.
            JULLIARD, 1952. MORALISTES ET PROPHETES , PART II.
            ALBERT CAMUS , PP. 183-191. BO 126, FR VII 7123.

2150   KANTERS, ROBERT. EN CHUTE LIBRE. 'LA CHUTE'. EXPRESS, NO.
            258 (JUNE 1, 1956), P. 19. CR 951.

2151   KANTERS, ROBERT. LA COMMUNION DES DAMNÉS. 'REQUIEM POUR UNE
            NONNE' (THÉÂTRE DES MATHURINS). CAMUS, LE PRÉDESTINÉ.
            EXPRESS, VOL. 4, NO. 275 (SEPT. 28, 1956), PP. 16, 17. CR

968.

KANTERS, ROBERT. CHRONIQUES. LE THÉÂTRE. ('REQUIEM POUR UNE   2152
   NONNE' DE WILLIAM FAULKNER ET ALBERT CAMUS.) CAHIERS DU
   SUD, 43RD YEAR, VOL. 44, NO. 340 (APRIL 1957), PP.
   465-466. CR 1036.

KANTERS, ROBERT. 'LES POSSÉDÉS', CONTRE-EXPERTISE. EXPRESS,   2153
   VOL. 6, NO. 399 (FEB. 5, 1959), PP. 30-31. CR 1139.

KANTERS, ROBERT. CAMUS, PRINCE DES BIEN PENSANTS OU DE LA   2154
   RÉVOLTE? EXPRESS, VOL. 9, NO. 568 (MAY 3, 1962), PP.
   32-33.

KANTERS, ROBERT. CAMUS S'ÉLOIGNE. REVIEW OF 'CARNETS'. FIGARO   2155
   LITTERAIRE, VOL. 17, NO. 839 (MAY 19, 1962), P. 2. FR VII
   29385.

KARLGREN, B. ALLOCUTION À CAMUS AU BANQUET NOBEL, LE 10   2156
   DÉCEMBRE 1957, À STOCKHOLM. IN LILJESTRAND, G. (EDITOR),
   LES PRIX NOBEL EN 1957. STOCKHOLM. P. A. NORSTEDT AND
   SONER, 1958, P. 44.

KARSCH, W. DER MACHTGEDANKE IN DER DRAMATIK DER GEGENWART.   2157
   MASKE UND KOTHURN, VOL. 6, NO. 3 (1960), PP. 201-211. FR
   VII 23634.

KASTERSKA, MARYA. FRANCUSKA KRONIKA LITERACKA-WIEKSZE I   2158
   MNIEJSZE NAGRODY. HORYZONTY, NO. 20 (JAN. 1958), PP.
   37-38.

KATEB, GEORGE. CAMUS' LA PESTE. A DISSENTING VIEW. SYMPOSIUM,   2159
   VOL. 17, NO. 4 (WINTER 1963), PP. 292-303. FR VII 33958.

KAUFMANN, WALTER. EXISTENTIALISM FROM DOSTOEVSKY TO SARTRE.   2160
   NEW YORK. MERIDIAN BOOKS, 1957. CHAPTER X.   CAMUS: 'THE
   MYTH OF SISYPHUS' , PP. 312-315. FR VII 14806.

KAY, C. E. M. THE PLAGUE, BY ALBERT CAMUS. DELPHIC REVIEW,   2161
   VOL. 1, NO. 1 (WINTER 1949), PP. 47-49. FR VII 34010.

KAZIN, A. CONDEMNED MAN. (REVIEW OF RESISTANCE, REBELLION,   2162
   AND DEATH BY ALBERT CAMUS. TRANSLATED BY JUSTIN O'BRIEN.
   KNOPF.) REPORTER, VOL. 24, NO. 4 (FEB. 16, 1961), PP.
   54-58.

KEE, R. COMMUNITY OF DEATH. 'THE PLAGUE'. TIME (ATLANTIC   2163
   OVERSEAS ED.), VOL. 52, NO. 7 (AUG. 16, 1948), P. 96. BO
   414.

KEE, ROBERT. FICTION. REVIEW. 'THE PLAGUE'. SPECTATOR, VOL.   2164
   181, NO. 6271 (SEPT. 3, 1948), P. 314. BO 415.

KEMP, ROBERT. LA VIE DES LIVRES. ÉCRITS RÉSISTANTIALISTES .   2165
   NOUVELLES LITTÉRAIRES, NO. 953 (AUG. 11, 1945), P 3. BO
   376, CR 529.

KEMP, ROBERT. ALBERT CAMUS. ÉRASME, VOL. 1, NO. 10 (OCT.   2166
   1946), PP. 401-404. BO 9, CR 565, FR VII 2704.

KEMP, ROBERT. LA VIE DES LIVRES. PRIX DES CRITIQUES. (LA   2167

PESTE). NOUVELLES LITTÉRAIRES, NO. 1033 (JUNE 19, 1947),
P. 2. CR 606.

2168 KEMP, ROBERT. LE THÉÂTRE. 'L'ÉTAT DE SIÈGE'. MONDE FRANÇAIS,
VOL. 12, NO. 39 (DEC. 1948), PP. 476-477. BO 444, CR 663,
FR VII 2705.

2169 KEMP, ROBERT. 'L'HOMME RÉVOLTÉ'. NOUVELLES LITTÉRAIRES, VOL.
30, NO. 1263 (NOV. 15, 1951), P. 2. BO 485, CR 788.

2170 KEMP, ROBERT. LA VIE DES LIVRES. II. PARIS. ÉDITIONS ALBIN
MICHEL, 1962. L'HOMME RÉVOLTÉ, PP. 263-269.

2171 KEMP, ROBERT. LA DÉVOTION À LA CROIX DE CALDERÓN. MONDE, VOL.
10, NO. 2609 (JUNE 16, 1953), P.9. FITCH.

2172 KEMP, ROBERT. LA VIE DU THÉÂTRE. PARIS. ALBIN MICHEL, 1956.
LES JUSTES DE CAMUS, PP. 266-271. FR VII 15030, KL I 273.

2173 KEMP, ROBERT. REQUIEM POUR UNE NONNE DE WILLIAM FAULKNER AU
THÉÂTRE DES NATIONS. MONDE, VOL. 10, NO. 446 (MAY 2-8,
1957), P. 5.

2174 KEMP, ROBERT. THÉÂTRE. UN FESTIVAL ALBERT CAMUS. 'CALIGULA'.
'LE CHEVALIER D'OLMEDO'. EXPRESS, NO. 314 (JUNE 28, 1957),
PP. 22-23. CR 1052.

2175 KEMP, ROBERT. AU NOUVEAU THÉÂTRE. CALIGULA D'ALBERT CAMUS.
MONDE, VOL. 11, NO. 487 (FEB. 13-19, 1958), P. 5.

2176 KEMP, ROBERT. LA VIE DES LIVRES. DISCOURS DE STOCKHOLM.
NOUVELLES LITTÉRAIRES, NO. 1594 (MARCH 20, 1958), P. 2.
CR 1100, KL I 274.

2177 KEMP, ROBERT. LA VIE DES LIVRES. PERSONNAGES. 'L'ENVERS ET
L'ENDROIT', PAR ALBERT CAMUS. NOUVELLES LITTÉRAIRES, NO.
1604 (MAY 29, 1958), P. 2. CR 1101.

2178 KEMP, ROBERT. LA VIE DES LIVRES. 'ACTUELLES III', PAR ALBERT
CAMUS. NOUVELLES LITTÉRAIRES, NO. 1610 (JULY 10, 1958),
P. 2. CR 1099.

2179 KEMP, ROBERT. AU THÉÂTRE ANTOINE. LES POSSÉDÉS DE DOSTOIEVSKY
ADAPTÉ PAR ALBERT CAMUS. MONDE, VOL. 12, NO. 537 (JAN.
29-FEB. 4, 1959), P. 5.

2180 KENNEDY, EUGENE, M.M. AGGIORNAMENTO, ANXIETY AND THE SEMINARY.
CRITIC, VOL. 23, NO. 6(JUNE-JULY 1965), PP. 33-35.

2181 KESSOUS, MOHAMMED-EL-AZIZ. ALBERT CAMUS ET L'HONNEUR DE
L'HOMME. SIMOUN, VOL. 8, NO. 31 (JULY 1960), PP. 3-12.
FR VII 23573, KL II 389.

2182 KETMAN, GEORGES. SUR CAMUS. PARISIENNE, NO. 48 (NOV.-DEC.
1957), PP. 1076-1080. CR 1047 TER, KL I 272.

2183 KIJOWSKI, ANDRZEJ. KSIĄŻKA MIESIĄCA. DZUMA-TAK TYLKO DOSIĘGA
SIĘ DNA.... TWÓRCZOŚĆ, VOL. 13, NO. 6 (1957), PP.
117-124.

2184 KILLINGER, JOHN. EXISTENTIALISM AND HUMAN FREEDOM. ENGLISH
JOURNAL, VOL. 50, NO. 5 (MAY 1961), PP. 303-313. PMLA

7799 (1963).

KILLINGER, JOHN. THE FAILURE OF THEOLOGY IN MODERN LITERATURE.   2185
    NASHVILLE, TENN.. ABINGDON PRESS, 1963.   SCATTERED
    REFERENCES.

KILLINGSWORTH, KAY. AU-DELÀ DU DÉCHIREMENT. L'HÉRITAGE   2186
    MÉRIDIONAL DANS L'OEUVRE DE WILLIAM FAULKNER ET D'ALBERT
    CAMUS. ESPRIT,   VOL. 31, NOUVELLE SÉRIE NO. 320 (SEPT.
    1963), PP. 209-234. PMLA 7973 (1964), FR VII 33959.

KING, ADELE. STRUCTURE AND MEANING IN 'LA CHUTE'. PUBLICATIONS   2187
    OF THE MODERN LANGUAGE ASSOCIATION OF AMERICA,   VOL. 77,
    NO. 5 (DEC. 1962), PP. 660-667. PMLA 7980 (1963).

KING, ADELE. CAMUS. EDINBURGH AND LONDON. OLIVER AND BOYD,   2188
    1964. NEW YORK. BARNES AND NOBLE, 1965.

KING, ADELE. JONAS OU L'ARTISTE AU TRAVAIL. FRENCH STUDIES,   2189
    VOL. 20, NO. 3 (JULY 1966), PP. 267-280.

KINGERY, R. E. 'THE PLAGUE'. LITERARY JOURNAL,   VOL. 73,   2190
    (1948), P. 1088. BO 416.

KINGSTON, FREDERICK TEMPLE. FRENCH EXISTENTIALISM, A CHRISTIAN   2191
    CRITIQUE. TORONTO. UNIVERSITY OF TORONTO PRESS, 1961.
    SCATTERED REFERENCES.

KLINGNER, EDWIN. ALBERT CAMUS UND DAS ABSURDE DES SEINS.   2192
    JUNGBUCHHANDEL,   VOL. 14, NO. 10 (1960), PP. 475-478.   BDZ
    121-321 (1960).

KNIGHT, E. W. LITERATURE CONSIDERED AS PHILOSOPHY, THE FRENCH   2193
    EXAMPLE. LONDON. ROUTLEDGE AND PAUL, 1957. SCATTERED
    REFERENCES. KL I 231.

KNOPF, BLANCHE. MIS RECUERDOS DE CAMUS. ASOMANTE,   VOL. 17,   2194
    NO. 1 (JAN.-MARCH 1961), PP. 70-77. BUL SIGN 16-19-9735,
    FR VII 26347.

KNOPF, BLANCHE. ALBERT CAMUS IN THE SUN. ATLANTIC MONTHLY,   2195
    VOL. 207, NO. 2 (FEB. 1961), PP. 77-84. FR VII 26346.

KOESTLER, ARTHUR. IN COLLABORATION WITH JEAN BLOCH-MICHEL   2196
    AND ALBERT CAMUS REFLEXIONS SUR LA PEINE CAPITALE. PARIS,
    CALMANN-LEVY (COLL. LIBERTE DE L'ESPRIT), 1957. CR 284.
    SEE NO. 591.

KOHLER, ADOLF. DER MYTHOS DES MENSCHEN OHNE GOTT BEI ANDRÉ   2197
    MALRAUX UND ALBERT CAMUS. BEGEGNUNG,   VOL. 6, NO. 5
    (1951), PP. 138-143. BFZ 102-771 (51), BO 111.

KOHN, HANS. MAN THE UNDOER. THE REBEL. AN ESSAY ON MAN IN   2198
    REVOLT , BY ALBERT CAMUS. SATURDAY REVIEW,   VOL. 37, NO. 7
    (FEB. 13, 1954), PP. 14-15. BO 529.

KOPPENHAVER, ALLEN J. 'THE FALL' AND AFTER. ALBERT CAMUS AND   2199
    ARTHUR MILLER. MODERN DRAMA, VOL. 9, NO. 2 (SEPT. 1966),
    PP. 206-209.

KORG, JACOB. CULT OF ABSURDITY. NATION,   VOL. 181, NO. 24   2200

(DEC. 10, 1955), PP. 517-518. BO 329.

2201   KORN, KARL. ALLEGORIEN DER EXISTENZ. ZU ROMANEN VON CAMUS (LA
        PESTE) UND KASACK (STADT HINTER DEM STROM). MERKUR, VOL.
        3, NO. 1 (JAN. 1949), PP. 90-97. BDZ 99-167 (1949), BO
        264, CR 708.

2202   KORN, K. DER DICHTER DER REVOLTE. ZUM TODE CAMUS (NOBELPREIS
        FÜR LITERATUR 1957). FRANKFURTER ALLGEMEINE ZEITUNG,
        (JAN. 6, 1960), P. 14. KL II 394.

2203   KOSKO, M. À PROPOS DU MALENTENDU. COMPARATIVE LITERATURE,
        VOL. 10, NO. 4 (FALL 1958), PP. 376-377. FITCH.

2204   KOSTELANETZ, RICHARD (EDITOR). ON CONTEMPORARY LITERATURE. NEW
        YORK. AVON BOOKS, 1964.

2205   KREA, HENRI. LE MALENTENDU ALGÉRIEN. FRANCE OBSERVATEUR, VOL.
        12, NO. 557 (JAN. 5, 1961), P. 16. SEE NO. 3253.

2206   KRIEGER, MURRAY. THE TRAGIC VISION. NEW YORK. HOLT, RINEHART
        AND WINSTON, 1960. PART 2, CHAPTER 5.   ALBERT CAMUS.
        BEYOND NONENTITY AND THE REJECTION OF THE TRAGIC , PP.
        144-153.

2207   KRINGS, HERMANN. ALBERT CAMUS ODER DIE PHILOSOPHIE DER REVOLTE.
        PHILOSOPHISCHES JAHRBUCH DER GÖRRESGESELLSCHAFT, VOL. 62
        (1953), PP. 347-358. BDZ 108-306, BO 230, CR 858.

2208   KRISHNA, S. EXISTENTIALISM AND THE THEME OF ALIENATION. A STUDY
        OF ALBERT CAMUS'S L'ETRANGER. LITERARY CRITERION, VOL. 5,
        NO. 4 (SUMMER 1963), PP. 29-31. PMLA 7974 (1964).

2209   KRUMN, JOHN MCGILL. THEOLOGY AND LITERATURE. THE TERMS OF THE
        DIALOGUE ON THE MODERN SCENE. IN SCOTT, NATHAN A., JR.,
        THE CLIMATE OF FAITH IN MODERN LITERATURE, PP. 19-41 (CAMUS
        REF. PP. 25, 35-36). SEE NO. 3044.

2210   KUECHLER, W. 'CALIGULA'. NUEPHILOLOGISCHE ZEITSCHRIFT, VOL.
        1, NO. 4 (1949), PP. 17-24. BO 371, CR 707.

2211   KUHN, HELMUT. EXISTENTIALISM-CHRISTIAN AND ANTICHRISTIAN.
        THEOLOGY TODAY, VOL. 6, NO. 6 (OCT. 1949), PP. 311-323.
        FR VII 16575.

2212   KURTZ, PAUL W. KIERKEGAARD, EXISTENTIALISM, AND THE
        CONTEMPORARY SCENE. ANTIOCH REVIEW, WINTER 1961-1962, PP.
        471-487 (CAMUS REF. PP. 471, 485).

2213   KWIATKOWSKI, W. CAMUS, PROBLEMATYKA TWÓRCZOŚCI, EWOLUCJA
        POZLADÓW. ZESZYTY NAUKOWE KATOLICKIEGO UNIWERSYTETU
        LUBELSKIEGO, VOL. 3, NO. 3 (1960), PP. 39-55. BUL SIGN
        15-19-685, 15-19-13750, KL II 388.

2214   L., WALTHER. BEMERKUNGEN ÜBER ALBERT CAMUS. AUFBAU, VOL. 4,
        NO. 7 (1948), PP. 635-637. FR VII 23635.

2215   LABERGE, PIERRE. SOUVENIR DE CAMUS. CITÉ LIBRE, VOL. 11, NC.
        30 (OCT. 1960), P. 22. FR VII 23636.

2216   LABLÉNIE, EDMOND. RECHERCHES SUR LA TECHNIQUE DES ARTS

LITTÉRAIRES. PARIS.   SOCIÉTÉ D'ÉDITION D'ENSEIGNEMENT
SUPÉRIEUR, 1962. FR VII 28298.

LACRETELLE, JACQUES DE. HAUTE MER. NOUVELLE REVUE FRANÇAISE,   2217
VOL. 8, NO. 87 (MARCH 1960), PP. 591-593. FR VII 23575, KL
II 394.

LACROIX, JEAN. LE SENS DE L'ATHÉISME MODERNE. TOURNAI.   2218
CASTERMAN, 1959.

LAFON, NOËL. CAMUS DE 1945 A 1947. REVUE SOCIALISTE,   2219
(OCT.-NOV. 1966), PP. 370-389.

LAFORGUE, R. LA PESTE ET LA VERTU. PSYCHÉ, VOL. 3, NOS. 18-19   2220
(APRIL-MAY 1948), PP. 406-420. BO 417, CR 664.

LAFUE, PIERRE. L'ÉVOLUTION DU ROMAN RÉALISTE ET LE RÉALISME   2221
D'UNE ÉPOQUE INHUMAINE. HIER ET DEMAIN, NO. 2 (NOV. 9,
1942), PP. 159-169. BO 56, FR VII 12696.

LAHBABI, M. A. À PROPOS DE CAMUS. CONFLUENT (RABAT),   2222
(SEPT.-OCT. 1960), PP. 518-525. FR VII 29387.

LAISNER, LEONE. SEPT METTEURS EN SCÈNE PLAIDENT POUR LE 'PLEIN   2223
AIR'. SPECTACLES, VOL. 1, NO. 2 (JULY 1958), PP. 20-24.
CR 1102.

LAKICH, JOHN JOVAN. THE ESTHETICS OF ALBERT CAMUS.   2224
DISSERTATION ABSTRACTS, VOL. 25, NO. 9 (MARCH 1965), P.
5281.

L'ALLIER, PAUL. ALBERT CAMUS. RELATIONS, VOL. 20, NO. 230   2225
(FEB. 1960), P. 45. FR VII 23637.

LALO, C. L'HOMME RÉVOLTÉ. REVUE D'ESTHÉTIQUE, VOL. 5,   2226
(1952), PP. 443-444. BO 494, BUL SIGN 8-5117.

LALOU, RENÉ. FEUILLETON LITTÉRAIRE. DE LA RÉVOLTE. (L'HOMME   2227
RÉVOLTÉ). HOMMES ET MONDES, VOL. 7, NO. 67 (FEB. 1952),
PP. 287-293. CR 825.

LALOU, RENÉ. LE LIVRE DE LA SEMAINE. 'L'ÉTÉ', PAR ALBERT   2228
CAMUS. NOUVELLES LITTÉRAIRES, NO. 1386 (MARCH 25, 1954),
P. 3. CR 892.

LALOU, RENÉ. ALBERT CAMUS ET LA FIDÉLITÉ. ÂGE NOUVEAU, VOL.   2229
9, NO. 87 (MAY 1954), P. 81. BFZ 36-234 (1953-54), BO 156,
CR 891, FR VII 11226.

LALOU, RENÉ. LE LIVRE DE LA SEMAINE. 'LA CHUTE', PAR A. CAMUS.   2230
NOUVELLES LITTERAIRES, NO. 1501 (JUNE 7, 1956), P. 3. CR
952.

LALOU, RENÉ. ALBERT CAMUS, PRIX NOBEL DE LITTÉRATURE.   2231
EDUCATION NATIONALE, VOL. 13, NO. 28 (OCT. 24, 1957), PP.
16-17. FR VII 17321, KL I 274.

LALOU, RENÉ. UN TÉMOIN DE NOTRE ÉPOQUE. NOUVELLES LITTÉRAIRES,   2232
NO. 1688 (JAN. 7, 1960), P. 8. FR VII 23638, KL II 394,
PMLA 6830 (1961).

LALOU, RENÉ. ALBERT CAMUS. REVUE DE PARIS, VOL. 67, NO. 2   2233

(FEB. 1960), PP. 161-162. KL II 394.

2234   LAMANA, M. EL ABSURDO Y LA REBELIÓN EN ALBERT CAMUS.
        UNIVERSIDAD, NO. 40 (APRIL-JUNE 1959), PP. 5-22. BUL SIGN
        14-18202.

2235   LAMBRICHS, GEORGES. FIER ET ANXIEUX. NOUVELLE REVUE FRANÇAISE,
        VOL. 8, NO. 87 (MARCH 1960), P. 436. FR VII 23575, KL II
        394.

2236   LAMONT, ROSETTE C. THE ANTI-BOURGEOIS. FRENCH REVIEW, VOL.
        34, NO. 5 (APRIL 1961), PP. 445-453. FR VII 26348, PMLA
        7368 (1962).

2237   LANCELOTTI, MARIO A. CAMUS Y LA INTELIGENCIA. SUR, VOL. 17,
        NO. 173 (MARCH 1949), PP. 71-78. BO 140, BR, CR 709, FR
        VII 2706.

2238   LANCKROCK, RIK. ALBERT CAMUS, DE PEST. VERTAALD DOOR WILLY
        CORSARI. ARSENAAL, VOL. 5. NO. 2 (MARCH-APRIL 1949) P.
        38. BVT 7-110.

2239   LANCKROCK, RIK. ALBERT CAMUS, DE VREEMDELING. VERTAALD DOOR
        ADRIAAN MORRIEN. ARSENAAL, VOL. 5, NO. 6 (NOV.-DEC.
        1949), P. 41. BVT 7-111.

2240   LANDQUIST, JOHN. STUDIE I DET ABSURDA. SPEKTRUM, VOL. 3, NO.
        4 (1948), PP. 235-239. FR VII 29388.

2241   LANFRANCHI, G. GENÈSE D'UNE RÉPONSE À ALBERT CAMUS. ÉTUDES
        PHILOSOPHIQUES, VOL. 12, NO. 3 (JULY-SEPT. 1957), PP.
        289-292. BFZ 43-294, BUL SIGN 13-1207, CR 1037.

2242   LANG, RENÉE. TWO BOOKS, TWO CREEDS. ANDRE GIDE'S 'THESEUS',
        AND 'THE STRANGER' BY ALBERT CAMUS. BOOKS ABROAD, VOL.
        21, NO. 4 (FALL 1947), PP. 383-386.

2243   LANGEVIN, A. ALBERT CAMUS. LIBERTÉ, VOL. 2, NO. 1 (JAN.-FEB.
        1960), FR VII 23609.

2244   LANNES, ROGER. LES SPECTACLES DE PARIS. CALIGULA D'ALBERT
        CAMUS. FONTAINE, VOL. 6, NO. 47 (DEC. 1945), PP. 140-144.
        CR 531.

2245   LANNES, ROGER. LE THÉÂTRE. UNE HEURE DE RÉPÉTITION POUR 'L'ÉTAT
        DE SIÈGE , DE CAMUS. FIGARO LITTÉRAIRE, VOL. 3, NO. 131
        (OCT. 23, 1948), P. 6. CR 665.

2246   LANNES, ROGER. VU ET ENTENDU A UNE RÉPÉTITION DES 'JUSTES', LA
        NOUVELLE PIÈCE DE CAMUS. FIGARO LITTÉRAIRE, VOL. 4, NO.
        190 (DEC. 10, 1949), P. 8. BO 457, CR 710, FR VII 4416.

2247   LANOUX, ARMAND. UNE OEUVRE EN DÉBAT DEVANT LA NOUVELLE
        GÉNÉRATION. PAR LE TON, PAR LA VOIX, CET ÉTRANGER EST UN
        AMI. FIGARO LITTÉRAIRE, VOL. 12, NO. 601 (OCT. 26, 1957),
        P. 7. FITCH. SEE NO. 3251.

2248   LANSNER, KERMIT. ALBERT CAMUS. KENYON REVIEW, VOL. 14, NO. 4
        (FALL 1952), PP. 562-578. BFZ 37-266 (1953-55), BO 40, BUL
        SIGN 7-363, CR 826.

LANZA, GIUSEPPE. IL TEATRO: REQUIEM PER UNA MONACA.   2249
    OSSERVATORE POLITICO LETTERARIO,   VOL. 5, NO. 1 (JAN.
    1959), PP. 114-117. FR VII 34011.

LAPARADE, M. RÉFLEXIONS SUR 4 MÉDECINS DE ROMAN. ESSAI DE   2250
    DÉFINITION D'UN HUMANISME MÉDICAL CONTEMPORAIN. BORDEAUX.
    SAMIE, 1948. BO 418.

LA PENNA, ANTONIO. ALBERT CAMUS O LA CONVERSIONE DEGLI   2251
    INDIFFERENTI. BELFAGOR, VOL. 5, NO. 6 (NOV. 1950), PP.
    617-635. BO 205, FR VII 5751.

LAPLANE, G. LE PRIX NOBEL. BULLETIN DE L'INSTITUT FRANÇAIS EN   2252
    ESPAGNE, (1958), PP. 1-6. KL I 274.

LAPRADE, JACQUES DE. LA PESTE, (CHRONIQUE LITTÉRAIRE). ARTS,   2253
    NO. 123 (JULY 11, 1947), P. 2. BO 392, CR 609, FR VII
    11227.

LARGEAUD, MARCEL. INSTRUITS PAR LE MESSAGE... TEMPS DES   2254
    HOMMES, NO. 9 (JAN.-FEB.-MARCH 1960), PP. 7-9. KL II 394.

LAST, JEF. ALBERT CAMUS SCHRIJFT VOOR ONS. VLAM, VOL. 3, NO.   2255
    19 (MAY 16, 1947), P. 5. CR 610.

LAUER, QUENTIN. ALBERT CAMUS. THE REVOLT AGAINST ABSURDITY.   2256
    THOUGHT, VOL. 35, NO. 136 (SPRING 1960), PP. 37-56. BUL
    SIGN 15-19-7990, FR VII 26349, PMLA 6831 (1961).

LAURENT, JACQUES. HOMMES ABSURDES ET HOMMES PÉCHEURS. SEMEUR,   2257
    VOL. 45, NO. 3 (1946), PP. 274-282. BO 187.

LAURENT, JACQUES AND CLAUDE MARTINE. NEUF PERLES DE CULTURE.   2258
    PASTICHES DE GIRAUDOUX, SARTRE, AUDIBERTI, MONTHERLANT,
    CLAUDEL, COCTEAU, CAMUS, MAURIAC, ANOUILH. PARIS.
    GALLIMARD, 1952. PASTICHE D ALBERT CAMUS , PP. 237-256.
    FR VII 7326.

LAURENT, JACQUES. ALBERT CAMUS CONTRE GUILLOTIN. ARTS,   NO.   2259
    631 (AUGUST 7-13, 1957), PP. 1, 3. CR 1038.

LAURENT, JACQUES. LE NOBEL COURONNE UNE OEUVRE TERMINÉE. ARTS,   2260
    NO. 641 (OCT. 23-29, 1957), PP. 1, 3. BR, CR 1038 BIS.

LAURENZI, CARLO. MORTE E SOLITUDINE. HUMANITAS, VOL. 15, NO.   2261
    1 (JAN. 1960), PP. 68-69. FR VII 23639, KL II 394.

LAVAUD, GUY. L'HÉRÉSIARQUE ET LE PONTIFE. REVUE PALLADIENNE,   2262
    NO. 21 (1952), PP. 30-34. FR VII 15350.

LAZARON, HILDA R. GABRIEL MARCEL, THE DRAMATIST. COLUMBIA   2263
    UNIVERSITY (PH. D.), 1959. DISSERTATION ABSTRACTS, VOL.
    19, NO. 2 (AUG. 1959), P. 671.

LEAL, R. B. ALBERT CAMUS AND THE SIGNIFICANCE OF ART.   2264
    AUSTRALIAN JOURNAL OF FRENCH STUDIES, VOL. 3, NO. 1
    (JAN.-APRIL 1966), PP. 66 -78.

LEBACQZ, ALBERT. NOTE SUR ALBERT CAMUS. RENAISSANCES,   NO. 22   2265
    (JUNE 1946), PP. 66-70. BO 188, CR 566, FR VII 13308.

LEBESQUE, MORVAN. ALBERT CAMUS L'ALGÉRIEN. CANARD ENCHAÎNÉ,   2266

OCT. 23, 1957. P

2267   LEBESQUE, MORVAN. ALBERT CAMUS, PRIX NOBEL. CAMUS, HOMME DE
         THÉÂTRE. CARREFOUR, VOL. 14, NO. 684 (OCT. 23, 1957), P.
         7.

2268   LEBESQUE, MORVAN. BILAN POSITIF. LES POSSÉDÉS, D'ALBERT CAMUS,
         D'APRÈS DOSTOIEVSKY, AU THÉÂTRE ANTOINE. CARREFOUR, VOL.
         16, NO. 751 (FEB. 4, 1959), P. 11. FR VII 21399.

2269   LEBESQUE, MORVAN. UN HOMME DE MÉTIER. CARREFOUR, VOL. 17, NO.
         799 (JAN. 6, 1960), P. 21.

2270   LEBESQUE, MORVAN. ALBERT CAMUS IN SELBSTZEUGNISSEN UND
         BILDDOKUMENTEN. DARGESTELLT VON M. L. HAMBURG. ROWOHLT,
         1960. FR VII 26296. TRANSLATION OF NO. 2271. MEISTER,
         GUIDO. MEISTER, GERTRUD.

2271   LEBESQUE, MORVAN. ALBERT CAMUS PAR LUI-MÊME. PARIS. EDITIONS
         DU SEUIL, COLL. ÉCRIVAINS DE TOUJOURS. FR VII 33927, PMLA
         7975 (1964).

2272   LEBESQUE, MORVAN. LA PASSION POUR LA SCÈNE. IN ANONYMOUS,
         CAMUS, PP. 157-198. SEE NO. 940.

2273   LEBOIS, ANDRÉ. PESTE À URANA ET PESTE À ORAN. REVUE DE
         LITTÉRATURE COMPARÉE, VOL. 26, NO. 4 (OCT.-DEC. 1952), PP.
         465-476. BFZ 34-272 (1951-53), BO 258, BUL SIGN 8-1124, CR
         827, FR VII 9304.

2274   LEEFLANG, ED. DE ACTUALITEIT VAN ALBERT CAMUS. LITTERAIR
         PASPOORT, VOL. 9, NO. 73 (JAN. 1954), P. 14. BO 479, CR
         895.

2275   LEFEBVE, MAURICE-JEAN. DEUX ÉTATS D'UNE PENSÉE. NOUVELLE REVUE
         FRANÇAISE, VOL. 8, NO. 87 (MARCH 1960), PP. 491-495. FR
         VII 23575.

2276   LEGRAND, ALBERT. ALBERT CAMUS. FROM ABSURDITY TO REVOLT.
         CULTURE, VOL. 14, NO. 4 (DEC. 1953), PP. 406-422. BFZ
         38-280, BO 210, FR VII 11228.

2277   LEGRAND, ALBERT. THE ANGUISH OF THE LEFT. CULTURE, VOL. 15,
         NO. 2 (JUNE 1954), PP. 164-174. CR 893.

2278   LEGUÈBE, ERIC. LA MORT ET LA SAINTETÉ, OBSESSIONS DES
         ROMANCIERS CONTEMPORAINS. ARTS, NO. 741 (SEPT. 23-29,
         1959), P. 6. FR VII 20755.

2279   LEHAN, RICHARD. EXISTENTALISM IN RECENT AMERICAN FICTION. THE
         DEMONIC QUEST, TEXAS STUDIES IN LITERATURE AND LANGUAGE,
         VOL. 1, NO. 2 (SUMMER 1959), PP. 181-202. FR VII 32432.

2280   LEHAN, RICHARD DANIEL. EXISTENTIALISM AND THE MODERN AMERICAN
         NOVEL. DISSERTATION ABSTRACTS, VOL. 20, NO. 4 (OCT. 1959),
         P. 1365. FR VII 20723.

2281   LEHAN, RICHARD DANIEL. CAMUS' AMERICAN AFFINITIES. SYMPOSIUM,
         VOL. 13, NO. 2 (FALL 1959), PP. 255-270. BUL SIGN
         15-19-1930, FR VII 21400, KL II 392.

LEHAN, RICHARD. CAMUS AND HEMINGWAY. WISCONSIN STUDIES IN   2282
    CONTEMPORARY LITERATURE, VOL. 1, NO. 2 (SPRING-SUMMER
    1960), PP. 37-48. FR VII 23640, PMLA 6832 (1961).

LEHAN, RICHARD. CAMUS ET HEMINGWAY. REVUE DES LETTRES   2283
    MODERNES, VOL. 8, NOS. 64-66 (FALL, 1961), PP. 359-375
    (ALT. PP. 55-71). FR VII 26288. TRANSLATION OF NO. 2282.

LEHAN, RICHARD DANIEL. CAMUS Y LOS NOVELISTAS NORTEAMERICANOS.   2284
    AFINIDADES. ASOMANTE, VOL. 17, NO. 1 (JAN.-MARCH 1961),
    PP. 45-61. BUL SIGN 16-19-9851, 16-19-9951. TRANSLATION OF
    NO. 2281.

LEHAN, RICHARD. CAMUS' 'L'ÉTRANGER'. SOURCES AND ANALOGUES   2285
    (ABSTRACT). SOUTH-CENTRAL BULLETIN, VOL. 21, NO. 1 (FEB.
    1961), P. 14.

LEHAN, RICHARD. LEVELS OF REALITY IN THE NOVELS OF ALBERT   2286
    CAMUS. MODERN FICTION STUDIES, VOL. 10, NO. 3 (AUTUMN
    1964), PP. 232-244.

LEHAN, RICHARD. CAMUS'S L'ÉTRANGER AND AMERICAN NEOREALISM.   2287
    BOOKS ABROAD, VOL. 38, NO. 3 (SUMMER 1964), PP. 233-238.
    PMLA 8618 (1964).

LE HARDOUIN, MARIA. L'ESCAMOTEUR. TABLE RONDE, NO. 146 (FEB.   2288
    1960), PP. 154-162. BFZ 46-284, BUL SIGN 15-19-13773, FR
    VII 23569, KL II 394.

LEHMANN, JOHN. THE OPEN NIGHT. LONDON. LONGMANS GREEN AND CO., 2289
    1952. THE SEARCH FOR THE MYTH, PP. 1-14 FR VII 31508.

LEHTONEN, MAIJA. LUKIJALLE (TO THE READER), IN ESSEITÄ   2290
    (VALIKOIMA) BY ALBERT CAMUS. HELSINKI. OTAVA, 1963. PP.
    7-15.

LEMARCHAND, JACQUES. 'CALIGULA' D'ALBERT CAMUS. ARCHE, VOL.   2291
    3, NO. 10 (OCT. 1945), PP. 140-144. CR 532.

LEMARCHAND, JACQUES. LE THÉÂTRE. LE FESTIVAL D'ANGERS. LE   2292
    FESTIVAL D'AVIGNON. (LA DÉVOTION À LA CROIX, DE CALDERÓN
    DE LA BARCA. LES ESPRITS, DE PIERRE DE LARIVEY). PREUVES,
    NOS. 30-31 (AUG.-SEPT. 1953), PP. 135-137. CR 860.

LEMARCHAND, JACQUES. 'UN CAS INTÉRESSANT' DE DINO BUZZATI   2293
    (ADAPTATION D'ALBERT CAMUS), AU THÉÂTRE LA BRUYÈRE. FIGARO
    LITTÉRAIRE, VOL. 10, NO. 466 (MARCH 26, 1955), P. 12. BO
    254, FR VII 13309.

LEMARCHAND, JACQUES. 'REQUIEM POUR UNE NONNE' DE WILLIAM   2294
    FAULKNER (ADAPTATION D'ALBERT CAMUS) AU THÉÂTRE DES
    MATHURINS. FIGARO LITTÉRAIRE, VOL. 11, NO. 545 (SEPT. 29,
    1956), P. 12. CR 953, FR VII 15352.

LEMARCHAND, JACQUES. 'REQUIEM POUR UNE NONNE'. NOUVELLE REVUE   2295
    FRANÇAISE, VOL. 4, NO. 47 (NOV. 1956), PP. 896-900. CR
    954, FR VII 15351.

LEMARCHAND, JACQUES. CALIGULA, D'ALBERT CAMUS, AU VI FESTIVAL   2296

D'ANGERS. FIGARO LITTÉRAIRE, VOL. 12, NO. 584 (JUNE 29, 1957), P. 14. CR 1039, FR VII 17322.

2297   LEMARCHAND, JACQUES. THÉÂTRE D'ÉTÉ. NOUVELLE REVUE FRANÇAISE, VOL. 5, NO. 56 (AUG. 1957), PP. 323-326. FR VII 16955.

2298   LEMARCHAND, JACQUES. 'CALIGULA' D'ALBERT CAMUS, AU NOUVEAU THÉÂTRE. FIGARO LITTÉRAIRE, VOL. 13, NO. 618 (FEB. 22, 1958), P. 14. CR 1103, FR VII 19428.

2299   LEMARCHAND, JACQUES. 'LES POSSÉDÉS' D'ALBERT CAMUS, D'APRÈS DOSTOIEVSKY, AU THÉÂTRE ANTOINE. FIGARO LITTÉRAIRE, VOL. 14, NO. 668 (FEB. 7, 1959), P. 12. CR 1140, FR VII 21401.

2300   LEMARCHAND, JACQUES. LES IMAGES QUE L'ON REGARDE AU SOIR DE LA MORT D'UN AMI. FIGARO LITTÉRAIRE, VOL. 15, NO. 716 (JAN. 9, 1960), PP. 1, 6. BRHT 501 (1960), FR VII 26351, KL II 394.

2301   LEMARCHAND, JACQUES. THÉÂTRE DES NATIONS. CALIGULA EN ARABE.... FIGARO LITTÉRAIRE, VOL. 18, NO. 887 (APRIL 20, 1963), P. 18. FR VII 33960.

2302   LENNARTZ, FRANZ. AUSLÄNDISCHE DICHTER UND SCHRIFTSTELLER UNSERER ZEIT, EINZELDARSTELLUNGEN ZUR SCHÖNEN LITERATUR IN FREMDEN SPRACHEN. STUTTGART. A. KRÖNER, 1955. CAMUS, PP. 90-93. BDZ 112-299 (1956).

2303   LENOIR, THOMAS. L'HOMME DE LA SEMAINE. ALBERT CAMUS. EXPRESS, VOL. 3, NO. 259 (JUNE 8, 1956), PP. 1, 12-13. BR, CR 955.

2304   LENZ, JOSEPH. DER MODERNE DEUTSCH UND FRANZÖSISCHE EXISTENTIALISMUS. 2. ERWEITERTE AUFL. TRIER. PAULINUS-VERLAG, 1951. BO 208, FR VII 7168.

2305   LEPP, IGNACE. PSYCHANALYSE DE L'ATHÉISME MODERNE. PARIS. GRASSET, 1961. PP. 245-252. L'ATHÉISME DÉSESPÉRÉ D'ALBERT CAMUS. FITCH.

2306   LEPP, IGNACE. ATHEISM IN OUR TIME. NEW YORK. MACMILLAN, 1964. THE DESPAIRING ATHEISM OF ALBERT CAMUS, PP. 151-156. TRANSLATED BY BERNARD MURCHLAND.

2307   LERMINIER. GEORGES. JEAN-LOUIS BARRAULT DÉFEND 'L'ETAT DE SIÈGE'. ÂGE NOUVEAU, NO. 33 (JAN. 1949), PP. 108-109.

2308   LERMINIER, GEORGES. D'UNE PIÈCE DE CAMUS À L'ART DE JOUVET. ÂGE NOUVEAU, VOL. 1, NO. 47 (MARCH 1950), PP. 114-115. CR 757.

2309   LERMINIER, GEORGES. REQUIEM FÜR EINE NONNE DE WILLIAM FAULKNER. VERSION ALLEMANDE DE ROBERT SCHNORR. THÉÂTRE POPULAIRE, NO. 21 (NOV. 1, 1956), PP. 109-110.

2310   LERMINIER, GEORGES. BRECHT, CAMUS ET LE THÉÂTRE D'AUJOURD'HUI. ÂGE NOUVEAU, VOL. 12, NO. 99 (JAN. 1957), PP. 108-110. BUL SIGN 11-10184, CR 1040, FR VII 17323.

2311   LERMINIER, GEORGES. ALBERT CAMUS DRAMATURGE. PENSÉE FRANÇAISE, VOL. 17, NO. 5 (MAY 1958), PP. 55-57. FR VII 19429, KL II

389.

LERNER, MAX. ACTIONS AND PASSIONS, NOTES ON THE MULTIPLE   2312
    REVOLUTION OF OUR TIME. NEW YORK. SIMON AND SCHUSTER,
    1949.   CAMUS AND THE OUTSIDER , PP. 46-49. BO 305, FR VII
    7127, PMLA 20669.

LEROUVRE, CATHERINE. AMOUR DE LA VIE. SIMOUN, VOL. 8, NO. 31   2313
    (JULY 1960), PP. 34-37. FR VII 23573, KL II 394.

LESAGE, LAURENCE. ALBERT CAMUS AND STENDHAL. FRENCH REVIEW,   2314
    VOL. 23, NO. 6 (MAY 1950), PP. 474-477. BO 289, CR 758, FR
    VII 4417.

LESAGE, LAURENT. NOTEBOOKS 1935-1942 BY ALBERT CAMUS. (REVIEW).   2315
    MODERN DRAMA, VOL. 7, NO. 1 (MAY 1964), PP. 108-109.

LESCURE, PIERRE DE. ALBERT CAMUS. FRANCE NOUVELLE, NO. 742   2316
    (JAN. 7, 1960), P. 24.

LEVAL, GASTON. BAKOUNINE ET L'HOMME RÉVOLTÉ D'ALBERT CAMUS.   2317
    LIBERTAIRE, VOL. 57, NO. 308 (MARCH 28, 1952), P. 3.
    FITCH.

LEVAL, GASTON. BAKOUNINE ET L'HOMME RÉVOLTÉ D'ALBERT CAMUS. II.   2318
    LIBERTAIRE, VOL. 57, NO. 309 (APRIL 4, 1952), P. 3.
    FITCH.

LEVAL, GASTON. BAKOUNINE ET L'HOMME RÉVOLTÉ D'ALBERT CAMUS.   2319
    III. LIBERTAIRE, VOL. 57, NO. 310 (APRIL 11, 1952), P. 2.
    FITCH.

LEVAL, GASTON. BAKOUNINE ET L'HOMME RÉVOLTÉ D'ALBERT CAMUS. IV.   2320
    LIBERTAIRE, VOL. 57, NO. 311 (APRIL 18, 1952), P. 3.
    FITCH.

LEVIN, Z. SIPURIM SHEL ALBERT CAMUS (ALBERT CAMUS' STORIES).   2321
    HAARETZ, MAY 8, 1959, PP. 10, 12.

LÉVY, YVES. 'NOCES', PAR ALBERT CAMUS. PARU, NO. 12 (NOV.   2322
    1945), PP. 65-68. CR 534.

L(ÉVY), Y(VES). 'LETTRES À UN AMI ALLEMAND', PAR ALBERT CAMUS.   2323
    PARU, NO. 14 (JAN. 1946), PP. 75-77. CR 567.

LEWALTER, CHRISTIAN E. DER WELTLOSE MENSCH. BEMERKUNGEN ZU   2324
    ALBERT CAMUS. MERKUR, VOL. 4, NO. 12 (DEC. 1950), PP.
    1317-1320. BDZ, BO 143.

LEWALTER, CHRISTIAN E. SARTRE CONTRA CAMUS. MERKUR, VOL. 6,   2325
    NO. 12 (DEC. 1952), PP. 1174-1176. BO 173, BUL SIGN
    7-8594, FR VII 10383.

LEWIS, RICHARD W. B. THE PICARESQUE SAINT, REPRESENTATIVE   2326
    FIGURES IN CONTEMPORARY FICTION. PHILADELPHIA. J. B.
    LIPPINCOTT CO., 1959. CAMUS, THE COMPASSIONATE MIND , PP.
    57-108, 299-302. FR VII 20857, KL II 389.

LEWIS, RICHARD W. B. 'CALIGULA': OR THE REALM OF THE   2327
    IMPOSSIBLE. YALE FRENCH STUDIES, NO. 25 (SPRING 1960), PP.
    52-58. BUL SIGN 16-19-10096, FR VII 23568, KL II 380.

2328　LEWIS, THEOPHILUS. CALIGULA . AMERICA, VOL. 102, NO. 25
　　　　(2651) (MARCH 26, 1960), PP. 775-776.

2329　LEWIS, WYNDHAM. THE WRITER AND THE ABSOLUTE. LONDON. METHUEN,
　　　　1952. SCATTERED REFERENCES. BR, CR 463 BIS.

2330　LEYBURN, ELLEN DOUGLASS. TWO ALLEGORICAL TREATMENTS OF MAN.
　　　　'RASSELAS' AND 'LA PESTE'. CRITICISM, VOL. 4, NO. 3
　　　　(SUMMER 1962), PP. 197-209. FR VII 33961, PMLA 3559
　　　　(1963).

2331　LHERMINIER, GEORGES. LE THÉÂTRE. CALIGULA . ESPRIT, VOL.
　　　　13, NO. 12 (NOV. 1, 1945), PP. 815-817. CR 535.

2332　LIEBLING, A. J. THE RATS OF ORAN. REVIEW: THE PLAGUE. NEW
　　　　YORKER, VOL. 24, NO. 24 (AUG. 7, 1948), PP. 60-63. BO
　　　　419.

2333　LIEBLING, A. J. THE CAMUS NOTEBOOKS. NEW YORKER, VOL. 39, NO.
　　　　51 (FEB. 8, 1964), PP.128, 130, 133, 134-138.

2334　LINDBLOM, PAUL. MELLAN DET ABSURDA OCH DET ABSOLUTA. REVIEW OF
　　　　MYTEN OM SISYFOS , ÖVERSÄTTNING AV GUNNAR BRANDELL OCH
　　　　BENGT JOHN, BONNIERS, 1947. BONNIERS LITTERÄRA MAGASIN,
　　　　VOL. 16, NO. 8 (OCT. 1947), PP. 666-668.

2335　LINS, ALVARO. JORNAL DE CRITICA. (SÉTIMA SÉRIE.) RIO DE
　　　　JANEIRO. EDIÇÕES O CRUZEIRO, 1963. O HOMEM, A NÁUSEA E A
　　　　REVOLTA , PP. 75-82.

2336　LOBET, MARCEL. LA VIE LITTÉRAIRE. ALBERT CAMUS. SOIR, VOL.
　　　　65, NO. 145 (MAY 26, 1951), P. 7. CR 789.

2337　LOBET, MARCEL. LA VIE LITTÉRAIRE. A. CAMUS. ACTUELLES II .
　　　　SOIR, VOL. 67, NO. 309 (NOV. 7, 1953), P. 7. CR 861.

2338　LOBET, MARCEL. LA SCIENCE DU BIEN ET DU MAL, ESSAI SUR LA
　　　　CONNAISSANCE LITTÉRAIRE. BRUSSELS. ÉDITIONS DES ARTISTES,
　　　　1954. SARTRISME ET GIDISME, PP. 76-85.

2339　LOBET, MARCEL. LA VIE LITTÉRAIRE. ALBERT CAMUS OU L'INVINCIBLE
　　　　ÉTÉ. SOIR, VOL. 70, NO. 276 (OCT. 3, 1956), P. 7. CR
　　　　956.

2340　LOBET, MARCEL. AUX AMIS DE LA LANGUE FRANÇAISE, MALRAUX,
　　　　SARTRE, CAMUS. SOIR, VOL. 71, NO. 36 (FEB. 5, 1957), P.
　　　　2. CR 1041.

2341　LOBET, MARCEL. LA VIE LITTÉRAIRE. LES ESSAIS. 'L'ENVERS ET
　　　　L'ENDROIT'. SOIR, VOL. 72, NO. 105 (APRIL 16, 1958), P.
　　　　8. CR 1104.

2342　LOCKRIDGE, ERNEST H. A VISION OF THE SENTIMENTAL ABSURD. STERNE
　　　　AND CAMUS. SEWANEE REVIEW, VOL. 72, NO. 4 (FALL 1964),
　　　　PP. 652-667. PMLA 4371 (1964).

2343　LOEWEL, PIERRE. LE THÉÂTRE: 'CALIGULA'. LETTRES FRANÇAISES,
　　　　VOL. 5, NO. 76 (OCT. 6, 1945), P. 7. CR 536.

2344　LOKHORST, EMMY VAN. ALBERT CAMUS IN NEDERLAND. GROENE
　　　　AMSTERDAMMER, VOL. 78, NO. 41 (OCT. 9, 1954), P. 11. BO

49.

LOKHORST, EMMY VAN. ALBERT CAMUS, DE WAARACHTIGE MENS. GIDS,   2345
     VOL. 123, NO. 1 (1960), PP. 58-65. BFZ 47-280, FR VII
     26352, PMLA 6834 (1961).

LOMBARDI, OLGA. L'ARTISTA E IL SUO TEMPO SECONDO ALBERTO CAMUS.   2346
     FIERA LETTERARIA, VOL. 9, NO. 50 (DEC. 12, 1954), P. 6.
     BO 104, FR VII 13310.

LOOSE, JOHN. THE CHRISTIAN AS CAMUS'S ABSURD MAN. JOURNAL OF   2347
     RELIGION, VOL. 42, NO. 3 (JULY 1962), PP. 203-214. PMLA
     7981 (1963).

LORANQUIN, ALBERT. LA CHUTE PAR ALBERT CAMUS. BULLETIN DES   2348
     LETTRES, VOL. 18, NO. 179 (JUNE 15, 1956), PP. 233-234.
     CR 957, KL I 274.

LORANQUIN, ALBERT. L'EXIL ET LE ROYAUME PAR ALBERT CAMUS.   2349
     BULLETIN DES LETTRES, VOL. 19, NO. 187 (APRIL 15, 1957),
     PP. 147-148. FR VII 17325.

LORANQUIN, ALBERT. ALBERT CAMUS OU LES RAISONS DU COEUR.   2350
     BULLETIN DES LETTRES, VOL. 19, NO. 192 (NOV. 15, 1957),
     PP. 373-377. FR VII 17324, KL I 272.

LORANQUIN, ALBERT. ALBERT CAMUS.-- DISCOURS DE SUÈDE .   2351
     BULLETIN DES LETTRES, VOL. 20, NO. 196 (MARCH 15, 1958),
     P. 120. CR 1106.

LORANQUIN, ALBERT. ALBERT CAMUS.-- L'ENVERS ET L'ENDROIT .   2352
     BULLETIN DES LETTRES, VOL. 20, NO. 197 (APRIL 15, 1958),
     P. 163. CR 1107.

LORANQUIN, ALBERT. ALBERT CAMUS.-- ACTUELLES III . BULLETIN   2353
     DES LETTRES, VOL. 20, NO. 200 (JULY 15, 1958), PP.
     310-311. CR 1105.

LORANQUIN, ALBERT.HENRI BONNIER.--ALBERT CAMUS OU LA FORCE   2354
     D'ÊTRE . BULLETIN DES LETTRES, VOL. 21, NO. 212 (NOV. 15,
     1959), PP. 401-402. FR VII 21402.

LORANQUIN, ALBERT. ALBERT CAMUS. BULLETIN DES LETTRES, VOL.   2355
     22, NO. 214 (JAN. 15, 1960), PP. 1-3. FR VII 26353.

LOURIA, YVETTE. DÉDOUBLEMENT IN DOSTOEVSKY AND CAMUS. MODERN   2356
     LANGUAGE REVIEW, VOL. 56, NO. 1 (JAN. 1961), PP. 82-83.
     BFZ 47-390 (1961), PMLA 7369 (1962).

LUC-VERBON, PHILIPPE. RÉVOLTE ET REFUS. ÂGE NOUVEAU, NO. 78   2357
     (DEC. 1952), PP. 8-19.

LÜDERS, E. M. ALLES ODER NICHTS. ZUR WELTANSICHT ALBERT CAMUS   2358
     (DIE PEST). STIMMEN DER ZEIT, VOL. 76, NO. 2 (NOV. 1950),
     PP. 105-117. BDZ 101-208, BO 110, CR 760, FR VII 13311.

LUMLEY, FREDERICK. TRENDS IN 20TH CENTURY DRAMA. A SURVEY   2359
     SINCE IBSEN AND SHAW. FAIR LAWN, NEW JERSEY. ESSENTIAL
     BOOKS, 1960. FR VII 23144.

LUPO, VALERIA. LA RICERCA DEL GIUSTO IN CAMUS. 'LES JUSTES'.   2360

PONTE,   VOL. 10,   NO. 6 (JUNE 1954), PP. 906-921.   BO 471,
FR VII 11230.

2361   LUPO, VALERIA. I DUE VOLTI DI ALBERTO CAMUS.   IN CHE COSA PUÓ
DIRSI E NON DIRSI UN CRISTIANO.   NUOVA ANTOLOGIA,   89TH
YEAR, VOL. 461, NO. 1844 (AUG. 1954), PP. 487-506.   BFZ
37-266 (1953-55), BO 119, CR 897, FR VII 11229.

2362   LUPPÉ, ROBERT DE. ALBERT CAMUS.   PARIS.   TEMPS PRÉSENT, 1951.
BO 35, CR 464, FR VII 5734.

2363   LUPPÉ, ROBERT DE. ALBERT CAMUS.   PARIS.   ÉDITIONS
UNIVERSITAIRES, 1952.   BO 41, CR 465, FR VII 7690.

2364   LUPPÉ, ROBERT DE. LA PHILOSOPHIE.   LES NOUVEAUX CHEMINS
D'ALBERT CAMUS. REVUE FRANÇAISE, NO. 89 (MAY 1957), P. 48.
CR 1042.

2365   LUPPÉ, ROBERT DE. LA PHILOSOPHIE.   ALBERT CAMUS OU LE RETOUR
AUX SOURCES . REVUE FRANÇAISE, NO. 101 (MAY 1958), PP.
58-59.   CR 1108.

2366   LUPPÉ, ROBERT DE. ALBERT CAMUS.   PARIS.   ÉDITIONS
UNIVERSITAIRES, 1960.   FR VII 23577.

2367   LUPPÉ, ROBERT DE. ALBERT CAMUS EST MORT.   REVUE FRANÇAISE,   NO.
115 (FEB. 1960), P. 17.

2368   LUPPÉ, ROBERT DE. LA SOURCE UNIQUE D'ALBERT CAMUS.   TABLE
RONDE,   NO. 146 (FEB. 1960), PP. 30-40.   BFZ 46-283, BUL
SIGN 15-19-13764, FR VII 23569, KL II 393.

2369   LUPPÉ, ROBERT DE. ALBERT CAMUS (DÉBAT).   RECHERCHES ET DÉBATS
DU CENTRE CATHOLIQUE DES INTELLECTUELS FRANÇAIS,   NO. 31
(JUNE 1960), PP. 169-192.   (LUPPÉ CONTRIBUTION, PP.
169-176).   BUL SIGN 15-19-1009, 15-19-20058.

2370   LUTGEN, ODETTE. EN DÉPIT DE LEUR GLOIRE.   PARIS. DEL DUCA,
1961.   ALBERT CAMUS, PRIX NOBEL DE LITTÉRATURE, PP. 33-41.
FITCH.

2371   LUZI, MARIO. ASPETTI DELLA GENERAZIONE NAPOLEONICA ED ALTRI
SAGGI DE LETTERATURA FRANCESE.   PARMA.   GUANDA EDITORE,
1956.   FR VII 18827.

2372   MAALAND, SVERRE. CAMUS ABSURDITETSFILOSOFI OG 'PESTEN'.
VINDUET,   VOL. 4, NO. 4 (1950), PP. 316-318.   FR VII 29390.

2373   M(ACH), H(ELGA). CAMUS.   IN   DER ROMANFÜHRER   VOL. 9, PP.
38-42. STUTTGART. ANTON HIERSEMANN, 1958.

2374   MACKSEY, RICHARD. THE ARTIST IN THE LABYRINTH.   DESIGN OR
DASEIN.   MODERN LANGUAGE NOTES,   VOL. 77, NO. 3 (MAY 1962),
PP. 239-256. FR VII 28547.

2375   MACKWORTH, CECILY. LES COUPABLES.   TWENTIETH CENTURY,   VOL.
161, NO. 963 (MAY 1957), PP. 459-468.   FR VII 16691.

2376   MACLURE, MILLAR. ALLEGORIES OF INNOCENCE.   DALHOUSIE REVIEW,
VOL. 40, NO. 2 (SUMMER 1960), PP. 145-156.   KL II 389.

2377   MADARIAGA, SALVADOR DE. L'ESPRIT ET LE COEUR.   NOUVELLE REVUE

FRANÇAISE, VOL. 8, NO. 87 (MARCH 1960), PP. 539-544. FR
VII 23575, KL II 387.

MADARIAGA, SALVADOR DE. UN DES NÔTRES. PREUVES, NO. 110   2378
(APRIL 1960), PP. 10-13. FR VII 23642, KL II 394, PMLA
7370 (1962).

MADAULE, JACQUES. UN MORALISTE. ALBERT CAMUS. LEBENDEN   2379
FREMDSPRACHEN, VOL. 3, NO. 7 (1951), PP. 193-194. BDZ
103-263 (51), BO 125, CR 791.

MADAULE, JACQUES. CAMUS ET L'ACTUALITÉ. REVUE DU CAIRE, VOL.   2380
16, NO. 168 (MARCH 1954), PP. 232-235. FR VII 26354.

MADAULE, JACQUES. ALBERT CAMUS, ESCRITOR. INSULA, VOL. 9, NO. 2381
102 (JUNE 1, 1954), P. 4. BO 50, FR VII 11231.

MADAULE, JACQUES. CAMUS ET DOSTOÏEVSKI. TABLE RONDE, NO. 146   2382
(FEB. 1960), PP. 127-136. BFZ 46-284, BUL SIGN
15-19-13774, FR VII 23569, KL II 392.

MADISON, M. M. ALBERT CAMUS. PHILOSOPHER OF LIMITS. MODERN   2383
FICTION STUDIES, VOL. 10, NO. 3 (AUTUMN 1964), PP.
223-231.

MAGGIONI, MARY FARINA. LA PESTE DI BOCCACCIO, MANZONI E CAMUS. 2384
REALTÀ, VOL. 5, NO. 26 (MARCH-APRIL 1955), PP. 18-20. FR
VII 15353.

MAGNAN, HENRI, ET AL. FORAY THROUGH EXISTENTIALISM. YALE   2385
FRENCH STUDIES, NO. 16 (WINTER 1955-56). SEE NO. 960,
1115, 1920, 1981.

MAGNY, CLAUDE-EDMONDE. LA LITTÉRATURE FRANÇAISE DEPUIS 1940.   2386
(II). FRANCE LIBRE, VOL. 9, NO. 52 (FEB. 15, 1945), PP.
292-304. CR 537.

MAGNY, CLAUDE-EDMONDE. ROMAN AMÉRICAIN ET CINÉMA. POÉSIE 45,   2387
VOL. 6, NO. 25 (JUNE-JULY 1945), PP. 71-79. FR VII 235.

MAGNY, CLAUDE-EDMONDE. 'LE MALENTENDU', 'CALIGULA'. ESPRIT,   2388
VOL. 13, NO. 1 (1945), P. 274. BO 336, CR 538.

MAGNY, CLAUDE-EDMONDE. FRENCH LITERATURE SINCE 1940. PARTISAN 2389
REVIEW, VOL. 13, NO. 2 (SPRING 1946), PP. 145-154.
TRANSLATED BY MARTIN GREENBERG.

MAGNY, OLIVIER DE. ENTRETIEN SUR CAMUS ENTRE L. BERTHE, J.   2390
CHARPIER, O. DE MAGNY. LETTRES NOUVELLES, VOL. 4, NO. 2
(1956), PP. 357-363. KL I 271.

MAGNY, OLIVIER DE. UN JUGE QUI PLAIDE COUPABLE. MONDE NOUVEAU, 2391
VOL. 11, NO. 102 (JULY 1956), PP. 74-79. CR 958, FR VII
15354, KL I 273.

MAGRINI, LILIANA. L'UOMO COMO TESTIMONE. FIERA LITTERARIA,   2392
40TH YEAR, NO. 36 (SEPT. 19, 1965), P6.

MAHFOUZ, NAGUIB. HOMMAGE À ALBERT CAMUS DES ÉCRIVAINS ARABES. 2393
SEE NO. 3047.

MAIA, JOÃO. VIDA LITERARIA. CAMUS (NOTICE SUR LA MORT DE   2394

CAMUS). BROTÉRIA, VOL. 70, NO. 2 (FEB. 1960), PP.
205-206. KL II 395.

2395   MAIONE, ITALO. RITORNO A CAMUS. BARETTI, VOL. 1, NO. 2
(DEC.-JAN. 1960), PP. 59-64. FR VII 26355, PMLA 6835
(1961).

2396   MAIRE, GILBERT. ALBERT CAMUS ET L'IDÉE DE RÉVOLTE. TABLE
RONDE, NO. 146 (FEB. 1960), PP. 75-79. BFZ 46-284, BUL
SIGN 15-19-13767, FR VII 23569, KL II 389.

2397   MAJAULT, JOSEPH. DE LA RÉVOLTE À LA SERVITUDE. ÉDUCATION
NATIONALE, VOL. 12, NO. 24 (SEPT. 27, 1956), PP. 20-21.
KL I 273.

2398   MALABARD, JEAN. L'OEUVRE D'ALBERT CAMUS. REVUE DE L'UNIVERSITE
LAVAL, VOL. 1, NO. 2 (OCT. 1946), PP. 118-122. BO 10, CR
568, FR VII 5752.

2399   MALDONADO DENIS, MANUEL. SOBRE ALGUNOS TEMAS FUNDAMENTALES DE
ALBERT CAMUS. CUADERNOS AMERICANOS, 21ST YEAR, VOL. 121,
NO. 2 (MARCH-APRIL 1962), PP. 148-156. PMLA 7982 (1963).

2400   MALLET, ROBERT. SUR L'AUTRE VERSANT DE LA MONTAGNE. (EXTRACT
FROM JOURNAL OF ROBERT MALLET, JAN. 29, 1959). FIGARO
LITTÉRAIRE, VOL. 15, NO. 716 (JAN. 9, 1960), P. 6. FR VII
26356, KL II 386.

2401   MALLET, ROBERT. PRÉSENT À LA VIE, ÉTRANGER À LA MORT (PAGES DE
JOURNAL). NOUVELLE REVUE FRANÇAISE, VOL. 8, NO. 87 (MARCH
1960), PP. 440-448. FR VII 23575, KL II 394.

2402   MALORI, JACQUES. UNE CORRESPONDANCE. NOUVELLE REVUE FRANÇAISE,
VOL. 8, NO. 87 (MARCH 1960), PP. 583-586. FR VII 23575, KL
II 391.

2403   MALRAUX, ANDRÉ. DES ÉCRIVAINS NOUS DISENT. (HOMMAGES À CAMUS).
FIGARO, VOL. 134, NO. 4770 (JAN. 6, 1960), P.4. FR VII
23649.

2404   MANDER, JOHN. THE FATE OF THE JUST. NEW STATESMAN, VOL. 61,
NO. 1562 (FEB. 17, 1961), PP. 267-268. FR VII 26357.

2405   MANGINI, NICOLA. ALBERT CAMUS UOMO DI TEATRO. ITALIA CHE
SCRIVE, (MAGGIO), VOL. 44, NO. 5 (1961), PP. 87-88. BFZ
48-262 (1962), PMLA 7371 (1961).

2406   MANLY, WILLIAM M. JOURNEY TO CONSCIOUSNESS. THE SYMBOLIC
PATTERN OF CAMUS'S L'ETRANGER. PUBLICATIONS OF THE MODERN
LANGUAGE ASSOCIATION OF AMERICA, VOL. 79, NO. 3 (JUNE
1964), PP. 321-328. PMLA 8619 (1964).

2407   MANOS, HAROLD. NEW WRITING IN FRANCE, ALBERT CAMUS. 'LA PESTE'.
FORMES ET COULEURS, VOL. 9, NO. 4 (1947), PP. 2 (UN-
NUMBERED).

2408   MANZINI, GIANNA. PRIS AU PIÈGE DE LA POÉSIE. NOUVELLE REVUE
FRANÇAISE, VOL. 8, NO. 87 (MARCH 1960), PP. 549-555. FR
VII 23575, KL II 389.

MANZINI, GIANNA. RITRATTI E PRETESTI. MILANO. IL SAGGIATORE,   2409
    1960. CAMUS. INSIDIATO DALLA POESIA, PP. 69-77.

MAQUET, ALBERT. ALBERT CAMUS OU L'INVINCIBLE ÉTÉ. PARIS.   2410
    NOUVELLES ÉDITIONS DEBRESSE, 1955. BO 544, CR 466, FR VII
    1532, KL II 387.

MAQUET, ALBERT. ALBERT CAMUS. LA SYMPATHIE, DIMENSION   2411
    NÉCESSAIRE DE LA RÉVOLTE. GRIVE, VOL. 28, NO. 88 (OCT.
    1955), PP. 12-15. BO 240, FR VII 13312.

MAQUET, ALBERT. ALBERT CAMUS. THE INVINCIBLE SUMMER. NEW   2412
    YORK. GEORGE BRAZILLER, 1958. BR, CR 467, FR VII 19400.

MAQUET, ALBERT. ALBERT CAMUS, QUESTO FRATELLO MAGGIORE.   2413
    QUESTIONI, VOL. 8, NOS. 1-2 (JAN.-MARCH 1960), PP. 21-29.
    FR VII 26358, PMLA 7983 (1963).

MARA, JAN. CARREFOUR VOUS PRÉSENTE UNE SEMAINE THÉÂTRALE   2414
    CHARGÉE. LES JUSTES D'ALBERT CAMUS, AU THÉÂTRE HÉBERTOT.
    CARREFOUR, VOL. 16, NO. 275 (DEC. 20, 1949), P. 7.

MARCABRU, PIERRE. LE THEATRE: 'CALIGULA' D'ALBERT CAMUS.   2415
    ARTS, NO. 658 (FEB. 19-25, 1958), P. 7. CR 1109.

MARCABRU, PIERRE. NI CAMUS, NI DOSTOÏEVSKI. (L'ADAPTATION DES   2416
    POSSÉDÉS AU THÉÂTRE ANTOINE). ARTS, NO. 708 (FEB. 4-10,
    1959), PP. 1,5. CR 1141.

MARCEL, GABRIEL. LES DÉBUTS DE LA SAISON THÉÂTRALE. 'CALIGULA'   2417
    D'ALBERT CAMUS. ÉTUDES, VOL. 79, NO. 248 (JAN. 1946), PP.
    108-110. CR 569.

MARCEL, GABRIEL. 'L'ETAT DE SIEGE'. NOUVELLES LITTERAIRES,   2418
    VOL. 27 , NO. 1106 (NOV. 11, 1948), P. 8. BO 445, CR 667.

MARCEL, GABRIEL. 'LES JUSTES'. NOUVELLES LITTERAIRES, VOL.   2419
    28, NO. 1164 (1949), P. 8. BO 458, CR 711.

MARCEL, GABRIEL. DER EXISTENTIALISMUS UND DAS ZEITGENÖSSISCHE   2420
    THEATER. WISSENSCHAFT UND WELTBILD, VOL. 9, NO. 4 (DEC.
    1956), PP. 251-262. KL I 231.

MARCEL, GABRIEL. LE THÉÂTRE. 'REQUIEM POUR UNE NONNE'.   2421
    NOUVELLES LITTÉRAIRES, NO. 1518 (OCT. 4, 1956), P. 8.
    FITCH.

MARCEL, GABRIEL. L'HEURE THÉÂTRALE DE GIRAUDOUX À JEAN-PAUL   2422
    SARTRE. PARIS. PLON, 1959. ALBERT CAMUS, PP. 159-176.
    FR VII 20988, KL II 390.

MARCEL, GABRIEL. ALBERT CAMUS. NOUVELLES LITTÉRAIRES, NO.   2423
    1688 (JAN. 7, 1960), PP. 1, 8. FR VII 23643, KL II 395,
    PMLA 6836 (1961).

MARCEL, GABRIEL. L'HOMME RÉVOLTÉ. TABLE RONDE, NO. 146 (FEB.   2424
    1960), PP. 80-94. BFZ 46-283, BUL SIGN 15-19-13766, FR VII
    23569, KL II 391.

MARCHAND, JEAN-JOSÉ. CHRONIQUES. LES LIVRES. 'LE MYTHE DE   2425
    SISYPHE' PAR ALBERT CAMUS. CAHIERS DU SUD, VOL. 31

(FEB.-MARCH 1944), PP. 172-174. CR 504.

2426   MARCORELLES, LOUIS. LE REFUS DU MENSONGE. FRANCE OBSERVATEUR,
           VOL. 12, NO. 557 (JAN. 5, 1961), P. 16. SEE NO. 3253.

2427   MAREK, JOSEPH C. L'ABSENCE DE DIEU ET LA RÉVOLTE. CAMUS ET
           DOSTOÏEWSKI. REVUE DE L'UNIVERSITÉ LAVAL, VOL. 10, NO. 6
           (FEB. 1956), PP. 490-510. FR VII 17326, KL I 274.

2428   MARISSEL, ANDRÉ. LA CHUTE. REVUE SOCIALISTE, NO. 100 (OCTOBER
           1956), PP. 324-325.

2429   MARISSEL, ANDRÉ. ROGER QUILLIOT: 'LA MER ET LES PRISONS.
           ESSAI SUR ALBERT CAMUS'. REVUE SOCIALISTE, NO. 112 (DEC.
           1957), PP. 552-553. FR VII 26359.

2430   MARISSEL, A. LES ÉCRIVAINS ALGÉRIEN S'EXPLIQUENT, UNE ENQUÊTE.
           NOUVELLES LITTÉRAIRES, NO. 1728 (OCT. 13, 1960), PP. 1, 5.

2431   MARLET, J. J. C. VAN KAFKA TOT EN MET SARTRE. DEPERSONALISATIE
           EN DEREALISATIE IN DE LITERATUUR. STREVEN, KATHOLIEK
           CULTUREEL TIJDSCHRIFT, (1951-52), PP. 174-176, 265-267.
           BO 144.

2432   MARQUET, P. B. CAMUS, HOMME DE THÉÂTRE. COMBAT, (JULY 1,
           1960).

2433   MARRA-LÓPEZ, J. R. TESTIGO Y SIMBOLO DE EUROPA. INSULA, VOL.
           15, NO. 159 (FEB. 1960), P. 12. FR VII 23645.

2434   MARRERO, VICENTE. LA SECONDE PATRIE DE CAMUS. TABLE RONDE,
           NO. 146 (FEB. 1960), PP. 144-153. BFZ 46-284, BUL SIGN
           15-19-13760, FR VII 23569.

2435   MARTIN, ALAIN-GEORGES. ALBERT CAMUS ET LE CHRISTIANISME. REVUE
           REFORMEE, VOL. 12, NO. 4 (OCT. 1961), PP. 30-50. FR VII
           29393.

2436   MARTIN, PIERRE-OLIVIER. LE MINOTAURE. UNE DÉCLARATION D'AMOUR.
           SIMOUN, VOL. 4, NO. 19 (1955), PP. 66-68. FR VII 23646.

2437   MARTIN-CHAUFFIER, LOUIS. MERCURIALE, LES LETTRES. LA PESTE.
           MERCURE DE FRANCE, VOL. 301, NO. 1009 (SEPT. 1947), PP.
           127-130. BO 393, CR 611.

2438   MARTIN-CHAUFFIER, LOUIS. DES ÉCRIVAINS NOUS DISENT. (HOMMAGES
           À CAMUS). FIGARO, VOL. 134, NO. 4770 (JAN. 6, 1960), P.4.
           FR VII 23649.

2439   MARTIN DU GARD, ROGER. PERSONNE N'EST MOINS DUPÉ, PERSONNE PLUS
           INDÉPENDANT. FIGARO LITTÉRAIRE, VOL. 12, NO. 601 (OCT.
           26, 1957), P. 1. BR, CR 1043., FR VII 17327.

2440   MARTINE, CLAUDE. NEUF PERLES DE CULTURE. SEE NO. 2258.

2441   MARTINET, DANIEL. ALBERT CAMUS AUX GROUPES DE LIAISON
           INTERNATIONALE. TÉMOINS, VOL. 8, NO. 23 (MAY 1960), PP.
           6-7. KL II 386.

2442   MAS, E. G. EL PENSAMIENTO DE ALBERT CAMUS. STUDIUM (COLOMBIA),
           VOL. 2, NOS. 4-5 (JAN.-SEPT. 1958), PP. 9-20. FR VII
           23647.

MASCOLO, DIONYS. SUR DEUX AMIS MORTS. NOUVELLE REVUE   2443
    FRANÇAISE, VOL. 8, NO. 87 (MARCH 1960), PP. 451-460. FR
    VII 23575, KL II 394.

MASON, H. A. M. CAMUS AND THE TRAGIC HERO. SCRUTINY, VOL. 14,   2444
    NO. 2 (DEC. 1946), PP. 82-89. BO 189, CR 570, FR VII 2707.

MASSON, ANDRÉ. OEUVRE D'ALBERT CAMUS EN DÉBAT DEVANT LA   2445
    NOUVELLE GÉNÉRATION. UN TÉMOIGNAGE DE L'ÎLE MAURICE.
    FIGARO LITTÉRAIRE, VOL. 12, NO. 602 (NOV. 2, 1957), P. 11.
    FITCH. SEE NO. 3252.

MATET, MAURICE. UN NOUVEAU STOÏCISME. ALBERT CAMUS. BULLETIN   2446
    DE LA BIBLIOTHÈQUE DE L'INSTITUT FRANÇAIS EN ESPAGNE, NO.
    34 (1949), PP. 7-12. BO 199.

MATTHEWS, J. H. (EDITOR). ALBERT CAMUS - CONFIGURATION CRITIQUE   2447
    D'ALBERT CAMUS, I. 'L'ÉTRANGER' À L'ÉTRANGER. CAMUS DEVANT
    LA CRITIQUE ANGLO-SAXONNE. REVUE DES LETTRES MODERNES,
    VOL. 8, NOS. 64-66 (FALL 1961), PP. 305-496 (ALTERNATE
    PAGES 1-192). PMLA 26288 (1962), PMLA 7984 (1963), FR VII
    26288..

M(ATTHEWS), J. H. 'L'ETRANGER' À L'ÉTRANGER. CAMUS DEVANT LA   2448
    CRITIQUE ANGLO-SAXONNE. REVUE DES LETTRES MODERNES, VOL.
    8, NOS. 64-66 (FALL 1961), PP. 312-314 (ALT. PP. 8-10). FR
    VII 26288, PMLA 7984 (1963).

MATTHEWS, J. H. L'OEIL DE MEURSAULT. REVUE DES LETTRES   2449
    MODERNES, VOL. 8, NOS. 64-66 (FALL 1961), PP. 441-454
    (ALT. PP. 137-150). FR VII 26288.

MATTHEWS, J. H. CRITIQUE ANGLO-SAXONNE DE CAMUS, SÉLECTION   2450
    BIBLIOGRAPHIQUE. REVUE DES LETTRES MODERNES, VOL. 8, NOS.
    64-66 (FALL 1961), PP. 483-495 (ALT. PP. 179-191). SEE NO.
    1276.

MATTHEWS, J. H. FROM THE STRANGER TO THE FALL. CONFESSION AND   2451
    COMPLICITY. MODERN FICTION STUDIES, VOL. 10, NO. 3
    (AUTUMN 1964), PP. 265-273.

MATTHEWS, J. H. CONFIGURATION CRITIQUE D'ALBERT CAMUS, II.   2452
    CAMUS DEVANT LA CRITIQUE DE LANGUE ALLEMANDE, R. THIEBERGER
    (EDITOR). COMPARATIVE LITERATURE STUDIES, VOL. 1, NO. 3
    (1964), PP. 248-250.

MATHIEU, JEAN CLAUDE. DAS ABSURDE UND DIE SCHULD. ALBERT CAMUS'   2453
    AUSEINANDERSETZUNG MIT DER CHRISTLICHEN ETHIK.
    MONATSCHRIFT FUR PASTORALTHEOLOGIE, VOL. 48, NO. 6 (JUNE
    1959), PP. 196-208. BDZ 118-290 (1958), CR 1143.

MATHIEU, P. PETITE HISTOIRE DE LA KHÂGNE AFRICAINE. REVUE DE   2454
    LA MÉDITERRANÉE, VOL. 19, NOS. 5-6 (NOV.-DEC. 1959), PP.
    625-630. KL II 386.

MAUDUIT, JEAN. CHRONIQUE DU THÉÂTRE. LES JUSTES D'ALBERT   2455
    CAMUS. ÉTUDES, VOL. 264, NO. 2 (FEB. 1950), PP. 248-253.

BO 466, CR 762, FR VII 5753.

2456   MAULET, PIERRE. NOCES. (REVIEW). RENAISSANCES, NO. 16 (NOV.
        25, 1945), P. 172. BO 290, CR 540.

2457   MAULNIER, THIERRY. LE MYTHE DE SISYPHE. REVUE UNIVERSITAIRE,
        VOL. 53, (1943), PP. 394-397. BO 312, CR 496.

2458   MAULNIER, THIERRY. FEUILLETON LITTÉRAIRE. LA PESTE. HOMMES ET
        MONDES, VOL. 4 NO. 14 (SEPT. 1947), PP. 157-162. BO 394,
        CR 612.

2459   MAULNIER, THIERRY. LE THÉÂTRE. AU THÉÂTRE MARIGNY, LA PESTE
        PORTE L'UNIFORME NAZI... FIGARO LITTÉRAIRE, VOL. 3, NO.
        132 (OCT. 30, 1948), P. 6. CR 668.

2460   MAULNIER, THIERRY. LE THÉÂTRE. FAUT-IL DÉTRUIRE LES
        VIVANTES...? FIGARO LITTÉRAIRE, VOL. 4, NO. 192 (DEC. 24,
        1949), P. 8. CR 713.

2461   MAULNIER, THIERRY. LES CHOSES SONT CE QU'ELLES SONT. TABLE
        RONDE, NO. 59 (NOV. 1952), PP. 27-41. BO 279, FR VII
        7708.

2462   MAULNIER, THIERRY. UNE LIGNE COMPROMETTANTE. TABLE RONDE, NO.
        60 (DEC. 1952), PP. 19-33. BO 280, FR VII 7709.

2463   MAULNIER, THIERRY. LE THÉÂTRE. RACINE, CAMUS, BERNARD SHAW.
        REVUE DE PARIS, VOL. 65, NO. 3 (MARCH 1958), PP. 139-142.
        CR 1110.

2464   MAULNIER, THIERRY. DES ÉCRIVAINS NOUS DISENT. (HOMMAGES À
        CAMUS). FIGARO, VOL. 134, NO. 4770 (JAN. 6, 1960), P.4.
        FR VII 23649.

2465   MAULNIER, THIERRY. OUVERTURE. 'LE MALENTENDU' D'ALBERT CAMUS.
        REVUE DE PARIS, , VOL. 71, NO. 10 (OCT. 1964), PP. 113-
        116.

2466   MAURIAC, CLAUDE. 'L'HOMME RÉVOLTÉ' D'ALBERT CAMUS. TABLE
        RONDE, NO. 48 (DEC. 1951), PP. 98-109. BO 486, CR 791
        BIS, FR VII 5754.

2467   MAURIAC, CLAUDE. HOMMES ET IDÉES D'AUJOURD'HUI. PARIS. ALBIN
        MICHEL, 1953. BO 231, CR 468, FR VII 8673.

2468   MAURIAC, CLAUDE. ALBERT CAMUS. PREUVES, NO. 65 (JULY 1956),
        PP. 74-79. CR 960, FR VII 15355.

2469   MAURIAC, CLAUDE. HOMBRES Y IDEAS DE HOY. ALBERT CAMUS.
        CUADERNOS (DEL CONGRESO POR LA LIBERTAD DE LA CULTURA),
        NO. 20 (SEPT.-OCT. 1956), PP. 15-21. FR VII 15356.

2470   MAURIAC, CLAUDE. L'ALITTÉRATURE CONTEMPORAINE. PARIS. A.
        MICHEL, 1958. ALBERT CAMUS, PP. 107-120. FR VII 18828, KL
        I 272.

2471   MAURIAC, CLAUDE. L'HONNEUR D'ALBERT CAMUS. FIGARO, VOL. 132,
        NO. 4161 (JAN. 22, 1958), P. 10. FR VII 19430.

2472   MAURIAC, FRANÇOIS. LETTRE III. RÉPONSE À ALBERT CAMUS. TABLE
        RONDE, NO. 14 (FEB. 1949), PP. 198-206. BO 266, CR 714,

FR VII 2708.

MAURIAC, FRANÇOIS. LETTRES OUVERTES. MONACO. ÉDITIONS DU   2473
    ROCHER, 1952. LETTRE III. À ALBERT CAMUS , PP. 33-49.
    BO 67, FR VII 8675.

MAURIAC, FRANÇOIS. LETTERS ON ART AND LITERATURE. NEW YORK.   2474
    PHILOSOPHICAL LIBRARY, 1953. LETTRE III.   TO ALBERT CAMUS
    CAMUS, PP. 31-43. BO 75, FR VII 8674.

MAURIAC, FRANÇOIS. UNE JEUNE VOIX À LAQUELLE UNE GÉNÉRATION   2475
    FAIT ECHO. FIGARO LITTÉRAIRE, VOL. 12, NO. 601 (OCT. 26,
    1957), P. 1. BR, CR 1044, FR VII 17328.

MAURIAC, FRANÇOIS. DES ÉCRIVAINS NOUS DISENT (HOMMAGES À   2476
    CAMUS). FIGARO, VOL. 134, NO. 4770 (JAN. 6, 1960), P.4. FR
    VII 23649.

MAURIAC, FRANÇOIS. ALBERT CAMUS. FIGARO LITTÉRAIRE, VOL. 15,   2477
    NO. 717 (JAN. 16, 1960), P. 1. PMLA 6837 (1961), KL II
    394, FR VII 23648, 26360

MAURO, WALTER. ALBERT CAMUS FRA SAGGIO E ROMANZO. NOSTRO   2478
    TEMPO, VOL. 9, NO. 74-75 (JULY-AUG. 1960), PP. 1-3.

MAURO, WALTER. LA RESISTENZA NELLA LETTERATURA FRANCESE DALLA   2479
    2A GUERRA MONDIALE ALL'ALGERIA. ROME. CANESI, 1961.

MAUROIS, ANDRÉ. DE PROUST À CAMUS. PARIS. PERRIN, 1963.   2480
    ALBERT CAMUS, PP. 321-347. FR VII 31452.

MAUROIS, ANDRÉ. LE DERNIER MOT DE CAMUS. FIGARO LITTÉRAIRE,   2481
    VOL. 18, NO. 875 (JAN. 26, 1963), PP. 1, 2. FR VII 33964.

MAY, WILLIAM F. ALBERT CAMUS, POLITICAL MORALIST. CHRISTIANITY   2482
    AND CRISIS, VOL. 18, NO. 20 (NOV. 24, 1958), PP. 165-168.

MAYHEW, ALICE ELLEN. EARLY CAMUS. (REVIEW. NOTEBOOKS 1935-1942   2483
    BY ALBERT CAMUS). COMMONWEAL, VOL. 79, NO. 6 (NOV. 1,
    1963), PP. 173-174.

MAYNE, RICHARD. EX NIHILO. THE MYTH OF SISYPHUS. NEW STATESMAN   2484
    AND NATION, VOL. 50, NO. 1292 (DEC. 10, 1955), P. 806. BO
    330.

MAYNE, R. THE NOBEL SAVAGE. TIME AND TIDE, VOL. 39, NO. 2   2485
    (1958), PP. 46-47. BFZ 42-284.

MAZARS, PIERRE. ALBERT CAMUS SONGE À ÉCRIRE UN VRAI ROMAN.   2486
    FIGARO LITTÉRAIRE, VOL. 5, NO. 208 (APRIL 15, 1950), P. 1.
    BO 467, FR VII 4418.

MAZARS, PIERRE. EN ADAPTANT ET EN MONTANT 'LES POSSÉDÉS' ALBERT   2487
    CAMUS RÉALISE UN DE SES PLUS ANCIENS RÊVES. FIGARO
    LITTÉRAIRE, VOL. 14, NO. 666 (JAN. 24, 1959), PP. 4, 12.
    CR 1144, FR VII 21403.

MAZOYER, JEAN A. LA CRISIS DEL MUNDO OCCIDENTAL. A PROPÓSITO   2488
    DE 'LA CAÍDA', DE ALBERT CAMUS. CUADERNOS AMERICANOS,
    16TH YEAR, VOL. 93, NO. 3 (MAY-JUNE 1957), PP. 45-53. FR
    VII 21404, KL I 273.

2489   MAZOYER, JEAN A. À PROPOS DE 'LA CHUTE'. COMPRENDRE, NOS.
            17-18 (1957), PP. 220-222. KL II 390.

2490   MCCORMACK, ROBERT. AGEE, CAMUS, GARY. TAMARACK REVIEW, NO. 8
            (SUMMER 1958), PP. 82-87.

2491   MCCORMACK, ROBERT. THE SEASONS OF ALBERT CAMUS. TAMARACK
            REVIEW, NO. 19 (SPRING 1961), PP. 91-99. FR VII 26361.

2492   MCEACHRAN, F. THE LITERATURE OF EXISTENTIALISM. CONTEMPORARY
            REVIEW, VOL. 203, (MAY 1963), PP. 257-264. FR VII 32406.

2493   MCLAUGHLIN, RICHARD. BATTLE AGAINST THE FORCES OF DARKNESS.
            THE PLAGUE . SATURDAY REVIEW OF LITERATURE, VOL. 31, NO.
            31 (JULY 31, 1948), PP. 10-11. BO 420.

2494   MCMULLEN, ROY. HOW RELEVANT IS CAMUS TODAY? RÉALITÉS, NO. 126
            (MAY 1961), PP. 66-69.

2495   MCPHEETERS, D. W. CAMUS' TRANSLATIONS OF PLAYS BY LOPE AND
            CALDERÓN. SYMPOSIUM, VOL. 12, NOS. 1-2 (SPRING-FALL
            1958), PP. 52-64. BUL SIGN 14-9077, FR VII 19431, KL II
            392.

2496   MEHL, R. DE LA RÉVOLTE À LA VALEUR. A PROPOS DU LIVRE DE
            CAMUS: 'L'HOMME REVOLTE'. FOI ET VIE, VOL. 50, NO. 6
            (NOV.-DEC. 1952), PP. 516-532. BFZ 35-240 (1952-53), BO
            495, CR 829.

2497   M(EIJERS), J. A. DE PEST EN HET LEVEN. GROENE AMSTERDAMMER,
            VOL. 73, NO. 5 (JAN. 29, 1949), P. 8. BO 23, CR 715.

2498   MELCHINGER, SIEGFRIED. ALBERT CAMUS UND DER MITTAGSGEDANKE.
            ANTARES, VOL. 2, NO. 8 (DEC. 1954), PP. 87-90.

2499   MELCHINGER, SIEGFRIED (EDITOR). FRANZÖSISCHES THEATER, MIT
            EINEM NACHWORT. JEAN GIRAUDOUX. KEIN KRIEG IN TROJA, PAUL
            CLAUDEL. VERKUNDIGUNG, JEAN-PAUL SARTRE. BEI GESCHLOSSENEN
            TUREN, JEAN ANOUILH. JEANNE ODER DIE LERCHE, ALBERT CAMUS.
            DIE GERECHTEN, EUGENE IONESCO, DER NEUE MIETER. FRANKFURT
            AM MAIN. BÜCHERGILDE GUTENBERG, 1959. CR 184. SEE NO.
            384.

2500   MELCHINGER, SIEGFRIED. LES ÉLÉMENTS BAROQUES DANS LE THÉÂTRE DE
            CAMUS. REVUE DES LETTRES MODERNES, NOS. 90-93 (WINTER
            1963), PP. 175-183. PMLA 8608 (1964). SEE NO. 3207.
            TRANSLATED BY BERNARD LORTHOLARY.

2501   MELCHIORRE, VIRGILIO. CAMUS. I DUE ESTREMI O DELLA SINCERITÀ.
            VITA E PENSIERO, VOL. 44, NO. 8 (AUG. 1961), PP. 570-572.
            FR VII 29394.

2502   MELCHIOR-BONNET, CHRISTIAN. SORTI DES PRESSES. CARNETS II,
            JANVIER 1942-MARS 1951. À LA PAGE, NO. 10 (APRIL 1965), P.
            636.

2503   MEMMI, ALBERT. CAMUS OU LE COLONISATEUR DE BONNE VOLONTÉ. NEF,
            VOL. 14, NO. 12 (DEC. 1957), PP. 95-96. CR 1045.

2504   MÉNARD, RENÉ. CHRONIQUES. LE SECRET ET L'ÉTÉ. CAHIERS DU SUD,

41ST YEAR, VOL. 39, NO. 324 (AUG. 1954), PP. 282-290. BO
539, FR VII 11232, CR 898.

MÉNARD, RENÉ. D'UN PERPÉTUEL DÉBAT. ALBERT CAMUS, 'LA CHUTE'.   2505
CRITIQUE, VOL. 14, NO. 110 (JULY 1956), PP. 597-601. CR
961, FR VII 17329, KL I 274.

MÉNARD, RENÉ. CHRONIQUES. LE ROMAN. 'LA CHUTE', PAR ALBERT   2506
CAMUS. CAHIERS DU SUD, VOL. 43, NO. 337 (OCT. 1956), PP.
465-466. CR 962.

MÉNARD, RENÉ. ALBERT CAMUS ET LA RECHERCHE D'UNE LÉGITIMITÉ.   2507
CRITIQUE, 11TH YEAR, VOL. 14, NOS. 135-136 (AUG.-SEPT.
1958), PP. 675-689. BUL SIGN 14-9004, CR 1110 BIS, FR VII
19432, 23650.

MÉNARD, RENÉ. ALBERT CAMUS DEVANT UN SECRET. NOUVELLE REVUE   2508
FRANÇAISE, VOL. 8, NO. 87 (MARCH 1960), PP. 608-613. FR
VII 23575, KL 389.

MENDEL, WERNER M. THE PHENOMENON OF INTERPRETATION. AMERICAN   2509
JOURNAL OF PSYCHOANALYSIS, VOL. 24, NO. 2 (1964), PP.
184-189 (CAMUS REF. P. 186).

MENDES, JOÃO. 'A PESTE' DE ALBERTO CAMUS. BROTÉRIA, VOL. 62,   2510
NO. 4 (1956), PP. 468-473. BFZ 39-279 (1954-55), BO 442,
CR 963.

MENGOD, V. ALBERT CAMUS EN SU APARENTE SOLEDAD. ATENEA,   36TH   2511
YEAR, VOL. 135, NO. 386 (OCT.-DEC. 1959), PP. 20-27. FR
VII 23651.

MENNEMEIER, FRANZ NORBERT. DAS MODERNE DRAMA DES AUSLANDES.   2512
DUSSELDORF. AUGUST BAGEL VERLAG, 1961. BDZ.

MERAY, TIBOR. BUDAPEST (23 OCTOBRE 1956). PARIS, ROBERT   2513
LAFFONT, 1966. ALBERT CAMUS. KADAR A EU SON JOUR DE PEUR,
PP. 11-15.

MERCHANT, W. MOELWYN. CHRISTIANITY AND THE MODERN LITERARY   2514
IMAGINATION. A SURVEY OF ALLEGIANCES. IN. SCOTT, NATHAN
A., JR., THE CLIMATE OF FAITH IN MODERN LITERATURE, PP.
42-64 (CAMUS REF. PP. 45-47). SEE NO. 3044.

MERCIER, JEANNE. ALBERT CAMUS' NOTEBOOKS. THE MAKING OF A MIND.   2515
MILWAUKEE JOURNAL, VOL. 81 (JULY 14, 1963), PART V, P. 4.

MERTON, THOMAS. THE OTHER SIDE OF DESPAIR. NOTES ON CHRISTIAN   2516
EXISTENTIALISM. CRITIC, VOL. 24, NO. 2 (OCT.-NOV. 1965),
PP. 13-23.

MERWIN, W. S. THROUGH THE BLUR OF PAIN. NATION, VOL. 187, NO.   2517
4 (AUG. 16, 1958), PP. 74-75. FR VII 23652.

METER AMES, VAN. EXISTENTIALISM AND THE ARTS. JOURNAL OF   2518
AESTHETICS AND ART CRITICISM, VOL. 9, NO. 3 (MARCH 1951),
PP. 252-256. BO 171, BUL SIGN 6-4656.

MEYERS, J. A. HET EINDE ENER VRIENDSCHAP. DE BROEDERTWIST   2519
SARTRE-CAMUS. GROENE AMSTERDAMMER, VOL. 76, NO. 43 (OCT.

25, 1952), P. 7. CR 830.

2520   M'HAMSADJI, KADDOUR. LA GRANDE COLÈRE DE L'ABSURDE. SIMOUN,
            VOL. 8, NO. 31 (JULY 1960), PP. 52-53. FR VII 23573, KL II
            394

2521   MICHA, RENÉ. L'AGNEAU DANS LE PLACARD. NOUVELLE REVUE
            FRANÇAISE, VOL. 8, NO. 87 (MARCH 1960), PP. 501-505. FR
            VII 23575, KL II 388.

2522   MICHALSON, CARL. EXISTENTIALISM IS A MYSTICISM. THEOLOGY
            TODAY, VOL. 12, NO. 3 (OCT. 1955), PP. 355-368. FR VII
            16577.

2523   MICHALSON, CARL. CHRISTIANITY AND THE EXISTENTIALISTS. NEW
            YORK. SCRIBNER, 1956. CF. PP. 14, 66. KL I 231.

2524   MICHAUD, GUY. UN TEXTE DE CAMUS. SEE NO. 1335.

2525   MICHOT-DIETRICH, HELA. HOMO FABER. VARIATIONS SUR UN THÈME DE
            CAMUS. DISSERTATION ABSTRACTS, VOL. 26, NO. 6 (DEC.,
            1965), P. 3345.

2526   MILLER, HENRY. LEADING BOOKS OF THE OCCUPATION PERIOD. WORLD
            REVIEW, OCTOBER 1945, PP. 66-67, 69.

2527   MILLER, JUDITH. THE PROBLEM OF GUILT AND JUDGEMENT IN CAMUS'
            THE FALL. DISCOURSE, VOL. 6, NO. 4 (AUTUMN 1963), PP. 285-
            292.

2528   MILLET, RAYMOND. LE MORALISTE LE MOINS SUSPECT DE NOTRE TEMPS
            ...ÉCRIT LA PRESSE ITALIENNE. FIGARO, VOL. 134, NO. 4770
            (JAN. 6, 1960), P. 4. FITCH.

2529   MILLOT, J. LA DISPARITION D'ALBERT CAMUS. BULLETIN DU
            BIBLIOPHILE ET DU BIBLIOTHÈCAIRE, NO. 2 (1960), PP. 90-95.
            FR VII 23653, KL II 394, PMLA 7372 (1962).

2530   MILOSZ, CZESLAW. L'INTERLOCUTEUR FRATERNEL. PREUVES, NO. 110
            (APRIL 1960), PP. 14-16. FR VII 23654, KL II 393, PMLA
            7373 (1962).

2531   MINARD, MICHEL J. AVANT-PROPOS, CONFIGURATION CRITIQUE D'ALBERT
            CAMUS. REVUE DES LETTRES MODERNES, VOL. 8, NOS. 64-66
            (FALL 1961), P. 309 (ALT. P. 5).

2532   MINARD, MICHEL J. SISYPHE SUR SA PENTE. REVUE DES LETTRES
            MODERNES, NOS. 90-93 (WINTER 1963), PP. 5-6. SEE NO.
            3207.

2533   MONIN, J.-M. SOURCES ET REMANIEMENTS DU CALIGULA D'ALBERT
            CAMUS. REVUE DE L'UNIVERSITÉ DE BRUXELLES, VOL. 12, NOS.
            1-2 (OCT. 1959-FEB. 1960), PP. 145-149. BUL SIGN
            15-19-8646, FR VII 23655, KL II 390.

2534   MINOR, ANNE. THE SHORT STORIES OF ALBERT CAMUS. YALE FRENCH
            STUDIES, NO. 25 (SPRING 1960), PP. 75-80. FR VII 23568,
            KL II 391.

2535   MIRÓ QUESADA C., FRANCISCO. CAMUS Y EL MOVIMIENTO INTELECTUAL
            FRANCÉS CONTEMPORÁNEO. MERCURIO PERUANO, 27TH YEAR, VOL.

33, NO. 307 (OCT. 1952), PP. 452-480. BO 68, FR VII 9305.

MITTERAND, HENRI. LE STYLE DES ÉCRIVAINS CONTEMPORAINS. ALBERT   2536
   CAMUS, L'ETRANGER. FRANÇAIS DANS LE MONDE, NO. 18
   (JULY-AUGUST 1963), PP. 29-30. FR VII 33965.

MOELLER, CHARLES. EXISTENTIALISME ET PENSÉE CHRÉTIENNE. REVUE   2537
   NOUVELLE, VOL. 13, NO. 6 (JUNE 15, 1951), PP. 570-581. CR
   791 TER.

MOELLER, CHARLES. ALBERT CAMUS OF DE WANHOPIGE EERLIJKHEID.   2538
   (I). DIETSCHE WARANDE EN BELFORT, NO. 5 (JUNE 1952), PP.
   258-269. BO 42, CR 831.

MOELLER, CHARLES. ALBERT CAMUS OF DE WANHOPIGE EERLIJKHEID.   2539
   (II). LA PESTE. DIETSCHE WARANDE EN BELFORT, NO. 6 (JULY
   1952), PP. 336-345. BO 42, CR 832.

MOELLER, CHARLES. LITTÉRATURE DU XXE SIÈCLE ET CHRISTIANISME.   2540
   I. SILENCE DE DIEU. CAMUS, GIDE, HUXLEY, SIMONE WEIL,
   GRAHAM GREENE, JULIEN GREEN, BERNANOS. TOURNAI.
   CASTERMAN, 1953. ALBERT CAMUS , PP. 25-90. BO 118, BUL
   SIGN 15-19-7960, CR 469, FR VII 8677.

MOELLER, CHARLES. 'L'ÉTÉ' D'ALBERT CAMUS. REVUE NOUVELLE,   2541
   VOL. 10, NOS. 7-8 (JULY-AUG. 1954), PP. 127-130. BO 540,
   BUL SIGN 10-1203, FR VII 17330.

MOELLER, CHARLES. DIE SCHÖNHEIT UND DAS ABSURDE, ALBERT CAMUS.   2542
   L'ÉTÉ . DOKUMENTE, VOL. 10, NO. 5 (OCT. 1954), PP.
   431-433. BR, CR 899.

MOELLER, CHARLES. DES MANDARINS À LIVING ROOM. REVUE NOUVELLE,   2543
   VOL. 11, NO. 2 (FEB. 15, 1955), PP. 181-185. FR VII 16560.

MOELLER, CHARLES. OÙ EN EST ALBERT CAMUS? REVUE NOUVELLE,   2544
   14TH YEAR, VOL. 27, NO. 1 (JAN. 15, 1958), PP. 79-85. CR
   1111, FR VII 19433, KL I 272.

MOELLER, CHARLES. ALBERT CAMUS. THE QUESTION OF HOPE. CROSS   2545
   CURRENTS, VOL. 8, NO. 2 (SPRING 1958), PP. 172-184. FR
   VII 21405.

MOELLER, CHARLES. UNE OEUVRE QUI EXALTE LA PAUVRETÉ ET LA   2546
   LUMIÈRE. TABLE RONDE, NO. 146 (FEB. 1960), PP. 103-113.
   BFZ 46-284, BUL SIGN 15-19-13757, FR VII 23569, KL II 388.

MOENKEMEYER, HEINZ. THE SON'S FATAL HOME-COMING IN WERNER AND   2547
   CAMUS. MODERN LANGUAGE QUARTERLY, VOL. 27, NO. 1 (MARCH
   1966), PP. 51-67.

MOHRT, MICHEL. ETHIC AND POETRY IN THE WORK OF CAMUS. YALE   2548
   FRENCH STUDIES, VOL. 1, NO. 1 (SPRING-SUMMER 1948), PP.
   113-118. BO 121, CR 669, FR VII 4419.

MOINOT, PIERRE. UNE OEUVRE EN DÉBAT DEVANT LA NOUVELLE   2549
   GÉNÉRATION. IL EST MON COMPAGNON DE PLANÈTE. FIGARO
   LITTÉRAIRE, VOL. 12, NO. 601 (OCT. 26, 1957), P. 7.
   FITCH. SEE NO. 3251.

2550 MOLNAR, THOMAS. ALBERT CAMUS. GUIDE OF A GENERATION. CATHOLIC
WORLD, VOL. 186, NO. 1114 (JAN. 1958), PP. 272-277. FR
VII 19434, KL II 387.

2551 MOLNAR, THOMAS. ON CAMUS AND CAPITAL PUNISHMENT. MODERN AGE,
VOL. 2, NO. 3 (SUMMER 1958), PP. 298-306.

2552 MOLNAR, THOMAS. CAMUS, VOICE OF A SEARCHING GENERATION.
CATHOLIC WORLD, VOL. 191, NO. 1142 (MAY 1960), PP. 94-96,
101-103. FR VII 23656, PMLA 6838 (1961).

2553 MOLNAR, THOMAS. ALBERT CAMUS. UNIVERSITY BOOKMAN, VOL. 5, NO.
4 (SUMMER 1965), PP. 75-82.

2554 MÖNCH, WALTER. ALBERT CAMUS, EIN VERSUCH ZUM VERSTÄNDNIS SEINES
DRAMATISCHEN WERKES. ZEITSCHRIFT FÜR FRANZÖSISCHE SPRACHE
UND LITERATUR, VOL. 75, NO. 4 (DEC. 1965), PP. 289-308.

2555 MONETTE, ARCADE M. DE LAMARTINE À CAMUS. REVUE DE L'UNIVERSITÉ
LAVAL, VOL. 16, NO. 3 (1961), PP. 199-204. FR VII 26362,
PMLA 6966 (1961).

2556 MONTAGNA, GIANNI. 'CAMUS UNO E DUE', BY NICOLA DI GIROLAMO.
(REVIEW) AUSONIA, VOL. 15, NO. 4 (JULY-AUG. 1960), PP.
86-87. FR VII 26295, KL II 387.

2557 MONTALDI, DANILO. CRONACHE DELLA GAUCHE. QUESTIONI, NO. 3
(MAY 1956), PP. 4-11. FR VII 25553.

2558 MONTEL, MICHEL. COMPTE RENDU DE 'LA CHUTE' D'ALBERT CAMUS.
BULLETIN DE DOCUMENTATIONS, ÉCOLE SUPÉRIEURE DES
PROFESSEURS DE FRANÇAIS A L'ÉTRANGER. ASSOCIATION DES
ANCIENS ÉLÈVES, VOL. 37, NO. 1 (1957), PP. 5-6. BUL SIGN
14-9010.

2559 MOORE, HARRY T. TWENTIETH-CENTURY FRENCH LITERATURE TO WORLD
WAR II. CARBONDALE. SOUTHERN ILLINOIS UNIVERSITY PRESS,
1966. PP. 194-205.

2560 MORAVIA, ALBERTO. DES ÉCRIVAINS NOUS DISENT. (HOMMAGES À
CAMUS). FIGARO, VOL. 134, NO. 4770 (JAN. 6, 1960), P.4.
FR VII 23649.

2561 MORÉ, MARCEL. LES RACINES MÉTAPHYSIQUES DE LA RÉVOLTE. DIEU
VIVANT, NO. 21 (1952), PP. 35-59. BO 496, BUL SIGN
6-7148, FR VII 7710.

2562 MOREAU, ABEL. ALBERT CAMUS. ACTUELLES. CHRONIQUES 1944-48 .
FICHES BIBLIOGRAPHIQUES, (1950). CR 765.

2563 MOREAU, PIERRE. ASPECTS ROMANTIQUES. TABLE RONDE, NO. 146
(FEB. 1960), PP. 41-46. BFZ 46-283, BUL SIGN 15-19-13763,
FR VII 23569, KL II 388.

2564 MOREL, JACQUES. REQUIEM POUR UNE NONNE. ÉTUDES, VOL. 89, NO.
291 (DEC. 1956), PP. 403-410. BFZ 40-252, CR 964, FR VII
17331, KL I 273.

2565 MORTIMER, JOHN. CAMUS, DURRELL, WAIN AND KAVAN. ENCOUNTER,
VOL. 10, NO. 6, ISSUE NO. 57 (JUNE 1958), PP. 83-86. CR

1112.

MORVAN, JEAN-JACQUES. QUELQUES LIGNES SUR UN GRAND FRÈRE.   2566
   TEMOINS,   VOL. 8, NO. 23 (MAY 1960), PP. 16-19. KL II 394.

MOSCA. CAMUS SE PENCHE SUR LUI-MÊME. ANNALES,   VOL. 59, NO. 24   2567
   (OCT. 1952), P. 21. CR 833.

MOSELEY, EDWIN M. PSEUDONYMS OF CHRIST IN THE MODERN NOVEL.   2568
   MOTIFS AND METHODS. PITTSBURGH. UNIVERSITY OF PITTSBURGH
   PRESS, 1963. CHRIST AS EXISTENTIALIST ANTICHRIST. CAMUS
   THE STRANGER, PP. 195-203.

MOSTYN, R. J. TWO EXISTENTIAL PLAYS. HUMANIST,   VOL. 78, NO.   2569
   12 (DEC. 1963), PP. 358-360. FR VII 33966.

MOUNIER, EMMANUEL. CAMUS PARLE. ESPRIT,   VOL. 15, NO. 2 (JAN.   2570
   1947), PP. 156-157. BO 215, CR 613.

MOUNIER, EMMANUEL. ÉLÉGIE POUR 'COMBAT'. ESPRIT,   VOL. 18, NO.   2571
   1 (1950), PP. 655-657. BO 99.

MOUNIER, EMMANUEL. ALBERT CAMUS OU L'APPEL DES HUMILIÉS.   2572
   ESPRIT,   VOL. 18, NO. 163 (JAN. 1950), PP. 27-66. BFZ
   30-185 (1949-50), BO 206, BUL SIGN 6-7511, CR 766, FR VII
   11233, 4420.

MOUNIER, EMMANUEL. CARNETS DE ROUTE. L'ESPOIR DES DÉSESPÉRÉS.   2573
   PARIS. ÉDITIONS DU SEUIL, 1953.   ALBERT CAMUS OU L'APPEL
   DES HUMILIÉS , PP. 83-145. CR 470, FR VII 8680.

MOUSSY, MARCEL. SUR CAMUS. PARISIENNE,   NO. 48 (NOV.-DEC.   2574
   1957), PP. 1081-1083. CR 1047 TER, KL I 272.

MOUSSY, MARCEL. RENCONTRES. SIMOUN,   VOL. 8, NO. 31 (JULY   2575
   1960), PP. 25-28. FR VII 23573, KL II 394.

MUELLER, WILLIAM R. THE PROPHETIC VOICE IN MODERN FICTION. NEW   2576
   YORK. ASSOCIATION PRESS, 1959. THE THEME OF THE FALL.
   CAMUS' THE FALL , PP. 56-82. FR VII 20858, KL II 390.

MULLER, HENRY. ALBERT CAMUS A FAIT SON APPRENTISSAGE DE   2577
   ROMANCIER EN COMPTANT LES MILLIBARS ET DE JUSTICIER EN
   EMPÊCHANT UN INNOCENT D'ÊTRE CONDAMNÉ À MORT. CARREFOUR,
   VOL. 16, NO. 275 (DEC. 20, 1949), P. 9. FITCH.

MÜLLER-LAUTER, WOLFGANG. THESEN ZUM BEGRIFF DES ABSURDEN BEI   2578
   ALBERT CAMUS. THEOLOGIA VIATORUM, VOL. 8 (1961-1962), PP.
   203-215. FR VII 33967.

MÜNZ, ERWIN K. ALBERT CAMUS, DER AFRIKANER. BEGEGNUNG, VOL.   2579
   5, NOS. 6-7 (1950), PP. 179-183. BDZ 102-250 (51), BO 30,
   CR 763.

MÜNZ, ERWIN K. ALBERT CAMUS. DIE PEST. AUSSPRACHE.   2580
   DEUTSCH-FRANZÖSISCHE HEFTE,   NO. 4 (1950), PP. 75-81. CR
   764.

MURCHLAND, BERNARD G. CRITICS OF CAMUS. COMMONWEAL, VOL. 68,   2581
   NO. 7 (MAY 16, 1958), PP. 190-191. FR VII 19435.

MURCHLAND, BERNARD G. ALBERT CAMUS. REBEL. CATHOLIC WORLD,   2582

VOL. 188, NO. 1126 (JAN. 1959), PP. 308-314. FR VII 21406,
KL II 387.

2583   MURCHLAND, BERNARD G. ALBERT CAMUS: THE DARK NIGHT BEFORE THE
        COMING OF GRACE. IN   BREE, GERMAINE, CAMUS, A COLLECTION
        OF CRITICAL ESSAYS, PP. 59-64. SEE NO. 1293. REPRINT OF
        NO. 2582.

2584   MURRAY, JACK. THREE MURDERS IN THE CONTEMPORARY FRENCH NOVEL.
        TEXAS STUDIES IN LITERATURE AND LANGUAGE, VOL. 6, NO. 3
        (AUTUMN 1964), PP. 361-375. PMLA 8460 (1964).

2585   MURILLO BUSTAMANTE, HERNANDO. TÉCNICA DEL DETALLE EN ALBERT
        CAMUS Y ANDRÉ GIDE. BOLIVAR, VOL. 14, NO. 61 (JULY-SEPT.
        1961), PP. 97-109.

2586   MURY, GILBERT. CHRONIQUE DES ROMANS. SOLITUDE DE L'HOMME.
        POÉSIE 47, VOL. 8, NO. 41 (NOV. 1947), PP. 86-98. BO 191.

2587   MYHRE, AMUND. PÅ VEI MOT TABOR. ET MØTE MELLOM EN MODERNE
        SISYFOS OG TRE FRANSKE FORFÄTTERE. VINDUET, VOL. 10, NO.
        1 (1956), PP. 72-77. FR VII 28346.

2588   NADEAU, MAURICE. LITTÉRATURE PRÉSENTE. PARIS. CORREA, 1952.
        ALBERT CAMUS ET LA TENTATION DE SAINTÉTÉ , PP. 211-216. BO
        113, BR, CR 470 BIS.

2589   NADEAU, MAURICE. MERCURIALE, LETTRES, ALBERT CAMUS ET LA
        RÉVOLTE. 'L'HOMME RÉVOLTÉ'. MERCURE DE FRANCE, VOL. 314,
        NO. 1061 (JAN. 1952), PP. 106-111. BO 497.

2590   NADEAU, MAURICE. LA CHUTE. LETTRES NOUVELLES, VOL. 4, NO. 2
        (1956), PP. 153-154. KL I 274.

2591   NAHAS, HÉLÈNE. L'ÉVOLUTION DE LA PENSÉE D'ALBERT CAMUS DANS
        ACTUELLES . FRENCH REVIEW, VOL. 26, NO. 2 (DEC. 1952), PP.
        105-111. BO 477, BUL SIGN 8-5119, FR VII 7711.

2592   NAHAS, HÉLÈNE. LA FEMME DANS LA LITTÉRATURE EXISTENTIELLE.
        PARIS. PRESSES UNIVERSITAIRES DE FRANCE, 1957. KL I 231.

2593   NAKAMURA, MITSUO. A PROPOS OF 'L'ÉTRANGER' BY ALBERT CAMUS.
        JAPAN SCIENCE REVIEW, LITERATURE, PHILOSOPHY AND HISTORY,
        VOL. 5, (1954), PP. 34-38. BUL SIGN 11-5497.

2594   NATANSON, MAURICE. ALBERT CAMUS. DEATH AT THE MERIDIAN.
        CAROLINA QUARTERLY, VOL. 12, NO. 2 (SPRING 1960), PP.
        21-26, 65-69.

2595   NATANSON, WOJCIECH. KRYMINALISTYKA I TRAGEDIA. TEATR, VOL.
        17, NO. 20 (OCT. 16-31, 1962), PP. 9-12.

2596   NATOLI, GLAUCO. ALBERT CAMUS O LA LOTTA CONTRA L'ASSURDO.
        FIERA LETTERARIA, (SEPT. 18, 1947). FR VII 5755, 5170.

2597   NATOLI, GLAUCO. SCRITTORI FRANCESI, SITUAZIONI ED ASPETTI.
        FLORENCE. LA NUOVA ITALIA, 1950.   ALBERT CAMUS O LA LOTTA
        CONTRO L ASSURDO , PP. 161-173. BO 192, FR VII 5170.

2598   NAVARRO, OSCAR. CAMUS E LA RIVOLTA DEL PERSONAGGIO. AUT AUT,
        NO. 14, (MARCH 1953), PP. 157-169. BO 232, FR VII 9306.

NAVEL, GEORGES. CAMUS AU MARBRE. (PROPOS RECUEILLIS PAR GEORGES   2599
    NAVEL). TÉMOINS, VOL. 8, NO. 23 (MAY 1960), PP. 8-12.
    FITCH.

NEGRE, LOUIS. LES ÉTAPES D'ALBERT CAMUS. BULLETIN DE   2600
    L'ASSOCIATION GUILLAUME BUDÉ, VOL. 4, NO. 3 (OCT. 1955),
    PP. 101-110. BO 54, FR VII 13313.

NÉGRONI, JEAN. ALBERT CAMUS ET LE THÉÂTRE DE L'ÉQUIPE. REVUE   2601
    D'HISTOIRE DU THÉÂTRE, VOL. 12, NO. 4 (OCT.-DEC. 1960),
    PP. 343-349. FR VII 23570, PMLA 7374 (1962).

NELS, JACQUES. THÉÂTRE. 'LES POSSÉDÉS', PIÈCE EN 3 ACTES   2602
    D'ALBERT CAMUS, D'APRÈS LE ROMAN DE DOSTOÏEVSKI. BIBLIO,
    VOL. 27, NO. 4 (APRIL 1959), P. 25. CR 1145.

NETZER, JACQUES. UN DIALOGUE SUR LE DESTIN DE LA LITTÉRATURE.   2603
    SARTRE ET CAMUS. FRANÇAIS DANS LE MONDE, VOL. 1, NO. 8
    (APRIL 1962), PP. 16-19. FR VII 31078.

NEURINGER, CHARLES. THE PROBLEM OF SUICIDE. JOURNAL OF   2604
    EXISTENTIAL PSYCHIATRY, VOL. 3, NO. 9 (SUMMER-FALL 1962),
    PP. 69-73.

NGUYEN-VAN-HUY, PIERRE. LA MÉTAPHYSIQUE DU BONHEUR CHEZ ALBERT   2605
    CAMUS. NEUCHÂTEL. À LA BACONNIÈRE, 1962. PP. 241-246.
    FR VII 29343.

NICOLAS, ANDRÉ. LA PENSÉE EXISTENTIELLE D'ALBERT CAMUS OU LA   2606
    RÉVOLTE JUGULÉE PAR L'ABSURDE. GRENOBLE. THESIS OF
    UNIVERSITY, 1955. FR VII 15333.

NICOLAS, ANDRÉ. UNE PHILOSOPHIE DE L'EXISTENCE, ALBERT CAMUS.   2607
    PARIS. PRESSES UNIVERSITAIRES DE FRANCE, 1964.

NICOLETTI, GIANNI. LA 'CRONACA' DI CAMUS. CONVIVIUM, VOL. 28,   2608
    NO. 1 (JAN.-FEB. 1960), PP. 83-88. BFZ 46-283, FR VII
    23657, KL II 394, PMLA 6839 (1961).

NIEL, ANDRÉ. ALBERT CAMUS ET LE DRAME DU 'MOI'. REVUE DE LA   2609
    MÉDITERRANÉE, VOL. 17, NO. 82 (NOV.-DEC. 1957), PP.
    603-622. CR 1046, FR VII 21407, KL I 272.

NIEL, ANDRÉ. TOMBEAU D'ALBERT CAMUS. (POÈME). TEMPS DES   2610
    HOMMES, NO. 9 (JAN.-FEB.-MARCH 1960), PP. 10. FITCH.

NIMIER, ROGER. DES MORTS IRREGULIÈRES. ARTS, NO. 756 (JAN.   2611
    6-12, 1960), P. 1. FR VII 23658.

NORA, PIERRE. POUR UNE AUTRE EXPLICATION DE L'ÉTRANGER. FRANCE   2612
    OBSERVATEUR, VOL. 12, NO. 557 (JAN. 5, 1961), PP. 16-17.
    SEE NO. 3253.

NORD, MAX. HET GELOOF IN DE TOEKOMST. (I) BAANBREKER, VOL. 2,   2613
    NO. 5 (FEB. 2, 1946), P. 2. CR 572.

NORD, MAX. HET GELOOF IN DE TOEKOMST. (II) BAANBREKER, VOL.   2614
    2, NO. 6 (FEB. 9, 1946), P. 6. CR 573.

NORD, MAX. HET DRAMA VAN DE LOGICA. KRONIEK VAN KUNST EN   2615
    KULTUUR, VOL. 7, NO. 8 (JUNE 1946), PP. 240-241. CR 571.

2616   NORD, MAX. LEVEN ZONDER HOOP. HET WERK VAN ALBERT CAMUS.   STEM
       VAN NEDERLAND,   VOL. 8, NO. 21 (NOV. 29, 1947), P. 9.   BO
       16, CR 615.

2617   NOURISSIER, FRANÇOIS. 'L'ÉTÉ', 'ACTUELLES II'.   NOUVELLE REVUE
       FRANÇAISE,   VOL. 2, NO. 17 (MAY 1954), PP. 893-895.   CR 899
       BIS.

2618   NOURISSIER, FRANCOIS. UN HOMME DE MES VINGT ANS. FRANCE
       OBSERVATEUR,   VOL. 12, NO. 557 (JAN. 5, 1961), P. 16.   SEE
       NO. 3253.

2619   NOVAK, MICHAEL. PHILOSOPHY AND FICTION. CHRISTIAN SCHOLAR,
       VOL. 47, NO. 2 (SUMMER 1964), PP. 100-110 (CAMUS REF. PP.
       104-105, 108-109).

2620   NOYER-WEIDNER, ALFRED. DAS FORMPROBLEM DER 'PEST' VON ALBERT
       CAMUS. GERMANISCH-ROMANISCHE MONATSSCHRIFT (NEUE FOLGE),
       VOL. 8, NO. 3 (JULY 1958), PP. 260-285. BDZ 117-307
       (1958), FR VII 19436, KL I 273.

2621   NOYER-WEIDNER, ALFRED. ALBERT CAMUS IM STADIUM DER NOVELLE.
       ZEITSCHRIFT FÜR FRANZÖSISCHE SPRACHE UND LITERATUR, VOL.
       70, NOS. 1-2 (JUNE 1960), PP. 1-38. BDZ 121-321 (1960), FR
       VII 23659, KL II 391, PMLA 6840 (1961).

2622   O'BRIEN, EDWARD. CAMUS AND CHRISTIANITY. PERSONALIST, VOL.
       44, NO. 2 (APRIL 1963), PP. 149-163.

2623   O'BRIEN, JUSTIN. PRESENTING A NEW FRENCH WRITER. NEW YORK
       HERALD TRIBUNE WEEKLY BOOK REVIEW, VOL. 22, NO. 34 (APRIL
       14, 1946), P. 4.

2624   O'BRIEN, JUSTIN. A MODERN PLAGUE. PARTISAN REVIEW, VOL. 14,
       NO. 4 (JULY-AUG. 1947), PP. 431-434.

2625   O'BRIEN, JUSTIN. WORLD CONTAGION. 'THE PLAGUE'. NEW REPUBLIC,
       VOL. 119, NO. 7 (AUG. 16, 1948), PP. 23-24. BO 422.

2626   O'BRIEN, JUSTIN. NOBEL PRIZE-WINNER CAMUS. A MAN COMMITTED YET
       ALOOF. NEW YORK TIMES BOOK REVIEW, VOL. 62 NO. 49 (DEC.
       8, 1957), P. 3.   FR VII 21408.

2627   O'BRIEN, JUSTIN. AN ENTRY IN CAMUS' BIBLIOGRAPHY. NEW YORK
       TIMES BOOK REVIEW, JAN. 5, 1958, P. 14.

2628   O'BRIEN, JUSTIN AND LEON S. ROUDIEZ. CAMUS. SATURDAY REVIEW,
       VOL. 43, NO. 7 (FEB. 13, 1960), PP. 19-21, 41. FR VII
       23661, PMLA 6841 (1961).

2629   O'BRIEN, JUSTIN. DE MÉMOIRE DE FRANCOPHILE AMÉRICAIN...
       NOUVELLE REVUE FRANÇAISE, VOL. 8, NO. 87 (MARCH 1960), PP.
       559-561. FR VII 23575, KL II 394.

2630   O'BRIEN, JUSTIN. INTRODUCTION TO RESISTANCE, REBELLION AND
       DEATH BY ALBERT CAMUS. LONDON. HAMISH HAMILTON, 1961. PP.
       IX-XI.

2631   O'BRIEN, JUSTIN. INTRODUCTION TO RESISTANCE, REBELLION AND
       DEATH BY ALBERT CAMUS. NEW YORK. ALFRED A. KNOPF, 1961.

PP. V-VIII.

O'BRIEN, JUSTIN. ALBERT CAMUS, MILITANT. COLUMBIA UNIVERSITY   2632
    FORUM, VOL. 4, NO. 1 (WINTER 1961), PP. 12-15. FR VII
    23660, PMLA 7375 (1962).

O'BRIEN, JUSTIN. ALBERT CAMUS. MILITANT. IN BRÉE,   2633
    GERMAINE, CAMUS, A COLLECTION OF CRITICAL ESSAYS, PP.
    20-25. FR VII 29338. SEE NO. 1293. REPRINT OF NO. 2632.

OCAMPO, VICTORIA. DOS AMIGOS. ALFONSO REGES, MEXICANO Y   2634
    EUROPEO, ALBERT CAMUS, FRANCÉS Y AFRICANO. SUR, NO. 264
    (MAY-JUNE 1960), PP. 3-10. FR VII 23662, KL II 392.

O'DONNELL, DONAT. FRANCE AS THE CONSCIENCE OF EUROPE.   2635
    LISTENER, VOL. 53, NO. 1351 (JAN. 20, 1955), PP. 105-106.
    FR VII 28266.

O'DONNELL, DONAT. ALBERT CAMUS. A REJOINDER. SPECTATOR, VOL.   2636
    204, NO. 6870 (FEB. 26, 1960), PP. 293-294.

OEDINGEN, KARLO. DIE ERFAHRUNG DER 'NICHTUNG' UND IHRE DEUTUNG   2637
    BEI CAMUS UND HEIDEGGER. TIJDSCHRIFT VOOR FILOSOFIE, VOL.
    27, NO. 1 (MARCH 1965), PP. 68-83.

OLAFSON, FREDERICK A. ALBERT CAMUS. 'THE MYTH OF SISYPHUS'.   2638
    PHILOSOPHICAL REVIEW, VOL. 66, NO. 1 (1957), PP. 104-107.
    BUL SIGN 12-945.

OLIASS, H. G. DER FREMDE. WELT UND WORT, VOL. 4, NO. 7 (JULY,   2639
    1949), P. 247. BO 306.

OLLIVIER, ALBERT. LE MALENTENDU (3 ACTES D'ALBERT CAMUS).   2640
    CONFLUENCES, VOL. 4, NO. 33 (JULY 1944), PP. 101-104. BO
    333, CR 506.

OLLIVIER, ALBERT. ALBERT CAMUS ET LE REFUS DE L'ETERNEL.   2641
    ARCHE, VOL. 2, NO. 6 (OCT.-NOV. 1944), PP. 158-163. BO
    106, CR 505, FR VII 754.

OLLIVIER, ALBERT. 'CALIGULA'. TEMPS MODERNES, VOL. 1, NO. 3   2642
    (DEC. 1945), PP. 574-576. BO 348, CR 541.

OLLIVIER, ALBERT. DES ÉCRIVAINS NOUS DISENT. (HOMMAGES À   2643
    CAMUS). FIGARO, VOL. 134, NO. 4770 (JAN. 6, 1960), P.4.
    FR VII 23649.

OLLIVIER, ALBERT. DE LA RÉSISTANCE À COMBAT. MONDE, VOL. 17,   2644
    NO. 4652 (JAN. 6, 1960), P. 2. FR VII 23663.

ONIMUS, JEAN. L'HOMME ÉGARÉ. NOTES SUR LE SENTIMENT   2645
    D'ÉGAREMENT DANS LA LITTÉRATURE ACTUELLE. ÉTUDES, VOL. 87,
    NO. 283 (OCT.-NOV.-DEC. 1954), PP. 320-329. FR VII 22904.

ONIMUS, JEAN. 'LA CHUTE', D'ALBERT CAMUS. CIVITAS, VOL. 12,   2646
    NO. 9 (1957), PP. 411-417. CR 1047.

ONIMUS, JEAN. D'UBU À CALIGULA OU LA TRAGÉDIE DE   2647
    L'INTELLIGENCE. ÉTUDES, VOL. 91, NO. 297 JUNE 1958), PP.
    325-338. BFZ 43-294, CR 1113, FR VII 19134, KL I 273.

ONIMUS, JEAN. CAMUS ADAPTE À LA SCÈNE FAULKNER ET DOSTOÏEVSKI.   2648

REVUE DES SCIENCES HUMAINES, NO. 104 (OCT.-DEC. 1961), PP.
607-621. BUL SIGN 16-19-24621, FR VII 26363.

2649 ORLANDIS, JOSÉ. EL HOMBRE EN REBELDIA. NUESTRO TIEMPO, (NOV.
1956). BR, CR 964 BIS.

2650 ORLANDIS, JOSÉ. UN PORTRAIT DE SISYPHE. TABLE RONDE, NO. 146
(FEB. 1960), PP. 69-74. BFZ 46-283, BUL SIGN 15-19-13753
(685), FR VII 23569, KL II 394.

2651 ORMESSON, JEAN D'. SUR CAMUS. PARISIENNE, NO. 48 (NOV.-DEC.
1957), PP. 1083-1086. CR 1047 TER, KL I 272.

2652 ORTIZ DE URTARAN, FÉLIX. ALBERT CAMUS, 'MARTIR' DESESPERADO DE
LA SOLIDARIDAD HUMANA. LUMAN, NO. 2 (MARCH-APRIL 1958),
PP. 135-148. FR VII 21409.

2653 OTTINO, GEORGES. ALBERT CAMUS TROUVE LA MORT DANS UN ACCIDENT
D'AUTO. JOURNAL DE GENÈVE, NO. 3 (JAN. 5, 1960), P. 1.

2654 OYEN, HENDRICK VAN. DE MENS IN OPSTAND. WENDING, VOL. 8, NO.
8 (OCT. 1953), PP. 534-549. BO 510.

2655 OYEN, HENDRICK VAN. ALBERT CAMUS UND DIE BOTSCHAFT DES
EMPÖRTEN. REFORMATIO, VOL. 2, NO. 6 (JUNE 1953), PP.
297-310. TRANSLATION OF NO. 2654.

2656 OYEN, HENDRIK VAN. LE MESSAGE DU REVOLTE. REVUE DES LETTRES
MODERNES, NOS. 90-93 (WINTER 1963), PP. 73-89. PMLA 8608
(1964). TRANSLATION OF NO. 2654, 2655. SEE NO. 3207.
TRANSLATED BY BERNARD LORTHOLARY.

2657 PACHECO, LEON. ALBERT CAMUS Y LA FILOSOFÍA DEL ABSURDO.
CAUDERNOS AMERICANOS, VOL. 147, NO. 4 (JULY-AUG. 1966),
PP. 84-115.

2658 PAEPCKE, FRITZ. DER ATHEISMUS IN DER SICHT VON ALBERT CAMUS.
ECKART, VOL. 27, NO. 8 (OCT.-DEC. 1958), PP. 278-283. BDZ
117-307 (58), FR VII 26364, KL I 272.

2659 PAEPCKE, FRITZ. LE SENS DE L'ATHÉISME CHEZ ALBERT CAMUS. REVUE
DES LETTRES MODERNES, NOS. 90-93 (WINTER 1963), PP. 91-99.
PMLA 8608 (1964). TRANSLATION OF NO. 2658. SEE NO. 3207.
TRANSLATED BY BERNARD LORTHOLARY.

2660 PAEPCKE, FRITZ. ALBERT CAMUS UND DER FRIEDE. ECKART, VOL. 29,
NO. 1 (JAN.-MARCH 1960), PP. 7-12. FR VII 23664, KL II
389, PMLA 6842 (1961).

2661 PAEPCKE, FRITZ. MASS UND REVOLTE. ZUM POLITISCHEN ETHOS VON
ALBERT CAMUS. MONATSCHRIFT FUR PASTORALTHEOLOGIE, VOL. 51
(SEPT. 1962), PP. 438-451.

2662 PAINTER, GEORGE D. NEW NOVELS. (REVIEW. THE PLAGUE). LISTENER,
VOL. 40, NO. 1025 (SEPT. 16, 1948), P. 426.

2663 PAMPALONI, GENO. IL SANGUE DELLO SPIRITO. MONDO, VOL. 2, NO.
43 (OCT. 28, 1950), P. 9. FR VII 17332.

2664 PANDOLFI, VITO. SPETTACOLO DEL SECOLO. IL TEATRO DRAMMATICO.
PISA. NISTRI-LISCHI, 1953. IL MALINTESO DI CAMUS , PP.

279-281. BO 343, FR VII 10922.

PAPADOPOULO, ALEXANDRE. ALBERT CAMUS ET LA BONNE CONSCIENCE.   2665
     REVUE DU CAIRE, VOL. 44, NO. 237 (MAY 1960), PP. 345-367.
     FR VII 23665. SEE NO. 3259.

PARADES, R.-G. 'EL EXTRANGERO', DE CAMUS. UNIVERSAL, (OCT.   2666
     22, 1957). BR, CR 1047 BIS.

PARAIN, BRICE. UN HÉROS DE NOTRE TEMPS. NOUVELLE REVUE   2667
     FRANÇAISE, VOL. 8, NO. 87 (MARCH 1960), PP. 405-408. FR
     VII 23575, KL II 394.

PARINAUD, ANDRÉ. LE THÉÂTRE. VOCATION D'ALBERT CAMUS. ARTS,   2668
     NO. 415 (JUNE 12-18, 1953), P. 12. CR 863.

PARINAUD, ANDRÉ. LA VIE D'UN ÉCRIVAIN ENGAGÉ. IN ANONYMOUS,   2669
     CAMUS, PP. 7-56. SEE NO. 940.

PARKER, SAMUEL EMMETT. ALBERT CAMUS. THE ARTIST IN THE ARENA--   2670
     THE DIALECTICS OF COMMITMENT. BEYOND LEFT AND RIGHT.
     DISSERTATION ABSTRACTS, VOL. 24, NO. 8 (FEB. 1964), P.
     3342. PMLA 8620 (1964).

PARKER, EMMETT. ALBERT CAMUS. THE ARTIST IN THE ARENA.   2671
     MADISON. UNIVERSITY OF WISCONSIN PRESS, 1965.

PAROUTAUD, J.-M.-A. 'L'ETRANGER', PAR ALBERT CAMUS.   2672
     CONFLUENCES, VOL. 2, NO. 13 (OCT. 1942), PP. 209-210. BO
     293, CR 492.

PAROUTAUD, J.-M.-A. LE MYTHE DE SISYPHE PAR ALBERT CAMUS.   2673
     CONFLUENCES, VOL. 2, NO. 15 (DEC. 1942), PP. 458-460. BO
     311, CR 493.

PARPAGNOLI, J. A. S. DE. EL EJEMPLO DE ALBERT CAMUS (A   2674
     PROPÓSITO DE ACTUELLES). HUMANITAS (TUCUMAN), VOL. 9, NO.
     14 (1961), PP. 197-200. FR VII 33968.

PARQUIN, JEAN. 'LES JUSTES', D'ALBERT CAMUS. GAZETTE DES   2675
     LETTRES, VOL. 5, NO. 104 (DEC. 24, 1949), P. 16. CR 716.

P(ASEYRO), R(ICARDO). CAMUS MASSACRE CALDERÓN. CAHIERS DES   2676
     SAISONS, NO. 20 (NUMERO SPECIAL 1960), PP. 601-611. FR
     VII 26365.

PASSERI PIGNONI, V. LA FILOSOFÍA DELL ASSURDO DI ALBERT CAMUS.   2677
     SAPIENZA (ROMA), (MAY-AUG. 1960). FR VII 29396.

PASTORE, ANNIBALE. IL SURRESISTENZIALISMO DI FRANCIA.   2678
     HUMANITAS, VOL. 1, NO. 5 (MAY 1946), PP. 449-452. BO 161,
     FR VII 9036.

PATRI, AIMÉ. NOTE SUR UN SENTIMENT D'ÉTRANGETÉ. ARCHE, VOL.   2679
     2, NO. 5 (1944), PP. 115-117. BO 296, CR 508.

PATRI, AIMÉ. 'LA PESTE'. PARU, NO. 33 (AUG. 1947), PP. 17-19.   2680
     BO 395, CR 616.

PATRI, AIMÉ. ACTUELLES. MONDE NOUVEAU-PARU, VOL. 7, NO. 48   2681
     (1951), P. 108. BO 473.

PATRI, A. L'HOMME RÉVOLTÉ. MONDE NOUVEAU-PARU, VOL. 7, NOS.   2682

53-54 (1951), PP. 152-155.   BO 487.

2683   PATRI, AIMÉ. DIALOGUE ENTRE ANDRÉ BRETON ET AIMÉ PATRI À PROPOS
       DE 'L'HOMME RÉVOLTÉ', D'ALBERT CAMUS. ARTS, NO. 333 (NOV.
       16, 1951), PP. 1, 3.   CR 782, FR VII 13304. SEE NO. 1304.

2684   PAULHAN, JEAN AND DOMINIQUE AURY (EDITORS). LA PATRIE SE FAIT
       TOUS LES JOURS. PARIS. ÉDITIONS DE MINUIT, 1947.
       PREMIÈRE LETTRE À UN AMI ALLEMAND, PP. 209-214.

2685   PAUTAL, C. ALBERT CAMUS. WORT UND TAT, NO. 6 (SEPT. 1947),
       PP. 65-66. CR 617.

2686   PAUTHE, JACQUELINE. LETTRE À CAMUS. ESPRIT, VOL. 22, NO. 214
       (MAY 1954), PP. 644-651. BFZ 36-234 (1953-54), BO 541, CR
       900, FR VII 11234.

2687   PAUWELS, LOUIS. À PROPOS DE 'L'HOMME REVOLTE'. ARTS, NO. 338
       (DEC. 21, 1951), P. 3.   BO 488, FR VII 13314.

2688   PAUWELS, LOUIS. ON MÉPRISE ET L'ON S'EN VA. ARTS, NO. 349
       (MARCH 7, 1952), PP. 1, 3.   BO 498, FR VII 13315.

2689   PELEGRI, JEAN. L'EXIL ET LE ROYAUME. SIMOUN, VOL. 8, NO. 31
       (JULY 1960), PP. 45-51. FR VII 23573, KL II 394.

2690   PELZ, MANFRED. DIE BEIDEN STILWEISEN BEI ALBERT CAMUS.
       ZEITSCHRIFT FÜR FRANZÖSISCHE SPRACHE UND LITERATUR, VOL.
       73, NOS. 1-2 (APRIL 1963), PP. 59-65. PMLA 7979 (1964), FR
       VII 33969.

2691   PÉREZ MARCHAND, MONELISA L. DEL PESIMISMO-NIHILISTA AL
       HUMANISMO MORALISTA DE ALBERT CAMUS. ASOMANTE, 15TH YEAR,
       VOL. 15, NO. 4 (OCT.-DEC. 1959), PP. 7-27. BUL SIGN
       14-18203, FR VII 23666.

2692   PÉREZ MARCHAND, MONELISA L. ¿ES CAMUS UN ESCRITOR FILOSÓFICO?
       ASOMANTE, VOL. 17, NO. 1 (JAN.-MARCH 1961), PP. 32-44.
       BUL SIGN 16-19-109, 16-19-2381, FR VII 26366.

2693   PERLADO, JOSÉ JULIO. EN TORNO A ALBERT CAMUS. CUADERNOS
       HISPANOAMERICANOS, NO. 105 (SEPT. 1958), PP. 295-315. FR
       VII 19437, KL I 273.

2694   PERRIN, OLIVIER. LES POSSÉDÉS. PIÈCE EN TROIS PARTIES.
       SPECTACLES, NO. 4 (DEC. 1958), PP. 34-37.

2695   PERRINE, LAURENCE. CAMUS' 'THE GUEST'. A SUBTLE AND DIFFICULT
       STORY. STUDIES IN SHORT FICTION, VOL. 1, NO. 1 (FALL
       1963), PP. 52-58. PMLA 8621 (1964).

2696   PERROS, GEORGES. L'HOMME FATIGUÉ. NOUVELLE REVUE FRANÇAISE,
       VOL. 8, NO. 87 (MARCH 1960), PP. 614-620. FR VII 23575, KL
       II 387.

2697   PERROUD, ROBERT. ALBERT CAMUS DELFINO DELL'ESISTENZIALISMO.
       VITA E PENSIERO, VOL. 33, NEW SERIES NO. 2 (FEB. 1950),
       PP. 97-108. BO 168, FR VII 11235.

2698   PERROUD, ROBERT. TRA BAUDELAIRE E SARTRE. MILAN. VITA E
       PENSIERO, 1952. ALBERT CAMUS DELFINO DELL ESISTENZIALISMO.

PP. 155-192. BO 69, FR VII 8685.

P(ERROUD), R(OBERT). ULTIME NOTIZIE ESISTENZIALISTE. LA   2699
    ROTTURA SARTRE E CAMUS. VITA E PENSIERO, VOL. 35, (NOV.
    1952), PP. 641-642. BO 281, FR VII 10392.

PERROUD, ROBERT. DA MAURIAC A GLI ESISTENZIALISTI. MILAN.   2700
    VITA E PENSIERO, 1955. FR VII 14788.

PERROUD DE POCCADAZ, ROBERT. ALBERT CAMUS, PREMIO NOBEL 1957.   2701
    VITA E PENSIERO, VOL. 40, (OCT. 1957), PP. 739-740. FR
    VII 19438.

PERRUCHOT, HENRI. LES HOMMES ET LEURS OEUVRES. L'INTERROGATION   2702
    D'ALBERT CAMUS. COURRIER GRAPHIQUE, NO. 40 (1949), PP.
    47-49. BO 25.

PERRUCHOT, HENRI. ALBERT CAMUS. RÉALITÉS, NO. 42 (JULY 1949),   2703
    PP. 73-77, 84, 90. BO 24, CR 717, FR VII 7691, 5757.

PERRUCHOT, HENRI. ALBERT CAMUS. REVUE DE LA MÉDITERRANÉE,   2704
    VOL. 11, NO. 6 (NOV.-DEC. 1951), PP. 641-657. BO 36, FR
    VII 7712.

PERRUCHOT, HENRI. ACTUALITÉ D'ALBERT CAMUS. DÉFENSE DE   2705
    L'HOMME, VOL. 7, NO. 68 (JUNE 1954), PP. 40-48. BO 51, FR
    VII 17333.

PERRUCHOT, HENRI. ACTUALITÉ D'ALBERT CAMUS. (EXTRAIT DE DÉFENSE   2706
    DE L'HOMME , JUNE 1954). CANNES. IMPR. AEQUITA, 1954. CR
    900 BIS, FR VII 11215.

PERRUCHOT, HENRI. LA HAINE DES MASQUES. PARIS. LA TABLE RONDE,   2707
    1955. ALBERT CAMUS, PP. 111-155. BO 255, BR, CR 471, FR
    VII 12606.

PERRUCHOT, HENRI. LA FRANCE ET SA JEUNESSE. PARIS. HACHETTE,   2708
    1958.

PERRUCHOT, HENRI. ALBERT CAMUS OU L'INNOCENCE TRAGIQUE. PENSÉE   2709
    FRANÇAISE, VOL. 19, NO. 3 (MARCH 1960), PP. 15-18. FR VII
    23668.

PETERSEN, CAROL. ALBERT CAMUS. BERLIN. COLLOQUIUM VERLAG,   2710
    1961. FR VII 26297, PMLA 7376 (1961).

PETRONI, LIANO. LE 'ACTUELLES' DI ALBERT CAMUS. RIVISTA DI   2711
    LETTERATURE MODERNE, VOL. 2, NO. 2 (APRIL-JUNE 1951), PP.
    287-311. BO 474, FR VII 5758.

PETRONI, LIANO. CAMUS. 'ACTUELLES II'. PONTE, VOL. 10, NO. 3   2712
    (MARCH 1954), PP. 503-506. BO 480, FR VII 11236.

PETRONI, LIANO. ALBERT CAMUS'LA CHUTE'; 'L'EXIL ET LE ROYAUME'.   2713
    PONTE, VOL. 13, NO. 12 (DEC. 1957), PP. 1875-1877.

PETRONI, LIANO. RICORDO DI ALBERT CAMUS. PONTE, VOL. 16, NO.   2714
    1 (JAN. 1960), PP. 11-12. FR VII 23669, KL II 394.

PEUCH, JACQUES. EXISTENTIALISME ET BIOLOGIE. REVUE DU CAIRE,   2715
    VOL. 10, NO. 102 (SEPT. 1947), PP. 48-56. FR VII 25307.

PEUCHMAURD, JACQUES. ALBERT CAMUS SERAIT-IL LE DUHAMEL DE SA   2716

GÉNÉRATION? ARTS, NO. 376 (SEPT. 12-18, 1952), PP. 1, 5.
BO 70, CR 835, FR VII 13316.

2717   PEYDRO, MIGUEL. ALBERT CAMUS Y LA PERSPECTIVA PERMANENTE DE LA
        MORAL. MADRID. ALCANTACILLA, 1958. FR VII 19401, KL II
        387.

2718   PEYRE, HENRI. THE RESISTANCE AND LITERARY REVIVAL IN FRANCE.
        YALE REVIEW, VOL. 35, NO. 1 (SEPT. 1945), PP. 84-92. BO
        92, CR 574, FR VII 2239.

2719   PEYRE, HENRI. EXISTENTIALISM--A LITERATURE OF DESPAIR? YALE
        FRENCH STUDIES, VOL. 1, NO. 1 (SPRING-SUMMER 1948), PP.
        21-32. CR 670.

2720   PEYRE, HENRI. FRIENDS AND FOES OF PASCAL IN FRANCE TODAY. YALE
        FRENCH STUDIES, NO. 12 (FALL-WINTER 1953), PP. 8-18. BO
        268, FR VII 10678.

2721   PEYRE, HENRI. THE CONTEMPRARY FRENCH NOVEL. NEW YORK. OXFORD
        UNIVERSITY PRESS, 1955. CHAPTER IX, PP. 240-251.

2722   PEYRE, HENRI. ALBERT CAMUS, AN ANTI-CHRISTIAN MORALIST.
        AMERICAN PHILOSOPHICAL SOCIETY PROCEEDINGS, VOL. 102, NO.
        5 (OCT. 20, 1958), PP. 477-482. FR VII 21410, KL I 272.

2723   PEYRE, HENRI. COMMENT ON CAMUS. VIRGINIA QUARTERLY REVIEW,
        VOL. 34, NO. 4 (FALL 1958), PP. 623-629. BFZ 44-283, FR
        VII 19439, KL II 388.

2724   PEYRE, HENRI. AN ALGERIAN SUN LIGHTS EUROPE'S FOG. 'CAMUS' BY
        GERMAINE BRÉE. NEW YORK TIMES BOOK REVIEW, APRIL 5, 1959,
        PP. 1, 30.

2725   PEYRE, HENRI. THE IDEAS MEN LIVED BY WOULDN'T DO. 'ALBERT CAMUS
        AND THE LITERATURE OF REVOLT' BY JOHN CRUICKSHANK. NEW
        YORK TIMES BOOK REVIEW, OCT. 4, 1959, P. 4.

2726   PEYRE, HENRI. HOMAGE TO CAMUS. MASSACHUSETTS REVIEW, VOL. 1,
        NO. 2 (FEB. 1960), PP. 209-211. PMLA 6843 (1961).

2727   PEYRE, HENRI. CAMUS THE PAGAN. YALE FRENCH STUDIES, NO. 25
        (SPRING 1960), PP. 20-25. BUL SIGN 16-19-9741 (1962), FR
        VII 23568, KL II 394.

2728   PEYRE, HENRI. CAMUS THE PAGAN. IN BRÉE, GERMAINE, CAMUS, A
        COLLECTION OF CRITICAL ESSAYS, PP. 65-70. FR VII 29338.
        SEE NO. 1293. REPRINT OF NO. 2727.

2729   PEYRE, HENRI. ALBERT CAMUS MORALISTE. LYNCHBURG, VIRGINIA.
        RANDOLPH-MACON COLLEGE, 1962.

2730   PEYRE, HENRI. THE STUDY OF MODERN FRENCH LITERATURE. WHERE DO
        WE STAND? WHERE DO WE GO FROM HERE? MODERN LANGUAGE
        QUARTERLY, VOL. 26, NO. 1 (MARCH 1965), PP. 16-39.

2731   PHILIPE, ANNE ET CLAUDE ROY. GÉRARD PHILIPE. PARIS. GALLIMARD,
        1960. CALIGULA, PP. 54-60, ET PASSIM.

2732   PIA, PASCAL. UN HOMME DE MÉTIER. CARREFOUR, NO. 799 (JAN. 6,
        1960), P. 21. FR VII 23670.

PIAZZOLLA, MARINO. CAMUS UOMO DELLA RINASCITA. FIERA   2733
    LETTERARIA, VOL. 17, NO. 2 (JAN. 14, 1962), PP. 1-2. FR
    VII 33971.

PICHER, RENÉ. CAMUS...UNE CONSCIENCE. REVUE DOMINICAINE, VOL.   2734
    66, NO. 1 (MAY 1960), PP. 203-207. FR VII 23671.

PICHON-RIVIÈRE, ARMINDA A. DE, AND WILLY BARANGER. RÉPRESSION   2735
    DU DEUIL ET INTENSIFICATIONS DES MÉCANISMES ET DES
    ANGOISSES SCHIZO-PARANOÏDES. REVUE FRANÇAISE DE
    PSYCHANALYSE, VOL. 23, NO. 3 (MAY-JUNE 1959), PP. 409-420.
    BUL SIGN 14-3892.

PICON, GAËTAN. ENTRETIEN AVEC ALBERT CAMUS. FIGARO LITTÉRAIRE,   2736
    VOL. 1, NO. 21 (AUG. 18, 1946), P. 1. BO 11, BR, CR 575.

PICON, GAËTAN. PANORAMA DE LA NOUVELLE LITTÉRATURE FRANÇAISE,   2737
    PARIS. ÉDITIONS DU POINT DU JOUR, 1949. CHAPTER III. 'LE
    NOUVEAU ROMAN FRANÇAIS'. 1. 'UN NATURALISME MÉTAPHYSIQUE'.
    'ALBERT CAMUS', PP. 96-102. BO 62, BR, CR 471 BIS.

PICON, GAËTAN. MERCURIALE. LES LETTRES. 'LA CHUTE', D'ALBERT   2738
    CAMUS. MERCURE DE FRANCE, VOL. 327, NO. 1116 (AUG. 1956),
    PP. 688-693. BUL SIGN 12-15854, CR 965.

PICON, GAËTAN. PANORAMA DES IDÉES CONTEMPORAINES. PARIS.   2739
    GALLIMARD, 1957. ALBERT CAMUS, AU-DELÀ DU NIHILISME , PP.
    721-723. CR 472.

PICON, GAËTAN. L'EXIL ET LE ROYAUME. MERCURE DE FRANCE, VOL.   2740
    330 NO. 1125 (MAY 1957), PP. 127-131. BFZ 42-284, CR 1048,
    FR VII 17334, KL I 273.

PICON, GAËTAN. EXILE AND THE KINGDOM. IN BRÉE, GERMAINE,   2741
    CAMUS, A COLLECTION OF CRITICAL ESSAYS, PP. 152-156. FR
    VII 29338. SEE NO. 1293. REPRINT OF NO. 2740.

PICON, GAËTAN. CE QUE FURENT EN 1957 LES LETTRES. NOUVELLES   2742
    LITTERAIRES, NO. 1584 (JAN. 9, 1958), PP. 1, 5. CR 1114.

PICON, GAËTAN. REMARQUES SUR 'LA PESTE' D'ALBERT CAMUS.   2743
    FONTAINE, VOL. 11, NO. 61 (SEPT. 1947), PP. 453-460. BO
    396, CR 620, FR VII 755.

PICON, GAËTAN. L'USAGE DE LA LECTURE. PARIS. MERCURE DE   2744
    FRANCE, 1960. REMARQUES SUR LA PESTE , PP. 79-87. FR VII
    22813. REPRINT OF NO. 2743.

PICON, GAËTAN. NOTES ON THE PLAGUE. IN BRÉE, GERMAINE,   2745
    CAMUS, A COLLECTION OF CRITICAL ESSAYS, PP. 145-151. FR
    VII 29338. SEE NO. 1293. TRANSLATION OF NO. 2743.

PICON, GAËTAN. L'USAGE DE LA LECTURE. PARIS. MERCURE DE   2746
    FRANCE, 1961. SUR ALBERT CAMUS. I. LA CHUTE .
    II. 'L'EXIL ET LE ROYAUME', PP. 163-174. FR VII 25241.

PIERCE, ROY. CONTEMPORARY FRENCH POLITICAL THOUGHT. NEW YORK.   2747
    OXFORD UNIVERSITY PRESS, 1966. SCATTERED REFERENCES.

PILLEMENT, GEORGES. ANTHOLOGIE DU THÉÂTRE FRANÇAIS   2748

CONTEMPORAIN. TOME 3. LE THÉÂTRE DES ROMANCIERS ET DES
POÈTES. PARIS. ÉDITIONS DU BÉLIER, 1948. ALBERT CAMUS,
PP. 296-302. CR 473.

2749   PILON, JEAN-GUY. POUR QUE LE MIROIR SOIT ESPACE (24 MARS 1960).
REVUE DE L'UNIVERSITÉ LAVAL, VOL. 14, NO. 9 (MAY 1960),
PP. 817-822 (CAMUS REF. P. 817). KL II 394.

2750   PINGAUD, BERNARD. UNE OEUVRE EN DÉBAT DEVANT LA NOUVELLE
GÉNÉRATION. L'AUTORITÉ DOIT S'EXERCER JUSQU'AU BOUT.
FIGARO LITTÉRAIRE, VOL. 12, NO. 601 (OCT. 26, 1957), P. 7.
FITCH. SEE NO. 3251.

2751   PINGAUD, BERNARD. UN PRÉDICATEUR INQUIET. PARISIENNE. NO. 48
(NOV.-DEC. 1957), PP. 1086-1089. CR 1047 TER.

2752   PINGAUD, BERNARD. ÉCRIVAINS D'AUJOURD'HUI 1940-1960. PARIS.
BERNARD GRASSET, 1960. ALBERT CAMUS, PP. 159-168.

2753   PINGAUD, BERNARD. LE MAL ENTENDU. ARC, VOL. 3 NO. 10 (APRIL
1960), PP. 92-93. KL II 394.

2754   PINNOY, M. ALBERT CAMUS. BRUGGE. DESCLÉE DE BROUWER, 1961.
FR VII 26298, PMLA 7377 (1961).

2755   PISELLI, FRANCESCO. CAMUS BY STELIO ZEPPI. PONTE, VOL. 18,
NO. 7 (JULY 1962), PP. 1693-1694.

2756   PITOU, SPIRE. SOME NOTES ON ALBERT CAMUS. BOOKS ABROAD, VOL.
34, NO. 2 (SPRING 1960), P. 125. BFZ 46-283, FR VII 23672,
KL II 394.

2757   PIZZORUSSO, ARNALDO. IN MORTE DI ALBERT CAMUS. NUOVA
ANTOLOGIA, 95TH YEAR, VOL. 478, FASC. 1910 (FEB. 1960),
PP. 177-182. BFZ 46-283, FR VII 23673, KL II 394,PMLA 6844
(1961).

2758   PLAGNOL, MAURICE. ALBERT CAMUS, ESPRIT MÉDITERRANÉEN. BULLETIN
DE L'ASSOCIATION GUILLAUME BUDÉ, SERIES 3 NO. 1 (MARCH
1953), PP. 101-112. BO 152, FR VII 13317.

2759   PLANT, RICHARD. BENIGN INDIFFERENCE. (REVIEW. 'L'ETRANGER').
SATURDAY REVIEW, VOL. 29, NO. 20 (MAY 18, 1946), P. 10.
BO 300.

2760   PLINVAL, GEORGES DE. LES IDÉES-PIÈGES DE L'EXISTENTIALISME.
ÉCRITS DE PARIS, NO. 141 (SEPT. 1956), PP. 57-73. KL I
231.

2761   POCH, M. PROCÉDÉS DE MISE EN RELIEF. LA PHRASE SEGMENTÉE DANS
QUELQUES OEUVRES D'ALBERT CAMUS. ORBIS, VOL. 8, NO. 1
(1959), PP. 161-168. FR VII 23674, KL II 390.

2762   PODHATSUR, D. ALBERT CAMUS, DEYOKANO SHEL MORED (ALBERT CAMUS.
A PORTRAIT OF A REBEL). LAMERHAV. MASAH, OCT. 25, 1957.

2763   PODHATSUR, D. DEYKAN YAHID OH 'GIBOR DORENU', AL 'HANEFILAH'
LE-ALBERT CAMUS (A PORTRAIT OF AN INDIVIDUAL OR 'A HERO
OF OUR GENERATION'. ABOUT ALBERT CAMUS' CHUTE). LAMERHAV.
MASAH, NOV. 27, 1959.

PODHORETZ, NORMAN. SOLITARY OR SOLIDARY. NEW YORKER, VOL. 34,   2764
    NO. 6 (MARCH 29, 1958), PP. 107-110, 113-114. FR VII
    21411.

PODHORETZ, NORMAN. SOLITARY OR SOLIDARY. IN   KOSTELANETZ,   2765
    RICHARD, ON CONTEMPORARY LITERATURE, PP. 315-321. SEE NO.
    2204. REPRINT OF NO. 2764.

POILVET LE GUENN, JEAN. NOTES CONJOINTES POUR UNE ÉTUDE SUR   2766
    ALBERT CAMUS. SIGNES DU TEMPS, NOS. 9-10 (1951),
    PP. 61-66. FR VII 17335.

POLYBIOS. ALBERT CAMUS. FREIDENKER, VOL. 41, NO. 12 (DEC. 1,   2767
    1958), PP. 366-377. BDZ 118-290 (1958).

POLITZER, HEINZ. DER WAHRE ARZT. FRANZ KAFKA UND ALBERT CAMUS.   2768
    MONAT, VOL. 1, NO. 132 (SEPT. 1959), PP. 3-13. FR VII
    21412, KL II 392.

POLITZER, HEINZ. LE VRAI MÉDECIN--KAFKA ET CAMUS. REVUE DES   2769
    LETTRES MODERNES, NOS. 90-93 (WINTER 1963), PP. 151-174.
    PMLA 8608 (1964). TRANSLATION OF NO. 2768. SEE NO. 3207.
    TRANSLATED BY BERNARD LORTHOLARY.

POLITZER, HEINZ. FRANZ KAFKA AND ALBERT CAMUS. PARABLES FOR   2770
    OUR TIME. CHICAGO REVIEW, VOL. 14, NO. 1 (SPRING 1960),
    PP. 47-67. FR VII 23675, PMLA 6845 (1961).

POLITZER, HEINZ. THE TRIAL AGAINST THE COURT. DAEDALUS, VOL.   2771
    93, NO. 3 (SUMMER 1964), PP. 975-997 (CAMUS REF. PP. 979,
    995).

POLLMANN, LEO. ALBERT CAMUS UND DAS LITERARISCHE PHÄNOMEN DES   2772
    SCHWEIGENS. NEUEREN SPRACHEN, VOL. 10, NO. 11 (NOV.
    1961), PP. 524-533. FR VII 26367, PMLA 7378 (1962).

POORE, CHARLES. BOOKS OF THE TIMES--ALBERT CAMUS. THE STRANGER.   2773
    NEW YORK TIMES, APRIL 11, 1946, P. 23.

POORTMAN, J. J. HET LIJDEN VAN KINDEREN ALS PROBLEEM. LA PESTE.   2774
    THEOSOFIA, VOL. 50, NO. 2 (1949), PP. 32-36. BO 432.

POPESCO, ELVIRE. DES PERSONNALITÉS DU THÉÂTRE... (HOMMAGES À   2775
    CAMUS). FIGARO, VOL. 134, NO. 4770 (JAN. 6, 1960), P. 4.
    FITCH. SEE NO. 3249.

POPKIN, HENRY. CAMUS AS DRAMATIST. PARTISAN REVIEW, VOL. 26,   2776
    NO. 3 (SUMMER 1959), PP. 499-503. FR VII 21413, KL II 389.

POPKIN, HENRY. CAMUS AS DRAMATIST. IN BRÉE, GERMAINE,   2777
    CAMUS, A COLLECTION OF CRITICAL ESSAYS, PP. 170-172. FR
    VII 29338. SEE NO. 1293. REPRINT OF NO. 2776.

POPMA, S. J. KRONIEK. HET AVONTUUR VAN DEN MENSCHELIJKEN   2778
    GEEST. (ALBERT CAMUS: BRIEVEN AAN EEN DUITSCHEN VRIEND).
    BEZINNING, VOL. 1, NO. 11 (DEC. 1946), PP. 170-172. CR
    576.

POPMA, S. J. ALBERT CAMUS EN ZIJN 'BRIEVEN AAN EEN DUITSCHEN   2779
    VRIEND'. BEZINNING, VOL. 1, (1947), PP. 170-172. BO 379.

2780   PORCARELLI, V. ALBERT CAMUS E LA TEORIA DELL'ASSURDISMO.
        RIVISTA DI FILOSOFIA NEO-SCOLASTICA,   VOL. 41, NO. 3
        (1949), PP. 308-319. BO 200.

2781   POUILLON, JEAN. L'OPTIMISME DE CAMUS. TEMPS MODERNES, VOL. 3,
        NO. 26 (NOV. 1947), PP. 921-929. BO 134, CR 621, FR VII
        757.

2782   POULET, ROBERT. LA LANTERNE MAGIQUE. PARIS. NOUVELLES
        ÉDITIONS DEBRESSE, 1956. ALBERT CAMUS, PP. 181-187. CR
        474, FR VII 14791, KL I 272.

2783   POULET, ROBERT. POURQUOI ADAPTE-T-IL AU LIEU D'ÉCRIRE? VOICI LE
        SECRET D'ALBERT CAMUS. CARREFOUR, VOL. 16, NO. 754 (FEB.
        25, 1959), P. 12. FR VII 21414.

2784   POULET, ROBERT. SUR ALBERT CAMUS. RIVAROL, NO. 470 (JAN. 14,
        1960), P. 13. FITCH.

2785   POULET, ROBERT. AVEUX SPONTANÉS, CONVERSATIONS AVEC... PARIS.
        PLON, 1963. ALBERT CAMUS OU LE MANQUE DE TEMPÉRAMENT, PP.
        155-160. FR VII 31455.

2786   PRAAG, SIEGFRIED E. VAN. FRANSCHE LITERATUUR VAN 1940 TOT 1945
        (I). CRITISCH BULLETIN, VOL. 13 (MARCH 1946), PP. 97-100,
        FR VII 28400.

2787   PRAAG, SIEGFRIED E. VAN. FRANSCHE LITERATUUR VAN 1940 TOT 1945
        (II). CRITISCH BULLETIN, VOL. 13 (APRIL 1946), PP.
        145-150. FR VII 28400.

2788   PRAAG, SIEGFRIED E. VAN. FRANSCHE LITERATUUR VAN 1940 TOT 1945.
        SLOT. CRITISCH BULLETIN, VOL. 13 (MAY 1946), PP. 193-198.
        FR VII 28400.

2789   PRAAG, SIEGFRIED E. VAN. NAAR EEN NIEUW FRANS HUMANISME. ALBERT
        CAMUS. 'LA PESTE'. CRITISCH BULLETIN, VOL. 15, NO. 3
        (MARCH 1948), PP. 132-137. BO 424, CR 671.

2790   PRAAG, SIEGFRIED E. VAN. CAMUS' PASSIONEEL EQUILIBRISME.
        CRITISCH BULLETIN, VOL. 19, NO. 8 (AUG. 1952), PP.
        370-375. BO 499, CR 836.

2791   PRASTEAU, JEAN. ALBERT CAMUS. PRIX NOBEL DE LITTERATURE 1957.
        FIGARO, VOL. 131, NO. 4079 (OCT. 18, 1957), P. 5.

2792   PRASTEAU, JEAN. ÉMOUVANT ET SIMPLE ADIEU À ALBERT CAMUS ...DANS
        LE PETIT CIMETIÈRE PROVENÇAL OÙ IL AVAIT CHOISI DE REPOSER.
        FIGARO, VOL. 134, NO. 4771 (JAN. 7, 1960), P. 9. FITCH.

2793   PRÉFONTAINE, YVES. CAMUS, REFUS ET CONSENTEMENT. LIBERTÉ,
        VOL. 2, NO. 1 (JAN.-FEB. 1960), PP. 51-52. FR VII 23609.

2794   PREMSELA, MARTIN J. DE MENS ALS ULTIMA RATIO. HET BOEK VAN NU,
        VOL. 1, NOS. 5-12 (1948), PP. 121-122. BO 137, CR 672.

2795   PREMSELA, MARTIN J. ERBARMEN VOOR DE RECHTVAARDIGEN. REVIEW OF
        LES JUSTES . CRITISCH BULLETIN, VOL. 17 (NOV. 1950). PP.
        584-586. BO 468, CR 769.

2796   PREMSELA, MARTIN J. ALBERT CAMUS EN ZIJN 'ACTUELLES'. HET BOEK

VAN NU, VOL. 4 (1951), P. 231. BO 475, CR 792.

PREMSELA, MARTIN J. ALBERT CAMUS. HET BOEK VAN NU, VOL. 11,   2797
    NO. 2 (OCT. 1957), PP. 27-28. CR 1049.

PREMSELA, MARTIN J. 'DE VREEMDELING'. HET BOEK VAN NU, VOL.   2798
    11, NOS. 10-11 (JUNE-JULY 1958), P. 197. CR 1115.

PRESCOTT, ORVILLE. OUTSTANDING NOVELS. YALE REVIEW, VOL. 38,   2799
    NO. 1 (SEPT. 1948), PP. 189-192 (CAMUS REF. P. 189). BO
    425.

PREVEO, V. P. ALBERT CAMUS. ROMANSIJER BOLA. KNJIŽEVNE   2800
    NOVINE, NOS. 1-2 (JAN. 21, 1954), P. 2745. CR 902.

PREVOST, J.-L. LE PRÊTRE, CE HÉROS DE ROMAN DE CLAUDEL À   2801
    CESBRON. I. PARIS. P. TEQUI, 1952. BO 243.

PRITCHETT, VICTOR S. THE PLAGUE. NEW STATESMAN AND NATION,   2802
    VOL. 36, NO. 911 (AUG. 21, 1948), P. 157. BO 426.

PRITCHETT, VICTOR S. BOOKS IN GENERAL. (ALBERT CAMUS.   2803
    L'ETRANGER). NEW STATESMAN AND NATION, VOL. 36, NO. 911
    (AUG. 21, 1948), P. 157. CR 673.

PRITCHETT, VICTOR S. A CONSCIENCE WITH A STYLE. NEW STATESMAN,   2804
    VOL. 59, NO. 1504 (JAN. 9, 1960), P. 34. BFZ 46-283, FR
    VII 23676.

PRITCHETT, V. S. TAUREAU QUI PENSE. NEW STATESMAN, VOL. 65,   2805
    NO. 1673 (APRIL 5, 1963), P. 492. FR VII 33972.

PRITCHETT, V. S. AN INTERESTING TIME. 'CARNETS 1942-1951' BY   2806
    ALBERT CAMUS. NEW STATESMAN, VOL. 71, NO. 1827 (MARCH 18,
    1966), PP. 378, 380.

PRITCHETT, U. P. NOTE ON FRENCH EXISTENTIALISM. BOOKS ABROAD,   2807
    VOL. 20, NO. 4 (1946), P. 381.

PROIX, R. L'IRREMPLAÇABLE AMI. TÉMOINS, VOL. 8, NO. 23 (MAY   2808
    1960), PP. 4-5. KL II 394.

PROKOP, JAN. O POEZJI CHARA. TWÓRCZOŚĆ, VOL. 15, NO. 8   2809
    (1960), PP. 163-168.

PROSCHWITZ, GUNNAR VON. CAMUS. 'LA CHUTE'. MODERNA SPRÅK,   2810
    VOL. 54, NO. 4 (DEC. 1960), PP. 384-395. KL II 390.

PUCCIANI, ORESTE F. THE FRENCH THEATER SINCE 1930, SIX   2811
    CONTEMPORARY FULL-LENGTH PLAYS EDITED BY ORESTE F.
    PUCCIANI (WITH AN INTRODUCTION AND NOTES ON EACH AUTHOR).
    BOSTON. GINN, 1954. FR VII 10926.

PUEL, G. ALBERT CAMUS ET NOUS. PARLER, VOL. 4, NOS. 12-13   2812
    (FALL-WINTER 1960), PP. 21-29. FR VII 29401.

PULETTI, RUGGERO. SAGGI E LETTURE, VOL. 1. PERUGIA. SIMONELLI,   2813
    1963. SITUAZIONE. LIBERTÀ E RIVOLTA IN ALBERT CAMUS , PP.
    111-119.

PUTIK, JAROSLAV. HRDINA NASÍ DOBY. IN CIZINEC-PÁD, PP.   2814
    181-188. SEE NO. 625.

QUASIMODO, SALVADORE. UNA COSCIENZA. HUMANITAS, VOL. 15, NO.   2815

1 (JAN. 1960), P. 69. FR VII 23677, KL II 394.

2816   QUENEAU, RAYMOND. HISTOIRE DES LITTÉRATURES. TOME III
       LITTÉRATURES FRANÇAISES, CONNEXES ET MARGINALES. VOLUME
       PUBLIÉ SOUS LA DIRECTION DE RAYMOND QUENEAU. PARIS.
       GALLIMARD (LA NOUVELLE REVUE FRANÇAISE), 1958. ALBERT
       CAMUS. PP. 1356-1357. CR 459.

2817   QUILLIOT, ROGER. AUTOUR D'ALBERT CAMUS ET DU PROBLÈME
       SOCIALISTE. REVUE SOCIALISTE, NO. 20 (APRIL 1948), PP.
       342-352. BO 95, CR 674, FR VII 2709.

2818   QUILLIOT, ROGER. LA MER ET LES PRISONS, ESSAI SUR ALBERT
       CAMUS. PARIS. GALLIMARD, 1956. BO 55, CR 475, FR VII
       15334, KL I 272.

2819   QUILLIOT, ROGER. LA CHUTE. REVUE SOCIALISTE, NO. 101 (NOV.
       1956), PP. 435-437. KL I 274.

2820   QUILLIOT, ROGER. ALBERT CAMUS, 'L'EXIL ET LE ROYAUME'. REVUE
       SOCIALISTE, NO. 109 (JULY 1957), PP. 217-218. FR VII
       17336.

2821   QUILLIOT, ROGER. LA QUERELLE EST POLITIQUE. NEF, VOL. 14, NO.
       12 (DEC. 1957), P. 96. CR 1051.

2822   QUILLIOT, ROGER. L'ALGÉRIE D'ALBERT CAMUS. REVUE SOCIALISTE,
       NO. 120 (OCT. 1958), PP. 121-131. FR VII 19440, KL I 274.

2823   QUILLIOT, ROGER. ALBERT CAMUS' ALGERIA. IN   BRÉE, GERMAINE,
       CAMUS, A COLLECTION OF CRITICAL ESSAYS, PP. 38-47. SEE NC.
       1293. TRANSLATION OF NO. 2822.

2824   QUILLIOT, ROGER. CAMUS CREATORE DI MITI. DRAMMA, VOL. 36, NO.
       280 (JAN. 1960), PP. 47-50.

2825   QUILLIOT, ROGER. TOMBEAU D'ALBERT CAMUS. REVUE SOCIALISTE,
       NO. 130 (FEB. 1960), PP. 175-180. FR VII 26368, KL II 394.

2826   QUILLIOT, ROGER. UN MONDE AMBIGU. PREUVES, NO. 110 (APRIL
       1960) PP. 28-38. FR VII 23678, KL II 394, PMLA 7379
       (1962).

2827   QUILLIOT, ROGER. AN AMBIGUOUS WORLD. IN   BREE, GERMAINE,
       CAMUS, A COLLECTION OF CRITICAL ESSAYS, PP. 157-169. FR
       VII 29338, REPRINTED FROM FR VII 23678. SEE NO. 1293.
       TRANSLATION OF NO. 2826.

2828   QUILLIOT, ROGER. ANNIVERSAIRE D'UNE ABSENCE. (SUIVI DE: ALBERT
       CAMUS, LETTRE A UN AMI 'DEÇU', 15 FÉVRIER 1953).
       DEMOCRATIE 62, (JAN. 4, 1962). FR VII 29403.

2829   QUILLIOT, ROGER. ALBERT CAMUS ET 'L'ETRANGER'. REVUE
       SOCIALISTE, NO. 265 (JUNE 1962), PP. 32-39. FR VII 29402.

2830   QUILLIOT, ROGER. GENÈSE DE 'LA PESTE'. PREUVES, NO. 142 (DEC.
       1962), PP. 30-37. FR VII 29404.

2831   QUILLIOT, ROGER (EDITOR). LES CARNETS D'ALBERT CAMUS,
       1942-1950. FIGARO LITTÉRAIRE, VOL. 19, NO. 969 (NOV.
       12-18, 1964), PP. 1, 8, 9. PMLA 8622 (1964).

QUILLIOT, ROGER. CAMUS,COMMANDEUR DE L'ORDRE DE LA LIBÉRATION.   2832
    REVUE SOCIALISTE,   NO. 193 (MAY 1966), PP. 471-473.

R(EILLE, JEAN FRANCIS). 'LES JUSTES' AVEC NOUS.   ARTS,   NO. 241   2833
    (DEC. 16, 1949), P. 7.   CR 720.

RADFORD, J. EXISTENTIALISM IN MODERN FRENCH LITERATURE.   2834
    MANITOBA ARTS REVIEW,   VOL. 10, NO. 3 (WINTER 1956), PP.
    16-31.   KL I 231.

RAEDEMAEKER, F. DE. OPSTAUDIGHEID EN REVOLUTIE.   STREVEN,   2835
    KATHOLIEK CULTUREEL TIJDSCHRIFT,   VOL. 6, NO. 3 (1952), PP.
    232-240.   BUL SIGN 7-5894.

RAINOIRD, MANUEL. LU ET VU.   REQUIEM POUR UNE NONNE . PIÈCE DE   2836
    WILLIAM FAULKNER.   ADAPTATION D'ALBERT CAMUS.   MONDE
    NOUVEAU,   VOL. 11, NO. 105 (NOV. 1956), PP. 138-139.   CR
    967.

RAJK, E. LE THÉÂTRE.   LE MALENTENDU, CALIGULA, PAR ALBERT   2837
    CAMUS.   PARU,   NO. 9 (JULY 1945), PP. 42-44.   CR 542.

RAMSEY, WARREN. ALBERT CAMUS ON CAPITAL PUNISHMENT. HIS   2838
    ADAPTATION OF 'THE POSSESED'.   YALE REVIEW,   VOL. 48, NO. 4
    (JUNE 1959), PP. 634-640.   BFZ 45-278, FR VII 21415, KL II
    392, PMLA 6846 (1961).

RANKE, H. ALBERT CAMUS. PRESSE,   NO. 21 (JAN. 1950).   BO 31.   2839

RANKE, H. V. DOSTOJEWSKIS 'DÄMONEN'--DRAMATISIERT VON ALBERT   2840
    CAMUS.   URAUFFÜHRUNG IN PARIS 1959.   UNIVERSITAS,
    ZEITSCHRIFT FÜR WISSENSCHAFT, KUNST UND LITERATUR,   VOL.
    14, NO. 5 (MAY 1959), PP. 553-554.   BDZ 118-352.

RAUHUT, FR. CAMUS ODER VOM NIHILISMUS ZU MASS UND   2841
    MENSCHENLIEBE. LUDWIGSBURGER BEITRAGE, VOL. 2 (1957), PP.
    189-205.   KL I 272.

RAUHUT, FRANZ. DU NIHILISME À LA 'MESURE' ET À L'AMOUR DES   2842
    HOMMES.   REVUE DES LETTRES MODERNES,   NOS. 90-93 (WINTER
    1963), PP. 17-40.   PMLA 8608 (1964).   TRANSLATION OF NO.
    2841. SEE NO. 3207.   TRANSLATED BY BERNARD LORTHOLARY.

RAY, SIBNARAYAN. ALBERT CAMUS.   QUEST,   NO. 25 (APRIL-JUNE   2843
    1960), PP. 9-18.

RAYMOND, LOUIS-MARCEL. LA RECHERCHE D'ALBERT CAMUS.   REVUE   2844
    DOMINICAINE,   VOL. 2, NO. 58 (JULY-AUG. 1952), PP. 35-47.
    BO 114, FR VII 13318.

RAZUM, HANNES. THÉÂTRE DE L'ABSURDE.   THE THEATRE OF THE   2845
    ABSURD.   WORLD THEATRE (BILINGUAL JOURNAL),   VOL. 10, NO. 4
    (1961), PP. 37-43.

READ, SIR HERBERT. 'FOREWORD'. IN ALBERT CAMUS 'THE REBEL'   2846
    (TRANSLATED FROM THE FRENCH BY ANTHONY BOWER), PP. 7-10.
    LONDON.   H. HAMILTON, 1953.

REARDON, B. M. G. ALBERT CAMUS'S PHILOSOPHY OF REVOLT.   2847
    THEOLOGY,   VOL. 63, NO. 480 (JUNE 1960), PP. 236-242.   BFZ

46-284.

2848   RECK, RIMA DRELL. THE THEATER OF ALBERT CAMUS. MODERN DRAMA,
       VOL. 4, NO. 1 (MAY 1961), PP. 42-53. FR VII 26369, PMLA
       7380 (1962).

2849   RECK, RIMA DRELL. ALBERT CAMUS. THE ARTIST AND HIS TIME.
       MODERN LANGUAGE QUARTERLY, VOL. 23, NO. 2 (JUNE 1962), PP.
       129-134. PMLA 7986 (1963).

2850   REDEKER, H. ALBERT CAMUS EN ZIJN 'DE MENS IN OPSTAND'. GROENE
       AMSTERDAMMER, VOL. 77, NO. 50 (DEC. 12, 1953), P. 13. BO
       512, CR 864.

2851   REED, PETER J. JUDGES IN THE PLAYS OF ALBERT CAMUS. MODERN
       DRAMA, VOL. 5, NO. 1 (MAY 1962), PP. 47-57. PMLA 7987
       (1963).

2852   REEVES, GEOFFREY. CAMUS AND THE DRAMA OF ASSASSINATION.
       ENCORE, VOL. 11, NO. 1 (JAN. 1964), PP. 6-15.

2853   RENARD, JEAN-CLAUDE. L'OEUVRE DE CAMUS EN DÉBAT DEVANT LA
       NOUVELLE GÉNÉRATION. UNE EXPÉRIENCE À LAQUELLE J'A-
       DHÈRE--EN CHRÉTIEN. FIGARO LITTÉRAIRE, VOL. 12, NO. 602
       (NOV. 2, 1957), P. 11. FITCH. SEE NO. 3252.

2854   RENAUD, ARMAND. QUELQUES REMARQUES SUR LE STYLE DE L'ÉTRANGER.
       FRENCH REVIEW, VOL. 30, NO. 4 (FEB. 1957), PP. 290-296.
       CR 1055, FR VII 17337, KL I 273.

2855   RENAUD, ARMAND. QUELQUES REMARQUES SUR LE STYLE DE L'ETRANGER.
       REVUE DES LETTRES MODERNES, VOL. 8, NOS. 64-66 (FALL
       1961), PP. 377-386 (ALT. PP. 73-82). FR VII 26288.
       REPRINT OF NO. 2854.

2856   REVOL, M. 'L'ETE' DE CAMUS. ESPRIT DES LETTRES, NO. 4
       (JULY-AUG. 1955), PP. 35-47. FR VII 15357.

2857   RHEIN, PHILLIP HENRY. A COMPARATIVE STUDY OF FRANZ KAFKA'S 'DER
       PROZESS' AND ALBERT CAMUS 'L'ETRANGER'. DISSERTATION
       ABSTRACTS, VOL. 21, NO. 12 (JUNE 1961), P. 3771. PMLA
       11746, PMLA 7988 (1963).

2858   RICAUMONT, JACQUES DE. DAS DRAMA DER BELAGERUNG. 'L'ÉTAT DE
       SIÈGE'. MONAT, VOL. 1, NOS. 8-9 (1948-49), PP. 135-137.
       BDZ 99-167 (1949), BO 446, CR 675.

2859   RICHTER, LISELOTTE. CAMUS E OS FILOSOFOS ATRAVES DOS SEUS
       DOCUMENTOS SOBRE O ABSURDO, IN. O MITO DE SISIFO. LISBOA.
       LIVROS DO BRASIL, N.D. (1961). PP. 131-165. TRANSLATED BY
       ANA DE FREITAS.

2860   RICKEY, H. WYNN. MALENTENDUS SUR CAMUS (ABSTRACT).
       SOUTH-CENTRAL BULLETIN, VOL. 21, NO. 1 (FEB. 1961), P. 20.

2861   RIDEAU, ÉMILE. PAGANISME ET CHRISTIANISME. TOURNAI.
       CASTERMAN, 1953. L'EXISTENTIALISME PAÏEN, III, PP.
       143-148. BO 233, FR VII 16550.

2862   RIEDER, HEINZ. VIERZIG JAHRE NACH KAFKA. ZUR GESCHICHTE SEINES

NACHRUHMS.   SCHWEIZER RUNDSCHAU,   VOL. 63, NO. 5 (MAY
1964), PP. 343-346.   PMLA 13618 (1964).   DUPLICATE OF NO.
2863.

RIEDER, HEINZ. VIERZIG JAHRE NACH KAFKA. ZUR GESCHICHTE SEINES   2863
NACHRUHMS.   WORT IN DER ZEIT (VIENNA),   VOL. 10, NO. 6
(1964), PP. 22-26.   PMLA 13618 (1964).   DUPLICATE OF NO.
2862.

RIEFSTAHL, HERMANN. ALBERT CAMUS.   'LE MYTHE DE SISYPHE'.   2864
ZEITSCHRIFT FÜR PHILOSOPHISCHE FORSCHUNG,   VOL. 2 (1947),
PP. 619-622.   BO 318, FR VII 5761.

RIES, JOACHIM SCHUTMANN. CAMUS THE ADAPTER. AN ANALYSIS OF   2865
CAMUS' DRAMATIZATION OF DOSTOEVSKY'S NOVEL 'THE
POSSESSED'.   DISSERTATION ABSTRACTS,   VOL. 26, NO. 8 (FEB.
1966), P. 4673.

RIESE, LAURE. ALBERT CAMUS.   QUEEN'S QUARTERLY,   VOL. 70, NO. 3 2866
(AUTUMN 1963), PP. 400-405.   PMLA 8623 (1964).

RILLA, PAUL. LITTERATUR. KRITIK UND POLEMIK.   BERLIN.   2867
HENSCHELVERLAG, 1952.   EXISTENTIALISMUS AUF DER BÜHNE,
CAMUS. 'CALIGULA', PP. 54-58.

RINIERI, J.-J. LA PESTE.   NEF,   VOL. 4, NO. 33 (AUG. 1947), PP. 2868
141-143.   BO 397, CR 622.

ROBERT, GUY. CAMUS.   CETTE LUCIDITÉ ARIDE.   MAINTENANT, NO. 4   2869
(APRIL 1962), PP. 151-152.   FR VII 29407.

ROBERTS, DAVID EVERETT. EXISTENTIALISM AND RELIGIOUS BELIEF.   2870
NEW YORK.   OXFORD UNIVERSITY PRESS, 1957.   CF. PP. 206,
329.   KL I 232.

ROBICHON, JACQUES. LE STYLE ET LA PROFONDEUR D'UN GRAND   2871
ROMANCIER. CARREFOUR, VOL. 14, NO. 684 (OCT. 23, 1957),PP.
7, 9.   BR, CR 1057 BIS.

ROBLÈS, EMMANUEL. JEUNESSE D'ALBERT CAMUS.   NOUVELLE REVUE   2872
FRANÇAISE,   VOL. 8, NO. 87 (MARCH 1960), PP. 410-421.   FR
VII 23573, KL II 386.

ROBLÈS, EMMANUEL. LA MARQUE DU SOLEIL ET DE LA MISÈRE.   IN   2873
ANONYMOUS, CAMUS, PP. 57-76.   SEE NO. 940.

ROBLÈS, EMMANUEL. VISAGES D'ALBERT CAMUS.   SIMOUN,   VOL. 8, NO. 2874
31 (JULY 1960), PP. 13-17.   FR VII 23573, KL II 386.

ROCHEFORT, A.-HENRY. 'L'ÉTRANGER'.   (REVIEW).   RENAISSANCES,   2875
VOL. 1, NO. 7 (AUG.-SEPT. 1944), PP. 150-152.   BO 294, FR
VII 13319.

ROCHEFORT, A.-HENRY. 'L'ETRANGER'.   (REVIEW).   RENAISSANCES,   2876
VOL. 1, NO. 7 BIS ANTHOLOGIQUE (NOV. 25, 1944), PP.
206-208.   BO 297, CR 503.

ROCHEFORT, A.-HENRY. ALBERT CAMUS.   PRIX NOBEL 1957.   2877
MARGINALES,   VOL. 12, NO. 57 (DEC. 1957), PP. 7-12.   CR
1058, KL II 186.

2878   ROCHEFORT, A.-HENRY. LA MORT DE CAMUS. THYRSE, NO. 62 (1960),
       PP. 49-51. KL II 395.

2879   RODEHAU, I. CAMUS ALS EXISTENZIALISTISCHER DICHTER.
       PHILOSOPHISCHE DISS. (HAMBURG), VOL. 8, (1952). BO 174.

2880   RODITI, EDOUARD. CRUMBS FROM CAMUS' TABLE. NEW LEADER, VOL.
       46, NO. 22 (OCT. 28, 1963), PP. 22-24.

2881   RODRÍGUEZ ROSO, RAFAELA. CAMUS, O LA PASION DEL HOMBRE. EIDOS,
       VOL. 4, NO. 7 (JULY-DEC. 1957), PP. 56-80. FR VII 21416.

2882   ROEMING, ROBERT F. THE CONCEPT OF THE JUDGE-PENITENT OF ALBERT
       CAMUS. TRANSACTIONS OF THE WISCONSIN ACADEMY OF SCIENCES,
       ARTS, AND LETTERS, NO. 48 (1959), PP. 143-149. BUL SIGN
       15-19-7992, FR VII 26370, PMLA 6847 (1961).

2883   ROEMING, ROBERT F. CAMUS SPEAKS OF MAN IN PRISON. TRANSACTIONS
       OF THE WISCONSIN ACADEMY OF SCIENCES, ARTS, AND LETTERS,
       NO. 49 (1960), PP. 213-218. PMLA 7381 (1962).

2884   ROGER, JUAN. FIGURAS DE LA LITERATURA FRANCESA CONTEMPORÁNEA.
       MADRID. RIALP, 1962. (LIBROS DE BOLSILLO RIALP, 17).
       ALBERT CAMUS, PP. 207-215. FR VII 28210.

2885   ROLAND, A. A REBIRTH OF VALUES IN CONTEMPORARY FICTION.
       WESTERN HUMANITIES REVIEW, VOL. 6, NO. 1 (WINTER 1957),
       PP. 59-69. FR VII 23679.

2886   ROLIN, DOMINIQUE. FESTIVAL. PREUVES, NO. 78 (AUG. 1957), PP.
       21-24. FR VII 16978.

2887   ROLIN, DOMINIQUE. L'OEUVRE DE CAMUS EN DÉBAT DEVANT LA NOUVELLE
       GÉNÉRATION. IL M'EST TOUJOURS PRÉSENT AU COEUR ET À
       L'ESPRIT. FIGARO LITTÉRAIRE, VOL. 12, NO. 602 (NOV. 2,
       1957), P. 11. FITCH. SEE NO. 3252.

2888   ROLO, CHARLES J. READER'S CHOICE. MAN IN REVOLT. ATLANTIC
       MONTHLY, VOL. 193, NO. 3 (MARCH 1954), PP. 85-56. BO 531.

2889   ROLO, CHARLES J. ALBERT CAMUS, A GOOD MAN. ATLANTIC MONTHLY,
       VOL. 201, NO. 5 (MAY 1958), PP. 27-33. BR, CR 1116 BIS, FR
       VII 19441, KL II 387.

2890   ROLO, CHARLES J. READER'S CHOICE. INTELLIGENT INTELLIGENCE.
       ATLANTIC MONTHLY, VOL. 207, NO. 3 (MARCH 1961), PP.
       110-112.

2891   ROM, PAUL. THE NOTION OF SOLIDARITY IN THE WORK OF ALBERT
       CAMUS. JOURNAL OF INDIVIDUAL PSYCHOLOGY, VOL. 16, NO. 2
       (NOV. 1960), PP. 146-150.

2892   ROM, PAUL. ZUSAMMENGEHÖRIGKEIT. ALFRED ADLERS
       'GEMEINSCHAFTSGEFÜHL' UND CAMUS' 'SOLIDARITÄT'. GEIST UND
       TAT, VOL. 16, NO. 3 (MARCH 1961), PP. 82-85. BDZ 123-307
       (1961).

2893   ROMEYER, BLAISE. LES 'AUTRES' D'APRÈS SARTRE, CAMUS ET BLONDEL.
       GIORNALE DI METAFISICA, VOL. 8, NO. 2 (15 MARCH-APRIL
       1953), PP. 185-206. BFZ 34-872 (51-53), BO 153, BUL SIGN

7-8595.

ROPARS, MARIE-CLAIRE. CONFIGURATION CRITIQUE D'ALBERT CAMUS.   2894
    CAMUS DEVANT LA CRITIQUE DE LANGUE ALLEMANDE. REVUE
    D'HISTOIRE LITTERAIRE DE LA FRANCE,   VOL. 65, NO. 4
    (OCT.-DEC. 1965), PP. 724-25.

ROSE, MARILYN GADDIS. MEURSAULT AS PHARMAKOS. A READING OF   2895
    L'ÉTRANGER. MODERN FICTION STUDIES,   VOL. 10, NO. 3
    (AUTUMN 1964), PP. 258-264.

ROSSI, A. IL PUNTO SULL'ATTUALITÀ LETTERARIA IN FRANCIA.   2896
    PARAGONE,   VOL. 11, NO. 124 (APRIL 1960), PP. 36-76.   FR
    VII 23038.

ROSSI, LOUIS R. ALBERT CAMUS. THE PLAGUE OF ABSURDITY.   KENYON   2897
    REVIEW,   VOL. 20, NO. 3 (SUMMER 1958), PP. 399-422.   CR
    1117, FR VII 19442, KL I 272.

ROSSI, LOUIS R. LA PESTE DE L'ABSURDE. REVUE DES LETTRES   2898
    MODERNES,   VOL. 8, NOS. 64-66 (FALL 1961), PP. 455-482
    (ALT. PP. 151-178). TRANSLATION OF ALBERT CAMUS.   THE
    PLAGUE OF ABSURDITY . FR VII 26288. SEE NO. 2897.

ROSSI, PAOLO. NICHILISMO E ATTIVISMO NELL OPERA DI ALBERT   2899
    CAMUS. PENSIERO CRITICO,   VOL. 1, NO. 4 (SEPT. 1951), PP.
    343-353. BO 145.

ROSTENNE, PAUL. SARTRE OU LA MAUVAISE CONSCIENCE ATHÉE.   REVUE   2900
    NOUVELLE,   VOL. 7, NO. 4 (APRIL 15, 1948), PP. 390-395.

ROSTENNE, PAUL. UN HONNÊTE HOMME. ALBERT CAMUS.   REVUE   2901
    NOUVELLE,   VOL. 11, NO. 3 (MARCH 15, 1950), PP. 234-243.
    BO 32.

ROSTENNE, PAUL. ALBERT CAMUS, L'HOMME RÉVOLTÉ. REVUE NOUVELLE,   2902
    8TH YEAR, VOL. 15, NO. 2 (FEB. 15, 1952), PP. 193-199.   BO
    501, FR VII 7713.

ROSTENNE, PAUL. LITTÉRATURE DU XXE SIÈCLE ET CHRISTIANISME ,   2903
    PAR CHARLES MOELLER, I.   SILENCE DU DIEU. CAMUS, GIDE,
    HUXLEY, SIMONE WEIL, GRAHAM GREENE, JULIEN GREENE,
    BERNANOS. REVUE NOUVELLE,   VOL. 9, NO. 5 (MAY 15, 1953),
    PP. 549-550. FR VII 16694.

ROTH, LEON. A CONTEMPORARY MORALIST. ALBERT CAMUS. PHILOSOPHY,   2904
    VOL. 30, NO. 115 (OCT. 1955), PP. 291-303. BFZ 39-279
    (54-56), BO 129, BR, BUL SIGN 11-173, CR 921, FR VII 19443.

ROTHERA, H. THE DEVELOPMENT OF SOCIAL CONSCIENCE IN THE   2905
    WRITINGS OF ALBERT CAMUS. PHILOSOPHICAL DISSERTATIONS
    (MANCHESTER), 1953. BO 102.

ROTHERA, H. A TRIBUTE TO ALBERT CAMUS. MODERN LANGUAGES,   VOL.   2906
    41, NO. 2 (JUNE 1960), PP. 44-45. BFZ 46-283, FR VII
    23680, KL II 395.

ROTHMUND, ALFONS. ALBERT CAMUS. 'LES MUETS'. NEUEREN   2907
    SPRACHEN,   VOL. 8, NO. 11 (NOV. 1959), PP. 522-528.   FR VII

21417, KL II 391.

2908 ROTHMUND, ALFONS. CAMUS ET LES LYCÉENS. REVUE DES LETTRES
MODERNES, NOS. 90-93 (WINTER 1963), PP. 185-200. PMLA
8608 (1964). SEE NO. 3207.

2909 R(OUDIEZ), L(EON) S. DISAGREEMENT ON CAMUS. FRENCH REVIEW,
VOL. 29, NO. 4 (FEB. 1956), P. 332.

2910 ROUDIEZ, LEON S. STRANGERS IN MELVILLE AND CAMUS. FRENCH
REVIEW, VOL. 31, NO. 3 (JAN. 1958,. PP. 217-226. FR VII
19445, KL I 274.

2911 ROUDIEZ, LEON S. LES ÉTRANGERS CHEZ MELVILLE ET CAMUS. REVUE
DES LETTRES MODERNES, VOL. 8, NOS. 64-66 (FALL 1961), PP.
343-357 (ALT. PP. 39-53). FR VII 26288. TRANSLATION OF
NO. 2910.

2912 ROUDIEZ, LEON S. THE LITERARY CLIMATE OF 'L'ETRANGER'. SAMPLES
OF A TWENTIETH-CENTURY ATMOSPHERE. SYMPOSIUM, VOL. 12,
NOS. 1-2 (SPRING-FALL 1958), PP. 19-35. BUL SIGN 14-9008,
FR VII 19444, KL II 390.

2913 ROUDIEZ, LEON S. 'L'ETRANGER', 'LA CHUTE', AND THE AESTHETIC
LEGACY OF GIDE. FRENCH REVIEW, VOL. 32, NO. 4 (FEB.
1959), PP. 300-310. BUL SIGN 15-19-14340, FR VII 21418, KL
II 390.

2914 ROUDIEZ, LEON S. GERMAINE BRÉE: 'CAMUS'. ROMANIC REVIEW,
VOL. 50, NO. 3 (OCT. 1959), PP. 235-237. FR VII 21419.

2915 ROUDIEZ, LEON S. JOHN CRUICKSHANK. 'ALBERT CAMUS AND THE
LITERATURE OF REVOLT'. ROMANIC REVIEW, VOL. 51, NO. 1
(FEB. 1960), PP. 77-78. FR VII 23681.

2916 ROUDIEZ, LEON S. CAMUS AND 'MOBY DICK'. SYMPOSIUM, VOL. 15,
NO. 1 (SPRING 1961), PP. 30-40. FR VII 26371, PMLA 7382
(1962).

2917 ROUSSEAU, LOUIS-B. CAMUS POUR NOUS. REVUE DOMINICAINE, VOL.
67, T. 2 (JULY-AUG. 1961), PP. 12-18. FR VII 26372.

2918 ROUSSEAUX, ANDRÉ. LES LIVRES. 'LA PESTE', PAR ALBERT CAMUS.
FIGARO LITTÉRAIRE, VOL. 2, NO. 61 (JUNE 21, 1947), P. 2.
CR 624.

2919 ROUSSEAUX, ANDRÉ. LES LIVRES. 'LA PESTE', D'ALBERT CAMUS.
FRANCE-ILLUSTRATION, VOL. 3, NO. 92 (JULY 5, 1947), P. 25.
BO 398, CR 625, FR VII 9308.

2920 ROUSSEAUX, ANDRÉ. ALBERT CAMUS ET LA PHILOSOPHIE DU BONHEUR.
CAHIERS DE NEUILLY, NO. 18 (1948), PP. 10-32. BO 138, CR
676.

2921 ROUSSEAUX, ANDRÉ. ALBERT CAMUS ET LA PHILOSOPHIE DU BONHEUR.
SYMPOSIUM, VOL. 2, NO. 1 (MAY 1948), PP. 1-18. BO 138, CR
677, FR VII 2710, 758.

2922 ROUSSEAUX, ANDRÉ. LITTÉRATURE DU VINGTIÈME SIÈCLE, VOL. 3.
PARIS. A. MICHEL, 1949. CAMUS ET LA PHILOSOPHIE DU

BONHEUR , PP. 73-105. BO 141, BR, CR 476.

ROUSSEAUX, ANDRÉ. LES LIVRES. LA MORALE D'ALBERT CAMUS.   2923
   FIGARO LITTÉRAIRE, VOL. 5, NO. 235 (OCT. 21, 1950), P. 2.
   BO 124, CR 770 BIS, FR VII 5760.

ROUSSEAUX, ANDRÉ. 'L'HOMME RÉVOLTÉ' D'ALBERT CAMUS. FIGARO   2924
   LITTÉRAIRE, VOL. 6, NO. 291 (NOV. 17, 1951), P. 2. BO
   489, CR 793, FR VII 5759.

ROUSSEAUX, ANDRÉ. ALBERT CAMUS ET LA RÉVOLTE.   2925
   FRANCE-ILLUSTRATION, VOL. 8, NO. 325 (JAN. 5, 1952), P.
   21. BO 225, FR VII 9307.

ROUSSEAUX, ANDRÉ. LITTÉRATURE DU VINGTIÈME SIÈCLE, VOL. 4.   2926
   PARIS. A. MICHEL, 1953. LA MORALE D'ALBERT CAMUS , PP.
   196-212. BO 128, CR 477, FR VII 8690.

ROUSSEAUX, ANDRÉ. LES VÉRITÉS D'ALBERT CAMUS. FIGARO   2927
   LITTÉRAIRE, VOL. 8, NO. 398 (DEC. 5, 1953), P. 2. BO 478,
   CR 865, FR VII 9309.

ROUSSEAUX, ANDRÉ. 'L'ÉTÉ' D'ALBERT CAMUS. FIGARO LITTÉRAIRE,   2928
   VOL. 9, NO. 413 (MARCH 20, 1954), P. 2. BR, CR 904.

ROUSSEAUX, ANDRÉ. L'ÉTÉ PAR ALBERT CAMUS. BIBLIO, VOL. 22,   2929
   NO. 5 (MAY-JUNE 1954), P. 19. FITCH. SEE NO. 2928.

ROUSSEAUX, ANDRÉ. 'LA CHUTE' D'ALBERT CAMUS. FIGARO   2930
   LITTÉRAIRE, VOL. 11, NO. 527 (MAY 26, 1956), P. 2. BO
   548, BR, CR 969, FR VII 15358, KL I 274.

ROUSSEAUX, ANDRÉ. LA CHUTE. BIBLIO, VOL. 24, NO. 7   2931
   (AUG.-SEPT. 1956), P. 15. CR 970.

ROUSSEAUX, ANDRÉ. 'L'EXIL ET LE ROYAUME' D'ALBERT CAMUS.   2932
   FIGARO LITTÉRAIRE, VOL. 12, NO. 569 (MARCH 16, 1957), P.
   2. FR VII 17339.

ROUSSEAUX, ANDRÉ. ALBERT CAMUS ET NOTRE ESPOIR. FIGARO   2933
   LITTÉRAIRE, VOL. 12, NO. 601 (OCT. 26, 1957), P. 2. BR,
   CR 1059, FR VII 17338, KL I 274.

ROUSSEAUX, ANDRÉ. LITTÉRATURE DU VINGTIÈME SIÈCLE, VOL. 6.   2934
   PARIS. A. MICHEL, 1958. ALBERT CAMUS PRIX NOBEL, PP.
   194-202. BUL SIGN 15-19-7959, FR VII 18845, KL I 274.

ROUSSEAUX, ANDRÉ. ALBERT CAMUS JADIS ET NAGUÈRE. FIGARO   2935
   LITTÉRAIRE, VOL. 13, NO. 625 (APRIL 12, 1958), P. 2. BR,
   CR 1118, KL I 273.

ROUSSEAUX, ANDRÉ. L'HOMME JUSTE. FIGARO, VOL. 134, NO. 4770   2936
   (JAN. 6, 1960), P. 1. FR VII 23682.

ROUSSEAUX, ANDRÉ. L'HOMME DE LUMIÈRE. TABLE RONDE. NO. 146   2937
   (FEB. 1960), PP. 174-177. BFZ 46-284, BUL SIGN
   15-19-13761, FR VII 23569, KL II 395.

ROUSSEL, J. LE SIÈCLE DE LA TRAHISON EST AUSSI LE TEMPS DU   2938
   NIHILISME. ÂGE NOUVEAU, VOL. 7, NO. 70 (FEB. 1952), PP.
   79-81. BO 502, BUL SIGN 6-9052, CR 838.

2939   ROUSSELOT, JEAN. CAMUS. PRIX NOBEL 1957. FRANCE-ASIE, VOL.
         14, NO. 140 (JAN. 1958), PP. 501-503. KL II 386.

2940   ROUSSELOT, JEAN. ALBERT CAMUS, SYMBOLE DE SON ALGÉRIE.
         FRANCE-ASIE, VOL. 17, NO. 165 (JAN.-FEB. 1961), PP.
         1715-1717. FR VII 26373.

2941   ROVIT, EARL H. THE AMBIGUOUS MODERN NOVEL. YALE REVIEW, VOL.
         49, NO. 3 (MARCH 1960), PP. 413-424. FR VII 23039.

2942   ROY, CLAUDE. LE PAPIER QU'ON MÂCHE EN 1945. POÉSIE 45, VOL.
         6, NO. 22 (JAN. 1945), PP. 83-89. BO 377, CR 545, FR VII
         2265.

2943   ROY, CLAUDE. LA PESTE. REMARQUES SUR LA RÉVOLTE D'ALBERT
         CAMUS. EUROPE, VOL. 25, NO. 22 (OCT. 1947), PP. 99-101.
         BO 399, CR 626.

2944   ROY, CLAUDE. GÉRARD PHILIPE. SEE NO. 2731.

2945   ROY, CLAUDE. CAMUS SOLIDAIRE ET SOLITAIRE. FRANCE-OBSERVATEUR,
         VOL. 11, NO. 505 (JAN. 7, 1960), P. 19. FITCH.

2946   ROY, JULES. DOUZE ANS APRÈS. CAMUS, PRIX NOBEL. NOUVELLES
         LITTÉRAIRES, NO. 1573 (OCT. 24, 1957), P. 1. BR, CR 1061,
         FR VII 17340, KL I 272.

2947   ROY, JULES. LA GUERRE D'ALGÉRIE. PARIS. RENÉ JULLIARD, 1960.

2948   ROY, JULES. UN AFRICAIN. MONDE, VOL. 13, NO. 585 (DEC. 31,
         1959-JAN. 6, 1960), P. 1. FR VII 23683.

2949   ROY, JULES. THE WAR IN ALGERIA (LA GUERRE D'ALGÉRIE). NEW
         YORK. GROVE PRESS, INC., 1961.

2950   ROY, JULES. LA TRAGÉDIE ALGÉRIENNE. IN ANONYMOUS, CAMUS, PP.
         199-216. SEE NO. 940.

2951   ROYCE, BARBARA. 'LA CHUTE' AND 'SAINT GENET'. THE QUESTION OF
         GUILT. FRENCH REVIEW, VOL. 39, NO. 5 (APRIL 1966), PP.
         709-716.

2952   ROYNET, L. ALBERT CAMUS CHEZ LES CHRÉTIENS. VIE
         INTELLECTUELLE, VOL. 17, NO. 4 (APRIL 1949), PP. 336-351.
         BO 109, CR 721.

2953   RUBÉ, PIERRE. WHO WAS ALBERT CAMUS? YALE FRENCH STUDIES, NO.
         25 (SPRING 1960), PP. 3-9. BUL SIGN 16-19-9734, FR VII
         23568, KL II 395, PMLA 6848 (1961).

2954   RUDICK, NORMAN. INDIVIDUAL AS MYTH. CHICAGO REVIEW, VOL. 13,
         NO. 2 (SUMMER 1959), PP. 94-119.

2955   RÜF, PAULA. BÜCHER ZU WEIHNACHTEN 1947. ALBERT CAMUS. 'LA
         PESTE'. DU (ZURICH), VOL. 7, NO. 12 (DEC. 1947), P. 62.
         BO 400, CR 623.

2956   RUGOFF, MILTON. PARABLE OF OUR WORLD SEEN IN A STRICKEN CITY.
         REVIEW. THE PLAGUE. NEW YORK HERALD TRIBUNE BOOK REVIEW,
         VOL. 24, NO. 50 (AUG. 1, 1948), P. 1. BO 427.

2957   RÜHLE, JÜRGEN. LITERATUR UND REVOLUTION, DIE SCHRIFTSTELLER
         UND DER KOMMUNISMUS. KÖLN. KIEPENHEUER UND WITSCH, 1960.

FR VII 25325.

RUPOLO, WANDA. ALBERT CAMUS. RIBELLIONE E MORTE. HUMANITAS   2958
    (BRESCIA), VOL. 17, NO. 3 (MARCH 1962), PP. 283-284. FR
    VII 29409.

RUPOLO, WANDA. LE CONTRADIZIONI DI ALBERT CAMUS. HUMANITAS   2959
    (BRESCIA), VOL. 18, NO. 11 (NOV. 1963), PP. 1161-1165. FR
    VII 33976.

S., C. D. ALBERT CAMUS, PRIX NOBEL DE LITTÉRATURE. CAHIERS DU   2960
    SUD, 44TH YEAR, T. 45, NO. 343 (NOV. 1957), P. 505. CR
    995.

SABA, GUIDO. ALBERT CAMUS, TESTIMONE DEL NOSTRO TEMPO. NUOVA   2961
    ANTOLOGIA, VOL. 471, NO. 1883 (NOV. 1957), PP. 345-354.
    BFZ 43-294, CR 1062, FR VII 19446, KL I 272.

SABA, GUIDO. PRESENZA DI CAMUS. AUSONIA, VOL. 9, NO. 4   2962
    (JULY-AUG. 1954), PP. 24-30. FR VII 15359.

SABATIER, ROBERT. L'OEUVRE DE CAMUS EN DÉBAT DEVANT LA NOUVELLE   2963
    GÉNÉRATION. IL LIVRE UNE BATAILLE CONTRE LA PEUR. FIGARO
    LITTÉRAIRE, VOL. 12, NO. 602 (NOV. 2, 1957). P. 11.
    FITCH. SEE NO. 3252.

SAHUGUET, M.-H. ALBERT CAMUS. 'LA CHUTE'. FICHES   2964
    BIBLIOGRAPHIQUES, (1956). CR 971.

ST. AUBYN, F. C. ALBERT CAMUS. DIALOGUE OR MONOLOGUE. BOOKS   2965
    ABROAD, VOL. 31, NO. 2 (SPRING 1957), PP. 122-125. BFZ
    42-284, CR 980, FR VII 17341, KL I 271.

ST. AUBYN, F. C. 'CAMUS' BY JEAN CLAUDE BRISVILLE, 'ALBERT   2966
    CAMUS AND THE LITERATURE OF REVOLT' BY JOHN CRUICKSHANK.
    FRENCH REVIEW, VOL. 33, NO. 2 (DEC. 1959), PP. 203-205.
    KL II 386.

ST. AUBYN, F. C. ANDRÉ PERRIN. THE NOSTALGIA OF OTHER.   2967
    SYMPOSIUM, VOL. 13, NO. 2 (FALL 1959), PP. 238-254.

ST. AUBYN, F. C. ALBERT CAMUS AND THE DEATH OF THE OTHER. AN   2968
    EXISTENTIALIST INTERPRETATION. FRENCH STUDIES, VOL. 16,
    NO. 2 (APRIL 1962), PP. 124-141. BFZ 49-262 (1960-62),
    PMLA 7989 (1963).

SAINT-CLAIR, M. ALBERT CAMUS. CAHIERS DE LA PLÉIADE, NO. 2   2969
    (APRIL 1947), PP. 125-126. BO 17, CR 627, FR VII 11240,
    759.

SAINT-CLAIR, M. GALÉRIE PRIVÉE. PARIS. GALLIMARD, 1947.   2970
    ALBERT CAMUS, PP. 143-146. BO 59, CR 478, FR VII 2080.

SAINT DENIS, MICHEL. REMEMBERING TWO FRIENDS--MATTHEW SMITH,   2971
    ALBERT CAMUS. QUARTERLY REVIEW (LONDON), VOL. 1, NO. 2
    (MARCH 1960), PP. 111-113. FR VII 26374, PMLA 6849 (1961).

SAINT-MORTIER, R. FRANSE LETTERKUNDE. EEN BLIK OP HET SEIZOEN.   2972
    DIETSCHE WARANDE EN BELFORT, NO. 4 (APRIL-MAY 1957), PP.
    240-244. CR 1063.

2973   SAINT-MORTIER, R. KRONIEK DER FRANSE LETTERKUNDE. (PRIX NOBEL
            1957). DIETSCHE WARANDE EN BELFORT, NO. 5 (JUNE 1958),
            PP. 301-305. CR 1119.

2974   SAISSELIN, RÉMY G. THE ABSURD, DEATH, AND HISTORY.
            PERSONALIST, VOL. 42, NO. 2 (APRIL 1961), PP. 165-177.
            BUL SIGN 16-19-7560.

2975   SAISSELIN, RÉMY G. L'ABSURDE, LA MORT ET L'HISTOIRE. BAYOU,
            VOL. 25, NOS. 85-86 (SPRING-SUMMER 1961), PP. 306-314.
            TRANSLATION OF NO. 2974.

2976   SALVET, A. LA PHILOSOPHIE D'ALBERT CAMUS. MÉRIDIEN,   NO. 8
            (1943), PP. 22-25. BO 130, CR 497.

2977   SAMSON, J. P. VON EINIGEN WESTEUROPEISCHEN BÜCHERN.
            DU(ZURICH), NO. 4 (1949). BO 433, BR, CR 722.

2978   SAMSON, J. P. HUMANISME ET PÉCHÉ. TÉMOINS, VOL. 5 , NOS.
            15-16 (WINTER-SPRING 1957), PP. 17-25. KL I 274.

2979   SAMSON, JEAN-PAUL. UNE SAGESSE À HAUTEUR D'HOMME. TÉMOINS,
            VOL. 8, NO. 23 (MAY 1960), PP. 23-24. KL II 395.

2980   SANDAUER, A. L. LA RÉALITÉ DÉGRADÉE (TRADUIT DU POLONAIS PAR V.
            ASCHER). LETTRES NOUVELLES, VOL. 7, NO. 68 (FEB. 1959),
            PP. 256-267. FR VII 23040.

2981   SANDBERG, H. ALBERT CAMUS VERDEDIGER DER VRIJHEID. VRIJ
            NEDERLAND (LONDON), (OCT. 16, 1954), P. 7. BO 237, CR
            905.

2982   SANDSTORM, GLENN. THE OUTSIDERS OF STENDHAL AND CAMUS. MODERN
            FICTION STUDIES, VOL. 10, NO. 3 (AUTUMN 1964), PP.
            245-257.

2983   SANOUILLET, MICHEL. ALBERT CAMUS OU LA RÉVOLTE MÉTHODIQUE.
            BEAUX-ARTS (BRUXELLES), NO. 553 (DEC. 28, 1951), P. 8.   BO
            220, FR VII 7715.

2984   SAPORTA, MARCEL. CARTA DE PARIS. CUADERNOS AMERICANOS,   12TH
            YEAR, VOL. 68, NO. 2 (MARCH-APRIL 1953), PP. 78-84.   FR VII
            8883.

2985   SAPORTA, MARCEL. CARTA DE PARIS. CUADERNOS AMERICANOS,   16TH
            YEAR, VOL. 92, NO. 2 (MARCH-APRIL 1957), PP. 233-239. BO
            283, FR VII 20713.

2986   SARGENT, LYMAN TOWER. PROLEGOMENA TO A STUDY OF THE POLITICAL
            PHILOSOPHY OF ALBERT CAMUS. MINNESOTA REVIEW, VOL. 4, NO.
            3 (SPRING 1964), PP. 365-369. PMLA 8624 (1964).

2987   SARRAUTE, CLAUDE. AU THÉÂTRE DES MATHURINS. LA RENCONTRE
            D'ALBERT CAMUS ET DE WILLIAM FAULKNER NOUS VAUDRA-T-ELLE
            UNE PREMIÈRE TRAGÉDIE MODERNE? MONDE, VOL. 9, NO. 411
            (AUG. 30-SEPT. 5, 1956), P. 8.

2988   SARTRE, JEAN-PAUL. EXPLICATION DE 'L'ETRANGER'. CAHIERS DU
            SUD, VOL. 30, NO. 253 (FEB. 1943), PP. 189-206. BO 295,
            CR 498.

SARTRE, JEAN-PAUL. EXPLICATION DE L'ÉTRANGER. PARIS. AUX   2989
    DEPENS DU PALIMUGRE, 1946. FR VII 739.

SARTRE, JEAN-PAUL. SITUATIONS I. PARIS. GALLIMARD, 1947.   2990
    EXPLICATION DE L'ÉTRANGER , PP. 99-121. BO 295, BR, CR
    479, FR VII 105.

SARTRE, JEAN-PAUL. AN EXPLICATION OF 'THE STRANGER'. IN   2991
    LITERARY AND PHILOSOPHICAL ESSAYS OF JEAN-PAUL SARTRE .
    NEW YORK. CRITERION BOOKS, 1955.

SARTRE, JEAN-PAUL. AN EXPLICATION OF 'THE STRANGER'. IN   2992
    BRÉE, GERMAINE, CAMUS, A COLLECTION OF CRITICAL ESSAYS,
    PP. 108-121. FR VII 29338. SEE NO. 1293. TRANSLATION OF
    NO. 2990.

SARTRE, JEAN-PAUL. RÉPONSE À ALBERT CAMUS. TEMPS MODERNES,   2993
    VOL. 8, NO. 82 (AUG. 1952), PP. 334-353. BO. 284, CR 839.

SARTRE, JEAN-PAUL. LITERARY AND PHILOSOPHICAL ESSAYS. NEW   2994
    YORK. CRITERION BOOKS, 1955. FR VII 18847. MICHELSON,
    ANNETTE.

SARTRE, JEAN-PAUL. LITERARY AND PHILOSOPHICAL ESSAYS, LONDON.   2995
    RIDER, 1955. FR VII 12609. MICHELSON, ANNETTE.

SARTRE, JEAN-PAUL. LITERARY ESSAYS. NEW YORK. PHILOSOPHICAL   2996
    LIBRARY, 1957. CHAPTER II. CAMUS 'THE OUTSIDER', PP.
    24-41. FR VII 18848.

SARTRE, JEAN-PAUL. ALBERT CAMUS. FRANCE-OBSERVATEUR, VOL. 11,   2997
    NO. 505 (JAN. 7, 1960), P. 17. FITCH.

SARTRE, JEAN-PAUL. ALBERT CAMUS. BONNIERS LITTERÄRA MAGASIN,   2998
    VOL. 29, NO. 2 (FEB. 1960), PP. 95-96. FR VII 23685.

SARTRE, JEAN-PAUL. EN LA MUERTE DE ALBERT CAMUS. INSULA, VOL.   2999
    15, NO. 159 (FEB. 1960), P. 1. FR VII 23686.

SARTRE, JEAN-PAUL. ALBERT CAMUS. MONAT, VOL. 12, NO. 137   3000
    (FEB. 1960), PP. 5-6. BDZ 120-311 (1960), FR VII 23684, KL
    II 395.

SARTRE, JEAN-PAUL. TRIBUTE TO ALBERT CAMUS. REPORTER, VOL.   3001
    22, NO. 3 (FEB. 4, 1960), P. 34.

SARTRE, JEAN-PAUL. TRIBUTE TO ALBERT CAMUS. IN BRÉE,   3002
    GERMAINE, CAMUS, A COLLECTION OF CRITICAL ESSAYS, PP.
    173-175. FR VII 29338. SEE NO. 1293.

SATO, S. QUESTION DE CAMUS. SOCIÉTÉ DE LA LITTÉRATURE   3003
    FRANÇAISE DU JAPON, NO. 1 (APRIL 1952), PP. 51-56. BO 43,
    FR VII 9310.

SATTLER, ANDREAS. DER UNERWARTETE NOBEL-PREISTRÄGER. ZEIT,   3004
    VOL. 12, NO. 43 (1957), P. 7. BDZ 115-350 (1958).

SAULNIER, ADAM. ALBERT CAMUS. PRIX NOBEL DE LITTÉRATURE... UN   3005
    HOMME. FORCE OUVRIÈRE, VOL. 14, NO. 608 (OCT. 24, 1957),
    P. 11. BR, CR 1063 BIS.

S., R. (SAUREL, RENÉE). LE THÉÂTRE. LES POSSÉDÉS D'ALBERT   3006

CAMUS, D'APRÈS DOSTOÏEVSKI AU THÉÂTRE ANTOINE. TEMPS
MODERNES,   VOL. 14, NOS. 156-157 (FEB.-MARCH 1959), PP.
1508-1509.   CR 1147.

3007   SAURIAT, ANDRÉ. LITTÉRATURE 51.   ACROPOLE,   VOL. 3, NO. 13
(SEPT.-OCT. 1951), PP. 2-7.   FR VII 10780, BO 65.

3008   SAUVAGE, LÉO. L'OPINION AMÉRICAINE SALUE EN CAMUS   CELUI QUI
DEMANDE AUX HOMMES DE DIRE OUI À LA VIE DE LA FAÇON LA PLUS
HÉROÏQUE . FIGARO, VOL. 134, NO. 4770 (JAN. 6, 1960), P.
4. FITCH.

3009   SAVAGE, EDWARD B. MASKS AND MUMMERIES IN ENRICO IV AND
CALIGULA. MODERN DRAMA, VOL. 6, NO. 4 (FEB. 1964), PP.
397-401. PMLA 10675 (1964).

3010   SCAPIN. LA PESTE (EXTRAIT). CONFÉRENCIA,   VOL. 36, NO. 8 (AUG.
15, 1947), PP. 349-351. CR 628.

3011   SCAPIN. 'LES JUSTES', EN SUÈDE.   ANNALES,   VOL. 58, NO. 3 (JAN.
1951), P. 43. CR 795.

3012   SCAPIN. NOS DRAMATURGES EN SUÈDE. 'CALIGULA'.   ANNALES,   VOL.
58, NO. 6 (APRIL 1951), P. 41. CR 794.

3013   SCAPIN. LA SOURCE.   ANNALES,   VOL. 58, NO. 10 (AUG. 1951), P.
23. CR 796.

3014   SCAPIN. ALBERT CAMUS, ADAPTATEUR DE 'LA DÉVOTION À LA CROIX' DE
CALDERÓN DE LA BARCA. ANNALES,   VOL. 60, NO. 33 (JULY
1953), P. 44. CR 866.

3015   SCHÄFER, W. E. VOM GLÜCK DER FORM. STUTTGARTER ZEITUNG,   VOL.
6, NO. 257 (NOV. 3, 1950), P. 2.

3016   SCHAERF, J. ALBERT CAMUS, EIN PHILOSOPH DER MENSCHLICHKEIT.
GEIST UND TAT,   VOL. 7, NO. 5 (MAY 1952), PP. 154-155.   BO
504, CR 840.

3017   SCHAJOWICZ, L. EL GRAN DIÓS PAN NO HA MUERTO. CAMUS Y EL
PENSAMIENTO DEL MEDIODÍA. ASOMANTE,   VOL. 17, NO. 1
(JAN.-MARCH 1961), PP. 19-31. BUL SIGN 16-19-109,
16-19-2382, FR VII 26375.

3018   SCHALEKAMP, J. A. IN EEN BAR AAN DE ZEEDIJK. CAMUS. LA CHUTE.
HAAGSE POST,   NO. 2168 (JUNE 30, 1956), P. 14. CR 972.

3019   SCHERER, OLGA. ILLOGICAL IMMORALIST. ALBERT CAMUS.
PERSPECTIVE,   VOL. 2, NO. 1 (AUTUMN 1948), PP. 53-60.

3020   SCHLETTE, HEINZ ROBERT. DER PHILOSOPH ALBERT CAMUS. HOCHLAND,
VOL. 52, NO. 4 (APRIL 1960), PP. 387-389. BDZ 121-321
(1960), FR VII 23687, KL II 387.

3021   SCHLETTE, HEINZ R. ALBERT CAMUS--DENKER DER FREIHEIT.
HOCHLAND,   VOL. 53, NO. 6 (AUG. 1961), PP. 561-567.   BDZ
123-307 (1961), FR VII 26376.

3022   SCHLUETER, PAUL. A MODEST OPTIMIST. (REVIEW. CAMUS BY NATHAN
A. SCOTT, JR.) CHRISTIAN SCHOLAR,   VOL. 47, NO. 3 (FALL
1964), PP. 263-267.

SCHLUMBERGER, JEAN. À PROPOS DE LA PEINE DE MORT, ('RÉFLEXIONS   3023
     SUR LA PEINE CAPITALE', PAR ALBERT CAMUS ET ARTHUR
     KOESTLER). FIGARO LITTÉRAIRE, VOL. 13, NO. 616 (FEB. 8,
     1958), PP. 1, 4. CR 1120.
SCHLUMBERGER, JEAN. DANS CETTE LUMIÈRE... FIGARO LITTÉRAIRE,   3024
     VOL. 15, NO. 716 (JAN. 9, 1960), P. 1. FR VII 26377.
SCHMIDT, PAUL. AKTUELLE STOFFE IN DER FRANZÖSISCHEN LEKTÜRE.   3025
     LEBENDEN FREMDSPRACHEN, VOL. 3, NO. 10 (OCT. 1951), PP.
     309-313. BO 469.
SCHNEIDER, PETER. MASS UND GERECHTIGKEIT. ZU A. CAMUS RECHTS   3026
     UND STAATSAUFFASSUNG. IN FESTGABE FÜR CARLO SCHMID,
     TÜBINGEN, 1962.
SCHNEIDER, PETER. MESURE ET JUSTICE. REVUE DES LETTRES   3027
     MODERNES, NOS. 90-93 (WINTER 1963), PP. 101-124. PMLA
     8608 (1964). TRANSLATION OF NO. 3026. SEE NO. 3207.
     TRANSLATED BY BERNARD LORTHOLARY.
SCHNIR, M.-R. CAMUS SOLIDAIRE DE CEUX QUI SOUFFRENT. CAHIERS   3028
     JEAN TOUSSEUL, VOL. 15, NO. 2 (APRIL-JUNE 1960), PP.
     41-45. KL II 395.
SCHOGT, H. G. LA SOLITUDE DU SOUTERAIN. IN DUTCH CONTRIBUTIONS   3029
     TO THE FOURTH INTERNATIONAL CONGRESS OF SLAVICISTS, MOSCOW,
     ŠEPTEMBER 1958, PP. 139-156. 'S-GRAVENHAGE. MOUTON, 1958.
SCHONAUER, FRANZ. SISYPHOS' THEOLOGISHER TRICK. ZU ALBERT   3030
     CAMUS' ROMAN 'DER FALL'. PANORAMA, VOL. 1 (MAY 1957), P.
     9. BDZ 123-307 (1961).
SCHRADER, GEORGE ALFRED. CAMUS AND OTHER EXISTENTIALISTS. YALE   3031
     REVIEW, VOL. 51, NO. 4 (JUNE 1962), PP. 644-649. FR VII
     29411.
SCHURMAN, DONALD M. SOME THOUGHTS ON ALBERT CAMUS. QUEEN'S   3032
     QUARTERLY, VOL. 68, NO. 3 (AUTUMN 1961), PP. 504-507.
     PMLA 7383 (1962).
SCHYLE, HANS-JOACHIM. DAS PROBLEM DES TODES BEI JEAN ANOUILH   3033
     UND ALBERT CAMUS. TÜBINGEN, PHIL. F. DISS., VOL. 13, NO.
     4 (JUNE 1959). CR 480.
SCHONAUER, FRANZ. CAMUS UND SEIN FALL . ECKART, VOL. 26, NO.   3034
     5 (JAN.-MARCH 1958), PP. 85-87. CR 1064, FR VII 26378, KL
     I 274, BDZ.
SCHRADER, GEORGE ALFRED. CAMUS AND OTHER EXISTENTIALISTS. YALE   3035
     REVIEW, VOL. 51, NO. 4 (JUNE 1962), PP. 644-649. FR VII
     29411.
SCHULTZ, HANS JÜRGEN. SIND CHRISTEN WELTVERBESSERER.   3036
     SONNTAGSBLATT DER WOCHENZEITUNG, NO. 25 (1959), P. 35.
     BDZ 120-311 (1960).
SCOLERI, DOMENICO. SOLITUDINE METAFISICA E SOLIDARIETÀ UMANA   3037
     REGGIO CALABRIA. EDIZIONI HISTORICA, 1953. CHAPTER IV.

CONDIZIONE UMANA ED IMPEGNO ETICO IN A. CAMUS, PP. 73-88.
BO 154.

3038   SCOLERI, D. A. CAMUS E LA RIVOLTA DEL MONDO MODERNO.
HISTORICA,   BO 226.

3039   SCOTT, NATHAN A., JR. THE MODEST OPTIMISM OF ALBERT CAMUS.
CHRISTIAN SCHOLAR,   VOL. 42, NO. 4 (DEC. 1959), PP.
251-274.

3040   SCOTT, NATHAN A., JR. THE BIAS OF COMEDY AND THE NARROW ESCAPE
INTO FAITH.   CHRISTIAN SCHOLAR,   VOL. 44 (SPRING 1961), PP.
9-39 (CAMUS REF. PP. 10-13).

3041   SCOTT, NATHAN A. ALBERT CAMUS.   LONDON. BOWES AND BOWES, LTD.,
1962.

3042   SCOTT, NATHAN A. ALBERT CAMUS.   NEW YORK. HILLARY HOUSE, 1962.

3043   SCOTT, NATHAN A., JR. THE TRAGIC VISION AND THE CHRISTIAN
FAITH. ANGLICAN THEOLOGICAL REVIEW, JAN. 1963, PP. 1-23
(CAMUS REF. PP. 5, 7).

3044   SCOTT, NATHAN A., JR. (EDITOR). THE CLIMATE OF FAITH IN MODERN
LITERATURE. NEW YORK. SEABURY PRESS, 1964. SEE NO. 1670,
1975, 2209, 2514.

3045   SCOTT, NATHAN A., JR. (EDITOR). FORMS OF EXTREMITY IN THE
MODERN NOVEL.   RICHMOND, VIRGINIA. JOHN KNOX PRESS, 1965.
CHAPTER III, PP. 55-74.   SEE NO. 1959.

3046   SCURANI, ALESSANDRO. LA RICERCA INTERROTTA DI ALBERT CAMUS.
LETTURE,   VOL. 17, NO. 1 (JAN. 1962), PP. 3-22 (+ 4 PAGE
INSERT, UNPAGINATED).   PMLA 7990 (1963).

3047   EL SEBAÏ, YOUSSEF, NAGUIB MAHFOUZ AND YOUSSEF IDRISS. HOMMAGE
À ALBERT CAMUS DES ÉCRIVAINS ARABES.   REVUE DU CAIRE,   23RD
YEAR, VOL. 44, NO. 237 (MAY 1960), PP. 368-370. SEE NO.
3259.

3048   SECRET, DANIEL. LA RENCONTRE DE CAMUS ET DE FAULKNER. MÉDECINE
DE FRANCE,   NO. 77 (1956), PP. 45-46.   CR 973.

3049   SECRET, DANIEL. LES LIMITES DU THÉÂTRE.   LES POSSÉDÉS,
MÉDECINE DE FRANCE,   NO. 101 (1959), PP. 47-48. CR 1148.

3050   SEGHERS, PIERRE. LETTER FROM PARIS. WORLD REVIEW, N.S., NO.
35 (JAN. 1952), PP. 39-42.

3051   SELLIER, PHILIPPE. LES ÉCRIVAINS DEVANT DIEU. 'CAMUS' PAR J.
ONIMUS. SIGNES DU TEMPS,   NO. 5 (MAY 1966), PP. 23-25.

3052   SELZ, JEAN. REQUIEM POUR UNE NONNE. LETTRES NOUVELLES,   VOL.
4, NO. 43 (NOV. 1956), PP. 622-627. FR VII 15360.

3053   SÉNARD, JEAN. UN CERTAIN JOURNALISTE. FIGARO LITTÉRAIRE,   VOL.
12, NO. 601 (OCT. 26, 1957), P. 5. BR, CR 1065, FR VII
17342, KL I 273.

3054   SÉNARD, JEAN. ALBERT CAMUS, PRIX NOBEL. PENSÉE FRANÇAISE,
VOL. 16, NO. 13 (DEC. 1957), PP. 3-7. FR VII 19447, KL II
386.

SÉNARD, JEAN. CAMUS PLUS PROCHE ENCORE... FIGARO LITTÉRAIRE,   3055
     VOL. 17, NO. 825 (FEB. 10, 1962), P. 7. FR VII 29413.

SÉNART, PHILIPPE. LE FEUILLETON LITTÉRAIRE. ALBERT CAMUS. 'LA   3056
     CHUTE'. ARTS, NO. 573 (JUNE 20-26, 1956), P. 7. CR 974.

SÉNART, PHILIPPE. LE FEUILLETON LITTÉRAIRE. ALBERT CAMUS.   3057
     L'EXIL ET LE ROYAUME. ARTS, NO. 615 (APRIL 17-23, 1957),
     P. 6. CR 1067.

SÉNART, PHILIPPE. ALBERT CAMUS SUCCÈDE À SULLY PRUDHOMME.   3058
     ARTS, NO. 641 (OCT. 23-29, 1957), P. 2.

SÉNART, PHILIPPE. CAMUS ET LE JUSTE MILIEU. TABLE RONDE, NOS.   3059
     174-175 (JULY-AUG. 1962), PP. 112-115. PMLA 7991 (1962).

SÉRANT, PAUL. LÀ EST LA QUESTION. PARISIENNE, NO. 16 (APRIL   3060
     1954), PP. 458-464. BO 78, FR VII 10781.

SÉRANT, PAUL. LES IDÉES-RÉALISME ET CIVILISATION. REVUE DES   3061
     DEUX MONDES, NO. 22 (NOV. 15, 1957), PP. 336-344. CR
     1068, FR VII 17343, KL I 273.

SERONI, ADRIANO. ALBERT CAMUS DALLA RIVOLTA AL CONFORMISMO.   3062
     RINASCITA, VOL. 17, NO. 2 (FEB. 1960), PP. 141-143. KL II
     387.

SÉROUYA, H. LES PHILOSOPHIES DE L'EXISTENCE. UNE NOUVELLE   3063
     CONCEPTION DE LA PHILOSOPHIE. PARIS. LIBRAIRIE
     FISCHBACHER, 1957. KL I 232.

SHAANAN, A. BEGAYHINOM SHEL HAHOVEH, AL ALBERT CAMUS (IN THE   3064
     HELL OF OUR PRESENT. ABOUT ALBERT CAMUS). MOZNAYIM, NO. 5
     (1958), PP. 387-389.

SHAANAN, A. HANEFILAH SHEL CAMUS (CAMUS' CHUTE). DAVAR, JUNE   3065
     11, 1959, P. 5.

SHAANAN, A. MITOH LABAT HAGAYHINOM (OUT OF HELL'S LAVA).   3066
     DAVAR, JUNE 19, 1959, P. 5.

SHAANAN, A. ALBERT CAMUS, HAMITOS SHEL SISYPHUS (ALBERT CAMUS: 3067
     THE SISYPHUS MYTH). DAVAR, JAN. 8, 1960.

SHARP, WILLIAM L. BOOKS IN REVIEW. 'CALIGULA AND THREE OTHER   3068
     PLAYS' BY ALBERT CAMUS. TRANSLATED BY STUART GILBERT.
     (NEW YORK. KNOPF, 1958). EDUCATIONAL THEATRE JOURNAL, VOL.
     11, NO. 2 (MAY 1959), PP. 160-161.

SHARP, WILLIAM. BOOKS IN REVIEW. 'CAMUS' BY GERMAINE BRÉE.   3069
     (RUTGERS UNIV. PRESS). EDUCATIONAL THEATRE JOURNAL, VOL.
     11, NO. 3 (OCT. 1959), PP. 245-246.

SHATTUCK, ROGER. TWO INSIDE NARRATIVES: BILLY BUDD AND   3070
     L'ÉTRANGER . TEXAS STUDIES IN LITERATURE AND LANGUAGE,
     VOL. 4, NO. 3 (FALL 1962), PP. 314-320. PMLA 5340 (1961).

SHATTUCK, ROGER. LOVE AND LAUGHTER. SURREALISM REAPPRAISED.   3071
     ARTS IN SOCIETY, VOL. 3, NO. 2 (1965), PP. 149-163 (CAMUS
     REF. PP. 150, 154, 157).

SHEED, WILFRID. A SOBER CONSCIENCE. JUBILEE, VOL. 8, NO. 12   3072

(APRIL 1961), PP. 48-50. FR VII 29338.

3073   SHEED, WILFRID. A SOBER CONSCIENCE. IN BRÉE, GERMAINE,
       CAMUS, A COLLECTION OF CRITICAL ESSAYS, PP. 26-30. FR VII
       29338. SEE NO. 1293. REPRINT OF NO. 3072.

3074   SHOIBESH, S. ALBERT CAMUS: L'HOMME RÉVOLTÉ, PARIS, 1951.
       IYUN,   VOL. 3, (JUNE 1952), PP. 173-175.

3075   SICARD, J. P. CHRONIQUE LITTÉRAIRE. LE MYTHE DE SISYPHE.
       RENAISSANCES,   VOL. 001, NO. 8 (1944), PP. 131-134. BO
       314, CR 546, FR VII 2711.

3076   SIEGMUND, GEORG. PHILOSOPHIE DES SELBSTMORDES. EINE
       AUSEINANDERSETZUNG MIT DEM FRANZÖSISCHEN EXISTENZIALISTEN
       ALBERT CAMUS. SEELSORGER, VOL. 31, (1960-61), PP. 52-60.
       BDZ 121-321 (1960).

3077   SIEGMUND, GEORG. DIE BEICHTE DES ATHEISTEN ZU ALBERT CAMUS 'DER
       FALL'. BEGEGNUNG,   VOL. 17, NO. 1 (JAN. 1962), PP. 7-11.
       BDZ 125-310 (1962).

3078   SIGAUX, GILBERT. AVEC ALBERT CAMUS. PREUVES, NO. 35 (JAN.
       1954), PP. 78-80. BO 52, CR 906, FR VII 11241.

3079   SIGAUX, GILBERT. SÉRÉNITÉ D'UN INSTANT. ALBERT CAMUS. L'EXIL ET
       LE ROYAUME. PREUVES,   NO. 77 (JULY 1957), PP. 72-73. CR
       1069, FR VII 17344.

3080   SIGAUX, GILBERT. UNE OEUVRE EN DÉBAT DEVANT LA NOUVELLE
       GÉNÉRATION. LES VIVANTS QUI ME SONT NÉCESSAIRES. FIGARO
       LITTÉRAIRE,   VOL. 12, NO. 601 (OCT. 26, 1957), P. 7.
       FITCH. SEE NO. 3251.

3081   SIGAUX, GILBERT. ALBERT CAMUS, PRIX NOBEL. TERRE RETROUVÉE,
       NO. 3 (NOV. 4, 1957). BR, CR 1069 BIS, FR VII 21420.

3082   SIGAUX, GILBERT. AU MILIEU DU CHEMIN... FIGARO LITTÉRAIRE,
       VOL. 15, NO. 716 (JAN. 9, 1960), P. 5. FR VII 26378, KL II
       395.

3083   SIGEAN, LOUIS. MANUEL DE RÉVOLTE POUR LE FRANÇAIS MOYEN.
       LIBERTÉ DE L'ESPRIT, VOL. 4, NO. 28 (FEB. 1952), PP.
       60-61. BO 227, FR VII 7716.

3084   SILVAIRE, ANDRÉ. LE THÉÂTRE. LE FEU ET LA CENDRE. ALBERT CAMUS,
       LES JUSTES (THÉÂTRE HÉBERTOT). LETTRES, VOL. 4, NO. 13
       (THIRD QUARTER, 1950), PP. 75-76. FITCH.

3085   SIMIOT, BERNARD. LE THÉÂTRE. 'L'ÉTAT DE SIÈGE', DE M. ALBERT
       CAMUS. HOMMES ET MONDES, VOL. 7, NO. 29 (DEC. 1948), PP.
       712-716. BO 447, CR 678.

3086   SIMON, ÉMILE. UNE RENCONTRE AVEC CAMUS. REVUE DU CAIRE, VOL.
       11, NO. 111 (JUNE 1948), PP. 271-278. FR VII 26380.

3087   SIMON, ÉMILE. UNE MÉTAPHYSIQUE TRAGIQUE. PARIS. GALLIMARD
       (COLLECTION ESPOIR), 1951. BO 146.

3088   SIMON, JOHN K. THE GLANCE OF IDIOTS. THE NOVEL OF THE ABSURD.
       YALE FRENCH STUDIES, NO. 25 (SPRING 1960), PP. 111-119.

BUL. SIGN 16-19-9948 (1962), FR VII 23568, KL II 391.

SIMON, JOHN K. CAMUS' KINGDOM. THE NATIVE HOST AND AN UNWANTED   3089
    GUEST. STUDIES IN SHORT FICTION,   VOL. 1, NO. 4 (SUMMER
    1964), PP. 289-291. PMLA 8625 (1964).

SIMON, PIERRE-HENRI. CAMUS OU LE RETOUR À L'HOMME. REVUE   3090
    GÉNÉRALE BELGE, NO. 47 (SEPT. 1949), PP. 767-777. BO 142,
    CR 723.

SIMON, PIERRE-HENRI. L'HOMME EN PROCÈS. NEUCHÂTEL. À LA   3091
    BACONNIÈRE, 1949. ALBERT CAMUS OU L'INVENTION DE LA
    JUSTICE , PP. 93-123. BO 218, BR, CR 482, FR VII 2082.

SIMON, PIERRE-HENRI. LES TÉMOINS DE L'HOMME. LA CONDITION   3092
    HUMAINE DANS LA LITTÉRATURE CONTEMPORAINE. PARIS. A.
    COLIN, 1951. ALBERT CAMUS ET L'HOMME , PP. 175-193. BO
    147, BR, CR 483, FR VII 5178.

SIMON, PIERRE-HENRI. ALBERT CAMUS ENTRE DIEU ET L'HISTOIRE.   3093
    TERRE HUMAINE, VOL. 2, NO. 2 (FEB. 1952), PP. 8-21. BO
    115, CR 840 BIS, FR VII 13320.

SIMON, PIERRE-HENRI. SARTRE ET CAMUS DEVANT L'HISTOIRE. TERRE   3094
    HUMAINE, NO. 23 (NOV. 1952), PP. 2-20. BO 286, FR VII
    14553.

SIMON, PIERRE-HENRI. L'ESPRIT ET L'HISTOIRE, ESSAI SUR LA   3095
    CONSCIENCE HISTORIQUE DANS LA LITTÉRATURE DU VINGTIÈME
    SIÈCLE. CAHIERS DE LA FONDATION NATIONALE DES SCIENCES
    POLITIQUES, NO. 64. PARIS. A. COLIN, 1954. CHAPTER V.
    POINTS DE VUE EXISTENTIALISTES SUR L'HISTOIRE. ALBERT
    CAMUS RENVERSE UNE IDOLE, PP. 182-193. LE DIALOGUE DE
    SARTRE ET DE CAMUS, PP. 193-208. BO 238, BO 285, FR VII
    12667.

SIMON, PIERRE-HENRI. HISTOIRE DE LA LITTÉRATURE FRANÇAISE AU   3096
    VINGTIÈME SIÈCLE, 1900-1950. PARIS. A. COLIN, 1956.
    ALBERT CAMUS, DU NIHILISME À L'HUMANISME, PP. 183-187. CR
    481.

SIMON, PIERRE-HENRI. L'ATHÉISME CONTEMPORAIN. GENEVA.   3097
    ÉDITIONS LABOR ET FIDES, 1956. LA NÉGATION DE DIEU DANS
    LA LITTÉRATURE FRANÇAISE CONTEMPORAINE , PP. 37-65.

SIMON, PIERRE-HENRI. ALBERT CAMUS DEVANT LE PÉCHÉ. TÉMOIGNAGE   3098
    CHRÉTIEN, NO. 623 (JUNE 15, 1956), P. 5. P BR, CR 974
    BIS.

SIMON, PIERRE-HENRI. THÉÂTRE ET DESTIN. LA SIGNIFICATION DE LA   3099
    RENAISSANCE DRAMATIQUE EN FRANCE AU VINGTIÈME SIECLE.
    PARIS. A. COLIN, 1959. CHAPTER VIII.   ALBERT CAMUS ET LA
    JUSTICE , PP. 191-211. FR VII 20994, KL II 389.

SIMON, PIERRE-HENRI. PRÉSENCE DE CAMUS. BRUSSELS. LA   3100
    RENAISSANCE DU LIVRE, 1961. FR VII 26299, PMLA 7384
    (1962).

3101   SIMON, PIERRE-HENRI. CARNETS, D'ALBERT CAMUS. MONDE, VOL. 15,
        NO. 709 (MAY 17-23, 1962), P. 10.

3102   SIMON, PIERRE-HENRI. CAMUS ET SAINT-EXUPÉRY POUSSÉS EN ENFER.
        MONDE, VOL. 15, NO. 717 (JULY 12-18, 1962), P. 10.

3103   SIMON, PIERRE-HENRI. LE PREMIER VOLUME DE LA PLÉIADE CONSACRÉ À
        ALBERT CAMUS. MONDE, VOL. 20, NO. 5622 (FEB. 13, 1963),
        PP. 10-11. FR VII 33979.

3104   SIMON, PIERRE-HENRI. LE PREMIER VOLUME DE LA PLÉIADE CONSACRÉ À
        ALBERT CAMUS. MONDE (SÉLECTION HEBDOMADAIRE), VOL. 16,
        NO. 748 (FEB. 14-20, 1963), P. 10.

3105   SIMON, PIERRE-HENRI. LE COMBAT CONTRE LES MANDARINS. IN
        ANONYMOUS, CAMUS, PP. 107-156. SEE NO. 940.

3106   SIMON, PIERRE-HENRI. LANGAGE ET DESTIN. DIAGNOSTIC DES LETTRES
        FRANÇAISES CONTEMPORAINES. PARIS, LA RENAISSANCE DU LIVRE,
        1966. LES 'CARNETS' D'ALBERT CAMUS, PP. 133-139.

3107   SIMONOV, KONSTANTIN. THREE STORIES. PRAVDA, VOL. 3, NO. 2
        (1958), P. 3.

3108   SIMONOV, KONSTANTIN. THREE STORIES. (EXCERPT FROM 'PRAVDA')
        CURRENT DIGEST OF THE SOVIET PRESS, VOL. 10, NO. 9 (APRIL
        9, 1958), PP. 23-24.

3109   SIMPSON, LURLINE V. TENSIONS IN THE WORK OF ALBERT CAMUS.
        MODERN LANGUAGE JOURNAL, VOL. 38, NO. 4 (APRIL 1954), PP.
        186-190. BO 246, FR VII 11242.

3110   SMITH, ANNETTE. ALGERIA IN THE WORK OF ALBERT CAMUS. CLAREMONT
        QUARTERLY, VOL. 7, NO. 3 (SPRING 1960), PP. 5-13. PMLA
        7385 (1962).

3111   SMITH, WINIFRED. ALBERT CAMUS. 'LE MALENTENDU'. 'CALIGULA'.
        BOOKS ABROAD, VOL. 22, NO. 2 (SPRING 1948), PP. 157-158.
        CR 679.

3112   SMITH, WINIFRED. ALBERT CAMUS. TWO PLAYS: 'CALIGULA', 'CROSS
        PURPOSE'. BOOKS ABROAD, VOL. 23, NO. 2 (SPRING 1949), P.
        188. CR 724.

3113   SMITH, WINIFRED. ALBERT CAMUS. 'LES JUSTES'. BOOKS ABROAD,
        VOL. 25, NO. 1 (WINTER 1951), P. 29. CR 797.

3114   SÖDERGARD, ÖSTEN. UN ASPECT DE LA PROSE DE CAMUS. LE RYTHME
        TERNAIRE. STUDIA NEOPHILOLOGICA, VOL. 31, NO. 1 (1959),
        PP. 128-148. BFZ 48-280 (1961), FR VII 21421, KL II 390.

3115   SÖDERGARD, ÖSTEN. FRANSKA SNITT, STUDIER I FRANSK 1800-OCH
        1900-TALS LITTERATUR. STOCKHOLM. GEBERS, 1961. FR VII
        28368.

3116   SOFER, JOHANNES. ALBERT CAMUS (1913-1960). STIMMEN DER ZEIT,
        VOL. 165, NO. 6 (MARCH 1960), PP. 433-450. BDZ 120-311
        (1960), FR VII 26381, PMLA 6851 (1961).

3117   SOLIER, RENÉ DE. SENS DU JOURNALISME CRITIQUE. NOUVELLE REVUE
        FRANÇAISE, VOL. 8, NO. 87 (MARCH 1960), PP. 476-479. FR

VII 23575, KL II 389.

SOLSONA, BRAULIO. ALBERT CAMUS Y EL PROBLEMA DE ARGELIA.   3118
EXCELSIOR, (JULY 1958). BR, CR 1120 BIS.

SONNENFELD, ALBERT. ALBERT CAMUS AS DRAMATIST. THE SOURCES OF   3119
HIS FAILURE. TULANE DRAMA REVIEW, VOL. 5, NO. 4 (JUNE
1961), PP. 106-123. FR VII 26382, PMLA 7386 (1962).

SORENSON, SUSAN M. AN EXISTENTIAL UTOPIA. MINNESOTA REVIEW,   3120
VOL. 4, NO. 3 (SPRING 1964), PP. 356-364. PMLA 8626
(1964).

SORONDO JORGE AUGUSTO. CALÍGULA DESDE FUERA. NUMERO, VOL. 1,   3121
NO. 5 (NOV.-DEC. 1949), PP. 467-469. FR VII 34025.

SOULAIROL, JEAN. TRANSPOSITION ET SUGGESTION. DIVAN, VOL. 39,   3122
NO. 264 (OCT.-DEC. 1947), PP. 179-186. BO 135, CR 629.

SOULIÉ, MICHEL. ALBERT CAMUS ET LA RECHERCHE DU BONHEUR.   3123
LETRAS, NO. 13 (1964), PP. 71-95.

SPAAK, CLAUDE. LE THÉÂTRE À PARIS. MESSAGE, NO. 50 (DEC.-JAN.   3124
1945-1946), PP. 57-58. FR VII 34026.

SPECTOR, ROBERT DONALD. KAFKA AND CAMUS. SOME EXAMPLES OF   3125
RHYTHM IN THE NOVEL. KENTUCKY FOREIGN LANGUAGE QUARTERLY,
VOL. 5, NO. 4 (1958), PP. 205-211.

SPECTOR, ROBERT DONALD. 'EXILE AND THE KINGDOM' BY ALBERT   3126
CAMUS. VENTURE, VOL. 3, NOS. 1-2 (1959), PP. 73-75.

SPECTOR, ROBERT DONALD. CAMUS' ILLUMINATING ANSWERS TO   3127
SEARCHING QUESTIONS. (LATER PUBLISHED COMPLETE IN VENTURE.)
NEW YORK HERALD TRIBUNE BOOK REVIEW, VOL. 36, NO. 29
(FEB. 21, 1960), P. 1. SEE NO. 3129.

SPECTOR, ROBERT DONALD. ALBERT CAMUS' LAST DRAMA. NEW YORK   3128
HERALD TRIBUNE BOOK REVIEW, VOL. 36, NO. 32 (MARCH 13,
1960), P. 10.

SPECTOR, ROBERT DONALD. ALBERT CAMUS, 1913-1960. A FINAL   3129
INTERVIEW. VENTURE, VOL. 3, NO. 4 (1960), PP. 26-38. FR
VII 26383, PMLA 6852 (1961).

SPECTOR, ROBERT DONALD. MELVILLE'S 'BARTLEBY' AND THE ABSURD.   3130
NINETEENTH CENTURY FICTION, VOL. 16, NO. 2 (SEPT. 1961),
PMLA 5040 (1962).

SPENDER, STEPHEN. ALBERT CAMUS, CITIZEN OF THE WORLD. THE   3131
PLAGUE. NEW YORK TIMES BOOK REVIEW, AUG. 1, 1948,PP. 1,
20. BO 428.

SPENS, WILLY DE. CAMUS ET LE PESSIMISME. TABLE RONDE, NO. 165   3132
(OCT. 1961), PP. 128-133. BUL SIGN 16-19-24253, FR VII
26384, PMLA 7387 (1962).

SPERBER, M. THE PILGRIMAGE OF A THINKING MAN. THE REBEL. NEW   3133
YORK TIMES BOOK REVIEW, JAN. 10, 1954, PP. 1, 20. BO 532.

SPIEGELBERG, HERBERT. FRENCH EXISTENTIALISM, ITS SOCIAL   3134
PHILOSOPHIES. KENYON REVIEW, VOL. 16, NO. 3 (SUMMER 1954),

PP. 446-462. BO 177.

3135   SPIGT, P. DE IRONIE VAN ALBERT CAMUS.   NIEUWE STEM,   VOL. 18,
       NO. 5 (MAY 1963), PP. 259-269.   PMLA 7983 (1964).

3136   SPIRE, G. LA PENSÉE D'ALBERT CAMUS.   TRAVAIL ET DOCUMENTATION,
       NOS. 5-6 (1947), PP. 33-36.   BO 136, CR 630.

3137   SPYCHER, PETER C. ALBERT CAMUS   L'ÉTRANGER, EINE STUDIE ÜBER
       DEN EINZIGEN CHRISTUS, DEN WIR VERDIENEN.   NEUEREN
       SPRACHEN,   VOL. 14, NO. 4 (APRIL 1965), PP. 159-180.

3138   STAELS, J. NATIONAAL THEATER EN 'EXISTENTIALISTISCH' TOONEEL TE
       PARIJS.   SPECTATOR (BRUSSELS),   (DEC. 30, 1945), P. 10.   CR
       547.

3139   STÅHLE, NILS K. NOBEL ET LES PRIX NOBEL.   REVUE FRANÇAISE DE
       L'ÉLITE EUROPÉENNE,   NO. 125 (JAN. 1961), PP. 47-53.

3140   STANFORD, DEREK. ALBERT CAMUS.   CONTEMPORARY REVIEW,   VOL. 193,
       NO. 1108 (APRIL 1958), PP. 191-195.   BFZ 45-278, FR VII
       19449, KL I 272.

3141   STANGERUP, HENRIK. DIGTEREN OG SOLEN.   SAMMENHAENGEN I ALBERT
       CAMUS FORFATTERSKAB.   PERSPEKTIV (COPENHAGEN),   VOL. 9, NO.
       4 (DEC. 1961), PP. 23-28.   PMLA 7992 (1963).

3142   STANGERUP, HENRIK. DIGTEREN OG SOLEN.   SAMMENHAENGEN I ALBERT
       CAMUS FORFATTERSKAB. (II).   PERSPEKTIV (COPENHAGEN),   VOL.
       9, NO. 5 (FEB. 1962), PP. 41-46.   PMLA 7992 (1963).

3143   STAROBINSKI, JEAN. DANS LE PREMIER SILENCE.   NOUVELLE REVUE
       FRANÇAISE,   VOL. 8, NO. 87 (MARCH 1960), PP. 496-500.   FR
       VII 23575, KL II 388.

3144   STAROBINSKI, JEAN. ALBERT CAMUS AND THE PLAGUE.   CIBA
       SYMPOSIUM,   VOL. 10, NO. 2 (1962), PP. 62-70.

3145   STARRATT, ROBERT J. AN ANALYSIS OF ALBERT CAMUS 'THE FALL'.
       CITHARA,   VOL. 1 (1961), PP. 27-38.   PMLA 7389 (1962).

3146   STAVROU, C. N. CONRAD, CAMUS, AND SISYPHUS.   AUDIENCE,   VOL. 7,
       NO. 1 (WINTER 1960), PP. 80-96.   PMLA 3866 (1961).

3147   STEFFEN, GÜNTHER. DIE FRANZÖSISCHE LINKE.   MYTHOS UND REALITAT.
       MERKUR,   VOL. 10, NO. 5 (MAY 1956), PP. 471-481.   FR VII
       14877.

3148   STEIGER, VIKTOR. JAHRESBERICHT DER AARGAUISCHEN KANTONSSCHULE,
       1951-52.   KANTONSCHULE, 1951-52.   'LA PESTE' D'ALBERT
       CAMUS. ESSAI D'INTERPRETATION, PP. 53-74.   BO 438, FR VII
       7692.

3149   STÉPHANE, R. 'LA PESTE'.   REVUE INTERNATIONALE,   VOL. 3, NO. 16
       (JUNE 1947), PP. 464-468.   BO 401, CR 631.

3150   STÉPHANE, ROGER. À DÉFAUT DE MALRAUX...   FRANCE-OBSERVATEUR,
       VOL. 8, NO. 389 (OCT. 24, 1957), P. 18.

3151   STERN, ALFRED. CONSIDERATIONS OF ALBERT CAMUS' DOCTRINE.
       PERSONALIST,   VOL. 41, NO. 4 (FALL 1960). PP. 448-457.   BUL
       SIGN 15-19-20062, FR VII 23688, PMLA 6853 (1961).

STERN, ALFRED. NOTICES NECROLOGIQUES, ALBERT CAMUS (1913-1960).   3152
    REVUE PHILOSOPHIQUE DE LA FRANCE ET DE L'ÉTRANGER, VOL.
    150, NO. 3 (JULY-SEPT. 1960), PP. 423-424. KL II 395.

STOCKWELL, H. C. R. ALBERT CAMUS. CAMBRIDGE JOURNAL, VOL. 7,   3153
    NO. 11 (AUG. 1954), PP. 690-704. BO 53, FR VII 11243.

STOLPE, SVEN. ALBERT CAMUS OCH •VÅR TIDS HJÄLTE . NYA ARGUS,   3154
    NO. 21 (DEC. 16, 1956), PP. 307-308. FR VII 34027.

STOLTZFUS, BEN. CAMUS AND THE MEANING OF REVOLT. MODERN   3155
    FICTION STUDIES, VOL. 10, NO. 3 (AUTUMN 1964), PP.
    293-302.

STORZER, GERALD H. LA GENÈSE DU HÉROS DE L'ETRANGER. FRENCH   3156
    REVIEW, VOL. 37, NO. 5 (APRIL 1964), PP. 542-553. PMLA
    8627 (1964).

STOURZH, GERALD. THE UNFORGIVABLE SIN. AN INTERPRETATION OF   3157
    THE FALL . CHICAGO REVIEW, VOL. 15, NO. 1 (SUMMER 1961),
    PP. 45-57. FR VII 26385, PMLA 7390 (1962).

STRATEN, HANS VAN. CAMUS' AFREKENING MET DE OORLOG. LA PESTE.   3158
    PCDIUM (AMSTERDAM), VOL. 1, NO. 3 (DEC. 19, 1947), PP.
    165-169. BO 402, CR 632.

STRAUSS, WALTER A. ALBERT CAMUS'S 'CALIGULA'. ANCIENT SOURCES   3159
    AND MODERN PARALLELS. CAMBRIDGE. HARVARD UNIVERSITY,
    1949. BO 372, BR, CR 484, FR VII 2693.

STRAUSS, WALTER A. ALBERT CAMUS' 'CALIGULA'. ANCIENT SOURCES   3160
    AND MODERN PARALLELS. COMPARATIVE LITERATURE, VOL. 3, NO.
    2 (SPRING 1951), PP. 160-173. CR 798, FR VII 5762.

STRAUSS, WALTER A. ALBERT CAMUS, STONE-MASON. MODERN LANGUAGE   3161
    NOTES, VOL. 77, NO. 3 (MAY 1962), PP. 268-281. PMLA 7993
    (1963).

STREM, GEORGE G. THE THEME OF REBELLION IN THE WORKS OF CAMUS   3162
    AND DOSTOIEVSKY. REVUE DE LITTÉRATURE COMPARÉE, VOL. 40,
    NO. 2 (APRIL-JUNE 1966), PP. 246-257.

STROMBERG, KJELL. L'INOUBLIABLE MESSAGE DU POÈTE. FIGARO,   3163
    VOL. 134, NO. 4770 (JAN. 6, 1960), P. 4. FITCH.

STUART, ROBERT LEE. THE WRITER-IN-WAITING. CHRISTIAN CENTURY,   3164
    VOL. 82, NO. 20 (MAY 19, 1965), PP. 647-649.

SUCHODOLSKI, B. TRADYCJE I PERSPEKTYWY PRZYMIERZA TECHNIKI I   3165
    HUMANISTYKI. (TRADITIONS ET PERSPECTIVES DE L'ALLIANCE
    TECHNIQUE-SCIENCES HUMAINES). KULTURA SPOLECZENSTWO, VOL.
    VOL. 5, NO. 3 (1961), PP. 3-19. BUL SIGN 16-19-8441.

SUFFERT, GEORGES. LE DERNIER GRAND LIVRE ROMANTIQUE. EXPRESS,   3166
    NO. 647 (NOV. 7, 1963), P. 40.

SURER, PAUL. ÉTUDES SUR LE THÉÂTRE FRANÇAIS CONTEMPORAIN. LE   3167
    THÉÂTRE DEPUIS LA LIBÉRATION. INFORMATION LITTÉRAIRE,
    VOL. 13, NO. 2 (MARCH-APRIL 1961), PP. 54-62. BUL SIGN
    16-19-16160.

3168   SURER, PAUL. ÉTUDES SUR LE THÉÂTRE FRANÇAIS CONTEMPORAIN. XI.
        LE THÉÂTRE DEPUIS LA LIBÉRATION (SUITE ET FIN).
        INFORMATION LITTÉRAIRE,   VOL. 13, NO. 4 (SEPT.-OCT. 1961),
        PP. 145-153. BUL SIGN 16-19-16160, FR VII 25831, FR VII
        27883.

3169   SÜSKIND, W. E. DIE PEST ALS SYMBOL.   EPISCHES THEATER NACH DEM
        BERÜHMTEN ROMAN VON CAMUS.   WIRTSCHAFTS-ZEITUNG
        (STUTTGART),   VOL. 5, NO. 50 (1950), P. 15.   BO 453.

3170   SWANSON, ROY ARTHUR. HEART OF REASON.   MINNEAPOLIS. T. S.
        DENISON, 1963.   CHAPTER IX. ALBERT CAMUS. COUNTERSTATEMENT
        TO DESPAIR, PP. 168-186, ET PASSIM.

3171   SYLVESTRE, GUY. ALBERT CAMUS, JOURNALISTE.   REVUE DOMINICAINE,
        VOL. 1, NO. 57 (JAN. 1951), PP. 34-41.   BO 100, FR VII
        13321.

3172   SYPHER, WYLIE. LOSS OF SELF IN MODERN LITERATURE AND ART.   NEW
        YORK. RANDOM HOUSE, 1962.   SCATTERED REFERENCES (NO INDEX).
        FRENCH VII 31598.

3173   SZASZ, THOMAS S. PORTRAIT OF A SECULAR MORALIST.   NEW REPUBLIC,
        VOL. 153, NO. 22 (NOV. 27, 1965), PP. 32-33.

3174   TACCA, OSCAR ERNESTO. EL ESPIRITU MEDITERRÁNEO EN LA OBRA DE
        ALBERT CAMUS.   UNIVERSIDAD (ARGENTINA),   NO. 37, (JAN.-JUNE
        1958), PP. 83-114.   BUL SIGN 14-13286.

3175   T., O. E. (TACCA, OSCAR ERNESTO). ALBERT CAMUS.   UNIVERSIDAD
        (ARGENTINA),   NO. 43 (JAN.-MARCH 1960), PP. 199-200.

3176   TAHA-HUSSEIN, M. LE TOMBEAU D'ALBERT CAMUS.   REVUE DU CAIRE,
        VOL. 44, NO. 237 (MAY 1960), PP. 393-396.   FR VII 23689.
        SEE NO. 3259.

3177   TANK, KURT L. EXPERIMENT MIT DER PEST.   KANN CAMUS UNS HELFEN?
        SONNTAGSBLATT,   VOL. 2, NO. 36 (1949), PP. 3-4.   BDZ
        100-256 (1950), BO 434, CR 725.

3178   TANS, J. A. G. ALBERT CAMUS. HEILIGHEID ZONDER GOD.
        KULTUURLEVEN (ANTWERPEN),   VOL. 18, NO. 9 (NOV. 1951), PP.
        718-728.   BO 172, CR 799.

3179   TANS, J. A. G. INTRODUCTION. IN L'EXIL ET LE ROYAUME.   SEE NO.
        302.

3180   TANS, J. A. G. LA POÉTIQUE DE L'EAU ET DE LA LUMIÈRE D'APRÈS
        L'OEUVRE D'ALBERT CAMUS.   IN GUIRAUD, PIERRE, ET AL. STYLE
        ET LITTÉRATURE, PP. 75-95.   SEE NO. 1927.

3181   TAOS, MARGUERITE. HOMMAGE À ALBERT CAMUS.   SIMOUN,   VOL. 8, NO.
        31 (JULY 1960), PP. 22-24.   FR VII 23573, KL II 395.

3182   TAUBMAN, ROBERT. ALBERT CAMUS. MORALIST.   SPECTATOR,   VOL.
        204, NO. 6870 (FEB. 26, 1960), P. 293.

3183   TAVARES DE ARANDA, SALETTE. A PROPÓSITO DE ALBERT CAMUS.
        OCIDENTE,   VOL. 54, NO. 237 (JAN. 1958), PP. 17-21.   CR
        1122.

TEGENBOSCH, LAMBERT. ALBERT CAMUS SCHAKELT TERUG. 'L'ETE'.   3184
    ROEPING (TILBERG),   VOL. 30, NO. 7 (1954), PP. 324-329. BO
    542, CR 907.

TEMKINE, RAYMONDE. LA PART DU DIABLE CHEZ CAMUS. POUR L'ART,   3185
    NO. 70 (JAN.-FEB. 1960), PP. 25-27. FITCH

TERNOO, E. LE MYTHE DU RÉVOLTÉ. GIDS (AMSTERDAM),   VOL. 118,   3186
    NO. 2 (NOV. 1955), PP. 319-328. BFZ 39-279 (1954-56), BO
    536, CR 922.

TERRACINI, ENRICO. L'AMICO ALBERT CAMUS. MONDO,   VOL. 17, NO.   3187
    25 (JUNE 22, 1965), PP. 9-10.

TERRIEN, SAMUEL. CHRISTIANITY'S DEBT TO A MODERN PAGAN. ALBERT   3188
    CAMUS (1913-1960). UNION SEMINARY QUARTERLY REVIEW,   VOL.
    15, NO. 3 (MARCH 1960), PP. 185-194.

TERZA, DAUTE DELLA. LA CHUTE. BELFAGOR,   VOL. 12, NO. 3 (MAY   3189
    1957), PP. 346-350. KL I 274.

TÊTE, ALAIN. CAMUS, JAMES DEAN DE LA PHILOSOPHIE.   3190
    C'EST-À-DIRE,   VOL. 5, NO. 27 (FEB. 1960), PP. 49-50.

TEULER, GABRIEL. LE MYTHE DE SISYPHE. NEW REPUBLIC,   NO. 29   3191
    (SEPT. 19, 1955).

TEULER, GABRIEL. SUR TROIS OEUVRES D'ALBERT CAMUS. REVUE DE LA   3192
    MÉDITERRANÉE,   VOL. 3, NO. 12 (MARCH-APRIL 1946), PP.
    197-211. BO 291, CR 577, FR VII 2712.

THEISS, RAIMUND. ALBERT CAMUS' RÜCKKEHR ZU SISYPHUS.   3193
    ROMANISCHE FORSCHUNGEN,   VOL. 70, NOS. 1-2 (1958), PP.
    66-90. BDZ 117-307 (1958), FR VII 19451, KL I 273.

THIÉBAUT, MARCEL. LES LIVRES DU MOIS. 'L'ÉTÉ'. ANNALES,   VOL.   3194
    61, NO. 45 (JULY 1954), P. 22. CR 908.

THIÉBAUT, MARCEL. LE THÉÂTRE EN FRANCE DE 1939 A 1946. REVUE   3195
    INTERNATIONALE DE THÉÂTRE,   VOL. 1 (OCT.-DEC. 1947), PP.
    41-47. FR VII 32819.

THIÉBAUT, MARCEL. LA PESTE. REVUE DE PARIS,   VOL. 54, NO. 8   3196
    (AUG. 1947), PP. 158-161. BO 403, CR 633.

THIÉBAUT, MARCEL. L'ENVERS ET L'ENDROIT. REVUE DE PARIS,   VOL.   3197
    65, NO. 6 (JUNE 1958), PP. 139-142. CR 1123, FR VII 19450,
    KL I 273.

THIEBERGER, RICHARD. RANDBEMERKUNG ZUR SUBJONCTIVITIS-KEINE   3198
    GRAMMATIKALISCHE ABHANDLUNG. ANTARES,   VOL. 5, NO. 8 (DEC.
    1957), PP. 36-37.

THIEBERGER, RICHARD. THEATER. I. DAS ABENTEUER IONESCU. II.   3199
    EIN NEUES THEATER IN PARIS-CAMUS INSZENIERT SEINEN
    CALIGULA . ANTARES, VOL. 6, NO. 2 (MARCH 1958), PP.
    143-146. FR VII 19142.

THIEBERGER, RICHARD. EIN NEUES THEATER IN PARIS, CAMUS   3200
    INSZENIERT SEINEN CALIGULA. ANTARES, VOL. 6, NO. 2 (MARCH
    1958), PP. 145-146.

3201 THIEBERGER, RICHARD. ALBERT CAMUS. ANTARES, VOL. 6, NO. 6
(SEPT. 1958), PP. 546-547.

3202 THIEBERGER, RICHARD. ALBERT CAMUS, SEIN WERK UND SEIN
KÜNSTLERTUM. UNIVERSITAS, ZEITSCHRIFT FÜR WISSENSCHAFT,
KUNST UND LITERATUR, VOL. 14, NO. 1 (JAN. 1959), PP.
21-30. BDZ 118-290 (1958), CR 1149, FR VII 19452, FR VII
21422, KL II 388.

3203 THIEBERGER, RICHARD. THEATER. ANTARES, VOL. 7, NO. 4 (JUNE
1959), PP. 346-349.

3204 THIEBERGER, RICHARD. PREFACE TO LES JUSTES, ALBERT CAMUS.
STUTTGART. KLETT, 1960. PP. 3-6.

3205 THIEBERGER, RICHARD. ALBERT CAMUS, EINE EINFÜHRUNG IN SEIN
DICHTERISCHES WERK. FRANKFURT-AM-MAIN. MORITZ DIESTERWEG
(DIE NEUEREN SPRACHEN, BEIHEFT 8), N. D.(1960).

3206 THIEBERGER, RICHARD. ALBERT CAMUS. FRANKFURT-AM-MAIN.
DIESTERWEG, 1961. PMLA 7391 (1962).

3207 THIEBERGER, RICHARD (EDITOR). CONFIGURATION CRITIQUE D'ALBERT
CAMUS, II. CAMUS DEVANT LA CRITIQUE DE LANGUE ALLEMANDE.
REVUE DES LETTRES MODERNES, NOS. 90-93 (WINTER 1963), PP.
1-208. SEE NO. 1217, 2001, 2114, 2500, 2532, 2656, 2659,
2769, 2842, 2908, 3027, 3208, 3209.

3208 THIEBERGER, RICHARD. L'ALLEMAGNE DEVANT CAMUS. REVUE DES
LETTRES MODERNES, NOS. 90-93 (WINTER 1963), PP. 13-16.
PMLA 8608 (1964). SEE NO. 3207.

3209 THIEBERGER, RICHARD. CRITIQUE ALLEMANDE DE CAMUS. SÉLECTION
BIBLIOGRAPHIQUE. REVUE DES LETTRES MODERNES, NOS. 90-93
(WINTER 1963), PP. 201-207. PMLA 8608 (1964). SEE NO.
3207.

3210 THIEBERGER, RICHARD. ALBERT CAMUS SEIT SEINEM TOD. ZEITSCHRIFT
FÜR FRANZÖSISCHE SPRACHE UND LITERATUR, VOL. 74, NO. 2
(SEPT. 1964), PP. 130-145. PMLA 8628 (1964).

3211 THIÉRIOT, J. ENSAYO DE UN PARALELO ENTRE SARTRE Y CAMUS.
LETRAS DEL ECUADOR, VOL. 14, NO. 118 (JAN.-JUNE 1960), PP.
10, 17. FR VII 23690, FR VII 24918.

3212 THODY, PHILIP. ALBERT CAMUS AND 'LA REMARQUE SUR LA RÉVOLTE'.
FRENCH STUDIES, VOL. 10, NO. 4 (OCT. 1956), PP. 335-338.
BFZ 40-252, CR 975, FR VII 17347, KL I 273.

3213 THODY, PHILIP. ALBERT CAMUS. CONTEMPORARY REVIEW, VOL. 190,
NO. 1092 (DEC. 1956), PP. 349-352. FR VII 17346, KL I 274.

3214 THODY, PHILIP. ALBERT CAMUS, A STUDY OF HIS WORK. NEW YORK.
MACMILLAN, LONDON. H. HAMILTON, 1957. BR, CR 485, KL I
272.

3215 THODY, PHILIP. A NOTE ON CAMUS AND THE AMERICAN NOVEL.
COMPARATIVE LITERATURE, VOL. 9, NO. 3 (SUMMER 1957), PP.
243-249. BFZ 42-284, BUL SIGN 15853, CR 1070, FR VII

17348, KL I 274.

THODY, PHILIP. ALBERT CAMUS. A STUDY OF HIS WORK. NEW YORK.   3216
    GROVE PRESS, 1959. FR VII 23578.

THODY, PHILIP. 'ALBERT CAMUS AND THE LITERATURE OF REVOLT', BY   3217
    JOHN CRUICKSHANK. FRENCH STUDIES, VOL. 14, NO. 3 (JULY
    1960), PP. 279-280. KL II 386.

THODY, PHILIP. ALBERT CAMUS, 1913-1960. LONDON. H. HAMILTON,   3218
    1961. FR VII 26300, PMLA 7994.

THODY, PHILIP. ALBERT CAMUS, 1913-1960. NEW YORK. MACMILLAN,   3219
    1962. FR VII 26300.

THODY, PHILIP. MEURSAULT ET LA CRITIQUE. REVUE DES LETTRES   3220
    MODERNES, VOL. 8, NOS. 64-66 (FALL 1961), PP. 315-327
    (ALT. PP. 11-23). FR VII 26288.

THOORENS, LÉON. ALBERT CAMUS. PARIS. LA SIXAINE (COLL. À LA   3221
    RENCONTRE), 1946. BO 12, CR 486, FR VII 740.

THOORENS, LÉON. 'L'EXIL ET LE ROYAUME' DE CAMUS. REVUE   3222
    GÉNÉRALE BELGE, VOL. 93 (MAY 1957), PP. 155-156. FR VII
    17349.

THORSON, THOMAS LANDON. ALBERT CAMUS AND THE RIGHTS OF MAN.   3223
    ETHICS, VOL. 74, NO. 4 (JULY 1964), PP. 281-291. PMLA
    8630 (1964).

TIJERAS, EDUARDO. CAMUS Y ARGELIA. CUADERNOS   3224
    HISPANOAMERICANOS, NO. 135 (MARCH 1961), PP. 360-365. FR
    VII 26387.

TILLION, GERMAINE. ALBERT CAMUS ET L'ALGÉRIE. PREUVES, NO. 91   3225
    (SEPT. 1958), PP. 69-72. BUL SIGN 14-18204, CR 1124, FR
    VII 19453, KL I 274.

TILLION, GERMAINE. DEVANT LE MALHEUR ALGÉRIEN. PREUVES, NO.   3226
    110 (APRIL 1960), PP. 25-27. FR VII 23691, KL II 392, PMLA
    7392 (1962).

TODD, OLIVIER. THE FRENCH REVIEWS. TWENTIETH CENTURY, VOL.   3227
    153, NO. 911 (JAN. 1953), PP. 36-42. BO 287, FR VII 8887.

TOENES, SARA. PUBLIC CONFESSION IN LA CHUTE. WISCONSIN STUDIES   3228
    IN CONTEMPRARY LITERATURE, VOL. 4, NO. 3 (FALL 1963), PP.
    305-318.

TOLSTRUP, KAMMA. ALBERT CAMUS. COPENHAGEN. DANSK   3229
    BIBLIOGRAFISK KONTOR, 1958. CR 487.

TOMA, V. ALBERT CAMUS, FILOSOOF DER MENSELIJKHEID. VLAM, VOL.   3230
    8, NO. 18 (MAY 3, 1952), P. 7. BO 150, CR 841.

TOUCHARD, PIERRE-AIMÉ. L'HOMME DE THÉÂTRE. MONDE, VOL. 13,   3231
    NO. 585 (DEC 31, 1959-JAN. 6, 1960), P. 1. FR VII 23692.

TOURAINE, Y. LE MYTHE DE LA CATASTROPHE DANS LE ROMAN ET LE   3232
    THÉÂTRE CONTEMPORAINS. TABLE RONDE, NO. 77 (1954), PP.
    122-126. BO 375.

TRACY, ROBERT. THE POSSESSED BY ALBERT CAMUS. CARLETON   3233

MISCELLANY,   VOL. 2, NO. 2 (SPRING 1961), PP. 70-77.

3234   TRAHAN, ELIZABETH. CLAMENCE VS. DOSTOEVSKY. AN APPROACH TO 'LA
       CHUTE'. COMPARATIVE LITERATURE,   VOL. 18, NO. 4 (FALL
       1966), PP. 337-350.

3235   TREADWELL, HUGH W. ALBERT CAMUS. 'L'HOMME RÉVOLTÉ'. BOOKS
       ABROAD,   VOL. 26, NO. 4 (FALL 1952), P. 352. CR 842.

3236   TREADWELL, HUGH W. ALBERT CAMUS. 'ACTUELLES II. CHRONIQUES
       1948-1953'. 'L'ETE'. BOOKS ABROAD,   VOL. 28, NO. 4 (FALL
       1954), P. 431. CR 909, CR 910.

3237   TREADWELL, HUGH W. ALBERT CAMUS. 'LA CHUTE'. BOOKS ABROAD,
       VOL. 31, NO. 1 (WINTER 1957), P. 32. CR 1071.

3238   TREADWELL, HUGH W. ALBERT CAMUS. 'REQUIEM POUR UNE NONNE'.
       PIECE EN DEUX PARTIES ET SEPT TABLEAUX, D'APRÈS WILLIAM
       FAULKNER. BOOKS ABROAD, VOL. 31, NO. 2 (SPRING 1957), P.
       141. CR 1073.

3239   TREADWELL, HUGH W. ALBERT CAMUS. 'L'EXIL ET LE ROYAUME'.
       BOOKS ABROAD, VOL. 31, NO. 4 (FALL 1957), P. 369. CR
       1072.

3240   TREADWELL, HUGH W. ALBERT CAMUS. 'L'ENVERS ET L'ENDROIT'.
       BOOKS ABROAD, VOL. 33, NO. 1 (WINTER 1959), P. 30. REF
       1404.

3241   TREADWELL, HUGH W. ALBERT CAMUS. 'ACTUELLES III. CHRONIQUE
       ALGERIENNE, 1939-1958'. BOOKS ABROAD, VOL. 33, NO. 2
       (SPRING 1959), P. 155. REF 1414.

3242   TREADWELL, HUGH W. JEAN-CLAUDE BRISVILLE. 'CAMUS'. (GALLIMARD).
       BOOKS ABROAD, VOL. 33, NO. 4 (FALL 1959), P. 418.

3243   TREADWELL, HUGH W. GERMAINE BRÉE. 'CAMUS'. (RUTGERS UNIVERSITY
       PRESS). BOOKS ABROAD, VOL. 33, NO. 4 (FALL 1959), P. 460.

3244   TREICH, L. THÉÂTRE FRANÇAIS. NOTES PARISIENNES. PIERRE
       DESCAVES OU ALBERT CAMUS? SOIR,   NO. 31 (FEB. 6, 1959), P.
       2. CR 1150.

3245   TREICH, L. NOTES PARISIENNES. POUR ALBERT CAMUS, LE THÉÂTRE
       EST UN 'DIEU DE VÉRITÉ'. SOIR,   NO. 116 (MAY 16, 1959), P.
       2. CR 1151.

3246   TREIL, CLAUDE. L'IRONIE D'ALBERT CAMUS. PROCÉDÉS
       PSYCHOLOGIQUES. TROIS ASPECTS. REVUE DE L'UNIVERSITÉ
       LAVAL,   VOL. 16, NO. 9 (MAY 1962), PP. 855-860. FITCH, FR
       VII 33984.

3247   TREIL, CLAUDE. ALBERT CAMUS, OU LA CERTITUDE DE L'INCERTITUDE.
       REVUE DE L'UNIVERSITÉ LAVAL,   VOL. 17, NO. 8 (APRIL 1963),
       PP. 687-697. PMLA 7986 (1964), FR VII 33983.

3248   TREIL, CLAUDE. RELIGION DE L'INDIFFÉRENCE CHEZ CAMUS. REVUE DE
       L'UNIVERSITÉ LAVAL,   VOL. 20, NO. 9 (MAY 1966), PP.
       808-815.

3249   (TRIBUTES TO ALBERT CAMUS). TANIA BALACHOVA, ET AL. DES

PERSONNALITÉS DU THEATRE... FIGARO,   VOL. 134, NO. 4770
(JAN. 6, 1960). P. 4.   SEE NO. 998, 1029, 1143, 1386, 1995,
2775.

(TRIBUTES TO ALBERT CAMUS). FRANÇOIS MAURIAC, ET AL. DES   3250
ÉCRIVAINS NOUS DISENT. FIGARO, VOL. 134, NO. 4770 (JAN.
6, 1960), P.4. FR VII 23649. SEE NO. 1395, 1825, 2010,
2403, 2438, 2464, 2476, 2560, 2643, 3282.

(TRIBUTES TO ALBERT CAMUS). ROGER IKOR, ET AL. UNE OEUVRE EN   3251
DÉBAT DEVANT LA NOUVELLE GÉNÉRATION (I). FIGARO
LITTÉRAIRE, VOL. 12, NO. 601 (OCT. 26, 1957), P. 7.
FRENCH VII 17316, FITCH. SEE NO. 1254, 1394, 2082, 2247,
2549, 2750, 3080, 3252.

(TRIBUTES TO ALBERT CAMUS). ROGER IKOR ET AL. L'OEUVRE DE   3252
CAMUS EN DÉBAT DEVANT LA NOUVELLE GÉNÉRATION (II). FIGARO
LITTERAIRE VOL. 12, NO. 602 (NOV. 2, 1957), P. 11. FRENCH
VII 17316, FITCH. SEE NO. 1662, 2445, 2853, 2887, 2963,
3251.

(TRIBUTES TO ALBERT CAMUS). GUY DUMUR ET AL. IL Y A UN AN,   3253
ALBERT CAMUS. FRANCE-OBSERVATEUR, VOL. 12, NO. 557 (JAN.
5, 1961), PP. 16-17. FITCH. SEE NO. 1641, 2205, 2426,
2612, 2618.

(TRIBUTES TO ALBERT CAMUS). L. P. DESROSIERS, ET AL. LIBERTÉ,   3254
VOL. 2, NO. 1 (JAN.-FEB. 1960), PP. 47-53. FR VII 23609.
SEE NO. 1137, 1584, 1669, 2243, 2793.

(TRIBUTES TO ALBERT CAMUS). M. M. MADISON, ET AL. ALBERT CAMUS   3255
SPECIAL NUMBER. MODERN FICTION STUDIES, VOL. 10, NO. 3
(AUTUMN 1964), PP. 223-314. SEE NO. 1064, 1733, 2087,
2286, 2383, 2451, 2895, 3155, 2982.

(TRIBUTES TO ALBERT CAMUS). MAURICE BLANCHOT, ET AL. HOMMAGE À   3256
ALBERT CAMUS. NOUVELLE REVUE FRANÇAISE (NUMERO SPECIAL),
VOL. 8, NO. 87 (MARCH 1960), PP. 403-620. FR VII 23575.
SEE NO. 791, 797, 949, 973, 978, 1031, 1070, 1102, 1103,
1162, 1167, 1316, 1333, 1397, 1569, 1587, 1640, 1697, 1713,
1750, 1889, 1893, 1903, 2006, 2030, 2031, 2133, 2141, 2217,
2235, 2275, 2377, 2401, 2402, 2408, 2443, 2508, 2521, 2629,
2667, 2696, 2872, 3117, 3143, 3318, 3329, 3358, 3394.

(TRIBUTES TO ALBERT CAMUS). SUR CAMUS. DES TEXTES DE DRISS   3257
CHRAÏBI, ET AL. PARISIENNE, NO. 48 (NOV.-DEC. 1957), PP.
1069-1096. FR VII 17345. SEE NO. 1444, 1455, 1761, 2077,
2182, 2574, 2651, 2751, 3299, 3424.

(TRIBUTES TO ALBERT CAMUS). RENÉ CHAR, ET AL. ALBERT CAMUS,   3258
HOMME DE THÉÂTRE. REVUE D'HISTOIRE DU THÉÂTRE (NUMÉRO
SPÉCIAL), VOL. 12, NO. 4 (OCT.-DEC. 1960), PP. 317-362. FR
VII 23570. SEE NO. 782, 930, 1411, 1706, 1707, 1873.

(TRIBUTES TO ALBERT CAMUS) YOUSSEF EL SEBAΫ ET AL. HOMMAGE À   3259

ALBERT CAMUS. REVUE DU CAIRE, 23RD YEAR, VOL. 44, NO. 237
(MAY 1960), PP. 345-396. SEE NO. 1461, 2015, 2079, 2393,
2665, 3047, 3176.

3260 (TRIBUTES TO ALBERT CAMUS). MOHAMMED-EL-AZIZ KESSOUS, ET AL.
CAMUS L'ALGÉRIEN. SIMOUN (NUMERO SPECIAL), VOL. 8, NO. 31
(JULY 1960), 68 PP. FR VII 23573. SEE NO. 974, 1144,
1327, 1462, 1554, 1588, 1720, 1770, 2181, 2313, 2520, 2575,
2689, 2874, 3181.

3261 (TRIBUTES TO ALBERT CAMUS). R.-M. ALBÉRÈS, ET AL. ALBERT CAMUS.
TABLE RONDE, NO. 146 (FEB. 1960). FR VII 23569, PMLA 6854
(1961). SEE NO. 765, 1030, 1062, 1097, 1299, 1551, 1578,
1746, 1872, 1908, 1919, 1934, 2005, 2039, 2288, 2368, 2382,
2396, 2424, 2434, 2546, 2563, 2650, 2937, 3317.

3262 (TRIBUTES TO ALBERT CAMUS). PIERRE RUBÉ, ET AL. YALE FRENCH
STUDIES, NO. 25 (SPRING 1960), PP. 3-143. FR VII 23568.
SEE NO. 1077, 1284, 1324, 1404, 1498, 1549, 1607, 1645,
1667, 1954, 1982, 2073, 2139, 2327, 2534, 2727, 2953, 3088,
3324, 3325, 3366, 3428.

3263 TRIOLET, ELSA. QUI EST CET ÉTRANGER QUI N'EST PAS D'ICI?
POÉSIE 43, VOL. 4, NO. 14 (MAY-JUNE 1943), PP. 11-26. BO
313, FR VII 7717.

3264 TRIOLET, ELSA. LE TYRAN MÉTAPHYSIQUE ET LE GENTILHOMME DE CHEZ
HERMÈS. 'CALIGULA', D'ALBERT CAMUS. LETTRES FRANÇAISES,
NO. 710 (FEB. 20-26, 1958), P. 6. CR 1125.

3265 TRIOLET, ELSA. ALBERT CAMUS OU L'ÉTRANGER. LETTRES FRANÇAISES,
NO. 806 (JAN. 7-13, 1960), PP. 1, 4. FR VII 23693, KL II
395.

3266 TRIPET, G. VON DER INNEREN REVOLTE ZUR THEOSOPHIE.
BETRACHTUNGEN ZU DEM BUCH 'DER REVOLTIERENDE MENSCH' VON
ALBERT CAMUS. ADYAR (GRAZ), VOL. 9, (1954), PP. 6-12.
BDZ 108-306, BO 533, CR 911.

3267 TROISFONTAINES, ROGER. WHAT IS EXISTENTIALISM? THOUGHT, VOL.
32, NO. 127 (WINTER 1957-58), PP. 516-532. BO 162, FR VII
18872.

3268 TROTZIG, BIRGITTA. DEN NYE CAMUS. REVIEW OF 'FALLET',
ÖVERSÄTTNING AV EVA ALEXANDERSON. BONNIERS 1957.
PANACHE-SERIEN. BONNIERS LITTERÄRA MAGASIN, VOL. 26, NO. 3
(MARCH 1957), PP. 279-281.

3269 TROYAT, HENRI. ALBERT CAMUS. 'CALIGULA'. (THÉÂTRE HÉBERTOT.).
NEF, VOL. 2, NO. 12 (NOV. 1945), PP. 149-153. BO 349, CR
548, FR VII 23694.

3270 TROYAT, HENRI. RÉPONSE À M. ALBERT CAMUS. NEF, VOL. 3, NO. 14
(JAN. 1946), PP. 144-148. BO 190, CR 578, FR VII 23695.

3271 TRUC, GONZAGUE. LA QUERELLE SARTRE-CAMUS. HOMMES ET MONDES,
VOL. 8, NO. 76 (NOV. 1952), PP. 370-375. BO 288, CR 843,

FR VII 8508, 7181.

TSEMAH, A. HAYAM VEHAEER BEETSIRAT CAMUS (THE SEA AND THE CITY   3272
   IN CAMUS'WORK). LAMERHAV. MASAH, SEPT. 2, 1960.

TUCHMAIER, H. S. ESSAI SUR L'ÉVOLUTION DE LA PENSÉE DE CAMUS.   3273
   THÈSE LAVAL, 1956. KL II 388.

TUCKER, HARRY, JR. A GLANCE AT 'WHITENESS' IN MELVILLE AND   3274
   CAMUS. PUBLICATIONS OF THE MODERN LANGUAGE ASSOCIATION OF
   AMERICA - PMLA, VOL. 80, NO. 5 (DEC. 1965), P. 605.

TURI, COSIMO. CAMUS UNO E DUE. CENOBIA, VOL. 10, NO. 4   3275
   (JULY-AUG. 1961), PP. 439-444. FR VII 26388.

TYLDEN-WRIGHT, DAVID. THE IMAGE OF FRANCE. LONDON. SECKER AND   3276
   WARBURG, 1957. FR VII 16553, KL I 274.

TYNAN, KENNETH. PERSONA GRATA. NEW YORK. PUTNAM, 1954. CF.   3277
   P. 30. BO 76. SEE NO. 1051.

UBERSFELD, ANNIE. ALBERT CAMUS OU LA MÉTAPHYSIQUE DE LA   3278
   CONTRE-RÉVOLUTION. NOUVELLE CRITIQUE, VOL. 10, NO. 92
   (JAN. 1958), PP. 110-130. CR 1125 BIS.

UBERSFELD, ANNIE. NOBEL PRIZEWINNER ALBERT CAMUS. MAINSTREAM,   3279
   VOL. 11, NO. 10 (OCT. 1958), PP. 1-17. FR VII 26389.

ULLMAN, STEPHEN. STYLE IN THE FRENCH NOVEL. CAMBRIDGE.   3280
   CAMBRIDGE UNIVERSITY PRESS, 1957.

ULLMANN, STEPHEN. THE IMAGE IN THE MODERN FRENCH NOVEL.   3281
   CAMBRIDGE. CAMBRIDGE UNIVERSITY PRESS, 1960. THE TWO
   STYLES OF CAMUS , PP. 239-299. FR VII 23006.

UNGARETTI, GIUSEPPE. DES ÉCRIVAINS NOUS DISENT. (HOMMAGES À   3282
   CAMUS). FIGARO, VOL. 134, NO. 4770 (JAN. 6, 1960), P. 4.
   FR VII 23649.

URMENETA, FERMÍN DE. SOBRE LA ESTÉTICA CAMUSIANA. REVISTA DE   3283
   IDEAS ESTÉTICAS. VOL. 18, NO. 70 (1960), PP. 165-169. FR
   VII 26390, PMLA 6855 (1961).

VAGNE, JEAN. ALBERT CAMUS. 'CALIGULA'. (THÉÂTRE HÉBERTOT).   3284
   LETTRES, VOL. 1, NO. 4 (1945), PP. 313-314. CR 549.

VAGNE, JEAN. ALBERT CAMUS. 'LE MALENTENDU'. (AUX MATHURINS).   3285
   LETTRES, VOL. 1, NO. 1 (1945), PP. 79-80. CR 550.

VAHANIAN, GABRIEL. THE DEATH OF GOD. THE CULTURE OF OUR   3286
   POST-CHRISTIAN ERA. NEW YORK. GEORGE BRAZILLER, 1961.
   SCATTERED REFERENCES.

VAHANIAN, GABRIEL. LA MORT DE DIEU. LA CULTURE DE NOTRE ÈRE   3287
   POST-CHRÉTIENNE. PARIS. BUCHET-CHASTEL, 1962. TRANSLATED
   BY BERNARD WILLERVAL.

VALGUY, J. 'L'ENVERS ET L'ENDROIT'. LIVRES ET LECTURES, VOL.   3288
   3, NO. 24 (JULY-AUG. 1958), P. 395. CR 1126.

VAN DER LINDEN, J. P. INTRODUCTION. IN L'EXILE ET LE ROYAUME,   3289
   PP. 5-6. SEE NO. 302.

VALLQUIST, GUNNEL. ENSAMHET ELLER GEMENSKAP. REVIEW.   3290

LANDSFLYKTEN OCH RIKET . ÖVERSÄTTNING AV EVA ALEXANDERSON.
PANACHE-SERIEN. BONNIERS, 1957. BONNIERS LITTERÄRA
MAGASIN,   VOL. 26, NO. 10 (DEC. 1957), PP. 927-928.

3291   VAN WETTER, G. LÉONARD, IBSEN, CAMUS. THYRSE,   VOL. 60, NO. 2
        (1958), P. 50. FR VII 26391.

3292   VARELA, JOSÉ LUIS. ALBERT CAMUS. PREMIO NOBEL DE LITERATURA.
        ARBOR,   VOL. 38, NO. 144 (DEC. 1957), PP. 417-422.

3293   VARIN, RENÉ. L'ÉROTISME DANS LA LITTÉRATURE FRANÇAISE, MORCEAUX
        CHOISIS DE PIERRE LOUYS À J.-P. SARTRE. PARIS. ÉDIT. DE
        LA PENSÉE MODERNE, 1953. FR VII 12668.

3294   VASOLI, CESARE. CAMUS E 'L'HOMME RÉVOLTÉ'. INVENTARIO, VOL.
        5, NO. 1-4 (JAN.-SEPT. 1953), PP. 214-220. BO 513, FR VII
        11244.

3295   VAZ DA SILVA, ALBERTO. NUNO DE BRAGANÇA. ALBERT CAMUS. TEMPO E
        O MODO,   NO. 7 (JULY-AUG. 1963), PP. 1-27. SEE NO. 1267.

3296   VEDALDI, A. ESISTENZIALISMO. VERONA. M. LECCE, 1947. BO 166,
        FR VII 5209.

3297   VELIKOVSKI, SAMIRI. 'LA PESTE' D'ALBERT CAMUS. RECHERCHES
        INTERNATIONALES À LA LUMIÈRE DU MARXISME,   VOL. 9, NO. 50
        (NOV.-DEC. 1965). PP. 142-174.

3298   VELOSO, A. O 'ABSURDISMO' DE CAMUS. BROTÉRIA,   NO. 70 (1960),
        PP. 129-139. KL II 387.

3299   VERALDI, GABRIEL. HEUREUX SUÉDOIS. PARISIENNE,   NO. 48
        (NOV.-DEC. 1957), PP. 1090-1093. CR 1047 TER, KL I 274.

3300   VERCRUYSSE, ROGER. VAN NEGATIEF TOT POSITIEF. NIEUW VLAAMS
        TIJDSCHRIFT,   VOL. 2, NO. 10 (1956), PP. 1014-1016. CR
        976.

3301   VERDOT, G. EN CETTE MAISON QUI FUT LA SIENNE... FIGARO
        LITTERAIRE,   VOL. 15, NO. 716 (JAN. 9, 1960), P. 6. FR VII
        26392, KL II 395.

3302   G.V. (VERDOT, GUY). IL ALLAIT COMMENCER UNE NOUVELLE
        EXPÉRIENCE. FIGARO LITTÉRAIRE, VOL. 15, NO. 716 (JAN. 9,
        1960), P. 6. FITCH.

3303   VERENO, M. VON DER LOGIK DER VERNICHTUNG. EINE BETRACHTUNG ZU
        CALIGULA . STANDPUNKT, VOL. 2, NO. 8-9 (1947), PP. 35-36.
        BO 354, CR 634.

3304   VERGA, LEONARDO. L'ESPERIENZA MORALE DI ALBERT CAMUS. RIVISTA
        DE FILOSOFIA NEOSCOLASTICA,   VOL. 50, NO. 1 (1958), PP.
        57-73. BFZ 43-294, CR 1127, KL I 272.

3305   VERMEER, H. TOONEEL TE BRUSSEL. ALBERT CAMUS. 'LE MALENTENDU'.
        SPECTATOR (BRUSSELS),   (MAY 12, 1946), P. 13. BO 339, CR
        579.

3306   VERNEAUX, R. DE L'ABSURDE. REVUE DE PHILOSOPHIE, 1946 ISSUE,
        PARIS. LIBRAIRIE P. TEQUI, (1947), PP. 165-197.

3307   VESTRE, BERNT. DEN SENTRALE IDÉ I ALBERT CAMUS' FORFATTERSKAP.

SAMTIDEN,   VOL. 69, NO. 2 (1960), PP. 104-113. FR VII
23697, PMLA 6856.

VESTRE, BERNT. NIHILISM OG LA PENSÉE DE MIDI. VINDUET,   VOL.   3308
12, NO. 4 (1958), PP. 315-320. FR VII 29422.

VESTRE, BERNT. FORORD IN DEN UOVERVINNELIGE SOMMER. OSLO.   3309
ASCHEHOUG, 1960. PP. 7-14.

VIATTE, AUGUSTE. ALBERT CAMUS DEVANT L'ATHÉISME. REVUE DE   3310
L'UNIVERSITÉ LAVAL,   VOL. 6, NO. 8 (APRIL 1952), PP.
642-647. BO 116, FR VII 7718.

VIATTE, AUGUSTE. ALBERT CAMUS. REVUE DE L'UNIVERSITÉ LAVAL,   3311
VOL. 14, NO. 8 (APRIL 1960), PP. 689-693. RFR, FR VII
23698, KL II 395, PMLA 6857.

VIDIL, CHARLES. 'L'HOMME RÉVOLTÉ' PAR ALBERT CAMUS. CAHIERS   3312
D'ÉTUDES CATHARES,   VOL. 3, NO. 11 (1951-1952), PP. 185-
186.

VIER, JACQUES. LITTÉRATURE À L'EMPORTE-PIÈCE (DEUXIÈME SÉRIE).   3313
PARIS. LES ÉDITIONS DU CÈDRE, 1961. CF. PP. 73-76.
DISCUSSES 'L'EXIL ET LE ROYAUME'. FITCH.

VIGÉE, CLAUDE. METAMORPHOSES OF MODERN POETRY. COMPARATIVE   3314
LITERATURE,   VOL. 7, NO. 2 (SPRING 1955), PP. 97-120.   BO
81, FR VII 12867.

VIGÉE, CLAUDE. LES ARTISTES DE LA FAIM. COMPARATIVE   3315
LITERATURE,   VOL. 9, NO. 2 (SPRING 1957), PP. 97-117. FR
VII 16667.

VIGÉE, CLAUDE. LES ARTISTES DE LA FAIM. PARIS. CALMANN-LEVY,   3316
1960.   LA NOSTALGIE DU SACRÉ CHEZ ALBERT CAMUS , PP.
249-273. FR VII 22819.

VIGÉE, CLAUDE. ALBERT CAMUS. L'ERRANCE ENTRE 'L'EXIL ET LE   3317
ROYAUME'. TABLE RONDE, NO. 146 (FEB. 1960), PP. 120-126.
BFZ 46-284, BUL SIGN 15-19-13772,   FR VII 23569,   KL II
391.

VIGÉE, CLAUDE. LA NOSTALGIE DU SACRÉ CHEZ ALBERT CAMUS.   3318
NOUVELLE REVUE FRANÇAISE,   NO. 87 (MARCH 1960), PP.
527-536. FR VII 23575, KL II 387.

VIGÉE, CLAUDE. 'CAMUS', BY GERMAINE BRÉE (RUTGERS UNIVERSITY   3319
PRESS, 1961). (REVIEW). SATURDAY REVIEW, (1961).

VIGÉE, CLAUDE. RÉVOLTE ET LOUANGES, ESSAIS SUR LA POÉSIE   3320
MODERNE. PARIS. JOSÉ CORTI, 1962. FR VII 28603.

VIGGIANI, CARL A. CAMUS' 'L'ÉTRANGER'. PUBLICATIONS OF THE   3321
MODERN LANGUAGE ASSOCIATION,   VOL. 71, NO. 5 (DEC. 1956),
PP. 865-887. BFZ 45-278, BR, CR 976 BIS,FR VII 15361, KL I
273.

VIGGIANI, CARL A. L'ÉTRANGER DE CAMUS. REVUE DES LETTRES   3322
MODERNES,   VOL. 8, NOS. 64-66 (FALL, 1961), PP. 407-440
(ALT. PP. 103-136). TRANSLATION OF 'CAMUS'S L'ÉTRANGER'.

SEE.   NO. 1884.

3323   VIGGIANI, CARL A. CAMUS IN 1936. THE BEGINNINGS OF A CAREER.
         SYMPOSIUM,   VOL. 12, NO. 1-2 (SPRING-FALL, 1958), PP. 7-18.
         BUL SIGN 14-9005, FR VII 19455, KL II 386.

3324   VIGGIANI, CARL A. CAMUS AND THE FALL FROM INNOCENCE. YALE
         FRENCH STUDIES,   NO. 25 (SPRING 1960), PP. 65-71. BUL
         SIGN 16-19-9950, FR VII 23568, KL II 390.

3325   VIGGIANI, C. A. CAMUS AND 'ALGER REPUBLICAIN', 1938-1939.
         (BIBLIOGRAPHIE DES ARTICLES DE CAMUS). YALE FRENCH
         STUDIES,   NO. 25 (SPRING 1960), PP. 138-143. KL II 392,
         FR VII 23568.

3326   VIGGIANI, CARL A. ALBERT CAMUS' FIRST PUBLICATIONS. MODERN
         LANGUAGE NOTES,   VOL. 75, NO. 7 (NOV. 1960), PP. 589-596.
         FR VII 23699, BFZ 47-280 (1961), KL II 388.

3327   VIGGIANI, CARL A. 'CAMUS LE JUSTE', BY GEORGES HOURDIN
         (ÉDITIONS DU CERF, 1960). REVIEW. ROMANIC REVIEW, VOL. 52,
         NO. 2 (APRIL 1961), PP. 156-158. KL II 387.

3328   VIGORELLI, GIANCARLO. CARTE FRANCESI. PT. 1. UN ANNO, PT. 2.
         ALTRE GIORNATE. TURIN. EDIZIONI RAI-RADIOTELEVISIONE
         ITALIANA, PT. 1-1958, PT 2-1959.   CAMUS , PP. 173-176. FR
         VII 22923.

3329   VILAR, JEAN. CAMUS RÉGISSEUR. NOUVELLE REVUE FRANÇAISE,   VOL.
         8, NO. 87 (MARCH 1960), PP. 506-508. FR VII 23575, KL II
         389.

3330   VILLELAUR, ANNE. LIVRES SUR CAMUS. LETTRES FRANÇAISES,   NO.
         813 (FEB. 25,-MARCH 2, 1960), P. 3. KL 386.

3331   VIRTANEN, REINO. CAMUS. 'LE MALENTENDU' AND SOME ANALOGUES.
         COMPARATIVE LITERATURE,   VOL. 10, NO. 3 (SUMMER 1958), PP.
         232-240. BFZ 44-282, BUL SIGN 14-2278, FR VII 19456, KL I
         273.

3332   VIVET, JEAN-PIERRE. ALBERT CAMUS OU L'AUTRE MALENTENDU. TERRE
         DES HOMMES,   VOL. 1, NO. 10 (DEC. 1, 1945), P. 6. BO 337,
         CR 551, FR VII 2713.

3333   VIVET, JEAN-PIERRE. CAMUS L'AFRICAIN. LIVRES DE FRANCE,   VOL.
         3, NO. 9 (NOV. 1951), PP. 3-4. CR 800.

3334   VIVET, JEAN-PIERRE. CAMUS L'AFRICAIN. BIBLIO, VOL. 19, NO. 9
         (NOV. 1951), PP. 3-4. BO 37, FR VII 5763.

3335   VOETS, GUY. CAMUS. DE MENS ALS KONING EN BANNELING OP DE
         AARDE. (L'EXIL ET LE ROYAUME). NIEUW VLAAMS TIJDSCHRIFT,
         VOL. 11, NO. 9 (SEPT. 1957), PP. 998-1001. CR 1077, KL I
         272.

3336   VOETS, GUY. EEN LANUS VOOR CAMUS. NIEUW VLAAMS TIJDSCHRIFT,
         VOL. 11, NO. 4 (APRIL 1957), PP. 446-448. CR 1076, KL I
         272.

3337   VOETS, GUY. UN CERTAIN SENS DE LA LIBERTÉ. NIEUW VLAAMS

TIJDSCHRIFT, VOL. 1, NO. 11 (1957), PP. 1110-1114. KL I
272.

VRACEM, PAUL VAN. THÉÂTRE ESTUDIANTIN.   LE MALENTENDU ,   3338
D'ALBERT CAMUS. CHANTIERS, VOL. 15, NOS. 7-8 (MAY-JUNE
1951), P. 8. CR 801.

WADE, GERALD E. ALBERT CAMUS, DON JUAN AND TIRSO DE MOLINA   3339
(ABSTRACT). SOUTH ATLANTIC BULLETIN, VOL. 22, NO. 3 (JAN.
1957), P. 11.

WADE, GERALD E. CAMUS' ABSURD DON JUAN. ROMANCE NOTES, VOL.   3340
1, NO. 2 (SPRING 1960), PP. 85-91. FR VII 26394, KL II
391.

WALKER, HAROLD BLAKE. (ON THE DEATH OF ALBERT CAMUS). CHICAGO   3341
SUNDAY TRIBUNE, SECT. 7 (MAY 26, 1963), P. 46.

WALKER, I. H. CAMUS AT THE CROSS-ROADS. TWENTIETH CENTURY,   3342
VOL. 166, NO. 990 (AUG. 1959), PP. 73-77. BFZ 45-278,
FR VII 21423, KL II 395.

WALKER LINARES, FRANCISCO. EL TEATRO DE ALBERT CAMUS. ATENEA,   3343
ANO 25, TOME 91, NO. 281-282 (NOV.-DEC. 1948), PP. 146-155.
FR VII 5765.

WALKER LINARES, FRANCISCO. EL TEATRO DE ALBERT CAMUS. VERBO,   3344
NO. 17 (OCT.-DEC. 1949), PP. 17-20. BO 341, FR VII 5764.

WALL, BERNARD. RECENT WORK OF ALBERT CAMUS. CHANGING WORLD,   3345
NO. 3 (WINTER 1947-48), PP. 86-92. FR VII 29423.

WALL, BERNARD. THE FRENCH REVIEWS. TWENTIETH CENTURY, VOL.   3346
153, NO. 914 (APRIL 1953), PP. 276-282. FR VII 8890.

WALRAVENS, JAN. ALBERT CAMUS, NOBELPRIJSWINNAAR. VLAAMSE GIDS,   3347
VOL. 41, NO. 12 (DEC. 1957), PP. 766-768. CR 1078, KL II
368.

WALRAVENS, J. DE DOOD VAN CAMUS. VLAAMSE GIDS, (1960), PP.   3348
101-107. KL II 395.

WALTERS, MARGARET. TWO FABULISTS: GOLDING AND CAMUS.   3349
MELBOURNE CRITICAL REVIEW, NO. 4 (1961), PP. 18-29. PMLA
4292.

WANG, JOAN PARSONS. JOSEPH CONRAD, PROTO-EXISTENTIALIST. A   3350
COMPARATIVE STUDY OF CONRAD, CAMUS, AND SARTRE.
DISSERTATION ABSTRACTS, VOL. 26, NO. 2 (AUG. 1965), PP.
1051-1052.

WARDMAN, H. W. PARODY IN CAMUS. ESSAYS IN FRENCH LITERATURE,   3351
NO. 2 (NOV. 1965), PP. 15-29.

WARNER, REX. BOOKS OF THE WEEK. THE MOTIVE OF THE REBEL.   3352
SPECTATOR, NO. 6545 (DEC. 4, 1953), PP. 674-676. BO 514,
CR

WARNER, REX. THE REBEL. SPRINGFIELD REPUBLICAN, (FEB. 7,   3353
1954), P. 5. BO 534.

WARNIER, RAYMOND. OUVRAGES FRANÇAIS TRADUITS ET ÉTUDIÉS EN   3354

ALLEMAGNE. REVUE DE LITTERATURE COMPARÉE, VOL. 33, NO. 4
(OCT.-DEC. 1959), PP. 573-584. FR VII 20808.

3355   WASSERSTROM, WILLIAM. IN GERTRUDE'S CLOSET. YALE REVIEW, VOL.
48, NO. 2 (DECEMBER-WINTER, 1959), PP. 245-265.

3356   WEBER, CARL AUGUST. DICHTUNG DER GEGENWART. FRANKREICH.
HERAUSGEGEBEN VON CARL AUGUST WEBER. MÜNCHEN. WEISMANN,
1947.   ALBERT CAMUS , PP. 127-129. CR 489.

3357   WEBER, CARL AUGUST. EHRUNG EINES MORALISTEN. NOBELPREIS FÜR
ALBERT CAMUS. WOCHE, VOL. 7, NO. 43 (1957), P. 15. BDZ
117-307 (1958).

3358   WEBER, JEAN-PAUL. DÉCOUVERTE DE MEURSAULT. NOUVELLE REVUE
FRANÇAISE, NO. 87 (MARCH 1960), PP. 575-580. FR VII
23575, KL II 391.

3359   WEBER, ROBERT. VOM INDIFFÉRENT ZUM ÉTRANGER: CAMUS ADAM.
NEUEREN SPRACHEN, VOL. 12, NO. 11 (NOV. 1963), PP.
485-498. PMLA 8633 (1964).

3360   WEBER, ROBERT W. RASKOL'NIKOV, ADDIE BUNDREN, MEURSAULT. SUR LA
CONTINUITÉ D'UN MYTHE. ARCHIV FÜR DAS STUDIUM DER NEUEREN
SPRACHEN UND LITERATUREN, VOL. 202, NO. 2 (AUG. 1965), PP.
81-92.

3361   WEIGHTMAN, J. G. THE NOVEL TODAY. ALBERT CAMUS' 'THE FALL'.
LISTENER, VOL. 71, NO. 1822 (FEB. 27, 1964), PP. 346-347.

3362   WEIGHTMAN, J. G. ALBERT CAMUS' THE FALL. LISTENER, VOL. 71,
NO. 1825 (MARCH 19, 1964), P. 474.

3363   WEIGHTMAN, JOHN. IMPRESSIONS AND INTUITIONS. 'NOTEBOOKS
1942-1951' BY ALBERT CAMUS. NEW YORK TIMES BOOK REVIEW,
NOV. 21, 1965, PP. 4, 54.

3364   WEIGHTMAN, J. G. THE FRENCH LITERARY SCENE. COMMENTARY, VOL.
41, NO. 2 (FEB. 1966), PP. 57-62.

3365   WEILER, MAURICE. ALFRED DE VIGNY ET ALBERT CAMUS. REVUE DE
PARIS, VOL. 71, NO. 8-9 (AUG.-SEPT. 1964), PP. 58-62.

3366   WEINBERG, KURT. THE THEME OF EXILE. YALE FRENCH STUDIES, NO.
25 (SPRING 1960), PP. 33-40. RFR, BUL SIGN 16-19-9737
(1962), FR VII 23568, KL II 389.

3367   WEINBERG, KURT. ALBERT CAMUS ET LE THÈME DE L'EXIL. REVUE DES
LETTRES MODERNES, VOL. 8, NOS. 64-66 (FALL 1961), PP.
329-341 (ALT. PP. 25-37). TRANSLATION OF 'THE THEME OF
EXILE'.SEE. NO. 1916.

3368   WEINSTEIN, LEO. THE METAMORPHOSES OF DON JUAN. STANFORD.
STANFORD UNIVERSITY PRESS, 1959 (ALSO LONDON. OXFORD
UNIVERSITY PRESS). CHAPTER XIV. THE CONTEMPORARY DON
JUAN, PP. 155-167.

3369   WEISS, LOUISE. ALBERT CAMUS OU L'HOMME DÉSINTEGRÉ. ÉCONOMIE
CONTEMPORAINE, VOL. 19, NO. 143 (1960), PP. 4-5. BFZ
46-283.

WELIKOWSKI, S. BEI DER GEGENUBERSTELLUNG MIT DER GESCHICHTE.   3370
    BEMERKUNGEN ÜBER DAS SCHAFFEN VON ALBERT CAMUS.
    SOWJETWISSENSCHAFT, KUNST UND LITERATUR.   VOL. 13, NO. 6
    (JUNE 1965), PP. 618-648.

WELLERSHOFF, DIETER. DER GLEICHGÜLTIGE.   COLOGNE. KIPENHEUER   3371
    UND WITSCH, 1963.   FR VII 31600.

WELLWARTH, G.E. ALFRED JARRY. THE SEED OF THE AVANT-GARDE DRAMA.   3372
    CRITICISM, VOL. 4, NO. 2 (SPRING 1962), PP. 108-119.

WENTINCK, CHARLES H. CAMUS EN ZIJN 'DUITSE VRIEND'.   3373
    LIBERTINAGE, VOL. 2, NO. 2 (MARCH-APRIL 1949), PP.
    118-124. BO 380, CR 727.

WENTINCK, CHARLES H. NASCHRIFT (BIJ DE BRIEF OVER CAMUS).   3374
    LIBERTINAGE, VOL. 2, NO. 6 (NOV.-DEC. 1949), PP. 459-460.
    CR 728. SEE NO. 1086.

WENTINCK, CHARLES H. BRIEF OVER CAMUS. CAMUS EN ZIJN DUITSE   3375
    VRIEND. MET NASCHRIFT D. CH. H. WENTINCK. LIBERTINAGE,
    VOL. 2, NO. 6 (1950), PP. 458-460. BO 381, CR 727.

WERNER, H. EINE TOPOGRAPHIE DER HÖLLE. ALBERT CAMUS. 'DIE   3376
    PEST'. STIMME DER GEMEINDE, VOL. 1, NO. 9 (1949), PP.
    14-15. BDZ 103-263 (1951), BO 435, CR 730.

WERNER, H. 'ICH WOLLTE DEN MOND'--DER UNFREIWILLIGE ZEUGE. ZU   3377
    DEM DRAMA VON CAMUS. 'CALIGULA'. STIMME DER GEMEINDE,
    VOL. 1, NO. 9 (1949), P. 16. BDZ 103-263 (1951), BO 373,
    CR 729.

WEST, PAUL. NEW WORLD WRITING. NEW YORK. THE NEW AMERICAN   3378
    LIBRARY OF WORLD LITERATURE, 1958.   ALBERT CAMUS AND THE
    AESTHETIC TRADITION , PP. 80-91. FR VII 18839, KL II 387.

WETHERILL, FRANK DOSTER. ALBERT CAMUS AND THE KINGDOM OF   3379
    NATURE. DISSERTATION ABSTRACTS, VOL. 26, NO. 1 (JULY
    1965), P. 378.

WETTER, GEORGES VAN. LÉONARD, IBSEN, CAMUS... THYRSE, VOL.   3380
    60, NO. 2 (FEB. 1958), PP. 50-52. CR 1128, FR VII 26391.

WEYERGANS, FRANZ. LE ROMAN DU MOIS. 'LA CHUTE', PAR ALBERT   3381
    CAMUS. REVUE NOUVELLE, VOL. 12, NOS. 7-8 (JULY-AUG.
    1956), PP. 121-124. FR VII 15362, KL I 274.

WEYERGANS, FRANZ. THÉÂTRE ET ROMAN CONTEMPORAINS. PARIS.   3382
    EDITIONS UNIVERSITAIRES, 1957. ALBERT CAMUS , PP. 65-77.
    KL II 387.

WHITEMAN, H. G. 'ALBERT CAMUS' BY ALBERT MAQUET. LISTENER,   3383
    VOL. 61, NO. 1576 (JUNE 11, 1959), P. 1034.

WHITEMAN, H. G. 'ALBERT CAMUS AND THE LITERATURE OF REVOLT' BY   3384
    JOHN CRUICKSHANK. LISTENER, VOL. 62, NO. 1586 (AUGUST 20,
    1959), P. 289.

WHITEMAN, H. G. ALBERT CAMUS AND FRANCIS PONGE. NONPLUS, VOL.   3385
    1, NO. 3 (SUMMER 1960), PP. 46-55.

3386   WHITEMAN, H. G. 'RESISTANCE, REBELLION AND DEATH', 'THE
          COLLECTED FICTION OF ALBERT CAMUS',   ALBERT CAMUS AND THE
          LITERATURE OF REVOLT . LISTENER, VOL. 65, NO. 1670 (MARCH
          30, 1961), P. 580.

3387   WILD, ALFRED. LA PHILOSOPHIE DE L'ABSURDE. SUISSE
          CONTEMPORAINE, NO. 12 (DEC. 1945), PP. 1136-1149. CR 551
          BIS.

3388   WILD, JOHN. EXISTENTIALISM. A NEW VIEW OF MAN (MARCEL,
          SARTRE). UNIVERSITY OF TORONTO QUARTERLY, VOL. 27, NO. 1
          (OCT 1957), PP. 79-95. KL I 232.

3389   WILLEMS, E. DE VREEMDELING VAN CAMUS EN HET PROCES VAN KAFKA.
          KRONIEK VAN HUNST EN KULTUUR, VOL. 11, NO. 1 (JAN. 1950),
          PP. 11-12. BO 308, CR 771.

3390   WILLHOITE, FRED H., JR. ALBERT CAMUS POLITICS OF REBELLION.
          WESTERN POLITICAL QUARTERLY, VOL. 14, NO. 2 (JUNE 1961),
          PP. 400-414. PMLA 7393 (1962).

3391   WILLIAMS, THOMAS A., JR. ALBERT CAMUS AND THE TWO HOUSES OF
          DESCARTES. ROMANCE NOTES, VOL. 5, NO. 2 (SPRING 1964), PP.
          115-117.

3392   WILLY, RENÉE. LA LITTÉRATURE. ALBERT CAMUS: L'HOMME ET
          L'OEUVRE. REVUE FRANÇAISE, NO. 97 (JAN. 1958), PP. 38-39.
          CR 1129.

3393   WILSON, ANGUS. ALBERT CAMUS. HUMANIST. SPECTATOR, VOL. 204,
          NO. 6870 (FEB. 26, 1960), P. 293.

3394   WILSON, ANGUS. ALBERT CAMUS. NOUVELLE REVUE FRANÇAISE, VOL.
          8, NO. 87 (MARCH 1960), PP. 545-548. FR VII 23575, KL II
          395.

3395   WILSON, COLIN. THE OUTSIDER. LONDON. GOLLANCZ, 1956. FR VII
          18865.

3396   WILSON, COLIN. THE AGE OF DEFEAT. LONDON. GOLLANCZ, 1959.
          THE CONTRIBUTION OF CAMUS , PP. 119-125.

3397   WILSON, COLIN. 'THE POSSESSED', A PLAY BY ALBERT CAMUS.
          LISTENER, VOL. 64, NO. 1636 (AUG. 4, 1960), P. 195. FR
          VII 26395.

3398   WILSON, EDMUND. ALBERT CAMUS-CHARLES DICKENS-LAFCADIO HEARN.
          NEW YORKER, VOL. 22, NO. 9 (APRIL 13, 1946), PP. 113-114.

3399   WINTZEN, RENÉ. ALBERT CAMUS OU L'OEUVRE D'UN JUSTE. SIGNES DU
          TEMPS, VOL. 2, NO. 2 (FEB. 1960), PP. 36-37.

3400   WOLF, ANDREAS. APHORISMEN VON ALBERT CAMUS. GEISTIGES
          FRANKREICH, VOL. 4, NO. 172 (1950).   CR 773.

3401   WOLF, ANDREAS. ALBERT CAMUS. BELAGERUNGSZUSTAND. KOMMENDEN,
          VOL. 4, NO. 16 (1950), P. 6. BDZ 101-208 (1950), BO 454,
          CR 772.

3402   WOLLHEIM, RICHARD. THE POLITICAL PHILOSOPHY OF EXISTENTIALISM.
          CAMBRIDGE JOURNAL, VOL. 7, NO. 1 (OCT. 1953), PP. 3-19.

BO 176, FR VII 10675.

WOLLHEIM, RICHARD. CORRESPONDENCE. LONDON MAGAZINE, VOL. 1,   3403
    NO. 3 (APRIL 1954), P. 72. SEE NO. 1501, 3402.

WUNBERG, GOTTHART. DAS ABSURDE UND DAS BEWUSSTSEIN BEI CAMUS.   3404
    SAMMLUNG, VOL. 1, NO. 3 (JUNE 1961), PP. 207-221. BDZ
    123-307 (1961).

WURMSER, ANDRÉ. LE DIAGNOSTIC DU CONFESSEUR. LETTRES   3405
    FRANÇAISES, NO. 624 (JUNE14-20, 1956), P. 2. CR 977, FR
    VII 15363, KL I 274.

WURMSER, ANDRÉ. L'ENVERS VAUT L'ENDROIT. LETTRES FRANÇAISES,   3406
    NO. 717 (APRIL 10-17, 1958), P. 2. CR 1130.

WUTHENOW, RAINER. ALBERT CAMUS. 'LA CHUTE'. ANTARES, VOL. 4,   3407
    NO. 7 (NOV. 1956), PP. 97-98.

WYNBENGA, J. DE MANLIKE KRÊFT FAN IT SUDEN. TSJERNE (DOKKUM), 3408
    VOL. 3, NO. 3 (MARCH 1948), PP. 67-71. BO 21, CR 680.

XURIGUERA, RAMÓN. LOS 'CARNETS' DE CAMUS. CUADERNOS (DEL   3409
    CONGRESO POR LA LIBERTAD DE LA CULTURA), NO. 63 (AUG.
    1962), PP. 81-82. FR VII 29428.

YALOM, MARILYN KOENICK. 'LA CHUTE' AND 'A HERO OF OUR TIME'.   3410
    FRENCH REVIEW, VOL. 36, NO. 2 (DEC. 1962), PP. 138-145.
    PMLA 7995 (1963).

YALOM, MARILYN K. ALBERT CAMUS AND THE MYTH OF THE TRIAL.   3411
    MODERN LANGUAGE QUARTERLY, VOL. 25, NO. 4 (DEC. 1964), PP.
    434-450.

YGLESIAS, JOSE. DECEPTION BY ALLEGORY. MASSES AND MAINSTREAM, 3412
    VOL. 1, NO. 8 (OCT. 1948), PP. 78-82. FR VII 26396.

YNDURAIN, FRANCISCO. GERMAINE BRÉE. 'CAMUS'. ARBOR, VOL. 44,   3413
    NOS. 163-164 (JULYAUG. 1959), PP. 477-478. FR VII 21424.

ZAHAREAS, ANTHONY. LA FEMME ADULTÈRE. CAMUS'S IRONIC VISION OF 3414
    THE ABSURD. TEXAS STUDIES IN LITERATURE AND LANGUAGE,
    VOL. 5, NO. 3 (FALL 1963), PP. 319-328.

ZAMPA, G. CALIGOLA DI CAMUS. MONDO (NEW YORK), NO. 20 (1946). 3415
    BO 351.

ZANTS, EMILY. CAMUS' DESERTS AND THEIR ALLIES, KINGDOMS OF THE 3416
    STRANGER. SYMPOSIUM, VOL. 17, NO. 1 (SPRING 1963), PP.
    30-41.

ZANTS, EMILY. RELATIONSHIP OF JUDGE AND PRIEST IN 'LA PESTE'. 3417
    FRENCH REVIEW, VOL. 37, NO. 3 (FEB., 1964), PP. 419-425.

ZEHM, GÜNTER ALBRECHT. ÜBER DEN NIHILISMUS BEI BRECHT, SARTRE 3418
    UND CAMUS. FRANKFURTER HEFTE, VOL. 17, NO. 7 (JULY 1962),
    PP. 474-482. PMLA 13460 (1963).

ZEIJEN, M. H. ALBERT CAMUS. NIEUWE EEUW, (JAN. 15, 1949). BO   3419
    26.

ZELTNER, GERDA. ZU ALBERT CAMUS' HOMME RÉVOLTÉ . SCHWEIZER   3420
    RUNDSCHAU, VOL. 52, NOS. 4-5 (JULY-AUG. 1952), PP.

278-280. BO 505.

3421   ZELTNER-NEUKOMM, GERDA. DAS WAGNIS DES FRANZÖSISCHEN
        GEGENWARTSROMANS, DIE NEUE WELTERFAHRUNG IN DER LITERATUR.
        HAMBURG. ROWOHLT, N.D. (C. 1960). DAS FALSCHE ICH
        (ALBERT CAMUS) , PP. 66-72. FR VII 25481.

3422   ZEPPI, STELIO. CAMUS. MILAN. NUOVA ACCADEMIA EDITRICE, 1961.
        PMLA 7996 (1963).

3423   ZERAFFA, MICHEL. LE THÉÂTRE ('REQUIEM POUR UNE NONNE',
        TRADUIT ET ADAPTÉ PAR ALBERT CAMUS, D'APRÈS LE'REQUIEM FOR
        A NUN', DE WILLIAM FAULKNER). EUROPE, VOL. 34, NOS.
        131-132 (NOV.-DEC. 1956), PP. 225-229 (CAMUS REF. PP.
        228-229). CR 978.

3424   ZERAFFA, MICHEL. CAMUS, CET INCONNU. PARISIENNE, NO. 48
        (NOV.-DEC. 1957), PP. 1094-1096. CR 1047 TER, KL I 272.

3425   ZEYGEN, M. H. JAC. DE GESEL VAN HET KWAAD. 'LA PESTE', VAN
        ALBERT CAMUS. NIEUWE EEUW, VOL. 30, NO. 207 (JAN. 15,
        1949), P. 7. CR 731.

3426   ZIMMER, DIETER E. AM 4. JANUAR VERUNGLÜCKTE ALBERT CAMUS
        TÖDLICH. ZEIT, VOL. 15, NO. 2 (1960), P. 6. BDZ 120-311
        (1960).

3427   ZINNES, HARRIET. CAMUS AND FREEDOM. ALBERT CAMUS. RESISTANCE,
        REBELLION AND DEATH . PRAIRIE SCHOONER, VOL. 36, NO. 2
        (SUMMER 1962), PP. 172-174. FR VII 29430.

3428   ZIOLKOWSKI, THEODORE. CAMUS IN GERMANY, OR THE RETURN OF THE
        PRODIGAL SON. YALE FRENCH STUDIES, NO. 25 (SPRING 1960),
        PP. 132-137. BUL SIGN 16-19-9745 (1962), FR VII 23568, KL
        II 392.

3429   ZIOLKOWSKI, THEODORE. ALBERT CAMUS AND HEINRICH BÖLL. MODERN
        LANGUAGE NOTES, VOL. 77, NO. 3 (MAY 1962), PP. 282-291.
        PMLA 7997 (1963).

3430   ZIZOLA, GIANCARLO. RITRATTO DI ALBERT CAMUS. HUMANITAS, VOL.
        13, NO. 1 (JAN. 1958), PP. 35-42. FR VII 19457, KL II 387.

3431   ZUCKERKANDL, ÉMILE. CALIGULA. REVUE DE LA MÉDITERRANÉE, VOL.
        3, NO. 11 (JAN.-FEB. 1946), PP. 103-108. BO 352, CR 581.

3432   ZUMALDE, I. (NOTICE SUR LA MORT DE CAMUS). NUESTRO TIEMPO,
        7TH YEAR, VOL. 12, NO. 67 (JAN. 1960), PP. 14-38. KL II
        395.

INDEXES

AUTHOR INDEX

By Country and Language

RANKE, H.   2839
RIEDER, HEINZ.   2863
SIEGMUND, GEORG.   3076
TRIPET, G.   3266
WOLF, ANDREAS.   3400

BELGIUM

FLEMISH
BENEDIC, DIRK.   1078
BERTELOOT, PIERRE.   1104
DAX, JEAN.   1552,1553
FLAM, L.   1735,1736,1737,1738
HEUGTEN, J. V.   2038
ITTERBEEK, EUGENE VAN.   2085
LANCKROCK, RIK.   2238,2239
MARLET, J. J. C.   2431
MOELLER, CHARLES.   2538,2539
RAEDEMAEKER, F. DE.   2835
SAINT-MORTIER, R.   2972,2973
STAELS, J.   3138
TANS, J. A. G.   3178
VERCRUYSSE, ROGER.   3300
VERMEER, H.   3305
VOETS, GUY.   3335,3336,3337
WALRAVENS, JAN.   3347
WALRAVENS, J.   3348

FRENCH
CAMUS.   91, 586, 604
ANDRIANNE, RENE.   794
ANONYMOUS.   822, 906, 927
AYGUESPARSE, ALBERT.   982
BLANCO AMOR, JOSÉ.   1164
BOISDEFFRE, PIERRE DE.   1195
BRINDEAU, SERGE.   1309
CAPPE, JEANNE.   1362
CHARLENT, J.-M.   1412
CHRISTOPHE, LUCIEN.   1450,1451
CORMEAU, NELLY.   1490,1491,
  1492
CRÉPIN, SIMONE.   1507
DELFOSSE, JEAN.   1566
DELMAS, C.   1570
DESMEDT, CL.   1582
DIERICKX, LOUIS.   1592
ESPIAU DE LA MAÊSTRE, A.   1685
FRÉMINVILLE, CLAUDE DE.   1769
GASCHT, ANDRE.   1817
GOTHOT, CLAUDINE.   1867,1868
HENDERICKX, PAUL.   2013
LOBET, MARCEL.   2338
MOELLER, CHARLES.   2537,2541,
  2543,2544
POCH, M.   2761
RAZUM, HANNES.   2845
ROCHEFORT, A.-HENRY.   2877,
  2878
ROSTENNE, PAUL.   2900,2901,
  2902,2903
SANOUILLET, MICHEL.   2983
SCHNIR, M.-R.   3028
SIMON, PIERRE-HENRI.   3090,
  3100
THIEBAUT, MARCEL.   3195

THOORENS, LÉON.   3222
VRACEM, PAUL VAN.   3338
WETTER, GEORGES VAN.   3380
WEYERGANS, FRANZ.   3381

GERMAN
OEDINGEN, KARLO.   2637

BRAZIL

PORTUGUESE
CAMUS.   210
CARPEAUX, OTTO MARIA.   1375
LINS, ALVARO.   2335

FRENCH
SOULIÉ, MICHEL.   3123

CANADA

ENGLISH
CAMUS.   99, 124, 125, 197,
  349, 350, 364, 382, 433, 439,
  440, 624, 728
BLOCK, HASKELL M.   1181
DAVIES, ROBERTSON.   1550
ESTALL, H. M.   1687
FAUCONNIER, R. L.   1711
GLICKSBERG, CHARLES I.   1852
GOBIN, P. B.   1856
H., M. A.   1944
HAMELIN, JEAN.   1960
JOHN, S.   2117
JONG, PIETER DE.   2130
KINGSTON, FREDERICK TEMPLE.
  2191
LEGRAND, ALBERT.   2276,2277
MACLURE, MILLAR.   2376
MCCORMACK, ROBERT.   2490,2491
RADFORD, J.   2834
RIESE, LAURE.   2866
SCHURMAN, DONALD M.   3032
WILD, JOHN.   3388

FRENCH
BLAISE, M.-C.   1137
CLOUTIER, CÉCILE.   1464
COSTA, JOHN.   1495
COTÉ, NICOLAS-M.   1496
DESROSIERS, L. P.   1584
ÉLIE, R.   1669
FONDA, CARLO.   1745
FREMONT, LAURENT.   1771
GUY, ROBERT.   1940
JEANSON, FRANCIS.   2107,2109
LABERGE, PIERRE.   2215
L'ALLIER, PAUL.   2225
LANGEVIN, A.   2243
MALABARD, JEAN.   2398
MAREK, JOSEPH C.   2427
MONETTE, ARCADE M.   2555
PICHER, RENE.   2734
PILON, JEAN-GUY.   2749
PRÉFONTAINE, YVES.   2793

RAYMOND, LOUIS-MARCEL.   2844
ROUSSEAU, LOUIS-B.   2917
SYLVESTRE, GUY.   3171
TREIL, CLAUDE.   3246,3247,3248
(TRIBUTES TO ALBERT CAMUS).
3254
TUCHMAIER, H. S.   3273
VIATTE, AUGUSTE.   3310,3311

CHILE

SPANISH
MENGOD, V.   2511
WALKER LINARES, FRANCISCO.
3343

COLOMBIA

SPANISH
MAS, E. G.   2442
MURILLO BUSTAMANTE, HERNANDO.
2585

CONGO

FLEMISH
FIEUW, ROGER.   1730

COSTA RICA

SPANISH
FERNANDEZ, G.   1723

CZECHOSLOVAKIA

CZECH
CAMUS.   126, 261, 625
PUTIK, JAROSLAV.   2814

DENMARK

DANISH
CAMUS.   100, 127, 152, 187,
211, 218, 225, 233, 237, 239,
262, 304, 373, 383, 441, 482,
486, 505, 506, 507, 508, 626
GARAUDY, ROGER.   1808
HANSEN, THORKILD.   1971
STANGERUP, HENRIK.   3141,3142
TOLSTRUP, KAMMA.   3229

ECUADOR

SPANISH
ADOUM, JORGE ENRIQUE.   752
THIERIOT, J.   3211

EGYPT

ARABIC
CAMUS.   540

FINLAND

FINNISH
CAMUS.   37, 68, 72, 128,
153, 182, 183, 188, 219, 221,
226, 235, 238, 240, 263, 305,
461, 462, 463, 483, 487, 509,
510, 627
LEHTONEN, MAIJA.   2290

FORMOSA

CHINESE
CAMUS.   264

FRANCE

FRENCH
CAMUS.   1,   2,   4,   5,
24, 36, 46, 47, 56, 58,
64, 65, 92, 93, 96, 97,
113, 117, 118, 119, 120, 121,
122, 148, 149, 150, 151, 171,
172, 186, 190, 191, 192, 193,
194, 195, 205, 206, 207, 208,
209, 222, 223, 228, 231, 232,
236, 245, 246, 247, 249, 250,
251, 253, 255, 256, 257, 298,
299, 300, 301, 327, 340, 344,
345, 346, 347, 365, 367, 369,
370, 371, 374, 376, 377, 378,
394, 395, 397, 398, 399, 401,
412, 414, 415, 416, 417, 434,
435, 436, 437, 460, 464, 468,
469, 470, 471, 472, 473, 490,
491, 492, 493, 494, 495, 496,
497, 498, 499, 500, 501, 502,
552, 557, 558, 561, 564, 566,
568, 571, 572, 573, 574, 578,
580, 584, 585, 588, 590, 591,
592, 593, 603, 607, 611, 612,
613, 614, 615, 616, 618, 619,
620, 621, 649, 650, 660, 661,
664, 668, 669, 670, 671, 673,
675, 677, 679, 680, 681, 682,
685, 686, 690, 691, 692, 693,
695, 696, 698, 699, 700, 704,
705, 706, 707, 708, 710, 713,
714, 715, 716, 717, 722, 723,
724, 725, 726, 734, 735, 737,
738, 739, 740
ALBÉRÈS, RENÉ-MARILL.   755,
757, 758, 759, 760, 761, 762,
763, 764, 765, 766, 767, 768,
769, 770, 771, 772
ALBERT, ALAN.   773

ALTER, ANDRÉ.   781, 782
ALTMAN, GEORGES.   784, 785
AMBRIÈRE, F.   789
AMBRIÈRE, FRANCIS.   790
AMER, HENRY.   791
ANEX, GEORGES.   796, 797
ANONYMOUS.   800, 801, 802,
    803, 804, 806, 807, 808, 812,
    816, 818, 819, 828, 830, 834,
    835, 838, 839, 841, 842, 844,
    845, 846, 849, 853, 854, 858,
    864, 865, 866, 867, 868, 872,
    875, 876, 877, 878, 879, 881,
    882, 883, 884, 885, 886, 887,
    888, 890, 892, 893, 895, 896,
    898, 900, 902, 903, 904, 908,
    909, 910, 911, 916, 917, 924,
    926, 928, 929, 930, 934, 940
ANTONINI, GIACOMO.   949
ARBAN, DOMINIQUE.   951
ARENDT, H(ANNAH).   953
ARENDT, HANNAH.   954
ARLAND, MARCEL.   956, 957,
    958
ARON, RAYMOND.   962
ARTAUD, ANTONIN.   963
ASTIER, E. D'.   965
ASTORG, BERTRAND D'.   966,
    967, 968
AUBARÈDE, GABRIEL D'.   969
AUDIBERTI, JACQUES.   971
AUDISIO, GABRIEL.   972, 973
AUDRY, COLETTE.   975
AURY, DOMINIQUE.   976
AURY, DOMINIQUE.   977, 978
AYRAUD, PIERRE.   983
B., L.   984
BAILLY, RENÉ.   988, 989, 990,
    991, 992, 993, 994, 995, 996
BALACHOVA, TANIA.   998
B(ALLARD), J(EAN).   999
B(ALLARD), J(EAN).   1000
B(ALLARD), J(EAN).   1001
BARJAVEL, RENÉ.   1007
BARJON, LOUIS.   1008,1009,1010,
    1011,1013,1014
BARJON, (LOUIS), R.P.   1015
BARJON, LOUIS.   1016,1017
BARNA-PAULI, EVA.   1019
BARRAULT, JEAN-LOUIS.   1028,
    1029,1030,1031
BARRIER, M. G.   1036
BATAILLE, GEORGES.   1039,1040,
    1041,1042,1043
BEAU DE LOMÉNIE, E.   1052
BECHTEL, GUY.   1056
BECKMANN, HEINZ.   1062
BÉDOUIN, JEAN-LOUIS.   1063
BÉGUIN, ALBERT.   1065
BEIGBEDER, MARC.   1067,1068,
    1069,1070
BELLE, G.   1072
BELLE, GEORGES.   1073,1074
BEN.   1076
BERGER, MARCEL.   1087
BERGER, PIERRE.   1090,1091,

1092
BERL, EMMANUEL.   1094,1095,
    1096,1097,1098,1099
BERNARD, JEAN-JACQUES.   1100
BERNARD, MARC.   1101,1102
BERNE-JOFFROY, ANDRÉ.   1103
BERTHE, LOUIS.   1105
BESPALOFF, RACHEL.   1107,1108
BILLY, ANDRÉ.   1118,1119,1120,
    1121
BIZET, RENÉ.   1128
BLANC-DUFFOUR, A.   1140,1141
BLANCHAR, PIERRE.   1143
BLANCHARD, MICHEL.   1145,1146
BLANCHET, ANDRÉ.   1147,1148,
    1150,1151,1154,1155,1156
BLANCHOT, MAURICE.   1157,1158,
    1159,1160,1161,1162,1163
BLANZAT, JEAN.   1167
BLOCH-MICHEL, JEAN.   1171,1172,
    1177,1178,1179,1180
BODIN, PAUL.   1189
BOER, MINNE G. DE.   1192
BOISDEFFRE, PIERRE DE.   1193,
    1194,1196,1197
BOISDEFFRE, PIERRE DE, ÉTIENNE
BORNE,   1199
BOISDEFFRE, PIERRE DE.   1201,
    1202,1203,1204,1205,1206,1207,
    1208,1209,1210,1211
BOIS-RABOT, GERARD.   1212
BOITOUZET, LUCIEN.   1213
BOLLNOW, OTTO F.   1217
BOLLONGIER, RENÉE.   1218
BONNEVILLE, GEORGES.   1228
BONNIER, HENRY.   1229
BOREL, JACQUES.   1233
BORGAL, CLÉMENT.   1235
BORNE, ÉTIENNE.   1236,1237,
    1238
BOSQUET, ALAIN.   1241,1242,
    1243,1244
BOUDOT, M.   1245
BOULLAYE, X. DE LA.   1246
BOURDET, CLAUDE.   1247
BOURDET, CLAUDE, AND GILLES
MARTINET.   1248
BOURDET, CLAUDE.   1249,1250
BOURDIN, ANDRÉ.   1251
BORGEAUD, GEORGES.   1254
BOURGET-PAILLERON, ROBERT.
    1255,1256,1257,1258
BOUTANG, PIERRE.   1259
BOYE, MAURICE-PIERRE.   1260,
    1261,1262,1263
BRASPART, M.   1268
B(RÉHIER), É.   1297
BRENNER, JACQUES.   1299,1300
BRETON, ANDRÉ.   1301,1302,1303
BRETON, ANDRÉ AND AIME PATRIE.
    1304
BRETON, ANDRÉ.   1305
BRINDEAU, SERGE.   1308
BRION, MARCEL.   1310
BRISSAUD, ANDRE.   1311
BRISVILLE, J.-C.   1312

JOURNAL INDEX

By Country and Language

TIJDSCHRIFT VOOR FILOSOFIE
  OEDINGEN, KARLO.   2637

BRAZIL

FRENCH
  LETRAS
    SOULIÉ, MICHEL.   3123

CANADA

ENGLISH
  CANADIAN JOURNAL OF THEOLOGY
    JONG, PIETER DE.   2130
  CULTURE
    LEGRAND, ALBERT.   2276,2277
  DALHOUSIE REVIEW
    MACLURE, MILLAR.   2376
  MANITOBA ARTS REVIEW
    RADFORD, J.   2834
  QUEEN'S QUARTERLY
    ESTALL, H. M.   1687
    FAUCONNIER, R. L.   1711
    GLICKSBERG, CHARLES I.   1852
    GOBIN, P. B.   1856
    RIESE, LAURE.   2866
    SCHURMAN, DONALD M.   3032
  SATURDAY NIGHT
    H., M. A.   1944
  TAMARACK REVIEW
    HAMELIN, JEAN.   1960
    MCCORMACK, ROBERT.   2490,
    2491
  UNIVERSITY OF TORONTO QUARTERLY
    BLOCK, HASKELL M.   1181
    JOHN, S.   2117
    WILD, JOHN.   3388

FRENCH
  CITÉ LIBRE
    LABERGE, PIERRE.   2215
  CULTURE
    COTÉ, NICOLAS-M.   1496
    FONDA, CARLO.   1745
  HUMANITIES ASSOCIATION OF CANADA
  BULLETIN
    CLOUTIER, CECILE.   1464
  LIBERTE
    BLAISE, M.-C.   1137
    DESROSIERS, L. P.   1584
    ÉLIE, R.   1669
    LANGEVIN, A.   2243
  RELATIONS
    L'ALLIER, PAUL.   2225
  REVUE DE L'UNIVERSITE LAVAL
    FREMONT, LAURENT.   1771
    MALABARD, JEAN.   2398
    MAREK, JOSEPH C.   2427
    MONETTE, ARCADE M.   2555
    PILON, JEAN-GUY.   2749
    TREIL, CLAUDE.   3246,3247,
    3248
    VIATTE, AUGUSTE.   3310,3311

REVUE DOMINICAINE
  GUY, ROBERT.   1940
  JEANSON, FRANCIS.   2107,2109
  PICHER, RENE.   2734
  RAYMOND, LOUIS-MARCEL.   2844
  ROUSSEAU, LOUIS-B.   2917
  SYLVESTRE, GUY.   3171

CHILE

SPANISH
  ATENEA
    MENGOD, V.   2511
    WALKER LINARES, FRANCISCO.
    3343

COLOMBIA

SPANISH
  BOLIVAR
    MURILLO BUSTAMANTE, HERNANDO.
    2585
  STUDIUM (COLOMBIA)
    MAS, E. G.   2442

CONGO

FLEMISH
  BAND
    FIEUW, ROGER.   1730

COSTA RICA

SPANISH
  REVISTA DE FILOSOFIA DE LA
  UNIVERSIDAD DE COSTA RICA
    FERNANDEZ, G.   1723

DENMARK

DANISH
  DANSKE MAGASIN
    CAMUS.   373
  DIALOG
    GARAUDY, ROGER.   1808
  PERSPEKTIV (COPENHAGEN)
    STANGERUP, HENRIK.   3141,
    3142

ECUADOR

SPANISH
  LETRAS DEL ECUADOR
    ADOUM, JORGE ENRIQUE.   752
    THIERIOT, J.   3211

WELTSTIMMEN (STUTTGART)
  CHRIST, E.   1446
WIRTSCHAFTS-ZEITUNG (STUTTGART)
  SÜSKIND, W. E.   3169
WORT UND TAT
  CAMUS.   576
ZEICHEN DER ZEIT
  BURGERT, HELMUTH.   1345
ZEIT
  BLÖCKER, GÜNTER.   1184
  BRAUN, HANNS.   1270
  ECKSTEIN, P.   1664
  IENS, WALTER.   2080
  SATTLER, ANDREAS.   3004
  ZIMMER, DIETER E.   3426
ZEITSCHRIFT FÜR FRANZÖSISCHE
SPRACHE UND LITERATUR
  NOYER-WEIDNER, ALFRED.   2621
  PELZ, MANFRED.   2690
  THIEBERGER, RICHARD.   3210
ZEITSCHRIFT FÜR PHILOSOPHISCHE
FORSCHUNG
  RIEFSTAHL, HERMANN.   2864
ZEITWENDE
  BECKMANN, HEINZ.   1061

FRENCH
  ARCHIV FÜR DAS STUDIUM DER
  NEUEREN SPRACHEN UND
  LITERATUREN
    WEBER, ROBERT W.   3360
  LEBENDEN FREMDSPRACHEN
    MADAULE, JACQUES.   2379
  MERKUR
    CHIAROMONTE, NICOLA.   1435
  NEUEREN SPRACHEN
    BALTES, A.   1003

GREAT BRITAIN

DUTCH
  VRIJ NEDERLAND (LONDON)
    SANDBERG, H.   2981

ENGLISH
  ADAM INTERNATIONAL REVIEW
    HERLING, GUSTAV.   2032
  BOOKS AND BOOKMEN
    BARISSE, RITA.   1006
  CAMBRIDGE JOURNAL
    STOCKWELL, H. C. R.   3153
    WOLLHEIM, RICHARD.   3402
  CHANGING WORLD
    WALL, BERNARD.   3345
  CONTEMPORARY REVIEW
    GASTER, BERYL.   1821
    MCEACHRAN, F.   2492
    STANFORD, DEREK.   3140
    THODY, PHILIP.   3213
  DELPHIC REVIEW
    KAY, C. E. M.   2161
  DOWNSIDE REVIEW
    ALLEN, LOUIS.   779

DUBLIN REVIEW
  COPLESTON, FREDERICK C.
  1487
  CRUICKSHANK, JOHN.   1517
ENCORE
  REEVES, GEOFFREY.   2852
ENCOUNTER
  CRANSTON, MAURICE.   1504
ENCOUNTER
  CAMUS.   672, 719
  CARACCIOLO, PETER L.   1363
  MORTIMER, JOHN.   2565
FRENCH STUDIES
  ALEXANDER, IAN W.   774
  BRÉE, GERMAINE.   1275
  BUSST, A.J.L.   1352
  CRUICKSHANK, JOHN.   1514,
  1524
  JOHN, S.   2121
  ST. AUBYN, F. C.   2968
  THODY, PHILIP.   3212
HORIZON
  AYER, A. J.   981
HUMANIST (LONDON)
  GREACEN, ROBERT.   1878
  MOSTYN, R. J.   2569
LISTENER
  ANONYMOUS.   857, 891
  FARLEY, CLIVE.   1709
  GERHARD, ROBERTO.   1833
  HEPPENSTALL, RAYNER.   2029
  WEIGHTMAN, J. G.   3361,3362
LONDON MAGAZINE
  CAMUS.   162, 330
  CRANSTON, MAURICE.   1500
MODERN LANGUAGE REVIEW
  HAGGIS, DONALD R.   1951
  LOURIA, YVETTE.   2356
MODERN LANGUAGES
  JOHN, S.   2118
  ROTHERA, H.   2906
NEW STATESMAN
  ALVAREZ, A.   786
  BRYDEN, RONALD.   1344
  PRITCHETT, V. S.   2806
NEW STATESMAN AND NATION
  CROSSMAN, R. H. S.   1512
  CURTIS, ANTHONY.   1531
  HEPPENSTALL, RAYNER.   2027
PENGUIN NEW WRITING
  HEPPENSTALL, RAYNER.   2026
PHILOSOPHY
  ROTH, LEON.   2904
QUARTERLY REVIEW (LONDON)
  SAINT DENIS, MICHEL.   2971
SCRUTINY
  MASON, H. A.   2444
THEOLOGY
  REARDON, B. M. G.   2847
TIME AND TIDE
  ANONYMOUS.   894
  CRUICKSHANK, JOHN.   1526
TWENTIETH CENTURY
  CRUICKSHANK, JOHN.   1521
  MACKWORTH, CECILY.   2375
  TODD, OLIVIER.   3227

PROKOP, JAN.   2809
ZESZYTY NAUKOWE KATOLICKIEGO
UNIWERSYTETU LUBELSKIEGO
    KWIATKOWSKI, W.   2213

FRENCH
    KWARTALNIK NEOFILOLOGICZNY
        EHRET, H.   1666

PORTUGAL

PORTUGUESE
    BROTÉRIA
        MAIA, JOÃO.   2394
        MENDES, JOÃO.   2510
        VELOSO, A.   3298
    OCIDENTE
        DINIZ, MARIA EMILIA.   1595
        TAVARES DE ARANDA, SALETTE.
        3183

PUERTO RICO

SPANISH
    ASOMANTE
        BAYON, D. C.   1049
        BRÉE, GERMAINE.   1288
        ENGUIDANOS, MIGUEL.   1679
        KNOPF, BLANCHE.   2194
        LEHAN, RICHARD DANIEL.   2284
        PÉREZ MARCHAND, MONELISA L.
        2692
        SCHAJOWICZ, L.   3017

RUMANIA

RUMANIAN
    VIATA ROMANEASCA
        CASSIAN, N.   1385

SPAIN

SPANISH
    ALCALA
        HERRERO, JAVIER.   2035
    ARBOR
        ALONSO, JULIO LAGO.   780
        GAMBRA, RAFAEL.   1798
        VARELA, JOSÉ LUIS.   3292
        YNDURAIN, FRANCISCO.   3413
    CUADERNOS HISPANOAMERICANOS
        HORIA, VINTILA.   2057
        PERLADO, JOSÉ JULIO.   2693
        TIJERAS, EDUARDO.   3224
    ESTAFETA LITERARIA
        BONET, LAUREANO.   1227
    ESTUDIOS
        BOASSO, FERNANDO.   1188
    FILOLOGÍA MODERNA
        ENGLER, WINFRIED.   1678

HUMANIDADES
    ALVAREZ, D.   788
INDICE DE ARTES Y LETRAS
    FERNANDEZ-SANTOS, FRANCISCO.
    1724,1725
    GAMBRA, RAFAEL.   1799
INSULA
    GULLÓN, RICARDO.   1936,1937
    IBERT, JEAN-CLAUDE.   2078
    MADAULE, JACQUES.   2381
    MARRA-LOPEZ, J. R.   2433
    SARTRE, JEAN-PAUL.   2999
NUESTRO TIEMPO
    GAMBRA, RAFAEL.   1800
    ORLANDIS, JOSÉ.   2649
PAPELES DE SON ARMADANS
    ARANGUREN, JOSE LUIS.   950
    CELA, CAMILO JOSÉ.   1396
RAZON Y FE
    BLAJOT, JORGE, S. J.   1138
    DELGADO, F.   1567,1568
REVISTA DE IDEAS ESTÉTICAS
    URMENETA, FERMIN DE.   3283
REVISTA DE LA UNIVERSIDAD DE
MADRID
    BENITEZ CLAROS, R.   1079
SAPIENTIA
    JOLIVET, REGIS.   2125
VERBO
    WALKER LINARES, FRANCISCO.
    3344

FRENCH
    BULLETIN DE L'INSTITUT FRANÇAIS
    EN ESPAGNE
        LAPLANE, G.   2252
    BULLETIN DE LA BIBLIOTHÈQUE DE
    L'INSTITUT FRANÇAIS EN ESPAGNE
        MATET, MAURICE.   2446

SWEDEN

SWEDISH
    BONNIERS LITTERÄRA MAGASIN
        CAMUS.   166, 229, 243, 326,
        559, 718
        BJURSTRÖM, CARL GUSTAF.
        1129,1130
        BJURSTRÖM, C. G.   1131
        EKELÖF, GUNNAR.   1668
        HOLMQUIST, BENGT.   2051
        JAENSSON, KNUT.   2089
        LINDBLOM, PAUL.   2334
        SARTRE, JEAN-PAUL.   2998
        TROTZIG, BIRGITTA.   3268
        VALLQUIST, GUNNEL.   3290

FRENCH
    MODERNA SPRAK
        CAMUS.   674
        PROSCHWITZ, GUNNAR VON.
        2810

FRENCH STUDIES
  CLAYTON, ALAN J.   1458
  KING, ADELE.   2189
THE HARVARD ADVOCATE
  CAMUS.   678
HUMANIST (OHIO)
  CARLSON, ERIC W.   1372
JERUSALEM POST
  CARR, MAURICE.   1376
JOURNAL OF AESTHETICS AND ART
CRITICISM
  DURFEE, HAROLD A.   1647
  METER AMES, VAN.   2518
JOURNAL OF EXISTENTIAL
PSYCHIATRY
  GARNER, HARRY H. AND ROBERT
  F. JEANS.   1811
  NEURINGER, CHARLES.   2604
JOURNAL OF INDIVIDUAL
PSYCHOLOGY
  ROM, PAUL.   2891
JOURNAL OF RELIGION
  DURFEE, HAROLD A.   1648
  HANNA, THOMAS L.   1966
  LOOSE, JOHN.   2347
JUBILEE
  SHEED, WILFRID.   3072
KENTUCKY FOREIGN LANGUAGE
QUARTERLY
  BECK, THEODORE TOULON.   1057
  BREARLEY, KATHERINE.   1273
  JONES, ROBERT EMMET.   2128
  JOYAUX, GEORGES J.   2138,
  2140
  SPECTOR, ROBERT DONALD.
  3125
KENYON REVIEW
  BENTLEY, ERIC.   1084
  FEIBLEMAN, JAMES K.   1717
  LANSNER, KERMIT.   2248
  ROSSI, LOUIS R.   2897
  SPIEGELBERG, HERBERT.   3134
LIBRARY JOURNAL
  BARRETT, MARY L.   1033
  BARRON, LOUIS.   1037
  FREEDLEY, GEORGE.   1766
LITERARY JOURNAL
  KINGERY, R. E.   2190
MAINSTREAM
  GUTIERREZ, FELIX.   1939
  UBERSFELD, ANNIE.   3279
  YGLESIAS, JOSE.   3412
MASSACHUSETTS REVIEW
  HOFFMAN, STANLEY.   2048
  PEYRE, HENRI.   2726
MILWAUKEE JOURNAL
  MERCIER, JEANNE.   2515
MINNESOTA REVIEW
  ARNETT, CARROLL.   961
  FREUND, JOHN B.   1774
  SARGENT, LYMAN TOWER.   2986
  SORENSON, SUSAN M.   3120
MODERN AGE
  MOLNAR, THOMAS.   2551

MODERN DRAMA
  ABRAHAM, CLAUDE K.   748
  BEHRENS, RALPH.   1066
  KOPPENHAVER, ALLEN J.   2199
  LESAGE, LAURENT.   2315
  RECK, RIMA DRELL.   2848
  REED, PETER J.   2851
  SAVAGE, EDWARD B.   3009
MODERN FICTION STUDIES
  BEEBE, MAURICE.   1064
  FITCH, BRIAN T.   1733
  HARTSOCK, MILDRED.   1983
  JACKSON, NAOMI C.   2087
  LEHAN, RICHARD.   2286
  MADISON, M. M.   2383
  MATTHEWS, J. H.   2451
  ROSE, MARILYN GADDIS.   2895
  SANDSTORM, GLENN.   2982
  STOLTZFUS, BEN.   3155
MODERN LANGUAGE JOURNAL
  SIMPSON, LURLINE V.   3109
MODERN LANGUAGE NOTES
  COHN, ROBERT GREER.   1475
  HAROUTUNIAN, LULU.   1974
  HOLDHEIM, WILLIAM W.   2050
  MACKSEY, RICHARD.   2374
  STRAUSS, WALTER A.   3161
  VIGGIANI, CARL A.   3326
  ZIOLKOWSKI, THEODORE.   3429
MODERN LANGUAGE QUARTERLY
  GRUBBS, HENRY A.   1904
  HARTSOCK, MILDRED E.   1984
  KAMBER, GERALD.   2146
  MOENKEMEYER, HEINZ.   2547
  PEYRE, HENRI.   2730
  RECK, RIMA DRELL.   2849
  YALOM, MARILYN K.   3411
NATION
  CLURMAN, HAROLD.   1469,1470
  GOLDBERG, HARVEY.   1857
NEW ENGLAND MODERN LANGUAGE
ASSOCIATION BULLETIN
  GALAND, RENE.   1791
NEW LEADER
  CRUICKSHANK, JOHN.   1523
  IONESCU, GHITA.   2083
  RODITI, EDOUARD.   2880
NEW MEXICO QUARTERLY
  COSMAN, MAX.   1494
NEW REPUBLIC
  HOWE, IRVING.   2064
  SZASZ, THOMAS S.   3173
NEW YORKER
  ANONYMOUS.   809, 852
  PODHORETZ, NORMAN.   2764
NEWSWEEK
  ANONYMOUS.   824, 851
NINETEENTH CENTURY FICTION
  SPECTOR, ROBERT DONALD.
  3130
OPTIMATE
  BURKE, KATHLEEN.   1347
PARTISAN REVIEW
  CAMUS.   185, 343, 372, 456,
  457, 458
  ABEL, LIONEL.   746

CHRONOLOGICAL INDEX

By Country and Language

1936

ALGERIA

FRENCH
CAMUS.   741

1937

ALGERIA

FRENCH
CAMUS.   170

FRANCE

FRENCH
DERMENGHEM, ÉMILE.   1576

1939

ALGERIA

FRENCH
CAMUS.   466

1942

FRANCE

FRENCH
CAMUS.   246, 434
FIESCHI.   1729
HELL, HENRI.   2002
LAFUE, PIERRE.   2221
PAROUTAUD, J.-M.-A.   2672,
2673

1943

ALGERIA

FRENCH
BLIN, GEORGES.   1169

FRANCE

FRENCH
CAMUS.   397, 573, 590
BLANCHOT, MAURICE.   1157
GRENIER, JEAN.   1886
MAULNIER, THIERRY.   2457
SALVET, A.   2976
SARTRE, JEAN-PAUL.   2988
TRIOLET, ELSA.   3263

SWITZERLAND

FRENCH
CAMUS.   560

1944

ALGERIA

FRENCH
ROCHEFORT, A.-HENRY.   2875,
2876
SICARD, J. P.   3075

FRANCE

FRENCH
CAMUS.   92, 247, 398, 414,
561, 612
ANONYMOUS.   800
CHAMPROMIS, PIERRE.   1407
CLEMENT, A.   1460

FLEISCHMAN, J.   1739

ITALY

ITALIAN
  CAMUS.   709
  ARMELLINI, RINA ANNA.   959
  BARRA, G.   1027
  BO, CARLO.   1187
  BONORA, ETTORE.   1230
  JESCHKE, HANS.   2116
  NAVARRO, OSCAR.   2598
  PANDOLFI, VITO.   2664
  SCOLERI, DOMENICO.   3037
  VASOLI, CESARE.   3294

FRENCH
  ROMEYER, BLAISE.   2893

JAPAN

JAPANESE
  CAMUS.   387, 408, 676

MEXICO

SPANISH
  SAPORTA, MARCEL.   2984

NETHERLANDS

DUTCH
  HOEVEN, P. V. D.   2045
  OYEN, HENDRICK VAN.   2654
  REDEKER, H.   2850

NORWAY

NORWEGIAN
  CAMUS.   449
  AARNES, ASBJØRN S.   745

SPAIN

SPANISH
  GULLÓN, RICARDO.   1936

SWEDEN

SWEDISH
  CAMUS.   358
  HOLMQUIST, BENGT.   2051

SWITZERLAND

GERMAN
  OYEN, HENDRICK VAN.   2655

TURKEY

TURKISH
  CAMUS.   289

UNITED STATES

ENGLISH
  DOMENACH, JEAN-MARIE.   1602
  DUHRSSEN, ALFRED.   1627
  GALAND, RENE.   1791
  GENÊT.   1824
  HEINEMANN, F. H.   1997
  MAURIAC, FRANÇOIS.   2474
  PEYRE, HENRI.   2720
  ROTHERA, H.   2905

1954

ALGERIA

FRENCH
  CAMUS.   324
  ALHEINC, RAOUL.   776

ARGENTINA

SPANISH
  BLANCO AMOR, JOSE.   1165

AUSTRIA

GERMAN
  ANONYMOUS.   850
  TRIPET, G.   3266

BELGIUM

FRENCH
  FRÉMINVILLE, CLAUDE DE.
    1769
  LOBET, MARCEL.   2338
  MOELLER, CHARLES.   2541

CANADA

ENGLISH
  CAMUS.   349
  JOHN, S.   2117
  LEGRAND, ALBERT.   2277

DENMARK

DANISH
  GARAUDY, ROGER.   1808

GREECE

GREEK
  CAMUS.   268

ITALY

ITALIAN
  MAGGIONI, MARY FARINA.   2384
  PERROUD, ROBERT.   2700

JAPAN

JAPANESE
  CAMUS.   48

NETHERLANDS

DUTCH
  HELWIG, W. L.   2007,2008
  HOEVEN, P. V. D.   2046
  TERNOO, E.   3186

NORWAY

NORWEGIAN
  GULLICHSEN, HARALD.   1935

PORTUGAL

PORTUGUESE
  CAMUS.   531

SWEDEN

SWEDISH
  AHLENIUS, HOLGER.   753

TURKEY

TURKISH
  CAMUS.   539

UNITED STATES

ENGLISH
  CAMUS.   63, 453, 646
  ANONYMOUS.   860
  ARNAUD, PIERRE.   960
  BARRETT, MARY L.   1033
  BARRETT, WILLIAM.   1034,1035
  BIEBER, KONRAD F.   1114
  BIEBER, KONRAD.   1115
  DURFEE, HAROLD A.   1647
  FRANK, WALDO.   1764
  GASSNER, JOHN.   1820
  GUICHARNAUD, JACQUES.   1920
  HARRINGTON, MICHAEL.   1978

HARTMAN, GEOFFREY, H.   1981
KAHLER, ERICH.   2143
KORG, JACOB.   2200
MAGNAN, HENRI, ET AL.   2385
MICHALSON, CARL.   2522
PEYRE, HENRI.   2721
SARTRE, JEAN-PAUL.   2991,
  2994
VIGÉE, CLAUDE.   3314

FRENCH
  CAMUS.   252

1956

AUSTRIA

GERMAN
  MARCEL, GABRIEL.   2420

BELGIUM

FLEMISH
  FLAM, L.   1735
  VERCRUYSSE, ROGER.   3300

FRENCH
  CAPPE, JEANNE.   1362
  WEYERGANS, FRANZ.   3381

CANADA

ENGLISH
  CAMUS.   350, 364, 439
  ESTALL, H. M.   1687
  RADFORD, J.   2834

FRENCH
  MAREK, JOSEPH C.   2427
  TUCHMAIER, H. S.   3273

FINLAND

FINNISH
  STOLPE, SVEN.   3154

FRANCE

FRENCH
  CAMUS.   118, 119, 340, 500,
    613, 681, 682, 734
  ALTMAN, GEORGES.   784
  ANONYMOUS.   803, 864, 865,
    866, 867, 868
  ARBAN, DOMINIQUE.   951
  ARLAND, MARCEL.   957
  BAILLY, RENÉ.   993
  BARJON, LOUIS.   1011
  BERL, EMMANUEL.   1094
  BERTHE, LOUIS.   1105

POLAND

POLISH
CAMUS.   366

PORTUGAL

PORTUGUESE
MENDES, JOÃO.   2510

SPAIN

SPANISH
ORLANDIS, JOSÉ.   2649

SWEDEN

SWEDISH
CAMUS.   326
BJURSTRÖM, C. G.   1133

SWITZERLAND

FRENCH
CAMUS.   651, 652
BRATSCHI, GEORGES.   1269
JOTTERAND, FRANK.   2132
SIMON, PIERRE-HENRI.   3097

UNITED STATES

ENGLISH
CAMUS.   363
CHAMPIGNY, ROBERT.   1401
FIEDLER, LESLIE A.   1728
GARVIN, HARRY R.   1815
GERSHMAN, HERBERT S.   1834
GERSHMAN, H. S.   1835
GOLDSMITH, J. H.   1860
HANNA, THOMAS L.   1966
HARTT, J. N.   1985
MICHALSON, CARL.   2523
R(OUDIEZ), L(EON) S.   2909
VIGGIANI, CARL A.   3321

YUGOSLAVIA

SLOVENE
CAMUS.   546

SERBO-CROATIAN
CAMUS.   545

1957

ALGERIA

FRENCH
BAUER, GERARD.   1047
GRENAUD, PIERRE.   1885
NIEL, ANDRÉ.   2609

ARGENTINA

SPANISH
CAMUS.   123, 303, 381, 420

AUSTRALIA

ENGLISH
BATT, JEAN.   1045

BELGIUM

FLEMISH
DAX, JEAN.   1552,1553
FLAM, L.   1736
ITTERBEEK, EUGENE VAN.   2085
SAINT-MORTIER, R.   2972
VOETS, GUY.   3335,3336,3337
WALRAVENS, JAN.   3347

FRENCH
CHRISTOPHE, LUCIEN.   1450
GASCHT, ANDRÉ.   1817
ROCHEFORT, A.-HENRY.   2877
THOORENS, LÉON.   3222

BRAZIL

PORTUGUESE
CAMUS.   210

CANADA

ENGLISH
CAMUS.   124
DAVIES, ROBERTSON.   1550
FAUCONNIER, R. L.   1711
WILD, JOHN.   3388

DENMARK

DANISH
CAMUS.   262, 506

ECUADOR

SPANISH
ADOUM, JORGE ENRIQUE.   752

GAMBRA, RAFAEL.   1799
GULLÓN, RICARDO.   1937
VARELA, JOSE LUIS.   3292

SWEDEN

SWEDISH
CAMUS.   108, 143, 229, 287,
 318, 390, 428, 452, 536,
 641
BJURSTRÖM, C. G.   1134,1135
TROTZIG, BIRGITTA.   3268
VALLQUIST, GUNNEL.   3290

FRENCH
KARLGREN, B.   2156

SWITZERLAND

FRENCH
ONIMUS, JEAN.   2646

GERMAN
CAMUS.   214, 244

U.S.S.R.

RUSSIAN
CAMUS.   217

UNITED STATES

ENGLISH
CAMUS.   144, 657
ANONYMOUS.   871, 874, 889
BAILEY, ANTHONY.   987
BRÉE, GERMAINE AND MARGARET
 GUITON.   1277
BRÉE, GERMAINE.   1278
CARR, MAURICE.   1376
CHAMPIGNY, ROBERT.   1402
COSMAN, MAX.   1494
CRUICKSHANK, JOHN.   1516
FERRATER MORA, JOSÉ.   1726
GOLDBERG, HARVEY.   1857
GUITON, MARGARET.   1933
HATZFELD, HELMUT.   1992
HOWE, IRVING.   2063
IONESCU, GHITA.   2083
KAUFMANN, WALTER.   2160
O'BRIEN, JUSTIN.   2626
OLAFSON, FREDERICK A.   2638
ROBERTS, DAVID EVERETT.
 2870
ROLAND, A.   2885
ST. AUBYN, F. C.   2965
SARTRE, JEAN-PAUL.   2996
THODY, PHILIP.   3214,3215
TREADWELL, HUGH W.   3237,
 3238,3239
TROISFONTAINES, ROGER.   3267
ULLMAN, STEPHEN.   3280

WADE, GERALD E.   3339

FRENCH
RENAUD, ARMAND.   2854
VIGÉE, CLAUDE.   3315

VENEZUELA

SPANISH
PARADES, R.-G.   2666

1958

ALGERIA

FRENCH
BURUCOA, CHRISTIANE.   1351

ARGENTINA

SPANISH
CAMUS.   173
ORTIZ DE URTARAN, FÉLIX.
 2652
TACCA, OSCAR ERNESTO.   3174

AUSTRIA

GERMAN
ESPIAU DE LA MAËSTRE, A.
 1681,1682

BELGIUM

FLEMISH
SAINT-MORTIER, R.   2973

FRENCH
BRINDEAU, SERGE.   1309
DELFOSSE, JEAN.   1566
MOELLER, CHARLES.   2544
WETTER, GEORGES VAN.   3380

BRAZIL

PORTUGUESE
CARPEAUX, OTTO MARIA.   1375

CANADA

ENGLISH
H., M. A.   1944
MCCORMACK, ROBERT.   2490

FRENCH
GUY, ROBERT.   1940

UNITED STATES   1959

SWITZERLAND

GERMAN
    CAMUS.   319, 325, 331
    ANONYMOUS.   905

TURKEY

TURKISH
    CAMUS.   291

UNITED STATES

ENGLISH
    CAMUS.   297, 454, 455, 599,
    712
    ADAMS, ROBERT M.   751
    ANONYMOUS.   907
    BARNES, HAZEL E.   1020
    BERGER, PETER L.   1088,1089
    BRÉE, GERMAINE.   1281
    CLOUGH, WILSON O.   1463
    COUCH, JOHN PHILIP.   1497
    DIRKS, J. EDWARDS.   1596
    GLICKSBERG, CHARLES I.   1850
    GRAEF, HILDA.   1876
    GREENE, MAXINE.   1880
    GREENMAN, MARTIN A.   1883
    HOLDHEIM, WILLIAM W.   2049
    JOYAUX, GEORGES J.   2135,
    2136,2137
    LAZARON, HILDA R.   2263
    LEHAN, RICHARD.   2279
    LEHAN, RICHARD DANIEL.   2280,
    2281
    LEWIS, RICHARD W. B.   2326
    MUELLER, WILLIAM R.   2576
    MURCHLAND, BERNARD G.   2582
    PEYRE, HENRI.   2724,2725
    POPKIN, HENRY.   2776
    RAMSEY, WARREN.   2838
    ROEMING, ROBERT F.   2882
    ROUDIEZ, LEON S.   2913,2914
    RUDICH, NORMAN.   2954
    ST. AUBYN, F. C.   2966,2967
    SCOTT, NATHAN A., JR.   3039
    SHARP, WILLIAM L.   3068
    SHARP, WILLIAM.   3069
    SPECTOR, ROBERT DONALD.
    3126
    THODY, PHILIP.   3216
    TREADWELL, HUGH W.   3240,
    3241,3242,3243
    WASSERSTROM, WILLIAM.   3355
    WEINSTEIN, LEO.   3368

FRENCH
    CHARNEY, HANNA.   1414
    JOYAUX, GEORGES J.   2134

YUGOSLAVIA

SERBO-CROATIAN
    CAMUS.   322

1960

ALGERIA

FRENCH
    AUDISIO, GABRIEL.   974
    BLANCHAR, PIERRE.   1144
    BRUA, EDMOND.   1327
    CLOT, RENÉ-JEAN.   1462
    DEBÈCHE, DJAMILA.   1554
    DIB, MOHAMMED.   1588
    FERAOUN, MOULOUD.   1720
    FRÉMINVILLE, CLAUDE DE.
    1770
    KESSOUS, MOHAMMED-EL-AZIZ.
    2181
    LEROUVRE, CATHERINE.   2313
    M'HAMSADJI, KADDOUR.   2520
    MOUSSY, MARCEL.   2575
    PELEGRI, JEAN.   2689
    ROBLÈS, EMMANUEL.   2874
    TAOS, MARGUERITE.   3181
    (TRIBUTES TO ALBERT CAMUS).
    3260

ARGENTINA

SPANISH
    CAMUS.   66, 595, 623, 736
    BLOCH-MICHEL, JEAN.   1176
    OCAMPO, VICTORIA.   2634
    T., O. E. (TACCA, OSCAR
    ERNESTO).   3175

AUSTRALIA

ENGLISH
    BATT, JEAN.   1046

AUSTRIA

GERMAN
    KARSCH, W.   2157
    SIEGMUND, GEORG.   3076

BELGIUM

FLEMISH
    WALRAVENS, J.   3348

FRENCH
    ANONYMOUS.   927
    CHRISTOPHE, LUCIEN.   1451
    CRÉPIN, SIMONE.   1507
    DESMEDT, CL.   1582

WEST GERMANY

GERMAN
  CAMUS.   8,   11,   15,   18,
     21,   39,   43,   59,   69,
     73,   76,   79,   80, 155,
    158, 405, 575, 581, 594,
    608, 630, 665, 701
  ANONYMOUS.   918, 919
  BECKMANN, HEINZ.   1060,1061
  BLANCHET, ANDRE.   1152,1153
  BLANK, J.   1166
  BONDY, FRANCOIS.   1224
  BRÉE, GERMAINE.   1282
  ESPIAU DE LA MAÉSTRE, A.
    1683
  FRITZ, WALTER HELMUT.   1779
  HARLASS, GERALD.   1973
  HORST, E.   2059
  KLINGNER, EDWIN.   2192
  KORN, K.   2202
  LEBESQUE, MORVAN.   2270
  NOYER-WEIDNER, ALFRED.   2621
  PAEPCKE, FRITZ.   2660
  RÜHLE, JÜRGEN.   2957
  SARTRE, JEAN-PAUL.   3000
  SCHLETTE, HEINZ ROBERT.
    3020
  SOFER, JOHANNES.   3116
  THIEBERGER, RICHARD.   3205
  ZELTNER-NEUKOMM, GERDA.
    3421
  ZIMMER, DIETER E.   3426

FRENCH
  CAMUS.   379
  CHIAROMONTE, NICOLA.   1435
  THIEBERGER, RICHARD.   3204

GREAT BRITAIN

ENGLISH
  CAMUS.   133, 267, 307, 549,
    632, 730
  ANONYMOUS.   920
  CRUICKSHANK, JOHN.   1521,
    1524
  GASTER, BERYL.   1821
  HARTLEY, ANTHONY.   1979
  O'DONNELL, DONAT.   2636
  PRITCHETT, VICTOR S.   2804
  REARDON, B. M. G.   2847
  ROTHERA, H.   2906
  SAINT DENIS, MICHEL.   2971
  TAUBMAN, ROBERT.   3182
  THODY, PHILIP.   3217
  WILSON, ANGUS.   3393
  WILSON, COLIN.   3397

FRENCH
  CAMUS.   396

GREECE

GREEK
  CAMUS.   269

INDIA

ENGLISH
  RAY, SIBNARAYAN.   2843

HINDI
  CAMUS.   135

IRELAND (EIRE)

ENGLISH
  WHITEMAN, H. G.   3385

ISRAEL

HEBREW
  BAR-NIR, D.   1026
  BISTRITSKY, N.   1126
  SHAANAN, A.   3067
  TSEMAH, A.   3272

ITALY

ITALIAN
  CAMUS.   103, 201, 386, 423,
    636
  ANGIOLETTI, GIOVANNI BATTISTA.
    799
  ANONYMOUS.   921
  CARLINI, ARMANDO.   1370
  CARSANIGA, G.   1380
  CASNATI, F.   1382
  CHIAROMONTE, NICOLA.   1436
  CHRISTINI, GIOVANNI.   1448
  CRISTINI, GIOVANNI.   1508
  FRESCAROLI, ANTONIO.   1773
  LAURENZI, CARLO.   2261
  MAIONE, ITALO.   2395
  MANZINI, GIANNA.   2409
  MAQUET, ALBERT.   2413
  MAURO, WALTER.   2478
  MONTAGNA, GIANNI.   2556
  NICOLETTI, GIANNI.   2608
  PASSERI PIGNONI, V.   2677
  PETRONI, LIANO.   2714
  PIZZORUSSO, ARNALDO.   2757
  QUASIMODO, SALVADORE.   2815
  QUILLIOT, ROGER.   2824
  ROSSI, A.   2896
  SERONI, ADRIANO.   3062

JAPAN

JAPANESE
  CAMUS.   279

TRACY, ROBERT.   3233
VAHANIAN, GABRIEL.   3286
VIGÉE, CLAUDE.   3319
VIGGIANI, CARL A.   3327
WILLHOITE, FRED H., JR.
3390

FRENCH
SAISSELIN, RÉMY G.   2975

VIETNAM (SOUTH)

FRENCH
JUN, ISHIKAWA.   2142
ROUSSELOT, JEAN.   2940

1962

ARGENTINA

SPANISH
CAMUS.   98

CANADA

ENGLISH
CAMUS.   99, 197, 382, 433,
624
HAMELIN, JEAN.   1960

FRENCH
TREIL, CLAUDE.   3246

DENMARK

DANISH
STANGERUP, HENRIK.   3142

EGYPT

ARABIC
CAMUS.   540

FRANCE

FRENCH
CAMUS.   113, 619, 620, 669
ALBÉRÈS, RENÉ-MARILL.   768,
769, 770
ALBERT, ALAN.   773
ANONYMOUS.   934
BARJON, LOUIS.   1017
BARRIER, M. G.   1036
BLANCHARD, MICHEL.   1146
BOISDEFFRE, PIERRE DE.   1208,
1209
BRISVILLE, JEAN-CLAUDE.
1317
CURNIER, PIERRE.   1529

DAIX, PIERRE.   1537
FERAOUN, MOULOUD.   1721
GRENIER, JEAN.   1890
GRENIER, ROGER.   1894
KANTERS, ROBERT.   2154,2155
KEMP, ROBERT.   2170
LABLENIE, EDMOND.   2216
NETZER, JACQUES.   2603
QUILLIOT, ROGER.   2828,2829,
2830
ROBERT, GUY.   2869
SÉNARD, JEAN.   3055
SÉNART, PHILIPPE.   3059
SIMON, PIERRE-HENRI.   3101,
3102
VAHANIAN, GABRIEL.   3287
VIGÉE, CLAUDE.   3320

WEST GERMANY

GERMAN
CAMUS.   157, 720
ALTGELT, ERIKA.   783
BAKKER, REINOUT.   997
BLÖCKER, GÜNTER.   1185
GAUTIER, J. M.   1823
HAAS, WILLY.   1946
HEMPEL, HANS PETER.   2011
PAEPCKE, FRITZ.   2661
SCHNEIDER, PETER.   3026
SIEGMUND, GEORG.   3077
ZEHM, GUNTER ALBRECHT.   3418

GREAT BRITAIN

ENGLISH
CAMUS.   361
ANONYMOUS.   935, 936
BRADBROOK, FRANK W.   1266
BUSST, A.J.L.   1352
COCKING, J. M.   1472
CRUICKSHANK, JOHN, (EDITOR).
1527
GASCOIGNE, BAMBER.   1818
HAGGIS, DONALD R.   1950
ST. AUBYN, F. C.   2968
SCOTT, NATHAN A.   3041

FRENCH
CAMUS.   551

IRAN

IRANIAN (PERSIAN)
CAMUS.   200

ISRAEL

HEBREW
CAMUS.   274, 516

FRENCH
    GADOUREK, CARINA.   1786

PORTUGAL

PORTUGUESE
    BRAGANÇA, NUNO DE.   1267
    VAZ DA SILVA, ALBERTO.   3295

SPAIN

SPANISH
    ALONSO, JULIO LAGO.   780
    BONET, LAUREANO.   1227

SWEDEN

SWEDISH
    CAMUS.   181, 216, 480, 642

UNITED STATES

ENGLISH
    CAMUS.   116, 145, 648
    ABRAHAM, CLAUDE K.   748
    BRÉE, GERMAINE.   1295
    CARRUTH, HAYDEN.   1379
    CROSS, LESLIE.   1511
    EMBLER, WELLER.   1673
    FEIBLEMAN, JAMES K.   1717
    FEUERLICHT, IGNACE.   1727
    FRIEDMAN, MAURICE.   1777
    GARGAN, EDWARD T.   1810
    GINGRAS, GEORGE E.   1841
    GLICKSBERG, CHARLES IRVING.
      1854
    GOLDBERG, M.A.   1859
    HAMMER, LOUIS Z.   1963
    HARTT, JULIAN N.   1987
    HASSAN, IHAB.   1989
    HUBBLE, THOMAS NEWMAN.   2067
    KATEB, GEORGE.   2159
    KILLINGER, JOHN.   2185
    MAYHEW, ALICE ELLEN.   2483
    MERCIER, JEANNE.   2515
    MILLER, JUDITH.   2527
    MOSELEY, EDWIN M.   2568
    O'BRIEN, EDWARD.   2622
    PERRINE, LAURENCE.   2695
    RODITI, EDOUARD.   2880
    SCOTT, NATHAN A.   3042
    SCOTT, NATHAN A., JR.   3043
    SWANSON, ROY ARTHUR.   3170
    TOENES, SARA.   3228
    WALKER, HAROLD BLAKE.   3341
    ZAHAREAS, ANTHONY.   3414
    ZANTS, EMILY.   3416

FRENCH
    CAMUS.   258, 721

1964

AUSTRIA

GERMAN
    RIEDER, HEINZ.   2863

BELGIUM

FRENCH
    HENDERICKX, PAUL.   2013

BRAZIL

FRENCH
    SOULIÉ, MICHEL.   3123

FRANCE

FRENCH
    CAMUS.   117
    ALBÉRÈS, RENÉ-MARILL.   772
    ANONYMOUS.   940
    BLOCH-MICHEL, JEAN.   1179
    BOISDEFFRE, PIERRE DE.   1211
    CHAPELAN, MAURICE.   1408
    DANIEL, JEAN.   1547
    FOUCHET, MAX-POL.   1753
    GASCAR, PIERRE.   1816
    GUISAN, GILBERT M.   1928
    LEBESQUE, MORVAN.   2272
    MAULNIER, THIERRY.   2465
    NICOLAS, ANDRÉ.   2607
    PARINAUD, ANDRÉ.   2669
    QUILLIOT, ROGER (EDITOR).
      2831
    ROBLÈS, EMMANUEL.   2873
    ROY, JULES.   2950
    SIMON, PIERRE-HENRI.   3105
    WEILER, MAURICE.   3365

WEST GERMANY

GERMAN
    CAMUS.   130
    THIEBERGER, RICHARD.   3210

FRENCH
    CAMUS.   259

GREAT BRITAIN

ENGLISH
    ANONYMOUS.   941
    BAXTER, K. M.   1048
    BRYDEN, RONALD.   1344
    FARLEY, CLIVE.   1709
    GERHARD, ROBERTO.   1833
    JARRETT-KERR, MARTIN.   2103
    JOHN, S. BEYNON.   2120

EAST GERMANY

GERMAN
  WELIKOWSKI, S.   3370

WEST GERMANY

GERMAN
  MONCH, WALTER.   2554
  SPYCHER, PETER C.   3137

FRENCH
  WEBER, ROBERT W.   3360

GREAT BRITAIN

ENGLISH
  ANONYMOUS.   943
  HAGGIS, DONALD R.   1951
  KING, ADELE.   2188

ITALY

ITALIAN
  BACCOLO, LUIGI.   985
  CHIAROMONTE, NICOLA.   1440
  DUSE,GASTONE.   1652
  MAGRINI, LILIANA.   2392
  TERRACINI, ENRICO.   3187

UNITED STATES

ENGLISH
  BEAUJOUR, MICHEL.   1054
  BLAMIRES, HENRY.   1139
  BONDY, FRANÇOIS.   1226
  BURKE, KATHLEEN.   1347
  CHARNEY, HANNA.   1415
  CLURMAN, HAROLD.   1470
  COHN, ROBERT GREER.   1475
  COHN, RUBY.   1476
  COX, HARVEY.   1499
  FUGAZY, IRENE MERCEDES.
   1781
  GALLOWAY, DAVID D.   1795
  GORE, KEITH O.   1865
  HAMILTON, WILLIAM.   1959
  HARTSOCK, MILDRED E.   1984
  HASSAN, IHAB.   1990
  HOCHBERG, HERBERT.   2043
  KENNEDY, EUGENE, M.M.   2180
  LAKICH, JOHN JOVAN.   2224
  MERTON, THOMAS.   2516
  MICHOT-DIETRICH, HELA.   2525
  MOLNAR, THOMAS.   2553
  PARKER, EMMETT.   2671
  PEYRE, HENRI.   2730
  SCOTT, NATHAN A., JR.
   (EDITOR).   3045
  SHATTUCK, ROGER.   3071
  STUART, ROBERT LEE.   3164
  SZASZ, THOMAS S.   3173

TUCKER, HARRY, JR.   3274
WANG, JOAN PARSONS.   3350
WEIGHTMAN, JOHN.   3363
WETHERILL, FRANK DOSTER.
  3379

1966

AUSTRALIA

ENGLISH
  LEAL, R. B.   2264

CANADA

FRENCH
  FONDA, CARLO.   1745
  TREIL, CLAUDE.   3248

CZECHOSLOVAKIA

CZECH
  CAMUS.   126, 261, 625
  PUTIK, JAROSLAV.   2814

FRANCE

FRENCH
  CAMUS.   580
  BERL, EMMANUEL.   1099
  CASTEX, PIERRE-GEORGES.
   1391
  DOUBROVSKY, SERGE.   1613
  HAGGIS, DONALD R.   1952
  LAFON, NOEL.   2219
  MERAY, TIBOR.   2513
  QUILLIOT, ROGER.   2832
  SELLIER, PHILIPPE.   3051
  SIMON, PIERRE-HENRI.   3106

ENGLISH
  STREM, GEORGE G.   3162

GREAT BRITAIN

ENGLISH
  HARTLEY, ANTHONY.   1980
  HEPPENSTALL, RAYNER.   2029
  PRITCHETT, V. S.   2806

MEXICO

SPANISH
  PACHECO, LEON.   2657